Introduction to
Political Sociology

Introduction to Political Sociology

Power and Participation in the Modern World

FIFTH EDITION

Anthony M. Orum
UNIVERSITY OF ILLINOIS AT CHICAGO

John G. Dale
GEORGE MASON UNIVERSITY

New York   Oxford
OXFORD UNIVERSITY PRESS
2009

Oxford University Press, Inc., publishes works that further Oxford University's
objective of excellence in research, scholarship, and education

Oxford · New York
Auckland   Cape Town   Dar es Salaam   Hong Kong   Karachi
Kuala Lumpur   Madrid   Melbourne   Mexico City   Nairobi
New Delhi   Shanghai   Taipei   Toronto

With offices in
Argentina   Austria   Brazil   Chile   Czech Republic   France   Greece
Guatemala   Hungary   Italy   Japan   Poland   Portugal   Singapore
South Korea   Switzerland   Thailand   Turkey   Ukraine   Vietnam

Copyright © 2009 by Oxford University Press, Inc.

Published by Oxford University Press, Inc.
198 Madison Avenue, New York, New York 10016
http://www.oup.com

Oxford is a registered trademark of Oxford University Press

Library of Congress Cataloging-in-Publication Data
Orum, Anthony M.
    Political sociology : power and participation in the modern world. —5th ed. /
    Anthony M. Orum, John G. Dale.
        p. cm.
    Rev. ed. of: Introduction to political sociology / Anthony M. Orum. 4th ed.
    ISBN 978-0-19-537115-4 (alk. paper)
    1. Political sociology. I. Dale, John G. II. Orum, Anthony M.
    Introduction to political sociology. III. Title.
JA76.O78 2009
306.2—dc22   2008035167

Printed in the United States of America
on acid-free paper

Dedicated to my parents, Alma and Maury Orum—Anthony M. Orum.

Dedicated to my son, Elijah—John Dale.

Contents

Preface

This is a new edition of a textbook that was first published in 1977. This book, through its several editions and many changes, has remained a popular introduction to the field of political sociology both in the United States as well as in countries like China. But this edition is in important respects different and, we hope, superior to the previous editions.

John Dale has now joined Tony Orum as the co-author on the book. At Tony's request, John agreed to take on the chapters on social movements as well as to add a new chapter on Karl Polanyi. We believe these chapters make a substantial contribution to the earlier version. In addition, Tony has revised a number of chapters from the previous edition, for example, those on parties and the metropolis, plus he has added two new chapters: a chapter on the mass media as well as a concluding chapter on the importance of political participation in democratic regimes.

As to our acknowledgments: John is grateful for having the opportunity to learn at the feet of many insightful political sociologists whose work has greatly influenced the field and his understanding of it. They include Fred Block, Charles Tilly, Andrew Arato, Jack Goldstone, Michael Peter Smith, John Walton, and the late Arthur Vidich. John adds that they, however, are in no way accountable for any misunderstanding of their teachings that he may have expressed in this book.

He would also like to thank his co-author Tony Orum for giving him this opportunity to contribute to this fifth edition of what has heretofore been his sole project. He is honored and, after coming to understand what it has entailed, humbled.

Finally, he wishes to thank his best friend, colleague, and partner, Daniela Kraiem, with whom he shares his own quotidian politics, countless rough drafts, good times (and others), two-year-old son Elijah, and any future royalties.

Tony wishes to thank his own teachers and friends, including Neil Smelser and Mayer Zald, who helped in the original formulation of this book, as well as the many students who have shared their thoughts with him about politics and political sociology over the years. In addition, he wants to thank his children, Hannah, Rebekah, and Nicholas, for leaving the nest and thus allowing him to complete this edition without too many distractions, but also, of course, for spreading their wings and beginning their own lifelong journeys. And to Susan, who for the past twenty years has accompanied him on his own journey—thanks for making it all the more fun and giving life greater joy.

Chapter 1

Introduction

Today we live in a time of great and rapid change. Old nations have collapsed. New states arise from their ashes. Capitalism, and the pursuit of profit, thrives in a world no longer centrally occupied by the forces of communism. Democracy has been victorious, but older democracies still seek ways to revitalize themselves. Territorial barriers between nations have broken down, allowing tens of thousands of immigrants to travel freely across the globe. The world no longer is threatened by the great wars, but acts of terrorism by small bands of individuals lurk as an imminent danger, more ominous and potentially more catastrophic than the military force of earlier times.

In this book we shall describe the ways in which political sociologists think about these matters. Political sociology, a subfield of the broader discipline of sociology, originated in the writings of several great nineteenth-century social theorists. All of them lived, as we do today, in a world that was undergoing vast changes and upheavals. Revolutions abounded; old regimes died; new social classes surfaced. And these thinkers tried, as we do today, to make sense of these changes.

Certain themes today dominate the work of political sociologists, making it different from other ways of studying politics. For one thing, political sociologists take a panoramic view of the world, seeking to see the connections between political and other institutions, especially economic ones. For another, political sociologists believe that while political institutions, like the state, can take on a life all their own, such institutions also are necessarily grounded in some fashion in the other institutions of the world. Democracies, to take one example, do not spring up full-blown, but depend on a set of special historical and social circumstances to emerge. Likewise, old regimes, like authoritarian governments or totalitarian dictatorships, disappear (though often not completely overnight) not simply because of the personal failures of their leadership, but also because of their inability to navigate the often treacherous waters of international relations. Finally, political sociologists are very interested in the temporal construction and unfolding of political institutions. Thus, time and history are important elements in their calculations, far more so than they would be in the analytical tools employed, let us say, by many modern political scientists.

Today, more than ever before, the vital lessons political sociology has to teach us are lessons that must be shared and publicized among all citizens. These are lessons about the success and failure of political institutions—how, for instance, human agents can work to create new durable and responsive democracies. This book will do its best to make these fundamental lessons clear and compelling even for those among you who at this point possess a limited background in the study of politics.

Power and Authority

Two basic concepts guide the thinking of political sociologists. These concepts are represented by terms familiar to us from everyday life: *power* and *authority*. They provide the central direction and animate the key questions raised by political sociologists. Thus, it is important to understand them at the outset of this book.

Power generally refers to the capacity of a person or, more often, a group and institution to be able to manipulate and shape the views and actions of people. When a parent can make his children behave, following his orders, we say that the parent has power over his children. Likewise, when a government is able to collect taxes from its citizens, we also say that the government exercises power over its citizens.

Authority is like power except that it always refers to a set of institutions, and institutionalized arrangements, in which it operates. If a bully beats up a coward, using force and violence to subdue him, we say that the bully has been victorious because of his greater power. But the bully has no authority, no set of institutions to back up his force, no set of institutionalized arrangements that compel the coward to obey him. He wins by virtue of his sheer exercise of muscle.

A basic premise of modern sociology is that the social world would not work effectively—it would, in fact, be sheer anarchy—if obedience were simply grounded in the force, or muscle power, of people. It would be a world occupied only by bullies, one in which eventually only the persons with the biggest muscles would survive. We know, however, that the world is filled with both bullies and cowards and all sorts of other people as well. And it works because of the set of social arrangements and institutions that guide it, working almost behind the scenes of our everyday lives. Social institutions operate to establish the set of rules that provide guidance to our lives and that, in the case of our illustration, permit the cowards of the world to secure compensation if they have been attacked and beaten by bullies.

These rules represent authority. They are the institutional guidelines that dictate the conditions under which one person may fairly ask another to comply with his wishes. If the chairman of an academic department asks a faculty member to teach certain courses, the faculty member does so not because the chairman is stronger, but because it is part of the faculty member's contract with the university as a teacher. The university delegates authority to the chairman of the department, and, as chairman, he can demand that the faculty member teach courses. If the faculty member were to reject that claim and disobey, then the chairman could fire him as an official of the university because of the authority he exercises within the structure of the university.

Power and authority, then, refer to the exercise of one person or group's ideas to shape the views, and/or actions, of another. Authority is the routine everyday medium of such relationships in nations. It is the layered and multidimensional element that fundamentally keeps our world working. When large-scale institutions break down, as did the government of the former Soviet Union, it is their fundamental authority that collapses. Power, then, takes over in these circumstances precisely because, in the absence of institutions, there are no rules to follow. The bullies win.

The real trick, as some political sociologists point out, is not the precise nature of the rules that are to be created when old governments collapse, but how to secure the *legitimacy* of the authority of the regimes that will arise. Legitimacy becomes a key element in the further unfolding from power to authority because it essentially is the sense of trust that is the foundation for the durable and continuing construction and operation of social and political institutions. Where it exists, or can be created, then so, too, can institutions and the authority they exercise; where legitimacy fails, so, too, will authority and its various rules. Certain modern social philosophers, such as Jürgen Habermas, pay a great deal of attention to the entire process of *legitimation*, or the creation of legitimate regimes, precisely because of the importance it has for the construction of durable social institutions.

To sum up, then, all political sociologists come to their study of politics, and the world in general, bearing a strong awareness of matters of power and of authority. For them, these are the common coin of their intellectual realm, playing a role similar to that of atoms (or even quarks) for physicists. They are the basic terms that guide their search of the dominant patterns of the social and political world. In the chapters that follow we shall often use the terms power and authority, relying essentially on the definitions we have provided here. At times we also will use them interchangeably, mainly because in many contexts it is more felicitous to write and speak of power rather than authority. Nevertheless, the distinctions we draw here—between power and authority and the importance of legitimacy—are critical ones; we urge you to keep them in mind as you read this book.

Institutions, Networks, and Culture

Besides the elements of power and authority, three other concepts are crucial to the work of political sociologists. We have already introduced you to one of them—the concept of *institution*. The early sociological theorists were very attentive to the nature of social institutions. Max Weber, about whom you shall learn in Chapter 3, more or less created his understanding of sociology according to his focus on the nature of social institutions and how they were created, even destroyed. For a period of time in the mid–twentieth century, sociologists tended to disregard the nature of social institutions, preferring to focus their attention instead on various forms of social behavior. But now the nature and form of social institutions have come back into popularity. You will find throughout this book various discussions about the nature of social institutions, such as political parties, governmental regimes, and business firms. In general, social institutions represent *the established and organized practices of a given society*. Moreover, once formed, they can exercise a profound shape and direction over the course of history and the lives of individuals.

A second major theme of the study of modern political sociology is that of *social networks*. Social networks represent social ties and bonds among people, the organized set of relationships that link individuals to one another. There is a growing awareness among sociologists that much of our everyday life can be thought of in terms of the social networks in which we are embedded. Again, you will discover in the following pages that the idea of social networks recurs in a number of different ways among the topics of political sociology. For example, students of voting behavior have looked at a voter's social networks in order to understand the process whereby he or she arrives at a decision as to which political candidate to support. Or, to take another example, analysts of social movements turn to the nature of various social networks in a society as a means of gaining insight into how movements originate and develop over the course of time.

The third and final concept on which political sociologists have come to rely is that of the *culture*, or beliefs among large groups of people. Culture, as a tool to be used for understanding the dynamics of societies, has become increasingly helpful for contemporary sociologists. We shall point to several ways in which the political dimensions of societies can be better understood by tracking the nature of their culture. One very visible way involves the form of nationalism exhibited by different countries. Nationalism represents the form of culture peculiar to territorial-bounded organizations of nations. In the United States, it has taken the form of a distinctive emphasis on equality and individualism, beliefs that have developed and taken root among Americans over the course of the past two centuries. Another way in which culture makes itself felt is in the manner in which modern social movements, such as feminism and environmentalism, emphasize the importance of central beliefs and the creation of new identities for their members. Such an emphasis stands in contrast to older social movements, such as trade unionism or even the civil rights movement, whose main stress was on the specific benefits to be achieved by the movement in concessions gained from management and the government.

The three concepts, then—institution, network, and culture—provide a way for thinking about the larger issues of politics. They help sociologists to frame their discoveries and also aid in directing their search for new findings. We urge you to be aware of how these concepts are used in the following topical sections as well as how large a role they play in the analyses of political sociologists.

Visions of Societies and Politics: Marx, Weber, Durkheim, de Tocqueville, and Polanyi

Five major scholars have provided an intellectual legacy that helps to shape how political sociologists think about politics today. Contemporary political sociologists have moved beyond this legacy, but it also has left a very deep imprint on our view of the world.

Chapters 2 through 5 will introduce you to the writings of these men. Chapter 2 takes up the major themes of Karl Marx. Marx was the first of the great nineteenth-century social theorists, and his writings on social class and modern capitalism have left their mark on many political sociologists. Though he did not have much to say about the nature of politics and the state—they were largely reflections of the dominance of capitalism—his basic imagery still animates the writings of a number of sociologists, as you shall discover in the chapters on American politics and on the development of the modern nation-state.

Chapter 3 considers the work of Max Weber. Weber is the preeminent political sociologist. He dealt with themes that Marx failed to treat and put an emphasis on political institutions and ideas that Marx considered relatively minor themes in the grander evolution of capitalism. Weber left us with our basic understanding of the state as well as the intimate ties of the state to other social institutions.

Emile Durkheim, a French sociologist, and Alexis de Tocqueville, one of the most insightful analysts both of America and of the French Revolution, left a somewhat different legacy. Unlike Marx and Weber, these scholars emphasized the common beliefs and institutions that animated societies. Durkheim turned his attention to the nature of social phenomena in general and created a set of ideas that help to focus our attention on what we today call civil society—that part of the social world that is neither the state nor the economy. Alexis de Tocqueville provided us with unparalleled insight into the workings of American democracy, furnishing a portrait that relies heavily on the links between democracy and the general pattern of civic associations and participation in America. In the past decade, the writings of these figures, plus others, have grown in popularity as scholars try to fathom what it is that constitutes an effective democratic government.

Chapter 5 introduces us to Karl Polanyi's still relevant critique of failed projects of economic globalization in the past. Like Marx, Polanyi denounced market liberalism as destructive to society. But, unlike Marx, Polanyi did not believe that there exists some transhistorical essence of capitalism that inevitably sows the seeds of its own destruction. Instead, Polanyi emphasized that the institutions underlying capitalism are historically contingent and therefore capable of being reorganized.

Polanyi, like Durkheim and de Tocqueville, emphasized the important role of civil society in protecting us from nondemocratic state action, policies, and institutions. But Polanyi simultaneously stressed that civil society must guard against the inequalities produced by markets. Thus, where Marxists like Lenin emphasized revolution, Polanyi remained optimistic about the possibility of reforming markets, depending on how civil society embeds markets in politics, law, and morality.

One can understand the work of modern political sociologists, we must confess, without delving deeply into the writings of these eminent scholars. Indeed, many political sociologists proceed with their work without taking the time to even consult their writings. Yet it is our conviction that these works, while in many ways now out of date, still provide wonderful models of how to create panoramic portraits of the world, portraits that make sense of the labyrinths of diverse facts. In this fashion they continue to inspire our work and imagination.

Pedagogical Guidelines

In our effort to present a broad and accurate portrait of political sociology, we have done a couple of things in this book that are a bit different from those that might have been done by my friends and colleagues. First, we have attempted to illuminate the abstract character of concepts by referring mainly to materials from the United States—its present as well as its past. Where possible, we also have tried to point out differences between the character of politics in the United States and elsewhere, particularly in Western Europe. Still, this attempt to draw in comparative materials has not gone quite as far as we would have wished—though it has gone a good deal further than twenty years ago. We hope that both students and instructors will introduce as many materials from other nations as possible to highlight the special features of the American setting and to flesh out the contents of the concepts used by political sociologists.

Second, we have presented the theories on particular subjects and then evaluate them in terms of the available evidence and, occasionally, in terms of the requirement of a good theory. Where it has been impossible to resolve the differences between theories on the basis of known facts or to dismiss a particular theory because it does not fit what we know about the world, then we have said as much. (Pay special attention to these considerations in Chapter 7.) Thus, in addition to the general diversity of ideas that we present in this book, you also will confront an effort to present differences among theories and unresolved issues. The world about us is not a neat and tidy place in which all our ideas are confirmed by our observations; there is no reason to sugarcoat a book about this world and, especially, its politics—such an act would demean your intelligence. The ideas in this book, just like those present in our world, demand that we think and reflect.

If there is any single lesson that we have tried to get across in this book, apart from the many substantive ones, it is this: one must approach the world in a state of curiosity and openness, be willing to arrive at conclusions about it, be sufficiently resilient to formulate tough statements of opinion, and be persistent enough to discover whether or not those judgments are accurate. This is what politics often proves to be about; it is what the enterprise of learning must be about.

Chapter 2

On the Economy and Politics
Karl Marx and the Neo-Marxists

One capitalist always kills many. Hand in hand with this centralisation, or this expropriation of many capitalists by the few, develop, on an ever-extending scale, the co-operative form of the labour-process, the conscious technical application of science, the methodical cultivation of the soil, ... the entanglement of all peoples in the net of the world-market, and with this, the international character of the capitalistic regime. Along with the constantly diminishing number of the magnates of capital, who usurp and monopolise all advantages of this process of transformation, grows the mass of misery, oppression, slavery, degradation, exploitation; but with this too grows the revolt of the working-class, a class always increasing in numbers, and disciplined, united, organised by very mechanism of the process of capitalist production itself. The monopoly of capital becomes a fetter upon the mode of production. ... The knell of capitalist private property sounds. The expropriators are expropriated.

Karl Marx, *Capital, Volume I*

How are we to explain the nature of politics to ourselves? What are the forces that will help us better understand the nature of politics and governmental institutions? Sociologists follow not one line, or point of view, but rather one of three different perspectives. In this and the following two chapters, we shall explain the nature of each one. We shall also try to provide a blend between the more classic statements about these views and recent contributions by eminent scholars.

The most well known of these views was offered more than a century ago in the writings of Karl Marx. Marx offered a very powerful and comprehensive view of the modern world. And it is a view that continues to inspire the writings and activities of many people today. Marx's main contribution was to locate the forces and energies of politics in the economy. Many scholars continue to follow the lead of Marx today. As the global economy of capitalism has spread across the world since the 1970s, economic inequalities between people have increased rather than diminished. The growth of economic inequalities—a central idea to the writings of Marx—has led many writers and scholars to believe that Marx's ideas are still essential to understanding the shape of the modern and its politics.

9

Karl Marx on the Economy and Politics

THE ESSENTIAL MARX

Karl Marx was born in Trier, Germany, in 1818 and died in London in 1883. Jewish by birth, his father converted the family to the Lutheran faith in 1817, a year before Karl was born. His father was an educated man and lawyer, but nothing exceptional. The family had several children, the most obstinate and intellectually aggressive among them being Karl. Marx matured easily. He did his academic work in the faculty of law at the University of Bonn. There he came under the influence of the neo-Hegelians, a group of very prominent German philosophers. Within a decade of the completion of his University education, he would become involved with his lifelong friend, Friedrich Engels, and the work of the newly created Communist Party. Together they would leave an indelible mark on humankind.[1]

In writing of the influence of Karl Marx, Isaiah Berlin remarks:

> If to have turned into truisms what had previously been paradoxes is a mark of genius, Marx was richly endowed with it. His achievements in this sphere are necessarily ignored in proportion as their effects have become part of the permanent background of civilized thought.[2]

Many of us believe, for example, that there exist some groups of which we are aware and with which we identify based on common levels of wealth and property, or, more succinctly, social classes. Marx helps us to understand the importance of this idea. Many of us also believe that people's ideas about politics or about religion are in some way shaped by the level of their wealth, that is, by how rich or poor they are. Marx has had a major influence over how we think about this connection. Finally, there are many of us who believe that there are marked inequalities of wealth and power in modern societies and that these inequalities can become the basis of major ideological struggles. Again, Marx helped give birth to this idea.

Ironically, many people whose own intellectual heritage owes the most to the theories of Marx are among his greatest enemies, mainly because his ideas have been used in the past as the basis of political parties or the programs of entire nations, such as the former Soviet Union. His ideas, in effect, became the basis for Marxism and countries built upon the ideas of Communism, such as the People's Republic of China. But while true, this should not become the basis for discrediting such ideas. Indeed, as we shall see, Marx's writings continue to provide important insight into the forces that energize nations today as well as the economic divisions that have emerged within them.

Marx believed that there is an inherent conflict between the role of people in their everyday lives and their role as scholars, or students of history. The first requires people to take practical action and to assume certain moral commitments towards the world. The second, however, demands that people be dispassionate and objective about the world so that they can achieve an unbiased observation of the world as it works. There are sociologists like Max Weber who also were aware of the tensions springing from these two contradictory roles but who chose to divorce the roles from one another. Weber, like many scholars today, insisted that the two roles had to be kept separate so that the scholar could render an objective opinion: it is perfectly all right, he argued, for each of us to hold political views, but those views should not be allowed to enter the classroom. (One wonders what Weber would have thought of universities and colleges today where the general view of the faculty is so liberal.)

Marx chose to resolve the conflict between these two roles by merging them into one. For example, as both a historian and sociologist, Marx believed that a scholar could discover the main principles of historical change and development by very careful and thorough study. He also claimed that he and Engels had discovered these basic principles with their theory of *dialectical materialism*. Later in this chapter we touch on certain important features of this theory. But for now let us simply note that the theory claims that the proletariat, or working classes, would emerge victorious from a revolutionary confrontation with the capitalists, or owners of industrial enterprises, during modern capitalism.

As a philosopher Marx thought that his theory of change was itself the product of historical development—that is, the development of society under capitalism in the nineteenth century had allowed some people, like himself and Engels, to grasp the major principles of historical change. When change in society was about to happen, he argued, some people would become armed with a theoretical understanding of it much like other people would become armed with weapons.[3]

(We should note, too, that Marx thought that all people's ideas were the result of social and historical circumstances. Most people—rich as well as poor—were so shaped by the interests of their particular social class background that even during periods of major social and economic change they could not comprehend the principles and the coming of change by themselves. There were, however, a few people who were able to achieve such an understanding, and naturally that group included Marx and Engels themselves.)

For Marx, then, it was only a small step to synthesizing his understanding of change, gained by virtue of his theoretical efforts, and his moral commitment to change that grew out of his own revolutionary convictions. Since he understood the dynamics of change at work—in particular, the growth of capitalism across the world and the inevitable inequalities it bred—he believed it important for intellectuals like himself to educate the working classes and to thereby hasten the inevitable social revolution itself. In effect, then, his theory of change and his commitment to action became wed to one another. Or, as he wrote in *Contribution to the Critique of Hegel's Philosophy of Right*, "Just as philosophy finds its *material* weapons in the proletariat, so the proletariat finds its *intellectual* weapons in philosophy."[4]

If we understand that Marx was able to achieve this remarkable synthesis between his commitments to rational thought and revolutionary action simultaneously, then many of the seemingly paradoxical elements of his writings become clarified. There are some thinkers, for instance, who believe that Marx's emphasis on determinism, that is, the inevitability of historical change, and his advocacy of revolution on behalf of the working classes contradict one another. Why should one organize for revolution if change is inevitable? Yet Marx created a marriage of the two points of view: determinism, on the one hand, and free will, on the other. Lewis Feuer writes of Marx's doctrine:

> It called upon human beings for a supreme deed of free will, that of intervening in their history with a revolutionary act and creating their own society. But it did so with a necessitarian vocabulary, so that the working class in its highest moment of freedom was fulfilling historical necessity. Freedom and determinism were joined in a dialectical unity. The language of liberty always had its deterministic semantic commentary, and the mystic revolutionist became one with the scientist.[5]

Like many marriages, this was not always a happy one, and on occasion one role, such as that of the scientist, took priority over the other, such as that of the revolutionary. Yet on the whole Marx managed to unify them as few scholars, before or since, have done. He was probably the first example of what sociologists today call a public intellectual.

Another key to understanding Marx is that certain ideas preoccupied him throughout his life. The most important one was that of alienation. He believed that humans, as social beings, are alienated—that is, they are estranged from their own unique creative capacities and from their capacity to empathize with one another. The principal causes of alienation, Marx maintained, are the institutions of society, in particular social classes and the division of labor. Further, he argued that the principal manifestation of alienation is the belief of people that social institutions are immutable and cannot be changed. Other sociologists have adopted somewhat similar ideas, though with a different slant. For example, the French sociologist Emile Durkheim maintains that the division of labor, like all social facts, represents a phenomenon of a genre or kind unto itself (see Chapter 4).

Marx's position has its own special twist. In truth, he believed, social institutions are *not* immutable, but rather they are continually being created and recreated by human beings. Further, he assumed, all history, in particular the continuous unfolding and changing of social institutions, is moving toward a single goal of eliminating alienation among men and, thus, eventually revealing to them that they are the masters and creators of their own social world. Each major stage in historical development brings with it greater progress toward this goal—an increasing capacity for societies to permit people to be freed from the constraints of alienation, to be freed from social institutions. The final attainment of this goal, Marx thought, would come about with the collapse of capitalism and the advent of communist society. Communism for Marx *had* to be a society without social classes, since it was classes that gave birth to the alienation of people.

THE ECONOMY AND SOCIAL STRATIFICATION

Man's primary role in life is that of a producer, or so Marx thought. The products which are created and the manner in which they are created—whether an agrarian system of production or industrial one—represent the foundations of the economy. To Marx it was these foundations that were central to the operations of society. Until the writings of Marx, the study of the economy was left at that— simply to understand the nature of production and the mode of production. But Marx introduced a very important new wrinkle. He maintained that out of the natural course of production social inequalities also arose, inequalities that had nothing to do with the nature of the human beings themselves. If some people were poor, and others rich, it was the effect of the process of production—and in modern society it was the result of the very foundations of capitalism itself. Although today many of us take this point for granted, when Marx made the assertion it was indeed revolutionary.

Social groups, or strata, come about because of the manner and mode of production in society. Such groups together represent the social stratification hierarchy of society, and they are called specifically *social classes*. In mature capitalist society, Marx believed, there are two principal classes: the *capitalists*, a small minority of the population, and the *proletariat*, the large majority. The two groups differ in one essential fact—the capitalists own the means of production, that is, the technological and scientific apparatus, and the proletariat own nothing but their own labor power. Ownership of property, moreover, entitles the owners to be the sole beneficiaries of the fruits of that process—profit or, technically, surplus value.

Though Marx would come to rely on this specific conception of social class throughout the course of much of his work, we must also realize that his notion of social class contained certain ambiguities. In *The Communist Manifesto*, a political manuscript Marx wrote and published with Friedrich Engels in 1848, in addition to the capitalists, or industrial bourgeoisie, and the proletarians, or working classes, the authors spoke of the "lower-middle class, the small man-ufacturer, the shopkeeper, the artisan, the peasant...[the] 'dangerous class,' the social scum."[6] In *The Class Struggles in France*, a historical analysis of the regimes of Louis Philippe and Louis Bonaparte, Marx wrote of the "finance aristocracy...[the] industrial bourgeoisie...[the] petty bourgeoisie... and the peasantry."[7] There are other instances when Marx wrote of these additional classes as well, and this inevitably raises questions about what he had in mind when he wrote of social class.

Since Marx died before he was able to clarify this confusion, a great deal of controversy as well as scholarship has developed around it. For our purposes here, we shall rely mainly on the social class division between capitalists and proletarians, but we do so with good reason. This is the conception that is used throughout Marx's abstract analysis of the economic development of capitalism.[8] In addition, this same conception figures prominently in his political analyses of capitalism. In *The Communist Manifesto*, for instance, Marx and Engels por-trayed the two final political camps of capitalism as the industrial bourgeoisie, or capitalists, and the proletariat. All additional classes, they claimed, would be incorporated into one of these groups. Finally, this conception is the one that is most compatible with Marx's overall definition of capitalism, namely, private ownership of the means of production. Defining social class and the founda-tions of capitalism in the very same terms was a deliberate ploy that allowed Marx to predict the collapse of capitalism and the capitalist class at one and the same historical instant.[9]

SUBSTRUCTURE AND SUPERSTRUCTURE

Marx possessed a broad and expansive vision of the social and political world. It was one that spoke not only about the present but also about the past. The economy, to Marx, represented the key to unlocking the mysterious founda-tions of this world. In other words, people's connections to the economy shaped their lives. Marx viewed the economy as having a deep and profound impact on virtually every feature and institution of the world. Thus, not only did the eco-nomic processes of a society shape its politics, for example, but they also shaped the nature of its religious ideas, its philosophical premises, its educational insti-tutions—indeed, the full and entire range of its way of life. "The ideas of the ruling class," Marx once wrote, "are in every epoch the ruling ideas."[10] Hence, under modern capitalism, the ruling ideas of this age, and societies that are capitalist, are the ideas of the class of capitalists.

Marx's view of the nature of politics extended his notion about the role and importance of the economy in any society. In general, he believed that politics were simply a reflection of the underlying nature of the form and relations of production under modern capitalism. Thus, since capitalists represented the dominant social class under capitalism, they also were the dominant political force as well. By the same token, their opposite number, the proletariat, was the mere subordinate, or powerless, group under modern capitalism.

One useful way to think about all of this is in terms of a metaphor that has become common among scholars of Marx—the link between the *substructure* and *superstructure* of a society. Consider Figure 2.1—the substructure consists entirely of the economic foundations of modern capitalism, hence the nature and form of its production. It would include both the means of production, or such elements as the material kinds of production that occur, as well as what Marx termed the relations of production, that is, the nature and form of social classes. The superstructure that is built on top of the substructure consists, among other things, of the political regimes under capitalism, as well as such specific elements as political parties. As a general rule Marx believed that the economic substructure exercised powerful limits over what could and could not be done by political institutions and leaders.

POLITICS AS A REFLECTION OF THE CLASS STRUGGLE

To most of us politics seems to be a continuing battle and struggle among different people, groups, and parties. For example, American politics today seems to be a struggle fought in purely partisan terms, between conservatives and liberals, Republicans and Democrats, and similar groups. To understand the nature of the battle for most people means simply understanding the specific political terms and issues in which the battles are fought. If Republicans and Democrats differ on the aims of the federal government, following this line of thought, it is simply a matter of understanding the different approaches they take to income tax and other such federal policies—the Republicans lowering such taxes in order to promote greater investment in business, the Democrats seeking to raise such taxes in order to provide more resources from the federal government for people in need.

To Marx, however, the differences among and between contesting political groups are in reality based upon differences in class and/or forms of property. For example, he noted in nineteenth-century France several different political

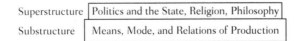
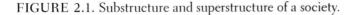

| Superstructure | Politics and the State, Religion, Philosophy |
| Substructure | Means, Mode, and Relations of Production |

FIGURE 2.1. Substructure and superstructure of a society.

factions and parties within the National Assembly that contended with one another for control of the government and manifested little unity among themselves. The absence of harmony among the political groups, Marx insisted, simply reflected underlying social class differences, and the opposing political programs came about from *different forms* of property:

> Legitimists and Orleanists, as we have said, formed the two great sections of the Party of Order. Was that which held these sections fast to their pretenders and kept them apart from one another nothing but lily and tricolour, house of Bourbon and house of Orleans, different shades of royalty, was it the confession of faith in royalty at all?... What kept the two sections apart... was not any so-called principles, it was their material conditions of existence, two different kinds of property, it was the old contrast of town and country, the rivalry between capital and landed property.[11]

Continuing in the same vein, he then furnished one of the clearest expositions of his theory about the connections between material conditions and political views:

> Upon different forms of property, upon the social conditions of existence rises an entire superstructure of distinct and characteristically formed sentiments, illusions, modes of thought and views of life. The entire class creates and forms them out of its material foundations and out of the corresponding social relations.... If Orleanists and Legitimists, if each section sought to make itself and the other believe that loyalty to their two royal houses separated them, it later proved to be the case that it was rather their divided interests which forbade the uniting of the two royal houses. And as in private life one distinguishes between what a man thinks and says of himself and what he really is and does, still more in historical struggles must one distinguish the phrases and fancies of the parties from their real organism and their real interests, their conception of themselves with their reality. Orleanists and Legitimists found themselves side by side in the republic with equal claims. If each side wished to effect the *restoration* of its *own* royal house against the other, that merely signifies that the *two great interests* into which the bourgeoisie is split—landed property and capital—sought each to restore its own supremacy and the subordination of the other.[12]

If the state does not clearly govern in favor of the capitalists, Marx believed, that means only that there is not yet a single dominant social class, but there are contending ones whose power derives from different forms of property and wealth.

STATE POWER AND ITS LIMITS

The state machinery of capitalist societies is comprised of "organs of standing army, police, bureaucracy, clergy and judicature," plus the parliament.[13] This machinery develops policies that generally serve to the advantage of the capitalists. In *Capital*, for instance, he claimed that the British Parliament passed many laws that were principally designed to extend the work day of the laborers and, thus, to increase the profits, or surplus value, of the capitalists.[14]

To Marx, as to many modern neo-Marxists, the state is a very powerful social institution. It concentrates a considerable amount of power and resources in the hands of a relatively small number of officials and institutions. To all appearances it would seem that such institutions can exercise decisive power over the lives of people. The executive branch of the United States federal government, for instance, can make declarations of War, veto decisions by the Congress, and provide for a general and vigorous political leadership for the United States.

But in Marx's view, the power and leadership of the state, and its officials, is ultimately determined and limited by the nature of capitalism itself. States, and state leaders, cannot make decisions that, in the long run, run counter to or undermine the interests of capitalism itself. The system of capitalism, which is a system of private property in which the benefits of ownership belong to private individuals and groups, and the capitalist class itself limits the freedom and exercise of power by the state. As Marx and Engels observed, "[t]he executive of the modern State is but a committee for managing the common affairs of the whole bourgeoisie."[15] (In later writings, these general claims would be updated and made more subtle by neo-Marxists.)

SUSTAINING CAPITALISM AND THE RULE OF CAPITALISTS

What is it that keeps modern capitalism going, especially in the face of the deep inequalities of wealth and material well-being that exist? Many people have written about this issue, seeking to discover the nature of its hegemony and integrity. To Marx, capitalism was sustained by two central forces: the power of its ideology and the durability and versatility of its economy. *Ideology* is one of the central features of the superstructure of capitalism. It represents the ideas, or ideals, that sustained capitalism. To Marx it also represented a form of "false consciousness" insofar as the ideas of capitalism were not those that served the best interests of the workers, but rather those that served the best interests of the capitalists and modern capitalism itself. Any belief, or set of beliefs, that serves to further the interests of capitalism—for example, the dream that many of us have that everyone and anyone can become rich in America—constitute the ideology of capitalism.

But at a deeper level it is the features of the system itself that are self-sustaining. Marx maintained that capitalists secured their profit, or surplus value, simply by providing workers only minimal wages while they reaped huge amounts of profits, much like many corporate CEOs today. The effect then is to prevent the working class from accumulating sufficient capital to become independent of the process of production itself. Thus, in Marx's view, workers only possess their own labor power, and they are forced on a daily, weekly, and monthly basis to work simply because they cannot accumulate any capital themselves. The free market system, a term used today to describe the nature of modern capitalism, is, in fact, anything but free for the working class!

REVOLUTION AND CHANGE

In the past two decades, more and more sociologists have turned their attention to studying movements for political change and those movements, in particular, whose aim is to promote revolutions, or fundamental changes in political and social institutions. The collapse of the Soviet Union and, along with it, its Eastern European allies represents just a few of the major political changes which have occurred and which interest many political sociologists.

Marx himself furnished a very powerful portrait of revolutions that drew upon his general sense of the nature of capitalist societies. He believed that the ultimate foundations for revolution are to be found in the nature of the economy and economic relations. Moreover, he believed that every society ultimately contains the materials within it that would spell its own doom. Societies to him were self-contradictions, forces that are promoted by one social class but that, in the course of development, lay the foundations for their own demise.

There are three general sets of factors that promote the rise of revolutions, according to Marx: critical economic factors, social factors, and the emergence of class consciousness among the working class. The economic factors were most important to Marx, but the others also play a significant role.

Economic Antecedents. Marx expected that the lust of the capitalists for profits would eventually produce an overabundance of commodities—a surplus that exceeded the capacity of the world market to absorb it. Most of the economic antecedents of revolution stem from this central premise. The first of these are the periodic crises and falling profits of capitalists. As Marx and Engels observed in *The Communist Manifesto*:

> It is enough to mention the commercial crises that by their periodic return put on its trial, each time more threateningly, the existence of the entire bourgeois society. In these crises a great part not only of the existing products but also the previously created productive forces are periodically destroyed. In these crises there [appears] an epidemic that in all earlier epochs would have seemed an absurdity—the epidemic of over-production.[16]

Marx's second economic antecedent of revolution is the centralization of cap- ital; a diminishing proportion of the owners of industries come to possess an increasingly greater proportion of the wealth—an exaggeration of capitalism's tendency for wealth to be controlled by a minority. "That which is now to be expropriated is no longer the labourer working for himself, but the capitalist exploiting many labourers. This expropriation is accomplished by the action of the immanent laws of capitalist production itself by the centralization of cap- ital. One capitalist always kills many."[17] One of the effects of centralization is to make the source of oppression and the fact of oppression more visible to the working classes.

Another effect of centralization is *proletarization*. Expropriated from the means of production they formerly controlled, many capitalists are compelled to join the ranks of the working class in order to survive; in effect, they become downwardly mobile. "Entire sections of the ruling classes are, by advance of industry, precipitated into the proletariat, or are at least threatened in their con- ditions of existence. These also support the proletariat with fresh elements of enlightenment and progress."[18]

The last of the major economic antecedents of revolution is also open to the most diverse interpretations. According to Marx, the financial conditions of the average worker would worsen as a result of the growing numbers of eco- nomic crises and the steady displacement of workers by the introduction of technology. In particular, a large surplus population of laborers, an industrial reserve army, would be created, leading to a reduction in workers' wages and to a general burden on the working class.

This industrial reserve army, however, represents only one part of a much broader process, *Verelendung*, or increasing misery. "Accumulation of wealth at one pole is, therefore, at the same time accumulation of misery, agony of toil, slavery, ignorance, brutality, mental degradation, at the opposite pole, i.e. on the side of the class that produces its own product in the form of capital."[19] Disputes occur among scholars about whether Marx intended to argue that the *absolute* wages of the working classes would diminish, that is, that there would be a decline in the general wage level of the working class, or whether he meant to claim that there would be an absolute rise in the general wage levels through- out society but a decline in the *relative* wage level of the proletariat, that is, their share in the national income. The former has become known as the "vulgar" reading of Marx, the latter as the "relative deprivation" reading. This dispute indeed is more than simply an academic one; if Marx meant to imply that the lot of the working class would become progressively worse in absolute terms, then he was clearly mistaken, and this might well account for the absence of the revolution he predicted would occur.

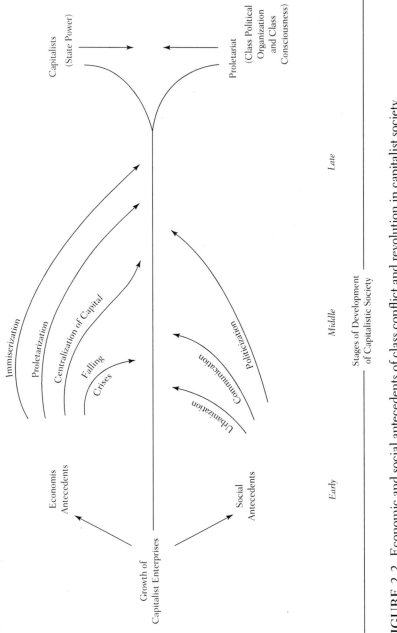

FIGURE 2.2. Economic and social antecedents of class conflict and revolution in capitalist society.

Social Antecedents. A leitmotif characteristic of Marx's thought is an alleged opposition between town and countryside. The theme is evident in Marx's emphasis on urbanization in promoting revolution. The masses of workers drawn into urban areas possess a far greater potential for revolution than the peasants and farmers in the country. There are two reasons for this: the workers in the urban centers are generally employed in factories, thus encountering the most degrading and dehumanizing forms of work, and sheer density of numbers presents a potential for the organization of revolutionary movements, a fact peculiarly characteristic of urban centers.

A second social antecedent of revolution stems from urbanization, namely communication. Communication among workers is essential to the formation of a revolutionary movement, mainly because it enables them to recognize the similarity of their experiences and to develop common beliefs:

> Now and then the workers are victorious, but only for a time. The real fruit of their battles lies not in the immediate result, but in the ever expanding union of the workers. This union is helped on by the improved means of communication that are created by modern industry and that place the workers of different localities in contact with one another.[20]

The importance of communication within the working class is that it serves to counteract the control of the capitalists over the means of communication in society as well as the general hegemony of the capitalist system of values.

The last of the major social antecedents required for the development of a revolutionary movement on the part of the working classes is their politicization. There are two sources of this politicization: one that occurs almost naturally as a result of the encounters between the workers and the capitalists is trade unionism; the other, which is brought into the working classes from without, is the effort by revolutionaries like Marx and his compatriots to direct the politics of the working class. Marx and Engels noted this latter process in *The Communist Manifesto*:

> Finally, in times when the class struggle nears the decisive hour, the process of dissolution going on within the ruling class, in fact within the whole range of old society, assumes such a violent, glaring character that a small section of the ruling class cuts itself adrift and joins the revolutionary class, the class that holds the future in its hands. [So] now a portion of the bourgeoisie goes over to the proletariat, and in particular a portion of the bourgeois ideologists, who have raised themselves to the level of comprehending theoretically the historical movement as a whole.[21]

The two sources, of course, are not necessarily compatible. Indeed, it is on matters of the precise form of this politicization that loyal followers of Marx's doctrines have become divided.

Class Consciousness and Political Action. Perhaps the most significant component in the Marxian scheme of revolution and, more broadly, of change is class consciousness. It is also the least understood component. In order for the working-class members to overthrow the capitalists, they have to become aware of themselves as a class. Adapting terminology from Ludwig Feuerbach, who himself adopted terms ultimately traceable to Kant, Marx asserted that the proletariat had to transform itself from a Klasse an sich, a class simply by virtue of similar economic and social conditions, to a Klasse für sich, a class whose members were aware of those conditions.

What precisely constitutes this phenomenon of class consciousness? Marx came closest to giving his most concise and clear conceptual exposition of it in *German Ideology*: "The separate individuals form a class only insofar as they have to carry on a common battle against another class; otherwise they are on hostile terms with each other as competitors."[22] Class consciousness consists of two elements: the shared awareness among a group of people that they are on hostile terms with another group of people, and a shared desire for united action against this group of people.[23] Class consciousness among the members of the proletariat, in particular, means that as a group they are aware that the capitalists are oppressing them and, further, that they are convinced of the need for collective action to be taken against the capitalists.

Political organization plays a major part in the formation of class consciousness. But what precise form does such an organization assume, especially among the proletariat? For many years it was assumed that trade unions, and the trade union movement, represented the kind of political form that Marx had in mind. Yet the trade union movement never fundamentally challenged the goals of Western capitalist governments, leading some Marxists to conclude that the movement simply represented another form of "false consciousness" under modern capitalism. Today, moreover, the trade union movement has basically disappeared as a force in most societies, thereby leaving a vacuum in political organization and leadership of the working class. The absence of such political organization may in fact be the central factor that has diminished the chances for revolution on the part of the working class. In any case, it certainly has led to greater compliance on the part of workers with the demands of capitalists and thereby sustained the force of capitalism itself.

The Neo-Marxists

V. I. LENIN

V. I. Lenin, born Vladimir Ilich Ulyanov in Russia in 1870, furnished vital and significant additions to the stream of the Marxist legacy in terms both of the meaning of revolutionary practice and the body of theory itself. Above and beyond his theoretical contributions, to which we shall turn shortly, Lenin and his collaborators, including Leon Trotsky, furnished a model for all subsequent revolutionaries. By virtue of their success, they showed how a revolution could be made, particularly in a country that had skipped over the stage of capitalism, ousting the Russian autocracy largely on the strength of a peasant revolution.[24] Under the regimes of the tsars, Russia had been largely an agricultural land, with a relatively small working class; the dominant class had not been one of capitalists but rather one of nobility whose power lay in land, nonproductive wealth, and heritage. Thus, once revolution came to this backward country—one that had not been predicted by Marx to be the first site of a major socialist revolution in the world—naturally all attention turned there. Much subsequent discussion and analysis thus came to be devoted by Communist theoreticians, both within and outside Russia, to the specific factors that contributed to the overthrow of the Tsar, and later the government of Alexander Kerensky, and to the conditions required in order to bring a socialist regime to full fruition. It was precisely on these points that Lenin and Trotsky divided, and that later Stalin and Trotsky separated, leading ultimately to the latter's death at the hands of an assassin in Mexico in 1941.

On Revolution. If Lenin's chief contribution to the Marxist legacy lay in his practical political successes in Russia, therein lay his chief theoretical contributions as well. In 1903 he published a famous pamphlet, What Is to Be Done?[25] This document was intended in part to be a polemic against his adversaries among the Social Democrats in Russia—Plekhanov, in particular—as well as against those who advocated anarchy, a style of political action that had gained much enthusiasm in Russia during the latter half of the nineteenth century, particularly among the narodniki, or Russian populists. Lenin in this pamphlet argues that the nature of the socialist revolution had to be carried out on several fronts—political and theoretical as well as economic. One could not assume, he insists, that the trade union efforts on behalf of the working classes would by themselves produce liberation for the workers. Such efforts, he argues, were alone insufficient. They were especially inadequate because they failed to cope with the existence of the Tsarist autocracy—itself a political, not an economic, institution. In arguing against simple efforts on behalf of better wages and trade unions in general, Lenin was arguing, too, against the reformist efforts that had occurred within various camps of socialists. Lenin's point was that those who sought revolution had to be prepared for it. The revolutionaries were almost compelled to help to create and mold the sentiments of the working class, to elevate them to a true consciousness of the whole movement of history in the doctrines of Marx and Engels. Thus, he believed, revolutionaries had to work to achieve theoretical innovations, and, at the same time, they had to devote themselves totally to the political effort—the effort of agitation against the government and preparation of a party to carry out the revolution.

For revolutionaries and lay scholars alike, Lenin's analysis of the nature of the revolutionary party holds particular fascination. In contrast to many of his contemporaries, Lenin insists that the revolutionary party must consist of a cadre of full-time revolutionaries, people so completely devoted to the revolutionary cause that it absorbs their entire lives. Lenin's own life became an example of such dedication as he gave his energies over entirely to the revolutionary effort in Russia, even during the many years he spent in exile abroad. It was full-time revolutionaries such as he, himself, who would make the revolution. They would train themselves by becoming steeped in the doctrines of Marx and Engels, by devoting their entire attention to the nature of the actual situations they confronted, and by fostering the appropriate understanding of the current historical situation among the masses of people who would constitute the revolutionary movement. Such revolutionaries, Lenin further insisted, must necessarily engage in a tireless campaign of agitation, both in an attempt to arouse the enthusiasm of the mass of supporters and in the difficult effort to unseat the powerful regime they confronted. The success of the Bolsheviks in Russia inevitably led many other potential revolutionaries to seek the answer to their own form of revolution in Lenin's *What Is to Be Done?*

With considerable admiration, Georg Lukács described Lenin as someone who was part theoretician—one who invents and elaborates the theories necessary to the success of the revolutionary party—and part politician—one who possesses a broad grasp of which tactics are to be used and when and how to use them most effectively. Nowhere is this delicate blend between attention to theory and to actual fact more evident than in Lenin's constant demand that revolutionaries seek to interpret the current state of affairs in light *both* of the unique historical situation and of the state of class conflict in a particular society. He condemned those so-called Marxists who blindly spoke of the working and bourgeois classes, and of class conflict in all societies, of failing to take into account the special concatenation of circumstances within them. He believed that the nature of the class struggle was not the same everywhere in the modern world. Thus, he observed that "a Marxist must take cognizance of actual events, of the precise facts of *reality*, and must not cling to a theory of yesterday, which, like all theories, at best only outlines the main and general, and only *approximates* to an inclusive grasp of the complexities of life."[26] Lenin's insistence on an acknowledgment of the actual state of affairs, construed with the aid of the theory of historical materialism—rather than an unreflective application of those theories—has become recognized as yet another of his important contributions to the Marxist legacy, and has particularly influenced such scholars as Louis Althusser and Nicos Poulantzas.[27]

On the State. As with his other contributions to Marxist theory and practice, Lenin's contributions in *State and Revolution,* a document completed in August 1917, but published after the October Revolution, took the form of political theory.[28] At length he explores the exact nature of a socialist or workers' state, something neither Marx nor Engels had been able to elaborate. It is here that Lenin seeks to discern the outlines of a revolutionary dictatorship of the proletariat, to determine how, in Engels' words, the state would ultimately "wither away." Lenin argues that in Russia the February Revolution, that which brought Alexander Kerensky to power but left the Parliament intact, was merely a preliminary step to the true socialist revolution. Indeed, he suggests, the February Revolution seemed to have all the characteristics of a bourgeois revolution, successfully overthrowing the Tsarist regime but, at the same moment, leaving the bourgeoisie in control of society. Thus, it was necessary that this regime, itself, be overthrown, and that it be overthrown in the name of the proletariat, the working classes of Russia. To do so, he further argues, there must be a joint effort on behalf of the peasants and the workers, the former largely outnumbering the latter save in a few urban places like Petrograd.

Having overthrown the despised Kerensky regime, Lenin argued, the Bolsheviks then must turn to the task of constructing an appropriate workers' state in Russia. But what did it mean to say that such a state would be a revolutionary dictatorship of the proletariat? Was it not true, in the writings of Marx and Engels alike, that the state was conceived merely as an instrument for the oppression of the ruled by the ruling classes and that with revolution it must necessarily disappear? On these issues Lenin had to struggle with the ambiguities found in the body of Marx's thought, to search for a way to remain consistent with the Marxist doctrine yet, at the same time, to develop novel principles to guide the workers' state in Russia. Hence, he came to argue that the workers' state had to take over the reins of power on behalf of the working classes, and that it had to be occupied by people who, themselves, came from the working classes. But such a state also had to be used as a weapon against the previously dominant ruling classes, the remnants both of the bourgeoisie and the Tsarist regime. Here Lenin went beyond that which Marx and Engels proposed. He insisted that the workers' state could become a weapon in the struggle for the emancipation of the workers, and with them the rest of society. He further suggested, again on the basis of his reading and understanding of where Russian society stood in mid-1917, that the workers' state would necessarily entail a concentration of power in the hands of the representatives of the workers—an armed movement, in other words. In contrast to those who proposed establishing a democratic republic, he claimed that such a democracy would not be suitable for Russia, at least for a time, because the remnants of the past society still displayed pronounced social and economic inequities.

Lenin sought to use the Paris Commune of 1871 and, in particular, Marx's analysis of it as a further device to furnish some sense of the socialist state. He found here support of his claim that the Russian state must be run on behalf of and entirely represent the workers rather than all citizens, as a simple reading of bourgeois democracy might suggest. Later, in the course of establishing a government on the heels of the Bolshevik Revolution of October, Lenin came to organize the new socialist regime on the basis of the soviets, the councils of workers who had helped to form the basis for the overthrow of the Kerensky government. The soviets, together with the development of the Communist Party apparatus, thus became the practical realization of the workers' state which Lenin sought to define in *State and Revolution*.

On Imperialism. Lenin made one additional—some even claim his most enduring—contribution to Marxist thought in the form of an analysis of imperialism. Imperialism, he argued, was the most advanced state of capitalism.[29] In his writings about mature capitalism, particularly in Capital, Marx seemed to have failed to keep pace with historical events much beyond the middle of the nineteenth century. Yet it was at this time that capitalism started to take on a novel appearance. Countries like Great Britain and France, for example, began to seek to extend their dominion over other parts of the world, particularly the lands of Asia and Africa. In need of ever more abundant supplies of raw materials and of cheap labor for manufacture, not to mention larger markets for their goods, these more advanced capitalist nations sought to make permanent subjects of unsuspecting inhabitants of other lands. The net effect was to commence a deep and growing division in the world at large, between the richer, capitalist countries and the poorer, colonial, or subject, nations, a division that remains vividly alive today.

Lenin sought to clarify and to explain these developments in his pamphlet entitled *Imperialism: The Highest State of Capitalism*. Drawing upon historical developments in the last quarter of the nineteenth and early years of the twentieth centuries, together with the pioneering analyses of J. A. Hobson and Rudolph Hilferding, Lenin argued that modern imperialism entailed the development of handfuls of monopolies within capitalist countries alongside the rise of finance capital to a place of paramount significance.[30] In search of ever-greater profit, the motive force of capitalism, the great industrialists in America, France, Germany, and the few other capitalist countries of the world turned to invest their capital in enterprises in the less developed lands and to further secure their dominance over these countries through large loans. Ultimately, Lenin argues, the world by the early twentieth century had become divided into the nations of owners, or capitalists, and nations of owned, or subjects. The division occurred in part at the initiation of the capitalist class itself, in part by the cooperative efforts of government officials who sought to make lawful the control of monopoly capitalism in occupied colonies.

Lenin's analysis represented a novel twist to the Marxist legacy insofar as it emphasized the growth of monopoly capitalism as a new state of capitalist development. Moreover, it was novel as well because of the way it portrayed the growing development of ties and alliances among the various countries of the world and of the deepening polarization between those countries that one might regard as bourgeois—including segments even of the working classes, as in Great Britain—and those countries that were largely, if not exclusively, made up of masses of laborers. This division, Lenin seemed to sense, was so powerful that it could provide the basis for the worldwide proletarian revolution earlier anticipated by Marx.

Antonio Gramsci

Like Lenin, the Italian radical Antonio Gramsci had become deeply involved with socialist politics even as a young man, but unlike Lenin, Gramsci never succeeded in participating in the overthrow of a regime on behalf of the working class. In fact, like so many other leftist radicals in the 1920s, Gramsci came to admire the Soviet regime for its great successes. Gramsci had taken up membership in the Italian Communist Party in 1926 after many years of active political and intellectual involvement with Italian left-wing groups. Only one year later, after flirting with capture for many years, Gramsci was seized by Benito Mussolini's police and put into prison. He remained there for the last decade of his life, subject to torture and to recurring physical ailments. This period also became the most intellectually creative of his life, a time when he attempted to deal with the possibility of proletarian revolution in Italy. In the course of his reflections he developed ideas that have had a profound influence over much subsequent Marxist thought.

On the Communist Party. One of Gramsci's principal ideas dealt with the role of the Communist Party in its efforts to oust the established powers. Departing from the seminal document of Niccolo Machiavelli, *The Prince*, Gramsci argued that in the modern world the prince actually represented not an individual person, but rather a corporate group, a collective will—or to be quite specific, a party such as the Italian Communist Party.[31] So understood, there were many lessons that the Communists could learn from the reflections of Machiavelli. Just like the prince, the party must learn when the moment is right for the effort to take and to secure power. Just like the prince, the party must stand firm in its political convictions, committed to specific lines of action designed to acquire power for itself and for the working classes. Most important, just like the prince, the party must appear as the "centaur—half-animal and half-human."[32] That is, the party must adapt to the circumstances of the world itself: it must be able to engage in the use of force as necessary, but also be able to take advantage of the widespread convictions and sympathies of the public. It must seek, in particular, to steer a delicate course between imposing itself as a collective will on the people from without and regarding itself as a simple expression of the will of the people.

On the Hegemony of Class Rule. Gramsci's analysis of the role of the party displayed an unusually acute and complete grasp of the strategic problems that confronted revolutionary parties such as that of the Communists. This very same sensitivity also helps to account for the power of his insight into those conditions that sustained established regimes, an analysis of the conditions of *hegemony*.[33] Troubled by the failure of working-class parties to secure power on behalf of the working classes, particularly in Italy, Gramsci argued that no party could come to power unless such power rested upon the hegemony of their rule. As in the case of his analysis of the modern prince, this meant that the regime must be regarded by the public not as an unsympathetic villain, but as the single, true expression of their wishes. The power of the state under its hegemony rested not on its force alone, but on a compliance more or less freely given by its subjects. Such a free and widespread public compliance, Gramsci reasoned, arose from the deep and complete entrenchment of a regime. Further, this entrenchment meant that a widespread loyalty must exist among the public for the regime, a loyalty that was manufactured by the panoply of social and cultural institutions.

The hegemony in the rule of a class thus came to rest on a highly complex and very diffuse set of sentiments within the public, sentiments virtually impervious to the occasional attacks of parties. "The superstructures of civil society," Gramsci wrote, "are like the trench-systems of modern warfare. In war it would sometimes happen that a fierce artillery attack seemed to have destroyed the enemy's entire defense system, whereas in fact it had only destroyed the outer perimeter; and at the moment of their advance and attack the assailants would find themselves confronted by a line of defense which was still effective."[34] Gramsci's analysis, of course, was extremely helpful to the effort to elaborate Marx's ideas in order to grasp the historic intransigence of regimes to the attempted radical penetration of them; at the same time it bore grave witness to the pessimism that overwhelmed him as he lay isolated and alone in prison.

THE FRANKFURT SCHOOL

Among contemporary Marxists there are few groups of scholars that can rival the influence of the Frankfurt School. Founded in 1934 in Germany by

Theodor Adorno and Max Horkheimer, later temporarily transplanted to the United States during the reign of Adolf Hitler, the Frankfurt School's principals interpreted Marx mainly as a philosopher rather than as a dedicated revolutionary thinker. In a sense, they returned to the early, younger Marx as a means of drawing out the main insights they believe he contributed; at the same time, they added new elements to Marxist thought, introducing ideas such as sublimation and repression from Sigmund Freud and rationality and legitimacy from Max Weber. Drawn toward a more philosophical rendering of the writings of Marx, they have fashioned a corpus of thought that is almost intellectually impenetrable—certainly a far remove from the needs of the working classes of the world today.

Herbert Marcuse. One of the main novelties of the Frankfurt School, particularly the writings of Herbert Marcuse and Jürgen Habermas, is the blending of ideas originally emphasized by Max Weber with the critical assessment of capitalism found in Marx. No longer concerned with the proletariat itself, or even with labor as productive activity, as in the classic Marxist formulations, Marcuse achieved great success and fame in the United States with his One-Dimensional Man.[35] He argues that modern civilization exhibits a radical divorce between the Reason sought after by the ancient Greeks and the reason that displays itself throughout modern society. The Reason of the ancient Greeks was associated intimately with the search for Truth, and mind, itself, was not divorced from nature but was viewed as part and parcel of it. The Greek philosophers had assumed an intimate harmony between mind and nature, the one the part of the other, and Reason represented the working of the mind as it sought, by virtue of deep reflection, to discover those principles that were essential to nature and those that merely were ephemeral. What modern capitalist civilization has done, in the eyes of Marcuse, is to create a fundamental alienation of man from nature, of reason from Reason, and it has accomplished this by suppressing all those qualities that are fundamentally and essentially human—man's need to reflect deeply on the world as well as his sensual nature, his Eros, or love. In assuming this sort of perspective, Marcuse, like Lukács before him, reintroduces dialectics into the nature of Marxist critical thought, so much so as to virtually disguise the essential Marxist twist to the thought itself.

Marcuse's indictment of modern capitalist civilization, with America taken as the supreme instance of this civilization, draws a certain inspiration from Weber's emphasis on the nature of rationality in the modern world.[36] Weber, as we shall learn in the next chapter, distinguished between technical rationality—that which seemed to characterize the essential element of modern capitalism, with a specific emphasis upon technique, efficiency, and calculability—and substantive rationality, that which was concerned with the ends, the goals, the values toward which action was targeted. That which is especially characteristic and, he implied, equally oppressive under modern capitalism is that all action, in virtually every sphere of society, has become dominated by a concern with the quantitative and calculable assessment of the costs involved in reaching a particular end, any end, rather than with the substantive meaning of the end itself. Marcuse compliments Weber on this basic insight; yet he then immediately condemns him for failing to carry through, in a true critical fashion, to ask why it is that technical and substantive rationality have become divorced from one another.

To Marcuse the answer lies, of course, in the fact that modern capitalist civilization displays a radical separation between the two forms of reason: technical reason becomes reason, and substantive reason stands for the Greek conception of Reason. In a fashion strongly reminiscent of Hegel as well as of Lukács, Marcuse argues that the objects created by man thus come to stand apart from, and apparently above, him, at the same time as his own capacity for deep reflection, or imagination, is itself repressed. In effect, man no longer represents man, but something dehumanized; his own sense of himself is seen through the objects and bodies of thought to analyze objects he has created. Hence, man comes to think of himself simply as a technical instrument, a worker on the assembly line divorced from a sense of self, because of the scientific principles of management in modern civilization. His language takes a form of immediate connection between a concept and a thing rather than an imaginative connection empowered by his mind; even his sexual passions come to be reified, in the form of appeals to his prurient interests and to his own body as a mere object of sexual passion rather than as a part of himself intimately involved in love. A good deal of this form of indictment of modern capitalism, it may be interesting to learn, found an even earlier expression in the very lucid and exceedingly insightful analysis of Antonio Gramsci.[37]

Jürgen Habermas. In perhaps his most well-known analysis, Jürgen Habermas, the current leading member of the Frankfurt School, too draws upon the work of Max Weber to critically understand the nature of modern capitalism. Taking up Weber's concern with the nature of legitimacy and legitimation, Habermas argues that the contradictions in modern society, in particular those engendered by the twin and paradoxical emphases on social welfare and mass democracy, have created a crisis in the assumed rightness and propriety of the decisions taken in modern capitalist nations. Both Weber and other scholars who shared with him an emphasis on the legalistic nature of legitimacy, Habermas claims, were misled into believing that the very nature of legal decision making in modern society was, itself, sufficient to secure proof of the propriety of decisions. That, in fact, is incorrect, Habermas claims—there is a deeper, or different, level upon which legitimacy rests, one of validity based upon peoples' shared normative understandings of what is to be valued in the social world. But this level of understanding is obscure both in modern society itself and in the theories about this society. Only a critical theory, he argues, one that holds as problematic the very foundations of modern capitalism, can penetrate to the truth of things in the world; in this effort, Habermas proposes a program of "universal pragmatics," which seeks to expose the distortions and contradictions under modern capitalism through a detailed analysis for discursive language and communication.[38]

NICOS POULANTZAS

The preeminent political sociologist among contemporary Marxists was Nicos Poulantzas, a theorist who died an untimely death in 1979. Poulantzas sought to extend the Marxist framework to twentieth-century capitalism and to an understanding of the twentieth-century state. In particular, he tried to understand how the state might become an independent actor in the history and development of the class struggle, and his ideas have become enshrined in discussions among Marxists about the "relative autonomy of the state."[39]

On Structures. Poulantzas provided some unique and special ways of thinking about capitalism and modern politics. Perhaps the most unique element of his vision was one that he adopted from his French mentor, another Marxist, Louis Althusser. Like Althusser, Poulantzas thought of societies in terms of structures. Structures represent more or less coherent ensembles of elements, and they serve to maintain the integrity of a social order. They are abstract forces, somewhat parallel, for example, to the notions of superstructure or civil society that we used earlier to explain Marx's imagery. They are much more than mere concepts, however, for, though abstract, they still serve to shape how the world works. Poulantzas, following Althusser, insisted that there are several structures at work in the operations of modern capitalism. They are the ideological, or the realm of ideas; the political, or the realm of politics and the state; the economic, or the realm of production; and the juridical, or the realm of law.[40] Thus, in the ideological realm, Poulantzas included such claims as the importance of individual rights, or the representation of multiple interests as instances of liberal political ideology under modern capitalism. Moreover, like Althusser, Poulantzas maintained that each of these structures could operate independently of one another and that in any given concrete historical society, say the United States in the twentieth century, one structure could dominate the others in the workings of the social order. For example, he maintained that in certain instances the ideological structure could prevail over the other three, whereas in other instances, the political and, in particular, the state could achieve dominance. Of course, the implication of this claim was that Poulantzas rejected any simple, or vulgar, reading of Marx, with its emphasis on economic determinism. The notion that the economic element determined the functioning of capitalism in the last instance was taken by Poulantzas in a very loose and liberal fashion.

On the State. A second, related element of the unique view of Poulantzas is his claim that the state, as a structure, can independently foster the survival and growth of a capitalist society. Here his argument is twofold. He asserts that the institutions of the state may intervene in the class struggle, particularly if and when there is a stalemate between the dominant and subordinate classes. Indeed, the state may even act to further the interests of the subordinate classes over and above those of the dominant capitalist class. He writes, for instance, that "the state aims precisely at the political disorganization of the dominated classes ... [and] ... where the political struggle of the dominated classes is possible, it is sometimes the means of maintaining the [hegemony of the dominant classes.]"[41] In other words, where the state permits the open competition and conflict among classes, this may simply serve to maintain the overall hegemony of capitalism in the economic, juridical, and ideological spheres of society. But there is another way that the state may serve as an independent actor in society. It does so by becoming a site itself on which the class struggle is fought. What Poulantzas means by this claim is that the state may be composed of different fractions of classes, including members of the dominant capitalist class but also members of the subordinate classes as well. Moreover, Poulantzas argues, sometimes the fate of capitalism is determined not by the hegemony of the capitalist class but by the hegemony of another class, one that more clearly unifies a capitalist society at a particular historical moment. It is in this sense that Poulantzas seeks to explain the modern welfare state, many of whose measures benefit the working class. The victory of the working class is only apparent, however. The benefits provided through the welfare state, such as Social Security, Medicare, and other measures, in Poulantzas's view simply insure that the other fundamental components of modern capitalism will escape attack.

The Relative Autonomy of the State: Poulantzas vs. Ralph Miliband. Poulantzas's imagery of society and of the state is obviously more complicated than that of Marx. Whereas Marx had once asserted that the "state is nothing but the executive of the ruling class," Poulantzas claims that the state can represent a battleground on which the conflicts and contradictions of capitalism are fought out among different classes. While this revision of Marx seems well taken, Poulantzas's argument about states as structures, and about their relative autonomy from the economic workings of capitalism, resulted in considerable debate with other contemporary Marxists, especially Ralph Miliband.[42] Miliband argues that in twentieth-century capitalist societies the state remains the central vehicle through which capitalism will survive. How? It happens, he claims, because members of the capitalist class constitute the key policy makers in such state institutions as the judiciary, the police force, the legislature, and, especially, the executive branch of government. Miliband provides very convincing documentation for his thesis. Poulantzas, however, asserts that Miliband's version of Marx—which clearly adheres to the "executive of the ruling class" notion—is much too simple-minded. It is the state as structure, not as people, that fosters and furthers the rise of modern capitalism. To reduce the state, or even capitalism as a whole, to individual agents, Poulantzas maintains, is to trivialize the fundamental ideas of Marx and to miss Marx's emphasis on capitalism as an impersonal, working system.

The intellectual battle between Poulantzas and Miliband over the nature and operations of the state in modern capitalism became quite heated in the 1970s. It also reflected some of the ambiguity evident in the ideas of Marx himself, an ambiguity to which we alluded in our discussion of Marx. One such point has to do with the role of people, or agents, in the Marxist scheme of things. Are they merely vehicles for the realization of the workings of the capitalist system, or do they serve somehow as independent forces? Indeed, are they, in fact, real? Poulantzas would deny them a reality altogether, while Miliband, though acknowledging their reality, would suggest they still serve to implement the long-term interests of capitalism. But the implication of Miliband's view, too, is that if the state were to be occupied by agents of other classes, then it could operate contrary to the interests of capitalism itself. It might even reform capitalism. That, clearly, is not at all the implication of Poulantzas's argument. Another point of ambiguity has to do with the role of the state itself. While Poulantzas wished to emphasize how the state could achieve an autonomy in the evolution of the class struggle, becoming dominated by classes other than the capitalist class, in the end his perspective provided no clearer view of this matter than did that of Marx. For, like Marx, he insisted that while the state structures might in a given historical circumstance favor some subordinate class—for example, the peasants during the regime of Louis Bonaparte in France—in the long run such actions continue to favor the growth of capitalism. In other words, the autonomy of the state for Poulantzas is just as much a fiction as it was for Marx; for both theorists the hegemony of the capitalist class, and with it, capitalism, escape untouched by the workings of the state.

Conclusion

The writings and ideas of Karl Marx continue to play a very important role in how sociologists think about politics. They animate some rather major views of history. And even where much of the Marxian paraphernalia has disappeared from view, including the notions of alienation and dialectical analysis, Marx's ghost still remains a powerful force over our view of the world. Perhaps the most potent idea is that of the deep injustice and misery that exists for so many citizens of the world. Marx focused on capitalism and its inequalities as a means of revealing how the system acted to make some people very rich, while others became incredibly poor. As capitalism has spread across the world, inequality remains. Indeed, there are new discoveries almost every day of the widening gap between the rich and the poor both within as well as across nations. The CEOs of corporations continue to accumulate new wealth while the average citizen can barely keep pace with the rising cost of living in most countries.

What is it about capitalism that leads to such great economic disparities? What must be done to help the poor and the needy to overcome their difficulties? These questions were central to Marx's economic analysis and thought, and they are the questions that remain his enduring legacy and vision for hope in the modern world.

NOTES

1. Isaiah Berlin, *Karl Marx: His Life and Environment* (London: Oxford University Press, 1963).
2. Tom Bottomore, ed., *Karl Marx* (Englewood Cliffs, NJ: Prentice-Hall, Inc., 1973), 68.
3. Georg Lukacs, *History and Class Consciousness*, translated by R. Livingstone (London: The Merlin Press, Ltd., 1971).
4. Robert C. Tucker, ed., *The Marx-Engels Reader* (New York: W.W. Norton Co., Inc., 1972), 23.
5. Lewis Feuer, ed., *Marx and Engels: Basic Writings on Politics and Philosophy* (Garden City, NY: Doubleday and Co., 1959), xi.
6. Feuer, *Marx and Engels*, 17–18.
7. Ibid., 282.
8. Since Marx, like every other sociologist, could not conduct such experiments in the real world, he conducted them in the abstract. The results, no less significant for being obtained in such a manner, indicated, among other things, the manner in which capitalist enterprises would grow. Defects in the actual economic principles

employed by Marx, owing largely to the source of them, David Ricardo, rendered many of his predictions wrong or indeterminate. For example, see Fred M. Gottheil, *Marx's Economic Predictions* (Evanston, IL: Northwestern University Press, 1977). Such is the fate of many of our scientific predictions, however good they might appear for a time.

9. Even when Marx wrote of the capitalist and proletariat classes, he seemed confused about what they represented. On occasion he wrote of them as though they were real groups. However, he usually viewed them as abstract entities that were useful for conducting analyses and making predictions [Stanislaw Ossowski, *Class Structures in the Social Consciousness* (New York: Free Press, 1963)]. More important, if Marx meant to define the capitalist and proletarian classes by their relationship to property, there must be one additional social class under capitalism, the landed aristocracy—a remnant of feudalism whose property consists not of the technical and scientific apparatus, but of land. There then appear to be three main social classes under capitalism, not two: the capitalists, owners of the technical and scientific apparatus of production; the landed aristocracy, owners of land; and the proletariat, owners of no property, simply their labor power. These, incidentally, were the three principal classes that Marx defined in the third volume of *Capital*. Nevertheless, if Marx had remained alive long enough he would probably have argued that as capitalist societies matured—and no capitalist society in the late nineteenth century could be considered mature, not even England—land would diminish in importance as a source of profit, thereby leaving only the two great classes, the capitalist and the proletariat.

10. Marx, "The German Ideology," in Tucker, *The Marx-Engels Reader*, 136.

11. Marx, "The Eighteenth Brumaire of Louis Bonaparte," in Tucker, *The Marx-Engels Reader*, 459.

12. Ibid., 459–60.

13. Marx, "The Civil War in France," in Tucker, *The Marx-Engels Reader*, 552.

14. Marx, *Capital*, I, Chapter 10.

15. Marx and Engels, "The Communist Manifesto," in Tucker, *The Marx-Engels Reader*, 337.

16. Feuer, *Marx and Engels*, 12.

17. Marx, *Capital*, I, 750.

18. Feuer, *Marx and Engels*, 19.

19. Marx, *Capital*, I, 644–45.

20. Feuer, *Marx and Engels*, 16.

21. Ibid., 17.

22. Tucker, *The Marx-Engels Reader*, 143.

23. There is one additional element that figures into class consciousness on a philosophical plane—the class of people must be aware of their coming ascendancy to power in society (Georg Lukacs, *History and Class Consciousness: Studies in Marxist Dialectics*. Cambridge, MA: The MIT Press, 1971, 83–222).

24. Isaac Deutscher, ed., *The Age of Permanent Revolution: A Trotsky Anthology* (New York: Dell Publishing, 1964), *passim*.

25. V. I. Lenin, "What Is to Be Done: Burning Questions of Our Movement," in *The Lenin Anthology*, ed. Robert C. Tucker (New York: W.W. Norton & Co., Inc., 1975), 12–114.
26. V. I. Lenin, "Letters on Tactics," in Lenin, *Marx-Engels-Marxism* (Moscow: Foreign Languages Publishing House, n.d.), 400.
27. Two works by Poulantzas which are particularly valuable are *Classes in Contemporary Capitalism* (London: Verso, 1978) and *Political Power and Social Classes* (London: Verso, 1978). Both reveal the influence of Lenin's thought on Poulantzas's own work.
28. V. I. Lenin, "The State and Revolution," in Tucker, *The Lenin Anthology*, 311–98.
29. V. I. Lenin, "Imperialism: The Highest State of Capitalism," in *The Lenin Anthology*, Tucker, 204–74.
30. Rudoph Hilferding, *Das Finanzkapital* (Vienna: I. Brand, 1910); and J. A. Hobson, *Imperialism* (Ann Arbor, MI: University of Michigan Press, 1902, 1965).
31. Antonio Gramsci, "The Modern Prince," in *Selections from the Prison Notebooks*, Antonio Gramsci, edited and translated Quintin Hoare and Geoffrey Nowell Smith (New York: International Publishers, 1971), 123–205.
32. Gramsci, *Prison Notebooks*, 170.
33. Gramsci, *Prison Notebooks*, 125 *et passim*.
34. Gramsci, *Prison Notebooks*, 235.
35. Herbert Marcuse, *One-Dimensional Man* (Boston: Beacon Press, 1964).
36. Herbert Marcuse, "Industrialization and Capitalism in the Work of Max Weber," in *Negations: Essays in Critical Theory*, Herbert Marcuse (Boston: Beacon Press, 1968), 201–26.
37. Antonio Gramsci, "Americanism and Fordism," in *Prison Notebooks*, Gramsci, 277–318.
38. See his various works, among them, Jürgen Habermas, *Legitimation Crisis* (Boston: Beacon Press, 1975); *Communication and the Evolution of Society* (Boston: Beacon Press, 1979); *Theory and Practice* (Boston: Beacon Press, 1973); and *Knowledge and Human Interests* (Boston: Beacon Press, 1971).
39. For a good introduction to the ideas of Nicos Poulantzas, read Bob Jessop, *Nicos Poulantzas: Marxist Theory and Political Strategy* (New York: St. Martin's Press, 1985). Poulantzas's own discussion of the relative autonomy of the state can be found in Poulantzas, *Political Power and Social Classes*, Part IV.
40. Poulantzas, ibid., Part I *et passim*.
41. Ibid., 191.
42. For interesting highlights on the debate, see David A. Gold, Clarence Y. H. Lo, and Erik Olin Wright, "Recent Developments in Marxist Theories of the Capitalist State: I" *Monthly Review Press*, 27 (October 1975), 29–43.

Chapter 3

On States and Societies
Max Weber and the Neo-Weberians

"Every state is founded on force," said Trotsky at Brest-Litovsk. That is indeed right...force is a means specific to the state....Today...we have to claim that a state is a human community that successfully claims the monopoly of the legitimate use of physical force within a given territory.... The state is considered the sole source of the 'right' to use violence. Hence, 'politics' for us means striving to share power or striving to influence the distribution of power, either among states or among groups within a state.

Politics As A Vocation

It seems to be a virtual truism that the institutions of the state, or government, exercise control over workings of politics. Certainly that claim is an integral part of the view of all those scholars who call themselves political scientists. But sociologists, at least since the time of Karl Marx, have taken a slightly different tack on the matter. Politics, they argue, cannot simply be understood by examining the internal operations of the state itself. Instead, one must work on a broader canvas—which, for many Marxists, would include social classes and the economy as well as the international setting of countries—in seeking to explain the nature of politics.

The thinker who functioned to turn our attention back to the force of the state and its connections to other social institutions was Max Weber. Weber, it is said, considered himself a kind of antithesis to Marx. He tried to correct Marx's materialist philosophy with one that also assigned an important, if not decisive, role to ideas and ideals in the study of history. In his famous conclusion to *The Protestant Ethic*, a work that traced the origins and consequences of the rise of ascetic Protestantism in the West, Weber observes that ". . . it is, of course, not my aim to substitute for a one-sided materialistic an equally one-sided spiritualistic causal interpretation of culture and of history. Each is equally possible, but each, if it does not serve as the preparation, but as the conclusion of an investigation, accomplishes equally little in the interest of historical truth."[1] In the realm of politics, Weber also tried to offset Marx's heavy emphasis on economic causes of social phenomena. Unlike Marx, he believed that the actual administration of politics in nations played a very significant part in shaping how power is exercised over people and other nations.

One other element that Weber brought to the study of politics is an emphasis on the role of great figures in the making of history. Most sociologists emphasize the long-term significance of fundamental organizations and social institutions, like the state, over historical outcomes. Weber, however, believed that individuals of great personal power and influence—*charismatic* personalities, he called them—could also exercise a decisive role in the shaping of modern nations. "Everywhere the development of the modern state is initiated through the action of the prince," he once wrote.[2] Figures like these often will arise under conditions of societal instability, providing the leadership necessary to take unstable institutions and to reshape them for future generations. In recent times, there are important figures like Mikhail Gorbachev in Russia and Nelson Mandela in South Africa who furnished precisely this kind of leadership in times of social and political upheaval.

Although sociologists disagree about the extent to which such figures can play a role—beyond institutions themselves—Weber tried to have it both ways. He argued that the strength of state institutions was due to the force of their law and administrative apparatus, as well as the singular figures who helped to furnish their direction and leadership. Such singular figures, he insisted, not only serve to sustain ongoing institutions, but they, and their immediate allies, have the energy and vitality to create them anew. "Weber shared with Nietzsche the conviction that only the individual, as a rule only the outstanding individual, was capable of setting new goals and of imparting a new drive to society," observes Wolfgang Mommsen.[3]

Max Weber on States and Politics

The Essential Weber

Max Weber was one of the world's last great polymaths. An expert in any number of fields, ranging from law to economics, Weber tried to unravel a number of mysteries about the development of the West. Unlike Marx, he never produced a grand theory. Nor did he believe such theories to be valid and important instruments for the development of the social sciences. He writes:

> Laws are important and valuable in the exact natural sciences, in the measure that those sciences are *universally valid*. For the knowledge of historical phenomena in their concreteness, the most general laws, because they are most devoid

of content are also the least valuable. The more comprehensive the validity,—or scope—of a term, the more it leads us away from the richness of reality since in order to include the common elements of the largest possible number of phenomena, it must necessarily be as abstract as possible and hence *devoid* of content. In the cultural sciences, the knowledge of the universal or general is never valuable in itself.[4]

Instead, he attacked specific, but broad problems with a kind of attention and historical rigor absent in the work of Marx. He believed that the history of human societies was such that it would be impossible to ever formulate some basic general laws or principles about such societies; at best one could offer specific explanations for particular historical events. Further, as time passed and the world changed, even the questions posed by social scientists would change, reflecting new issues and concerns.

Because of his many pursuits, Weber was compelled to engage in a delicate balancing act, seeking to sustain his work as a scholar and to continue with his active interest in everyday politics. Eventually he shaped a strategy for himself that has since become a model for many social scientists and historians. Above all else, he advocated, an intellectual must attempt to separate his life as a scholar from that as a man of action. The judgments involved in the two pursuits simply could not be mixed without endangering the effectiveness of each; as a scientist, in particular, one could not fairly or safely judge the proper course for the citizen. Along similar lines, the scholar, in his capacity as teacher, should not engage in polemics in the classroom, particularly if such a strategy is designed to achieve popularity rather than to educate. "The task of the teacher," he wrote, "is to serve the students with his knowledge and scientific experience and not to imprint upon them his personal political views....I am ready to prove from the works of our historians that whenever the man of science introduces his personal value judgment, a full understanding of the facts ceases."[5]

As serious scholarship and science make it imperative that polemics be removed from the setting of intellectual discourse, so, too, the political arena is marked by its own special rules. Politics, in essence, represents a continuing conflict over the control of scarce material and symbolic (or ideal) resources. Any person who wishes to engage in this arena must be prepared to struggle, to compromise, but eventually to emerge either on the side of the victors or on that of the vanquished. Thus, an ethics of ultimate ends, especially that of natural law that insists on the inherent rights and equality of all men, is doomed from the beginning to failure in politics. Obviously Weber's view of politics, as of its connections to scholarship, differs greatly from that of Marx; Marx sought to achieve a unity among the seemingly independent pursuits. Nevertheless, Weber's perspective, like that of Marx, must be understood in the broader context of his view of Western societies.

The nature of social and economic life in the West, according to Weber, represents the pinnacle of professionalism and routine activity. Each of the many and diverse kinds of activities is defined in the form of a profession, or vocation, thereby establishing a unique career path as well as a special set of rights and obligations. This theme, in turn, is part of a much broader and pervasive trend in the development of Western civilization; the theme is the *rationalization of life*. This, for Weber, means that all life is subject to a common form of assessment, calculability—that is, the assessment of the most technically efficient means for attaining particular ends. Thus, in the marketplace the most efficient means for purchasing goods and services can be calculated with precision; in the courts the form of penalty or obligation incumbent on the lawbreaker can be made almost exactly; in war the strategy best designed to accomplish quick and efficient naval or land victories can easily be assessed.

These patterns are embodied in rational bureaucracy, the most dominant and striking feature of the West. This form of administration, Weber claimed, has both advantages and its disadvantages. As the structural embodiment of the major themes of Western civilization, it represents major *technical* advances over all prior civilizations; it can accomplish tasks more quickly, precisely, and cheaply than any other form of organization. It also, however, invites the alienation of man; it represents the structural avenue through which modern life is administered, and the individual, lacking the ability to control this institution, is therefore unable to control the activities of his own life. Further, bureaucracy has become so pervasive an institution that the individual's options for action, and thus his freedom, have been reduced.

Although any individual's choice with regard to means has been reduced to a common measure of evaluation, it has not been similarly diminished with respect to ends. There are a finite number of values from among which men and women may choose to commit themselves. Such values represent an integral part of Weber's sociology, finding their expression as objects that could provide the basis for distinctive social groups, *status groups*, as well as sources of competition and conflict among groups in the political arena.

Weber's greatest intellectual achievement is to be found in his effort to explain the broad differences between the West and the Orient. Here he turned his attention and efforts to understanding the nature of religion. He made religion the centerpiece of much of his work and the study of the rise of ascetic Protestantism in the West the major part of it. He argued that ascetic Protestantism was a major fact of Western life, signifying a major difference between the West and the Orient. The tenets of ascetic Protestantism—its emphasis on salvation, the unceasing vigilance of the believer over his or her life, the abstinence from self-indulgence, the single-minded devotion to one's work and life—helped in a paradoxical fashion to secure the dominion of capitalism in the West by providing a moral foundation for the shrewd and relentless accumulation of wealth.[6]

Weber's sense of the possibilities and power of politics and political officials was far more astute and developed than that of Marx. He believed that administration, in general, and the modern state, in particular, could exercise as much influence as the workings of the economy. Unlike Marx, who believed that the activities of societies were grounded fundamentally in their mode of production and economic institutions, Weber believed that the exercise of authority, or domination, was central to modern societies. A large part of his intellectual agenda was devoted to deciphering the precise nature of that authority and how it worked in modern, feudal, and ancient societies.

Like Marx, Weber insisted that people are alienated, but from the means of administration rather than from those of material production. Unlike Marx, however, Weber was less certain that humankind could throw off the yoke of its alienation; he believed that virtually nothing can be done to reduce the encroachment of bureaucracies over the individual's life. Moreover, unlike Marx's writings, his work contained no teleological endpoint or purpose toward which humankind was moving. History and life moved on; at best one could understand the major themes that had constructed the past, but one could not easily discern the lineaments of the future. We are, he concluded, prisoners of the "iron cage" of the institutions of the modern world: "The Puritan wanted to work in a calling; we are forced to do so," he writes. "[The modern economic] order is now bound to the technical and economic conditions of machine production which to-day determine the lives of all...individuals....In Baxter's view the care for external goods should only lie on the shoulders of the 'saint like a light cloak, which can be thrown aside at any moment.' But fate decreed that cloak should become an iron cage."[7]

THE STATE

Weber bequeathed to his followers the outlines and main features of how to think about modern states and their operations in society. The principal feature of the modern state, according to him, is that it exercises the "monopoly of the legitimate use of physical force within a given territory."[8] Such a monopoly provides the state a power that no other institution or agency possesses in modern society; it enables the state, and its officeholders, to wield its power in a way no other group, including large social classes or firms, possibly could. On matters, then, of force and might, the state is the ultimate authority. In a sense, Weber insisted, the state in the modern world occupies the same place of prominence and centrality the Church did in the medieval world.

For Weber there were two critical features to the organizational dimensions of the state. The first is the *state bureaucracy* itself. From his point of view, this bureaucracy is central to the organization and administration of the state. It provides the articulation and implementation of the laws and policies on behalf of the larger society. Although the parliament, or Congress, represents the elected officials, the state bureaucracy, consisting of civil servants, remains decisive because it actually carries out the law formulated by political officials. In nineteenth-century Germany, in fact, the state bureaucracy was far more powerful than the elected officials, and Weber held out little hope that officials, even democratically elected ones, would ever prove as effective and competent as civil servants.[9]

The second principal dimension of power is that of particular *groups of officials* who gain ascendance over others. Such ascendance grows out of their expert knowledge and skill in the administration of politics. Since law—specifically, modern rational law—had become so important to the daily life of modern societies, those who understood the law—modern lawyers—would, Weber argued, become most central to politics and to the implementation of the force of the state.[10] Lawyers, to Weber, represented a powerful social alliance as societies modernized, far more potent perhaps than even the capitalist social class.

In a democratic society, Weber observed, the rule of law obtains. Citizens must obey the laws or suffer the penalties of disobedience. Each day moves smoothly, almost like clockwork, as people go about their routines and move in an orderly, rational fashion. Weber believed that beneath the surface of this order, however, lay the potential for deep internal threats to society, in general, and democratic society, in particular. The first such threat came from the very emphasis on rational norms and their application by the state, and also by other modern institutions. Such norms placed an emphasis on efficiency and calculability at the expense of deeper issues such as justice and equality. By shifting the emphasis to efficiency, Weber believed the deeper and more powerful ends of life—and questions about such ends—were pushed aside, lost in the array of rules and bureaucratic order.

The other threat came from the bureaucratic nature of the modern state, itself. Weber believed that as the state became more complex and powerful, the ability of any group of individuals to challenge the state, much less a single individual, diminished. The great threat to the future of democratic societies, in his eyes, lay not in the concentration and centralization of capital, as Marx had argued, but in the centralization of power under the state. A state without vigorous leadership, but only a smoothly working group of bureaucrats, poses as much harm to the long-term well-being of its citizens as a state ruled by a leader of ill will. "[T]here is only the choice between leadership democracy with a 'machine'," he wrote, "and leaderless democracy, namely, the rule of professional politicians without a calling, without the inner charismatic qualities that make a leader."[11]

THE POWER OF THE RULER

Can we really speak of a great man theory of history? Tension and ambivalence abound in the writings and thinking of Max Weber about the role of individual figures, or leaders, and the role of institutions.[12] This tension leads to vastly different readings of Weber. Some scholars will emphasize Weber's intellectual leanings toward the power of great figures, such as Bismarck in nineteenth-century Germany, emphasizing that Weber believed, as did Friedrich Nietzsche, that great personages could exercise enough power to overturn and transform the world, making institutions and customs the mere servants of the power of the individual.[13] Others will emphasize that while Weber admitted the power of individuals, he also believed that institutions did take on a life all their own (as he showed in his work on the Protestant Ethic), remaking society and life in their own outlines. It is this reading of Weber that makes much out of his emphasis on the role of the modern state and how it can reshape and remake societies.

The most judicious way to understand Weber—and to extend his view of politics—on the matter of leadership comes from the writings and interpretations of the German sociologist Wolfgang Mommsen. Mommsen argues that in Weber's thinking institutions and personal authority should not be thought of as dualities in opposition to one another, but rather as part of the actual workings of organizations and institutions. He firmly believed in democracy, but it was a democracy of institutional law and force, guided by benevolent leaders. "From a realistic perspective," writes Mommsen, "[Weber believed] democracy can at best mean domination by freely elected leaders, who are then in a position to proceed essentially at their own discretion. It can never mean the superseding of domination by a system of policy formation from the bottom up."[14] Thus, the power of the modern state lies not simply in the regular and efficient workings of the state bureaucracy, but also in the leadership and charisma given to the state by the power of individuals. In this sense, then, great figures, like Winston Churchill in wartime England, or Golda Meir in the fledgling state of Israel, provided a kind of voice and direction to the state that it would otherwise lack.

Some very recent organizational sociologists, such as Peter Blau, completely disavow the crucial significance of rulers and singular figures of influence and power, maintaining that the work of modern society is really done by the regular and routine activities of organizations and other structures. Yet to the end Weber himself insisted that "[p]olitical action is always determined by the 'principle of small numbers.'... In mass states, this caesarist element is ineradicable."[15]

AUTHORITY AND ITS LEGITIMACY

In the study of politics, one of Weber's most enduring contributions lies in his effort to understand how it is that large assemblages of individuals are held together and operate. For Marx, it had been partly a matter of ideology. For Weber it became a matter of authority or, as some sociologists put it, domination.[16]

The grounds for obeying authority are written into their very foundations. In modern societies such authority rests on the rational-legal foundations of law. Law is an instrument of universal and impersonal rule, and it furnishes many great advantages to the running of large-scale societies. For example, Weber insisted, it helped in the creation of modern democratic societies which, by their very nature, must rest on universal grounds rather than particular ones. But law possesses an even deeper significance. It provides the terms in which both the officials and the citizens of modern states make a contract to agree to the nature of rule.

Law by itself does not guarantee compliance, or domination, in modern society, however. There also must be an administrative apparatus that helps to implement the law, to carry it out. Administration helps to enforce the obedience of people to the ruler by providing punishment for noncompliance with commands, by levying and collecting taxes, by carrying on war, and by attending to related matters. "Organized domination," Weber remarked, "requires the control of those material goods which in a given case are necessary for the use of physical violence... [as well as] control of the executive staff and the material implements of administration."[17] Administration entails its own problems because major struggles for the position of dominance always occur between the ruler and his staff. To lessen the threat of usurpation of the ruler's power, there must also be a solidarity of interest between the ruler and the staff; the burden for establishing such solidarity falls on the shoulders of the ruler. As in similar instances, such solidarity is insured through the provision of material and ideal rewards by the ruler: "The fear of losing [material reward and social honor] is the *final* and *decisive* basis for solidarity between the executive staff and the power-holder."[18]

Although Weber characterized the modern state as exercising a monopoly over the means of violence in a given territory, the legitimacy on which the rule of the state was based in the long run may have been more important to him. Rulers, Weber avowed, could not simply exercise their rule without the willing obedience of their subordinates. Power was a matter of sheer domination, but authority was grounded in the compliance of citizens. If citizens were not compliant, no amount of force could compel them to be so. The recurring dualism of Weber's thought—between the power of individuals and of institutions, between the power of ideas and of material production—surfaced even on this matter of the legitimacy of rule. State rulers can rule, of course, because they hold the means of force behind them; but unless their followers fully believed in their right to lead, no exercise of power by rulers could ever succeed.

POLITICAL POWER AND CONTENDING SOCIAL GROUPS

Inasmuch as modern states exercise the legitimate control of force in modern societies, they are routinely considered the prize for contending social groups. Marx argued, as we recall, that such a prize was secured by the dominant class in a specific historical society, and in modern capitalism was controlled by the forces of the rich and the wealthy. To Weber the matter was not quite so simple. Indeed, to him it was a great deal more complex. Although he agreed with Marx that social classes existed, in his view they simply represented general aggregates of people who shared a similar position in the labor market. Social classes could never be organized to take decisive action because they lacked any common basis for such action. Instead Weber insisted that common and purposive action was more apt to occur for two other kinds of social alliances.

One is what he called *status groups*. Such groups consist of people who share a common occupational or professional position, like doctors or artists, or, as above, lawyers. As a result of their common position, such people can also come to share certain values and lifestyles. They may live in similar areas of a city, shop at similar grocery stores, or do work in a similar kind of manner. In the 1980s, observers wrote of *yuppies*, or young urban professionals. They were people who worked in urban areas, made a good deal of money, and lived in similarly upscale housing. They represented a classic example of a status group.

Sometimes status groups can become the basis for political action. They are able to do so precisely because their members share similar lifestyles and values. Hunters in modern society represent something of a status group in the sense that hunting and rifles represent a major part of their leisure activity. Moreover, when efforts are made to control the sale of guns, such hunters, through organizations like the American Rifle Association, can become very effective at preventing the passage of major laws that would control the sale and use of weapons.

More often, however, it is specific *political associations* and *parties* that are the main contenders for the power of the state. The party, unlike either a social class or status group, is organized specifically to pursue political ends and the exercise of power. "Parties live in a house of 'power,'" Weber once observed. "Their action is oriented toward the acquisition of social 'power,' that is to say, toward influencing a communal action no matter what its content may be."[19] Political parties focus their energies and plan their strategies to secure power. Sometimes they have long histories and records of successful campaigns as well as winning high political office, as in the case of the Democrats and Republicans in America. Other times they serve more limited ends and purposes, even emerging as contenders for power within bureaucracies and other kinds of organizations.

In the final analysis, Weber insisted, there is much conflict in modern society, but social classes prove much too large, unwieldy, and diverse to be effective at seizing the rewards of power. Status groups on occasion, but parties most often, are the prime contenders for the privilege to rule—and to wield the vast forces of the modern state.

The Neo-Weberians

Although Weber never created a large band of followers and ideologists in the same manner as Karl Marx, his writings on states and societies have proved influential for a number of sociologists in recent decades. Here we shall discuss three of the most notable—Reinhard Bendix, Charles Tilly, and Theda Skocpol.

REINHARD BENDIX

Coming as a refugee to America from Germany in 1938, Reinhard Bendix helped introduce to American sociology a strong emphasis on comparative and historical studies. He drew upon concerns and themes from Max Weber as well as from the French scholar, Alexis de Tocqueville (see Chapter 4). Bendix was interested in social and political change on a grand scale, and especially in the role that ideas played in the constitution of societies as well as in prompting such change. With the publication in 1960 of *Max Weber: An Intellectual Portrait*, he became the foremost interpreter of Weber's writings.[20]

On the Nature and Exercise of Authority. The central Weberian theme that Bendix helped to illuminate in his own writings was that of political authority. Authority played the same central role in Weber's work as the economy and ideology did in Marx's writings. Weber believed that differences in authority were key in distinguishing between different historical regimes and epochs. Moreover, he came to believe that the main innovation feature of modern society was not capitalism per se but rather the form of rational organization and the underpinnings that secured its authority over men and women. Bendix elaborated on these themes, blending them together with questions and issues raised by Tocqueville.[21]

In refashioning Weber's original concept, Bendix made it clear that authority does not simply represent the simple exercise of power, even legitimate power, by rulers. Instead, the exercise of authority represents a kind of delicate balancing act, a constant tension arising from the strong desire of leaders to get their commands implemented and the reluctant willingness of followers to obey those commands. Thus, if one wished to understand the nature of a society, one should not only investigate the nature of authority and who holds it, but also inquire into the grounds and reasons that enabled leaders to exercise their power over their followers. Authority could not simply be wielded by powerful figures with no sense of the nature or character of followers, themselves. In his biography of Weber, Bendix remarks:

> Domination involves a reciprocal relationship between rulers and ruled, in which the actual frequency of compliance is only one aspect of the fact that the power of command exists. Equally important is the meaning that rulers and ruled attach to the authority relationship. In addition to the fact that they issue commands, the rulers claim that they have legitimate authority to do so....In the same way, the obedience of the ruled is guided to some extent by the idea that the rulers and their commands constitute a legitimate order of authority.[22]

Indeed, to Bendix the exercise of authority said as much, if not more, about the mindset of followers as it did about leadership.

Work and Authority in Industry. Weber had emphasized that the integrity of societies arose not simply out of the material resources commanded by the wealthy, but also and often because of the dominant ideas and ideals. Bendix extended this argument further, insisting that political struggles took place over both ideal and material interests of competing social groups.[23] Ideal interests, in fact, played as major a part in the nature of politics as material interests did, although often they had to be discovered through a more subtle and nuanced historical analysis.

Bendix's major contribution to the study of ideal interests and their role in society's conflicts took the form of his study of the changes that occurred in the ideologies of managerialism exercised in the early part of the nineteenth century. He began his analysis from the collapse of the royal authority at the end of the eighteenth century. Once this collapse happened, a number of forces were unleashed. Bendix notes, among other things, that the lower classes were now free to pursue their own course of action, unfettered by the authority relations of the past. This created a kind of paradox in his reading of the situation: the individual was freed to pursue his interest, but in order to do so he was compelled to join with others in this pursuit.[24] A kind of tension ensued between the individualism unleashed by the collapse of the old regime and the need for workers to band together to pursue their material interests in common.

This situation of transition, from a society in which the relations between nobility and the peasants were fixed, to a society in which industry now arose and new occupations opened for the masses of people, presented a problem in the nature of labor itself. Now that the people were free, what would convince them to work in the new industries and for their new masters? Why should they even work for new masters? Bendix believed, with Weber, that ideas were the key here to the authority relationship, but what kind of ideas, or ideologies, were necessary to create the grounds for this new form of compliance by former peasants? This was the essential Bendix question posed both in his early writings on work and authority and in his later writings on kings and rulers.

In the case of labor, Bendix insisted that the different ideologies arose both in the West and in Russia to secure the loyalty of the worker.[25] Over time the nature of the ideological justifications for work would change in both countries. In the West, in particular, there came to be an increasing emphasis on the scientific character of work, and the best way that production could be done by the laborer. This culminated in the rise of the ideas and writings of Frederick Taylor in the 1920s and 1930s, ideas that claimed there was only one right way to do work and the trick for management was to get workers to perform in that manner. The underlying ideology of Taylorism replaced the earlier emphasis on laissez faire capitalism, and ideas that had stressed the basis laziness and idleness of workers. Such management ideologies, in Bendix's eyes, were crucial to the nature of labor itself, far more crucial than a simple material Marxian emphasis on labor and labor power under modern capitalism.

Kings or People. Bendix's broadest attack on understanding the nature of authority took the form of his last major work, *Kings or People*.[26] In this book he sets himself the goal of seeking to understand the transition from the authority of kings and nobles to the authority of the people, or the masses in the world of the eighteenth century and beyond. He examines the problem of political authority across the wide spectrum of history and in different national/cultural contexts, ranging from that of Russia to England to France and Japan. He argues, in a way strongly reminiscent of Weber, that the spread of ideas and the mobilization of intellectuals played a significant part in the construction of modern societies:

> [I]ntellectual mobilization—the growth of a reading public and of an educated secular elite dependent on learned occupations—(is) an independent cause of social change....For example, the invention of printing and the scientific revolution of the seventeenth century were part of an intellectual mobilization that

was facilitated by commercialization in the early modern period, but that also occurred well in advance of commercialization and provided a means to promote commerce and industry.[27]

Moreover, he argues on behalf of what he calls the "demonstration effect," namely that the collapse of the old regimes and inauguration of the power of the people takes place as one nation copies the achievements of another. Thus, the English revolution, and the rise of Parliament in the late seventeenth century, provided a model for other countries to emulate, particularly for those groups of intellectuals who aspired to democracy. The role of such groups of people, motivated as they were by the effort to copy the successes of other regimes, for Bendix plays a major part in the creation of new states and nations.

Bendix drew especially on a certain theme in the work of Weber—that which emphasized the role of *ideal forces* in the making and unmaking of societies. He believed that to comprehend the social order required that one understand the deep and underlying bases of authority, in other words, the grounds for why one group of people obeyed another group. His careful analysis helped to reveal the way that such ideal forces arose and worked, both for the power of kings and for the power of workplace management. Yet his work has had limited lasting influence on contemporary political sociologists. Perhaps the main reason is that he failed to leave us with a clear, systematic, and powerful model of how ideas and ideals continue to work their power in politics, a model that would serve to direct and to inspire the analyses of today's sociologists.

CHARLES TILLY

Charles Tilly, one of the leading historical sociologists of modern times, falls somewhere between Karl Marx and Max Weber in his theoretical style. He is not so much a direct intellectual descendant of either man as he is someone who has helped further our understanding of the very same questions they raised about politics and societies.[28] In his analysis of economic circumstances and class differences, he has helped to extend our detailed understanding of how such forces play a role in history—not through broad models, but through exacting and careful historical analysis.[29] And in his copious writings on the state—both state building and struggles over the authority of government—we find him adding to and refining the Weberian legacy.

Tilly believes that change is a major theme in the nature of societies, and he has devoted much of his body of work to its examination. Instead of taking a broad, overly theoretical view of change, his work focuses on how change comes about—especially how forces of protest and for change arise among the common people, whether they be peasants or the urban proletariat. His work is always deeply rooted in specific historical events, grounded in the vast detail of agony and discontent that arise among groups of aggrieved citizens; moreover, most of it has been devoted to studying the origins of dissent and disloyalty in France and Great Britain over the past several centuries. He is one of the most prolific of contemporary sociologists, and also one whose own ideas seem to evolve and change over time. Here I shall point to several key contributions he has made to understanding the nature of the modern state as well as the forces of resistance that arise to confront established political authority.

On the Origins of the Modern State. Almost three decades ago, Tilly was a member of a team of social scientists who were asked by the Social Science Research Council in America to draw together their research and observations on how European states came into existence.[30] What emerged from this task was a series of very interesting research papers on different features of state making and state building. Indeed, though there were considerable differences in the method and arguments of each of the scholars, they came to agree that the central focus for their work was state building, not nation building.[31]

Tilly's main contribution was to orchestrate and to synthesize the diverse research programs and papers. Four main contributions emerged from his synthesis at the time. The first was a very clear and coherent definition of the modern state:

> The structure which became dominant in Europe after 1500, the national state, (bore these features): (1) it controlled a well-defined, continuous territory; (2) it was relatively centralized; (3) it was differentiated from other organizations; (4) it reinforced its claims through a tendency to acquire a monopoly over the concentrated means of physical coercion within its territory.[32]

This definition clearly echoes key features of the concept of state to which Weber first drew attention. The second contribution was his effort to ask the question about the origins of the state in a way different from his fellow social scientists at the time. In particular, he insisted that any effort to understand the origins of the modern state had to inquire not only about the institution that actually emerged, but also had to inquire as to why alternative forms of the state, or government—e.g., the city-state—failed to survive.

His third contribution was the argument that origins of the modern state were closely connected to the development and success of political institutions in war. Essentially state making was war making: those governments that were successful in war also had the best chance to develop a modern state. His fourth and final contribution was perhaps the most important. He insisted that other analyses had emphasized the sequence and stages of state making— actually political development—far too much. Because modern states, he claimed, differed greatly from one another, it would be a mistake to somehow believe that one sequence, or one model, represented the way of all state making. In fact, he suggested, there was so much variation in the nature of modern states that any sound analysis must examine the origins of states more deeply and not be satisfied with the idea that all states moved through an identical set of stages.[33]

Tilly's 1975 statement on state making served as a preliminary sketch for work he undertook some years later. In this later treatment, published in 1990, he argued that modern states, such as France, England, or Holland, arose from a combination of two central factors: (1) the concentration and accumulation of capital and (2) the concentration and accumulation of coercion, or force.[34] Where political institutions were able to mobilize and to concentrate capital, there, too, they would be able to devote much of the apparatus of the modern state—in particular, the financial organization and devices for extracting resources from the population. Similarly, where political organizations were able to concentrate the means of force under a single authority, amassing both weapons and a strong military, the key elements of the modern national state would emerge.

Tilly argued that the variations among different modern states arose from different combinations of the elements of capital and the elements of coercion. For example, he observes, the Dutch state arose primarily because it was able to draw on the resources of capital and those of urban industry and financiers to create and solidify its base of power. In contrast, the modern German state was successful because it was able to mobilize both military and administrative forces through its exercise of force and coercion over various political rulers in the diverse and various principalities like Hanover and Prussia. In general, however, state making was always most successful and most likely because of war making:

> A ruler's creation of armed force generated durable state structure. It did so both because an army became a significant organization within the state and because its construction and maintenance brought complementary organizations—treasuries, supply services, mechanisms for conscription, tax bureaux, and much more—into life.[35]

War making was particularly decisive in the late fifteenth century. It was then that a number of major and critical wars were fought. Those states that were successful in such wars tended to be larger, to control more territory, and to be better administered—in other words, to look very much like the modern state, as Tilly had identified it in his 1975 work. Those states that failed tended to be smaller, on the order of city-states, and would later become the historical residue of state-like organizations that failed in the struggle to survive competition with other territorially based organizations.

Although the mobilization of capital and the exercise of coercion represented the key factors in the making of modern states, other forces also played a role. Thus, Tilly observes, the kind and strength of social classes in a country could affect the kind of state that emerged and the process through which the state was built. So, too, the geopolitics of a region were crucial, particularly in terms of the range of territory under dispute or under the governance of different and sometimes competing political authorities.

While Tilly's arguments and evidence have helped materially to move our understanding of the origins of modern states much further along than Weber's preliminary researches, and even those of other contemporary scholars, there is one critical point he fails to clarify—one that leaves his work both unsatisfying and unsatisfactory. He insists that the variation among states depends critically on the success of organizations in mobilizing both capital and coercion and that there exists a wide variety of states. But he never informs us of the nature of such variations by producing some kind of classification. How *do* states differ from one another? In what terms? And are such differences significant from one another? In what ways? In other words, how are we to classify states? In the end, Tilly says far too little about the differences among states to permit us to understand precisely how the main factors of capital and coercion, and the subsidiary ones of social classes and geopolitics, actually combine to produce such variations.

On the Politics of Contention and Mobilization. Among sociologists, the work for which Tilly is best known is his writing about social movements and revolution. His seminal work is a piece of scholarship now more than two decades old, devoted to understanding the nature of political mobilization.[36] This work is one of the more widely read and widely cited pieces of literature on social movements.

Tilly argues that sociologists must shift their attention from the grand paradigms of Marx and Weber to focus more on the dimensions of political contention itself. His life's work in the study of political protest is devoted to a proper conceptualization and empirical study of these dimensions. He introduces what he calls the "mobilization" model of collective action. There are several key elements to the model: *interests, organization, mobilization,* and *opportunity.* To understand how collective action arises, it is necessary to understand how each of these elements operates.

Interests refer to the advantages or disadvantages a particular population is likely to have relative to other groups in the population. Organization refers to the common identity and the social structure promoting such an identity. Mobilization refers to the resources that can be controlled by a group seeking new political advantages. And opportunity refers to the chances that a particular group has in mobilizing its resources and acting as a contender in the battle with the established political forces in a society.

Tilly notes a number of specific empirical features of each of these elements. For example, he notes that a population group's basic social structure can influence its ability to mobilize to challenge the authorities in a society. Thus, drawing on the pioneering work of sociologist Anthony Oberschall (1973), he notes that strong social links and connections among a group can facilitate the mobilization of that group for collective action. Opportunity is also a key factor in the ability of a group to effectively mobilize and counter established forces. If the authorities are successful in their efforts to repress challengers, then there are limited opportunities to mobilize. But if the current regime is undergoing powerful threats, or if general social conditions help to loosen the otherwise repressive forces of a regime, then the opportunity to mobilize increases significantly.

Much of Tilly's effort to think of collective action is an effort to draw up a different set of concepts and schemes from those earlier employed by the great social theorists like Weber. More than that, what he attempts to do is to show how radical collective action is a process that occurs in a sequence of steps. In this respect, he adds considerably to the visions created by both Marx and Weber, showing in greater historical detail what specific events must take place for radical mobilization to occur. Along the way, he helps to invent entirely new and important concepts.

Perhaps his most important concept—and one to which he often draws attention—is that of a *repertoire of collective action*. The notion of repertoire refers to the specific kinds of protest and discontent that emerge among common people in an historical epoch. Thus, in some periods street demonstrations represent the mode of collective action, whereas in others, especially in the United States during the midtwentieth century, the repertoire included such things as sit-ins and wade-ins. In his important analysis on discontent and protest in France, for instance, he notes that the change in repertoires was a critical one. Between 1650 and 1850, collective action tends to be *parochial* and *patronized*, taking the form of local actions, such as the seizure of grains, against local, or village, authorities. Between 1850 and 1980, however, the repertoire became *national* and *autonomous*, involving strikes and demonstrations that often were nationwide and directed against the whole panoply of French political authority.[37] Collective action, in other words, can exhibit alternative forms depending on the period in which it arises.

Perhaps most of all, Tilly takes the notion of revolution and protest out of the grand mists of history, as concocted by Marx and Weber, and makes it more amenable and accessible to the contemporary period. Collective action for him is no longer the major revolutionary events of great social classes, as in Marx, nor the charismatically or ideologicallyinspired movements, as he understands Weber, but it can involve a host of different populations, each engaged in different kinds of struggles. In this respect, then, the Tillyian vision is very much in keeping both with Marx and with Weber. Grievances, he has written, exist at all times; the key is to understand how in a continuing situation in which challengers and authorities are always at odds the challengers manage to create a situation in which their challenge can be effective. Such success depends on large causes, like opportunities provided by social openings, as well as on the strategic aims of actors that seek to mobilize for revolution. It is a canvas created both out of structural causes and out of specific strategies chosen by potential revolutionaries.

The greatest legacy of Tilly's work on collective action is his invention of certain key concepts that enable one to investigate collective action in a variety of different historical situations. Though his own main concern is with the classic issues of Marx and Weber—agrarian protests, the conflicts between peasants and nobles—the concepts he develops lend themselves to a variety of different possibilities and historical situations. This has permitted them to be used by a great number of contemporary researchers. And he has directly influenced a number of the more prominent younger scholars in the study of collective action today, including Doug McAdam and Aldon Morris.

THEDA SKOCPOL

Like Charles Tilly, Theda Skocpol is a student of Barrington Moore, Jr., a famous sociologist-historian who taught at Harvard. Moore's writings, particularly his work on dictatorships and democracies, provided a sociology that was strongly rooted in historical and comparative analyses (see Chapter 10). Skocpol has carried that emphasis forward in a number of significant writings over the past two decades.

The chief aim of Skocpol's work has been to revive the concept of the *state*, as construed by Weber and the historian, Otto Hintze, and to show how it could prove useful to understanding different historical issues.[38] The modern concepts of the state and social classes originated in the writings of the German philosopher Georg Hegel. It was Hegel who wrote of the nature of civil society and social classes, on the one hand, and the state, on the other.[39] Hegel's view of the world, one that later deeply influenced Marx, was that history was moving toward the emancipation of humankind and that the highest achievements of the modern world were to be the product of the thinking of the great philosophers—like himself—and the institution of the state. Marx picked up on these same themes, but, as often been noted, turned them upside down. Philosophy was a sham, or false consciousness, to Marx; material forces were the driving motor of history, not ideas; and social classes, and class emancipation, lay at the end of history, not the achievements of the state.

Skocpol has drawn much from Weber, Hintze, and Marx. From Weber, she has taken the view that the modern state is more than simply a reflection of the dominant class. The modern state, she believes, represents an autonomous institution, one that possesses a force and energy all its own. It consists of a variety of specific organizations and actors, including the legislature and legislators, the administrative bodies of government, and, in certain historical circumstances, royal authority. Adopting one of Weber's most crucial insights, she has come to believe that the state, like other institutions, can take on a life all its own, and actually direct the energies and decisions of society. Indeed, the question about which much of her work centers is the extent and circumstances under which the state furnishes the powerful directions for society itself.

There are several ways in which she has explored these themes, including her works on the origins and development of the New Deal administration of Franklin Delano Roosevelt. Unlike some theorists, who imputed the origins of this administration to the catastrophic collapse of the American economy, she argues that many policies preceded the origins of the New Deal administration and that state actors and institutions were sufficiently autonomous to develop actions that were the cause of the economic resurgence. In the discussion that follows, I shall point to two major instances in which Skocpol's treatments have expanded our understanding not only of the state but of two broader questions: the nature of social revolutions and the origins of welfare policy in America.

States and Social Revolutions. Skocpol's most famous and, to date, most influential work deals with the role that the state and other political forces played in the major revolutions of the past two centuries—the French, Russian, and Chinese revolutions.[40] Here she takes on the themes of her mentor, Barrington Moore, Jr., who himself sought to explain why the social and political history of some countries, like Japan, produced dictatorships, while others, like England, produced democratic regimes.[41] She argues that Moore, among other things, left major factors out of consideration, the chief one being the role that the state, or proto-state, forces played in the development of each of these countries.

Skocpol asserts that there are three essential points to take into account in explaining the origins of these revolutions: (1) causes of revolutions are to be found in the structural, or objective, conditions of a society, not in the expressed intentions or wishes of revolutionaries; (2) international conditions and circumstances play a major role in promoting revolutions, prominently influencing the capacity of the reigning authorities to direct and control a particular society; and (3) the state, through its agents and institutions, is a crucial factor in the success of a revolution and, contrary to Marxist interpretations, may act in ways autonomous of social classes, or other economic forces, to impede or to promote the success of a social revolution.[42] These several claims thus set her thesis apart from many other theses about the origins of reform or revolutionary movements, and they also establish her work as unique and novel today.

Skocpol draws a careful and important distinction between the conditions that promote the vulnerability of a society and state to revolution and those that, in fact, transform the existing institutions. As to the facilitating circumstances themselves, she closely examines the set of conditions in France, China, and Russia prior to revolutionary times and finds in all instances roughly similar circumstances. The state bureaucracies had all been relatively strong, control over the peasants and other groups had been effective, and wars and other external pressures eventually made the bureaucracies vulnerable to attack. In each of these instances, in fact, wars had been long and had taxed the capacities of state rulers to govern at all. Moreover, Skocpol goes on to show in other countries where revolutions might have taken place because of some roughly similar conditions—Prussia, for example—the international environments were very different, and the external pressures on the governments' ability to govern were not nearly as strong.[43] Likewise, she goes on to show how the economic and social conditions in each society were sufficiently encouraging to promote the organization and development of the peasantry into an effective revolutionary force. Again, in those countries that escaped revolution, such as Japan or Prussia, the peasants were unsuccessful at developing and sustaining solidarity—sometimes, as in Prussia, because the landed nobility held such a strong hand of control over the lands.[44] Ultimately, she argues, it is the peculiar historical conjunction of weakened and eviscerated state regimes coupled with the successful creation of strong and successful peasant organizations that creates the imminent likelihood of revolutions.

And yet, Skocpol rightly points out, it is only the possibility of revolution that originates from such conditions. Whether the fundamental transformations so essential to creating a revolution happen depends on the capacity of the insurgent forces to engage in successful social and political changes of a country. Here, again, Skocpol wishes to direct attention not to some vague and amorphous changes, but rather to the manner in which state building occurs. Indeed, among the very different circumstances that ensued on the heels of the revolutionary outbreaks, it was the common fact of the creation of far more powerful and successful state bureaucracies and administrations that, according to Skocpol, permit one to label the changes in China, France, and Russia as revolutionary.[45] In France, Napoleon introduced a whole range of new measures, including legal codes, more complex administrative forces, a deeper and more disciplined army—in brief, a greater centralization of political authority, which qualified as revolutionary state building. In Russia, roughly the same

thing happened, but in a more systematic and powerful fashion, aided principally through the activities and development of the Communist Party. Tougher
bureaucracies, greater central authority, and more uniform codes and activities
throughout the country also were the result of the victory of the Communist
Party in China, Skocpol shows. Finally, in a touch of irony, she claims, in all
three regimes the losers, in some sense, were the very forces that helped to
topple the old regime, the peasantry.

Skocpol's analysis proves to be a very compelling, indeed brilliant, one.
Nevertheless, her admirers, while legion, are not universal. Her argument can
be criticized on several grounds, including the fact that she leaves little room
in her perspective for the importance of ideological factors, or beliefs, and even
less for the activities of human agents. Indeed, one might ask of her: how is it at
all possible to have revolutionary movements, much less actual social transformations, if there are no human agents to perform the activities?

The Origins of the American Welfare State. Skocpol's other major contribution to studies of the modern state and its impact on society is her revision-
ist interpretation of the origins and development of welfare state policies in
America. Unlike other Western industrial democracies, such as those of
Germany, Scandanavia, or even Great Britain, the welfare state, with its variety
of associated benefits, for healthcare, pensions, and unemployment, developed
much differently and somewhat later in the United States. It was not until the
1930s, in the midst of the Great Depression, that substantial aid was provided
by the government to the needy. It took the form of the provision of the Social
Security Act of 1935 that furnished each American with a guaranteed pension
on retirement. The history of the development of the welfare state in America
and in other Western countries has led scholars to a set of explanations for the
origins of the differences. Some, beginning with Werner Sombart, trace the
absence of a strong welfare state in America to the absence of socialism here.[46]
Others trace the absence of a welfare state to a peculiar set of American values,
with their emphasis on individualism as opposed to collectivism, for example,
an emphasis, scholars argue, that simply led to a different historical trajectory
in America.[47]

Skocpol, in her usual fashion, takes on these arguments in her work
Protecting Soldiers and Mothers, offering new evidence on welfare measures in
America as well as a different interpretation of the development of the welfare
state here.[48] She agrees with other scholars that the welfare state in America
simply never became as strong as in Western European democracies. But her
interpretation of the differences takes a new tack.

Her argument is rather complicated, but, as all her work, it is rooted in an
understanding of the historical and institutional context of America. It begins

with her discovery that, in fact, the U.S. government at the end of the nineteenth century possessed an important building block for a strong welfare state—in the form of pensions and benefits provided for Civil War veterans. Here was a case in which the federal government provided aid to a needy group well before the invention of the New Deal welfare policies of the 1930s. Skocpol poses the question: if such a policy were in effect at the end of the nineteenth century, why did it not provide a "wedge" for the development of a full-fledged welfare state, composed of the kind of benefits and aids provided by governments like those of Sweden and Denmark?

Skocpol argues that the failure of the Civil War pensions to become the carrier for a larger social program for the needy and poor depended on several specific historical factors. First, the United States lacked a centralized and autonomous state apparatus that could become the vehicle for developing such a program. Rather, over the course of the nineteenth century the state in America consisted of a system in which the courts and political parties exercised the greatest power rather than the officials of the federal and state governments. Decisions, therefore, came from the bottom up rather than the top down, as in Europe. Political parties were important not as unifying national forces but for the programs they provided in local circumstances, in cities and states, to the poor. In addition, the elites and middle classes in America failed to provide the support necessary for social programs, instead turning their wrath and anger on immigrants and the poor during the late nineteenth and early twentieth centuries. Businessmen, rather than providing support for a broad social welfare program that could be organized and implemented by the government, provided their own piecemeal efforts, thus robbing the state of an opportunity to build on the Civil War pensions. In other words, there were a set of specific factors that discouraged welfare polices from above as happened in European states.

The other key part to Skocpol's argument is that the unique historical and institutional context in America that impeded the development of a strong *paternalist* state—one that was run by men and that benefited the male worker as the breadwinner of his family—actually facilitated the development of a strong *maternalist* state. Whereas white men were granted suffrage in nineteenth-century America, women were not. This helped to encourage a kind of extrapolitical activity on the part of women, forcing them to undertake extramural efforts on issues they deemed important. Here Skocpol also uncovers a new set of evidence. They show a broad and active array of voluntary associations and groups in American society among women, groups that would become vital to the success of their effort not only to gain suffrage in 1919 but to secure the passage of welfare policies that would benefit them as mothers and their children.

The state, in this rendering, is what Skocpol considers a "federated polity" of organizations and associations—groups consisting of women that were able to mobilize on behalf of benefits for mothers and other kinds of women's aid. In effect, American politics, by Skocpol's accounting, was organized less on the basis of classes and labor unions, as in Europe, and more on the basis of gender. And because it was so organized, and because women proved so forceful, measures here that would have benefited workers and labor failed, whereas those that benefited housewives and mothers succeeded. They succeeded, in part, because male legislators proved more sympathetic to them than they did to class-based measures that would have benefited male workers and their families. Accordingly, what would unfold in America, at least up until the 1930s, was a maternalist rather than a paternalist set of welfare policies.

Skocpol's view of the failure of a full-fledged welfare state in America to grow out of the Civil War pensions is novel, while her argument about the development of a maternalist state draws upon recent work among American historians. It is a novel melding and merging of different bodies of evidence and insight, though in the end it makes the state appear as far less autonomous and active than her earlier work on social revolutions. She notes, early on in this work, that the state is "any set of relatively differentiated organizations that claims sovereignty and coercive control over a territory and its population, defending and perhaps extending that claim in competition with other states," and therefore that the United States "has always had one."[49] But clearly the way the state unfolds in her story of welfare state policies in America is much different than the centralized and powerful state in so many European regimes. In fact, in her emphasis on voluntary associations and gender, she really mixes the state and civil society and invokes a kind of state that is only a short distance from the kind invoked in the writings of Alexis de Tocqueville (see Chapter 4).

Regardless, Theda Skocpol has invigorated the study of the state and political institutions among both sociologists and political scientists, drawing on a tradition of scholarship first begun in the nineteenth century by Max Weber.

Conclusion

Max Weber started sociologists on the path to understanding the nature and complexity of modern states, and the writings of several contemporary scholars have helped us better to understand the workings of these institutions.

States are vital to the modern world. Among other things, they remain powerful forces and they exercise legitimate control over the weapons of violence. Moreover, it is through states that the people have an opportunity to voice their opinions about the direction in which they wish societies to move and how, among other things, the body of citizens as a whole will meet the needs of the poor and the indigent. A great issue now looms ahead of us: how much authority can states continue to exercise, and how can they regulate the power of corporations and capital? There are those who argue that the forces of globalization are such that states may ultimately become something like bit players in the arena of money and politics. But if that is so, they would have to do so with the consent of those whom they serve—the citizens.

We can think of no questions or issues quite as significant for contemporary political sociology as those that concern the relative strength of states and of modern capitalism. Unlike Marx's early and rather crude image, states are not merely the handmaidens of great corporations. They often take actions that run counter to the interests of capitalists and the business class, especially when they engage in actions against many of their own citizens, as in the recent examples of Rwanda and Kosovo. Modern states also have provided over the course of the past fifty years or so important forms of welfare and other benefits to the most needy of citizens. As global capitalism increases, as more public enterprises are turned over to private sources, who will take care of the needy? Or the poor? Or the elderly?

NOTES

1. Max Weber, *The Protestant Ethic and the Spirit of Capitalism*, translated by Talcott Parsons (New York: Charles Scribner's Sons, 1958), 183.
2. Max Weber, "Politics as a Vocation," in Hans H. Gerth and C. Wright Mills (eds.), *From Max Weber: Essays in Sociology* (New York: Oxford University Press), 77.
3. Wolfgang J. Mommsen, *The Political and Social Theory of Max Weber: Collected Essays* (Chicago: University of Chicago Press, 1989), 26.
4. Max Weber, *The Methodology of the Social Sciences*. Translated and edited by Edward A. Shils and Henry A. Finch. With a Foreword by Edward A. Shils. (New York: The Free Press, 1949), 80.
5. Max Weber, "Science as a Vocation," in Gerth and Mills, *From Max Weber*, 146.
6. See, for example, the section on religion in Gerth and Mills, *From Max Weber*.
7. Weber, *The Protestant Ethic and the Spirit of Capitalism*, 183.
8. Weber, "Politics as a Vocation," in Gerth and Mills, *From Max Weber*, 78.
9. Max Weber, *Economy and Society: An Outline of Interpretive Sociology*, translated by Guenther Roth and Claus Wittich (New York: Bedminster Press, 1968), Volume III, 1393 ff.
10. Weber, "Politics as a Vocation," in Gerth and Mills, *From Max Weber*, 94–5.
11. Weber, ibid., 113.
12. Arthur Mitzman, *The Iron Cage: An Historical Interpretation of Max Weber* (New York: Alfred A. Knopf, 1970).
13. Chapter 9, "The Sociology of Charismatic Authority," in Gerth and Mills, *From Max Weber*.
14. Mommsen, *The Political and Social Theory of Max Weber*, 32.

15. Weber, *Economy and Society*, III, 1414.

16. See, for example, Reinhard Bendix, *Max Weber: An Intellectual Portrait* (Garden City, NY: Doubleday & Co., 1962), Chapter 9.

17. Weber, *Economy and Society*, I, 264.

18. Weber, "Politics as a Vocation," in Gerth and Mills, *From Max Weber*, 80.

19. Weber, "Class, Status and Party," in Gerth and Mills, *From Max Weber*, 194.

20. Bendix, *Max Weber: An Intellectual Portrait*.

21. Reinhard Bendix, *Nation-Building and Citizenship: Studies of Our Changing Social Order* (Berkeley: University of California Press, 1964).

22. Bendix, *MaxWeber: An Intellectual Portrait*, 292.

23. *State and Society: A Reader in Comparative Political Sociology*, Reinhard Bendix, ed. (Boston: Little Brown, 1968).

24. Reinhard Bendix, "The Extension of Citizenship to the Lower Classes," in Bendix, ibid., 233–56.

25. Reinhard Bendix, *Work and Authority in Industry* (Berkeley: University of California Press, 1956).

26. Reinhard Bendix, *Kings or People: Power and the Mandate to Rule* (Berkeley: University of California Press, 1978).

27. Bendix, ibid., 266.

28. See, for example, Charles Tilly, *From Mobilization to Revolution* (Reading, MA: Addison-Wesley Publishing Company, 1978), Chapter 2.

29. Charles Tilly, *The Contentious French* (Cambridge, MA: The Belknap Press of Harvard University Press, 1986), and *Popular Contention in Great Britain, 1758–1834* (Cambridge, MA: Harvard University Press, 1995).

30. Charles Tilly, ed., *The Formation of National States in Western Europe* (Princeton, NJ: Princeton University Press, 1975).

31. Ibid., 6.

32. Ibid., 27.

33. Also see Charles Tilly, *Big Structures, Large Processes, Huge Comparisons* (New York: Russell Sage Foundation, 1984), Chapter 2 especially.

34. Charles Tilly, *Coercion, Capital, and European States, AD 990–1990* (Cambridge, MA: Basil Blackwell, 1990).

35. Ibid., 70.

36. *From Mobilization to Revolution*.

37. *The Contentious French*, 392–93.

38. See Otto Hintze, "The State in Historical Perspective," in Reinhard Bendix, ed., *State and Society*, 154–69.

39. *Hegel's Philosophy of Right*, translated by T. M. Knox (New York: Oxford University Press, 1942); also see the excellent commentary by Charles Taylor in his *Hegel* (Cambridge, MA: Cambridge University Press, 1975), Chapter XVI.

40. Theda Skocpol, *States and Social Revolutions: A Comparative Analysis of France, Russia and China* (Cambridge, MA: Cambridge University Press, 1979).

41. Barrington Moore, Jr., *Social Origins of Dictatorship and Democracy: Lord and Peasant in the Making of the Modern World* (Boston: Beacon Press, 1966).

42. Skocpol, *States and Social Revolutions*, 14–33.

43. Ibid., 104–12; 155–57.

44. Ibid., 140–47.

45. Ibid., Chapters 5–7.

46. Werner Sombart, *Why is There No Socialism in the United States?* (White Plains, NY: International Arts and Sciences Press, 1976).

47. Louis Hartz, *The Liberal Tradition in America: An Interpretation of American Political Thought Since the Revolution* (New York: Harcourt Brace Jovanovich, Inc., 1955).

48. Theda Skocpol, *Protecting Soldiers and Mothers: The Political Origins of Social Policy in the United States* (Cambridge, MA: The Belknap Press of Harvard University Press, 1992).

49. Ibid., 43.

Chapter 4

On Civil Society and Politics

Emile Durkheim and
Alexis de Tocqueville

The system of signs I use to express my thought, the system of currency I employ to pay
my debts, the instruments of credit I utilize in my commercial relations, the practices
followed in my profession...function independently of my own use of them...Here,
then, is a category of facts with very distinctive characteristics: (they) consist of ways of
acting, thinking, and feeling, external to the individual and endowed with a power of
coercion, by reason of which they control him....They constitute...a new variety
of phenomena; and it is to them exclusively that the term 'social' ought to be applied.[1]

S ince the late 1950s, one of the major distinctions that writers make about
sociology is that between the "conflict" and "consensus" schools of sociology.[2] Though the distinction really is one of emphasis, it helps to highlight
the crucial differences among our leading theorists of society and politics. The
conflict school is said to date from the writings of Karl Marx and Max Weber.
It puts its emphasis on the divisions and battles in the nature of societies. The
basic conception of history is one of continuous conflict until, of course, as for
Marx, the working class achieves its great and lasting revolution.

   The consensus school sees the world vastly differently. Instead of an underlying division in the nature of societies, it presumes an underlying set of agree-
ments, or beliefs. Permanence and stability are achieved through the daily
workings of social institutions, most often through the schools, the family, and
religion. When politics is invoked, it is not a politics of division and exploitation, but a politics that creates and recreates the important institutions of
society through its celebration of key dates, events, and symbols. Paradoxically,
politics—which in everyday life we think of as a battleground pitting groups
against one another—is seen by the consensual theorists as an arena of fundamental harmony and manufactured unity, not as one of underlying division
and tension.

Two nineteenth-century French writers furnish us with the sociological basis for this consensual portrait of societies and politics. One, Emile Durkheim, is usually classified, along with Marx and Weber, as one of the greatest sociological theorists ever—certainly prior to the twentieth century. Durkheim's principal concern throughout his career was the nature of social solidarity and how it comes about in societies. The other scholar is Alexis de Tocqueville, a great political and intellectual figure of nineteenth-century France. Tocqueville's greatest contribution to political discourse was his work *Democracy in America*, which, most critics agree, stands as the most penetrating analysis ever of American politics.

Here we shall consider the important ideas of both scholars, using them to convey that sense of society and politics that imagines the world in terms of its common social underpinnings and understandings. Durkheim and Tocqueville emphasized *civil society* in the construction of politics, whereas Marx emphasized the economy and Weber the state.[3] This emphasis on civil society has lately been in ascendance, the result of powerful and fruitful research by, among others, the sociologists Robert Bellah and James Coleman and the political scientist Robert Putnam.

Emile Durkheim on Civil Society and Politics

THE ESSENTIAL DURKHEIM

Emile Durkheim was born in 1858 in the Alsace-Lorraine region of France, an area that came under dispute during the course of World War I. He was the model educator. Punctual to a fault, elegant in his deliveries, committed to reforming the French educational system, he saw himself not as a revolutionary nor even as a political figure, but as someone who would transform society through the strength of his teachings and the discoveries of his research.

He stood directly in the line of French scholars, dating from the writings of Jean-Jacques Rousseau, whose concern was with the nature of the "general will," or that set of understandings that bound civilized human beings to one another. If there is a common thread to the life's work of Durkheim it is his effort to use scientific methods to uncover the nature of this general will and how it came to make itself felt in the thinking and beliefs of humankind.

Durkheim thought of himself as a scientist and an educator. As a scientist, he took up the call of his French intellectual predecessor, Auguste Comte. Comte had insisted that there could be a science of society, a science of social facts which possessed the same permanence and force in the world as biological or physical facts. Sociology was the name Comte gave to this science. Durkheim took it upon himself to further Comte's agenda. Like Comte, Durkheim maintained that sociology is the study of social facts, those "collective and shared ways of thinking, feeling and acting" in the world that exist beyond both the psychology of the individual and the biological principles of humans as a species.[4] Social facts have a force and power over human beings much as psychological or biological facts do.

Much of Durkheim's writing over the course of his life was intended to provide the intellectual underpinnings for the significance of this approach. In one of his earliest and most famous works, *Suicide*, he took great pains to show that suicide was not the product of biological causes.[5] Nor was it simply a psychological fact, as he demonstrated that different societies varied in suicide rates across time and in different regions. In his last and greatest work, he took on, among others, the great German philosopher Immanuel Kant. Kant had insisted, in effect, that the nature of the physical universe was a product of "humankind's imagination and intelligence," shifting the emphasis in philosophy from the nature of the external world to the nature of the human being, or the subject.[6] Durkheim then sought to move beyond Kant. He insisted that the source of ideas about the physical universe, such as force, and about the social order, such as *mana*, was the result of the very power that society held over the thought of human beings. It was society, in general, and social institutions, in particular, Durkheim claimed, that created the intelligence of human beings and that gave birth to their picture of the universe and the moral order.[7]

Unlike Marx, who believed that the ongoing order of capitalism was inherently pernicious and, therefore, had to be overturned, Durkheim insisted that the conflict and disorder of modern society were brought about by the attenuation of its moral order. If one could discover the causes of this attenuation of the moral order, he argued, one would not need to overthrow the ongoing institutions but rather simply reform them. At the conclusion of his famous work, *The Division of Labor in Society*, he writes that profound "changes have been produced in the structure of our societies...(and because) certain of our duties are no longer founded on the reality of things, a breakdown has resulted.... [Therefore] our first duty is to make a moral code for ourselves."[8] This meant, to Durkheim, that great research effort had to be expended on discovering the fundamental character of the moral order, how it became diminished, and the directions in which society was likely to move.

Durkheim's sense of the nature of chaos and conflict thus was fundamentally at odds with the views of Marx and Weber. Whereas Marx understood the conflicts among workers in the nineteenth century to be a product of the evil exploitation by capitalists, Durkheim understood it to be a product of the failure of the major institutions of society to properly inculcate the norms and values of society. To Durkheim, social institutions needed a kind of moral rejuvenation; to Marx they needed to be completely leveled and entirely rebuilt from the ground up. The one took a conservative viewpoint, seeking to restore the social order; the other assumed a radical position, seeking to overthrow the social order, and then ultimately to remake it entirely.

Durkheim focused his energies on discovering the nature of that moral order, particularly in France. Certain fundamental norms and values, he believed, bound people together in society. Social change, or *modernization* as we now call it, had eaten away at the norms that people held in common, creating a greater fragmentation among groups and, at the same time, in Anthony Giddens' apt term, a greater *individuation* among human beings. Once those fundamental norms and values were revealed via empirical research, then Durkheim believed it was the responsibility of the sociologist to formulate an educational program to teach them to young people. He argued in *Moral Education* that the school is central to the reform of society.[9] It was less important for schools simply to teach "reading, writing and arithmetic," and much more important that they teach the basic rules and discipline of citizenship. The "general will" in the theories of Rousseau became the "collective conscience" of society that Durkheim sought to recover and restore through educational institutions.

SOCIETY

Just as the central focus for Marx is the nature of social class and class conflict, the central focus for Durkheim is the nature of society. Society is the object that the science of sociology treats and seeks to explain. In general it consists of several main features: norms and laws, institutions, symbols and rituals, and the division of labor. Each of these elements is discussed and examined at length by Durkheim.

Social Norms and Laws. The basic elements of societies are their norms and laws. Such elements act as the rules that guide the behavior and thinking of the members of societies. They are the fundamental social facts to which Durkheim addressed much of his attention. For any society to work properly, the norms and laws must carefully govern the behavior of its members. In smaller, more primitive societies, there are fewer such norms and laws, and they are enforced so that all people feel compelled to obey them. In larger societies, however, such laws become more fragmented, and their hold over all the members of society also becomes more tenuous.

The nature of punishment, or sanctions, also differs between the two forms of society. In smaller, primitive societies the laws seek retribution on behalf of the entire society, whereas in larger, more complex societies the laws seek to compensate the individual party. The more limited punishments in modern societies correspond to the increasing complexity and differences of such societies and the increasing "individualism" that also occurs. The differences are evident between penal law, on the one hand, and civil and corporate law, on the other. Penal law, which is characteristic of smaller, more inclusive societies, exacts harsh punishments from the offender, whereas civil law simply seeks restitution on behalf of the victim, restoring things, as Durkheim puts it, "to their original state."[10]

Institutions. Education, religion, and the economy represent the main institutions of society. Institutions provide the guiding norms and laws for a society, and they differ by virtue of the different tasks, or functions, they provide. Education is central because it furnishes the foundations for the instruction of children in the ways and norms of a particular society. If a society is not working properly, in the sense that there are high rates of crime, that failure, in Durkheim's view, can be traced to the weakness of schools. Teaching, he insisted, must be firm and strict in such institutions; it must cover the basic norms of society.[11]

Religious institutions are equally significant. Religion, in Durkheim's view, provides the basic glue to the social order. The core laws and values of a society are taught by its religious institutions. Durkheim introduces a number of important concepts to help clarify the nature of religion and its significance. The most critical and famous is that between the *sacred* and the *profane*.[12] The sacred refers to that special, or holy, quality that particular objects or practices hold, and which are so identified by religious institutions. They include special holidays, but also special figures and material objects, such as the cross for Christians or the shank of lamb for Jews on Passover. The profane stands entirely apart from the sacred: it deals with everyday activities and practices, such as the manner in which household or work activities are performed.

In his last great work, *The Elementary Forms of the Religious Life*, Durkheim traced the centrality and importance of religion.[13] Religion, he maintained, provides the core values for all societies and thus furnishes the material that binds its members to one another. Not only does Durkheim seek a sociological answer to questions raised by Kant, but he provides an interpretation of why the institutions of religion are so vital to the working of society. In this respect, his emphasis on religion stands in stark contrast to Marx's view of the economy.

Culture, Symbols, and Rituals. Norms and laws are critical to the working of societies. Sometimes they can be taught explicitly, as in the case of education and schools. But more often they are taught in very subtle ways.

Durkheim insists that there are common symbols around which the members of societies unite and which are crucial to sustaining societies over long periods of time. Such symbols might include the more common, as in the case of flags or national songs, as well as the more central, such the admiration and respect given to special figures, such as the founding figures of societies. In the case of a particular regime or nation, the symbols could be a flag, or even some special personage, like George Washington. They invoke images which, due to the constant repetition of lessons about them, serve to remind members that all of them belong to the same nation.

Ritual is vital in invoking and reminding people of these symbols. "[R]ites," Durkheim observes, "are means by which the social group reaffirms itself periodically."[14] In effect, rituals are the regular and periodic occasions in which the people gather together to celebrate themselves as a nation or society. Voting, for instance, can be considered such a ritual in the sense that it reminds people of the freedom they enjoy under democracy. Durkheim's most penetrating example concerns the case of rituals observed in more primitive groups, such as those that celebrate the origins and life of their gods:

> [M]en would be unable to live without gods, but, on the other hand, the gods would die if their cult were not rendered.... The real reason for the existence of the cults, even of those which are the most materialistic in appearance, is not be sought in the acts which they prescribe, but in the internal and moral regeneration which these acts aid in bringing about. The things which the worshipper really gives his gods are not the foods he places upon the altars, nor the blood which he lets flow from his veins: it is his thought.[15]

By gathering periodically and regularly to celebrate harvests, or the birth of particular animals, such groups not only commemorate specific events, but they also unintentionally engage in a rebirth of themselves as a social order.

These wonderful insights have had profound influence among social anthrologists as well as sociologists. As we shall learn shortly, they are used, for example, by the sociologist of religion, Robert Bellah, to speak about the *civil religion* of the United States.

The Division of Labor. The last critical element of Durkheim's view of the nature of societies lies in his conception of the division of labor. Whereas Marx and Weber had written of social classes, Durkheim wrote of something he called the division of labor. He picked up this theme, in part, from Herbert Spencer who argued that the division of labor of societies grows over time as those societies evolve and become more complex.

The division of labor consists essentially of the different tasks and functions done in a society to maintain the material survival of its members. Among primitive tribes, such tasks consist of the process of hunting and gathering by tribal members, whereas in more modern societies they consist of a diversity of tasks and practices—what we would call specific jobs and occupations today. The concept of the division of labor, rather than setting people apart as the concept of social class did for Marx, actually serves the same integrative function for Durkheim as norms and laws: it furnishes the basis for sustaining the social order. If each person has a particular position in the working of the social order, and all major tasks are fulfilled to keep the society an ongoing enterprise, then it would survive. Thus, by a kind of similar process as the "invisible hand," societies manage to sort and shuffle people into particular jobs and tasks that must be performed if they are to persist as societies. Moreover, as societies grow, by number and in complexity, there is also a growing division of labor. One of Durkheim's more profound, but also controversial, suggestions is that as the population density of a society, or group, increases, there will be an inevitable pressure for the division of labor to become more complex, thus sorting people into new and different positions. "[A]ll condensation of the social mass, especially if it is accompanied by an increase in population," he writes, "necessarily determines advances in the division of labor."[16]

STATES, POLITICS, AND SOCIETIES

Durkheim's sense of states and politics completely reflects his view of societies. States, or governments, are simply another kind of social institution. Rather than ruling on behalf of some illegitimate, or temporary, dominating class, or group, states represent the whole of society, and they seek to engender overall agreement and consensus. They embody, in a sense, the *volonte generale* of Rousseau. They represent the articulate norms and laws of the underlying social order. Thus, to oppose the state is to oppose the social order, or society, itself. In this reckoning, then, power and authority are not exercised illegitimately or on behalf of any class or other grouping; society is *the basis of authority*, and the state must be seen as representing its basic workings and operations.

Dissent, in Durkheim's view, is not the opposition of a group that represents the future of society, or some overall or higher good. Opposition is, in effect, deviance from the general norms of society.[17] States thus are compelled to act with force to impose their will and to put down any form of opposition. To Durkheim, then, the state is essentially a police force, responsible for ensuring that the norms and rules of society are, in fact, obeyed. Moreover, there never is any question of its illegitimacy or illegality—its authority is rooted in the very nature of society itself.

Nevertheless, Durkheim fully recognized that as societies modernized, the hold of the state, like that of society, lessens over the lives of individuals.

Deviance, in the form of suicides and of homicides, increases with modernization precisely because the common bonds that hold individuals to societies lessen in their strength and power. Thus, in modern societies integrity is based less on the general and total power of the social bonds, as of the states, and more on the manufacture of new bases for integrity and integration. States, like other social institutions, must work to sustain and develop themselves as societies become more complex.

Though Durkheim never fully explains or articulates this vision of the modern polity, he provides his clearest exposition of how it might work, in principle, toward the end of *Suicide*. Noting that the division of labor in modern societies had become more complex, he argues that the division of labor, one of the core elements of society, could furnish the basis for linking the state effectively to modern society and the lives of individuals:

> The only way to resolve [the antimony between excessive force and excessive neglect by the State] is to set up a cluster of collective forces outside the State, though subject to its action, whose regulative influence can be exerted with greater variety....To [such corporations]...falls the duty of presiding over companies of insurance, benevolent aid and pensions, the need of which are felt by so many good minds but which we rightly hesitate to place in the hands of the State, already so powerful and awkward; theirs it should likewise be to preside over the disputes constantly arising between the branches of the same occupation, to fix conditions...with which contracts must agree in order to be valid, in the name of the common interest to prevent the strong from unduly exploiting the weak, etc.[18]

The new modern society, in other words, is to be found in the proliferation of occupations among workers, and it is there that the lives of individuals will unfold. Social groups close to this experience, then, will be closest to the experience of individuals as social change happens and marks their lives. States will work best that best provide a means for organizations representing such occupations to voice the concerns of workers.

What is so remarkable about this passage from Durkheim is that it fits so neatly with a view that was propounded only decades earlier by his fellow Frenchman, Alexis de Tocqueville. The heart and soul of society should be the form and workings of the organizations around which the lives of individuals are fashioned, and such organizations must be connected integrally to the workings of the state, the highest level of authority in society. What Durkheim truly failed to appreciate—though he probably understood at some level—is that the state could come to have its own strong purposes, and that such purposes often ran deliberately counter to the needs and interests of the vast majority of citizens.

Alexis de Tocqueville on Civil Society and Politics

THE ESSENTIAL TOCQUEVILLE

Alexis de Tocqueville (18051859), born into the French aristocracy, has become justly famous as the author of arguably the most penetrating analysis ever of American democracy. In the space of fifty-four years, he created at least two memorable works of history and comparative analysis. Most of his life was spent as a politician and writer; his writings, on democracy and on the French Revolution, gained him both fame and wealth. Although he and Durkheim have much in common—in their emphasis on the civil basis of the political order and the underlying continuities of societies—they also differ markedly. Indeed, to many, Tocqueville is the more compelling thinker, for he managed to weave both an historical and a sociological imagination together at one and the same time. In the course of so doing, he also provided some of the earliest and still the very best of comparative historical and social analysis.

Tocqueville's major writings cast light on two important historical events. One concerns the French Revolution of 1789 and the collapse of the *ancien regime*.[19] Why, he asked, did the ancien regime collapse? In raising this question, he anticipated the analyses of revolution and change among many of his successors. He argued, in essence, that the old regime had collapsed because of the failure of the nobility, itself, and because of the changes engendered in French society over the course of the eighteenth century. It was not the simple acts of 1789, and shortly thereafter, that led to the revolutionary overthrow, but a set of sources that had earlier ripened and matured in French society. When the regime collapsed, it had basically exhausted its resources. Moreover, it failed in the middle of a general movement across the world for a greater social and political equality, a movement highlighted in the nineteenth century by the United States. The violence and terror of 1789 came about because citizens believed they needed to make a clean and abrupt break with their feudal and inegalitarian past: to do away with all remnants of the old society meant to do away completely and violently with that society.

The other related question for Tocqueville was this: Why and how did American society develop in the manner it had? How was it able to create a novel set of social and political institutions that were singular in their emphasis on equality and democracy, when all older societies—which should have had some edge—were unable to do so? Tocqueville set about answering this question in an extended and detailed comparative historical analysis, one that has come to rank alongside the historical writings of Max Weber in terms of its elegance and ambition.[20] Tocqueville managed to show how we can think of nations as whole entities, and therefore how we can compare nations in terms of their differences. And he did so with a subtlety and power that remains exemplary to this very day.

EQUALITY IN AMERICA

Democracy in America, Tocqueville claimed, represented a very special and unique accomplishment. Observing the nations of the nineteenth century, Tocqueville could find no other society that possessed the notable political institutions of America. The main feature of American democracy was its emphasis on the equality of its citizens. In his introduction to Volume 1 of *Democracy in America*, he wrote that in his visit to America "nothing struck me more forcibly than the general equality of condition among the people.... [I]t gives a peculiar direction to public opinion and a peculiar tenor to the laws; it impacts new maxims to the governing authorities and peculiar habits to the governed."[21] All people, he observed, were held to be equal before the law and deserving of equal respect and treatment by the law. The very nature of American republican institutions furnished the basis for this equality.

General political institutions provided the framework for political equality in America. All people—but, of course, at the time this meant all white men—were to be granted suffrage and the equal capacity to influence the outcomes of the political process. Tocqueville regarded suffrage as one of the central elements of democracy in America. The other was that of the abolition of the law of primogeniture, and the inheritance of wealth and privilege from one generation to another. Such a system, which characterized European countries at the time, fundamentally undercut the ability of people to pursue their own wishes and desires on an equal footing. Other features of the court system and law also upheld the condition of equality, requiring that all people be treated with respect and dignity in the legal system. The federal system of government provided the framework for institutional equality among the states and between men. The Constitution secured the basic principles, including the right of assembly, among others, permitting people to easily join with one another and to share their opinions in an equal and unfettered manner.

THE CONDITIONS (CAUSES) FOR EQUALITY

The key analytical problem for Tocqueville was to discover the conditions that promoted such equality. Why, among all nations, should the United States have managed to create this special and virtually unique situation? What was it about the American people, and the country of America, that enabled equality to be achieved?

In a fundamental sense, the basic answer to this question is simple: in all other societies people suffered under oppression, from the nobles or the growing wealth of the manufacturing class but in America, citizens in effect were born free. "The social condition of the Americans is eminently democratic; this was its character at the foundation of the colonies, and it's still more strongly marked at the present day," he would write.[22] A relatively new and unburdened set of peoples, most of whom came to America as immigrants and to escape oppression in Europe, reached this continent and found freedom. As Louis Hartz pointed out decades later, the critical notion of Rousseau—that men are born free and everywhere they are in chains—was simply not true, in Tocqueville's view, in America. In America, they were in effect born free since they had escaped the chains of their former existence abroad. Hereditary authority and the transmission of wealth and property did not operate in nineteenth-century America as they did in nineteenth-century Europe. Hence men were able to pursue wealth and material satisfaction, unburdened by the debts and chains of a feudal past.

Freedom, then, is the *sine qua non* of democratic equality in America. But by itself it is insufficient to secure such equality. After all, men could be free—but free for what? In Tocqueville's America men were not only free, they engaged in actions that constantly affirmed and reaffirmed this freedom. There were two critical components of this activity. The first, and to this day the most prominent, is the continuing activity of people to develop, support, and engage in voluntary associations. People voluntarily act with one another to secure their freedom: they engage in causes with one another in new organizations that pursue political ends; such organizations are critical, in fact, to the success of the American revolutionaries. "In their political associations the Americans, of all conditions, minds and ages, daily acquire a general taste for association and grow accustomed to the use of it," Tocqueville observed.[23]

Eventually, then, a strong social infrastructure emerged in America of voluntary associations of all stripes—political groups, social groups, cooking clubs, organizations among women to support the Revolutionary effort. This massive structure of organizations and associations, in Tocqueville's eyes, ensured that democracy would continue because all such organizations treated their members as equals and all such organizations became vehicles whereby the people could articulate their concerns and opinions to the reigning authorities. People cherished this freedom to act and to express their opinons almost in the same measure as they cherished their goals of wealth and material well-being. "The most natural privilege of man," Tocqueville wrote, "next to the right of acting for himself, is that of combining his exertions with those of his fellow creatures and of acting in common with them. The right of association therefore appears to me almost as inalienable in its nature as the right of personal liberty."[24]

Equally important to ensuring democratic equality in America is a free press and the freedom of speech, in the eyes of Tocqueville. Freedom of speech is the first principle on which American government had been established and founded. And in reality Tocqueville found it displayed in the many and various activities undertaken by newspapers in America. Here, unlike Europe, one could read and see the free opinions of Americans expressed, opinions that were shared among themselves and that were also available to be read and understood by their rulers. To Tocqueville the sheer number and variety of different publications underscored the importance of the principle of free speech and a free press enshrined in the First Amendment to the Constitution of the United States.

In the absence then of voluntary associations and a free press, freedom and democracy could not be sustained, or so Tocqueville argued. Their very absence in the nations of Europe, he maintained, accounted for the political differences between the United States and European countries such as France and England.

THREATS TO DEMOCRACY IN AMERICA

Just as America showed the path that other countries of the world could follow on the way to democracy, it also displayed the major challenges that could threaten democracy. Three such threats were of most concern to Tocqueville.

The first of these was the element of race. Though he wrote of widespread equality and the underpinnings of equality in American institutions, Tocqueville was not so naive to believe that equality existed everywhere. It did not. In fact, he pointed to three races in America, the differences among them revealing deep social and economic inequalities. The races were: the Indians, or indigenous Americans; black Americans; and white Americans. It was among blacks that Tocqueville found the most potent threat to widespread equalities. He noted that blacks lived under conditions of slavery and in far worse circumstances than most other Americans. The conditions of servitude might diminish, as in the North, but there still appeared to be deep and irreconcilable differences between blacks and whites in America. "Whoever has inhabited the United States must have perceived that in those parts of the Union in which Negroes are no longer slaves they have in no wise drawn nearer to the whites. On the contrary, the prejudice of race appears to be stronger in the states that have abolished slavery than in those where it still exists."[25] Such a powerful and prescient observer was Tocqueville that his observations on race sound as though they were written yesterday! One century later, Gunnar Myrdal and his colleagues would revisit Tocqueville's emphasis on equality in their master-piece on race and inequality in midtwentieth-century America.[26]

In addition, while America did not show the deep social and particularly economic inequalities of Europe, Tocqueville opined that if inequality ever did reach American shores, industry and manufacturing would be the culprits. Manufacturing, he argued, created divisions among people in terms of their wealth. And as businesses expanded and developed they could promote a new kind of inequality. "(T)he friends of democracy," he wrote, "should keep their eyes anxiously fixed in this direction; for if ever a permanent inequality of conditions and aristocracy again penetrates into the world, it may be predicted that this is the gate by which they will enter."[27]

Yet the most dangerous threat to equality in America, in Tocqueville's eyes, was the threat posed by the widespread equality itself:

> In my opinion, the main evil of the present democratic institutions of the United States does not arise, as is often asserted in Europe, from their weakness, but from their irresistible strength. I am not so much alarmed at the exceptional liberty which reigns in that country as at the inadequate securities which one finds there against tyranny.[28]

If all people were regarded as equal, then no one was more equal than any-one else. This meant that everyone's opinion and idea would count the same. Under these conditions, the policies and principles of the people would be implemented through majority rule—on any key question, the majority would govern. But what was to become of the opinions and ideas of the minority, Tocqueville wondered? He went on to speculate that the great danger of equality in the governance of a society was that of *the tyranny of the majority*. Since all were equal, only the greatest number could gain advantage, unlike in European countries where advantage came to those with inherited privileges of wealth and property. It was such tyranny that Americans would have to guard against, both in the development of their political institutions, and in the general manner of their social ways of doing things among themselves.

CONCLUDING OBSERVATIONS

In sum, Tocqueville provided both a vision and a map for the future of America. It rested upon the principles of equality and freedom, and was grounded in a sense of the general character of the society. When Tocqueville looked at America, moreover, he did not perceive a society divided by social classes nor one dominated by the state as Marx or Weber likely would have seen. Rather he saw a society possessed of a specific and unique culture, supported and maintained by an array of associations and organizations by which Americans gave voice and expression to their equality. It was, in essence, *a civil society through and through—civil in its nature and civil in its relations among its citizens.* Though it could come to harm through the divisions between the races and the looming danger of unbridled capitalism, it was a unique society, radically different in form from its European counterparts.

The Neo-Consensualists

SEYMOUR MARTIN LIPSET

One of the most interesting and provocative social scientists of the twentieth century—and the most widely cited—is Seymour Martin Lipset. He also is one of the principal founders of the field of political sociology. Lipset has been a prodigious and creative scholar, writing more than twenty books and countless articles. It was Lipset who first gave shape to the intellectual agenda of political sociology in his justly famous work, *Political Man.*[29] There he identified Marx, Weber, and Tocqueville as the main intellectual founders of political sociology.

Like Tocqueville, Lipset's main intellectual passion has been to study America and, in particular, the nature of democracy in America. He has used this interest as a kind of intellectual probe also to explore the nature of other societies and their political systems. Thus, in a pioneering comparative analysis he examined the character of democratic governments in a number of societies, concluding that the main condition making for democracy is a strong middle class and a prosperous economy. He also focuses on America as a way of asking what became for him a lifelong query—why no socialism in America? To answer this question he undertook to explore the origins of agrarian socialism in Canada, basing his analysis on the emergence of the Cooperative Commonwealth Federation in Saskatchewan, Canada. He argued that the unusually high rate of political interest and participation in the province helped to lay the foundations for the Federation's appearance. Years later he would add to this analysis by suggesting, too, that the Canadian system of proportional representation, as compared to America's winner-take-all system, greatly facilitated the rise of the socialist Federation in Canada.[30]

Though Lipset has been much influenced by the writings of Marx and Weber, it is the sensibility and passion of Tocqueville that seem to shine through his thought and writing most clearly. Consider the powerful and provocative analysis of the International Typographical Union in New York City, a work Lipset wrote in collaboration with James Coleman and Martin Trow.[31]

Taking this single case, they ask why the I.T.U. was able to sustain a democratic form of governance and administration whereas most other trades unions were unable to. His answer comes virtually straight from the pages of Tocqueville. Most other unions discouraged the active participation of their members in union activities, whereas because of the high level of education and skill of the printers, such participation became a way of life. "The printers' strong identification with (their) craft," the authors note, "...meant that they were more likely to be involved in the affairs of their organization than workers in other occupations.... [Moreover], their occupational community [further] stimulated the desire of the printers to participate in their union."[32] Democracy, so unique to this union, became grounded on a deep sense of comittment and widespread participation among the union members.

Lipset's analysis in *Union Democracy* represents an important illustration of the way that the civil institutions of a society—or in this instance, an organization—provide the means and foundations for politics, in particular, democratic politics. To Lipset, as to Tocqueville before him, such institutions assume the form of the voluntary organizations and the informal networks that exist among people, as well as the customs and values on which they are grounded and that they serve to express. Activity in such social groupings provides both a means for understanding the nature of the larger social group, and a way of communicating and securing a sense of trust among the others with whom one has contact.

Lipset's vision of democracy—a vision at one point illustrated with the claim of Joseph Schumpeter that democracy is "the free competition between elites for the right to govern"—is a vision that he continues to pursue and works hard to understand. Much of his writing makes sense only when understood as his passion and quest to understand the underpinnings of democratic governments. The central elements that he has found—a high degree of education; an advanced economy; a broad and deep middle class—represent the elements that he believes are necessary to sustain democratic governments.[33] Together they constitute one view of the way that civil society anchors democratic governments.

Moreover, his is a view that sees working democratic governments like that in the United States as good in and of themselves and does not consider them either as pursuing the ends of power or as ruling on behalf of a small and illegitimate class of capitalists. Democratic government works to effectively process the different and varied opinions of people in society. It is a perspective that, while recognizing the important changes and shifts which have taken place, is deeply indebted to the imagery and questions raised first by Alexis de Tocqueville. And it is also a perspective that has gone to great pains to temper the influence of Marx's ideas on modern sociology.[34]

Lipset's empirical expertise and knowledge has proven to be exceptional. His work on the International Typographical Union helped to show how useful single case studies could be to the sociological study of the world of politics. Much of his writing has been about sample surveys and employs the perspective of the modern behavioral sciences, with their emphasis on questionnaire construction, surveys, and the opinions of the public. Though he has crafted exceptional historical work, to some degree modern sociology, and other social sciences, have moved beyond him in their emphasis on the institutional and historical underpinnings of modern societies.

ROBERT BELLAH

Robert Bellah has been more often associated with the sociological study of religion than of politics. But, as a scholar who worked in the traditions of Emile Durkheim and Alexis de Tocqueville, what he has to say about sociology also has important bearing on one's view of politics. Indeed, Bellah's perspective on the world provides a distinctive way of talking about the bearing of civil society, or the civil order, on the character of politics.

Civil Religion. One of Bellah's main contributions to sociology is his thesis about the nature of *civil religion*.[35] Adopting an idea from Durkheim, Bellah has argued that politics in America has become what he calls a civil religion. Durkheim originally suggested the germ for this argument in discussions such as the following:

> There can be no society that does not feel the need of upholding and reaffirming at regular intervals the collective sentiments and the collective ideas which make its unity and its personality.... What essential difference is there between an assembly of Christians celebrating the principal dates of the life of Christ, or of Jews remembering the exodus from Egypt, or the promulgation of the decalogue, and *a reunion of citizens commemorating the promulgation of a new moral or legal system or some great event in the national life?*[36](italics added)

Bellah argues that one may think of politics not in the conventional sense, but as a kind of way of life, or religion, for American citizens.

The roots of American civil religion, Bellah claims, can be found in some of the major statements and interpretations of our leading political figures. One illustration he uses is the inauguration of President John F. Kennedy in 1961. He notes that Kennedy used the word "God" three times in his speech. But the American Constitution calls for a separation of the State and Church. How exactly then could one interpret Kennedy's invocation of the term in his national address? Bellah insists that "the separation of church and state has not denied the political realm a religious dimension.... [There are] certain common elements of religious orientation that the great majority of Americans share [and]...these have played a crucial role in the development of American institutions and still provide a religious dimension for the whole fabric of American life, including the political sphere."[37]

American civil religion is represented both by the symbols and by the rituals in which Americans engage to celebrate the nation and the elements they hold in common. Moreover, there are national crises that serve as tests of the state of nationhood and that offer the opportunity for restoring the sense of common fellowship among Americans. One such crisis was represented by the Civil War, when the North and South divided on the issue of slavery. It became both a moment of moral division and a moment that, when the War was over, provided an opportunity for healing. In many respects, such healing has happened. And yet, the nation must continue to live through the trauma and make efforts to heal its moral wounds. Racism, the modern-day equivalent of slavery, is a kind of crisis around which Americans are joined and through which they make efforts to heal and to make themselves common. Its continuing presence also provides the continuing sense of crisis, and the continuing possibility, that the nation will never be whole.[38] It is such elements as these, in the history and sense of nationhood, in which Bellah finds his sense of civil religion to be revealed.

Habits of the Heart. Bellah's most famous work is one on which he collaborated with several colleagues: fellow sociologists Richard Madsen, Stephen Tipton, and Ann Swidler, and philosopher William Sullivan. It is an original and important study of America, and it also became a bestseller, one of the few works by academic sociologists ever to achieve such recognition.[39]

Much like Alexis de Tocqueville, the authors endeavor to probe and to understand the nature of American culture. They do so by assembling a series of interviews with a group of middle-class white Americans, the "middling group of Americans," who, they believe, are representative of American customs and ways. They seek to discover what Tocqueville termed *habits of the heart*:

> I am very much convinced that political societies are created by not by their laws but by the feelings, beliefs, ideas, the habits of heart and mind of the men who compose those societies, by that which nature and education have made them, have prepared them to be.[40]

Theirs is a study, then, not of behavior or even of political events and institutions, but rather of the deep cultural roots of American society. It is these traditions, they argue, that can explain both the strengths of America circa 1990 and its weaknesses as well. And the tone of their work is deliberately moralistic: culture is not simply a set of habits and patterns, but a set of moral expectations for how people are to lead their lives.

The main pattern Bellah and his colleagues uncover is that of *individual-ism*. There are different varieties, the most often encountered of which in the activities of Americans takes the form of self-interested behavior and individual initiative, what they call *utilitarian* and *expressive individualism*. And there are two other forms, the *biblical* and *civic republican* traditions, that have receded from contemporary experience, but which the authors believe represent the most positive forms of individualism. The American tradition of individualism, which is responsible for the energy and activity of many in the business world, also has an impact on other spheres of life. Bellah and his colleagues portray various personal exemplars of individualism, some of whom reveal in very clear and graphic ways the value they attach to great personal success and ambition and, in the lingua franca of the day, "being their own person."

These deep cultural foundations of American life, the same as those to which Tocqueville pointed more than a century earlier, have important rever-berations in public life and politics. Americans, Bellah and his colleagues show, have a preference for individual pursuits as well as a reluctance to engage in broad civic activities. The strength of the American tradition is to foster the individual pursuit of excellence, but its weakness is to diminish the sense of charity and compassion Americans have for others. In a section in which they consider the activity of Americans in broad civic and public associations, they contrast the view of politics found in local government and the view advocated by a citizens' group:

> Two images of American life confronted each other: the efficient organizational society of private achievement and consumption versus the civic vision of work as a calling and contribution to the community, binding individuals together in a com-mon life.... This (latter) view of politics depends upon a notion of community and citizenship importantly different from the utilitarian individualist view. It seeks to persuade us that the individual self finds its fulfillment in relationships with others in a society organized through public dialogue.[41]

The consequence, then, of such a strong belief in individualism is that Americans tend to think of civic ventures only in terms of personal gain and achievement rather than in terms of promoting a stronger sense of community among themselves while acting to help others.

While Bellah and his co-authors decry the limits that individualism imposes on American public life today, they are careful to argue that the older, more sub-dued traditions, which emphasize a greater trust and commonality even among individuals, might always be resurrected. Such traditions exist as a kind of silent language, always available but mute in the face of utilitarian individualism's suc-cess. Moreover, though they do not link individualism much to signs of public inac-tivity, it also is clear that the authors believe such things as diminishing turnout for elections and the growing indifference of Americans to associational activity represent the "nihilism" to which individualism, when carried to an extreme, can lead.

JAMES S. COLEMAN AND ROBERT PUTNAM

Over the course of the past decade, there has been a virtual explosion of interest in the bearing of civil society on the nature of a nation's politics and political institutions. Much of this work has been stimulated by theoretical formulations that owe their origins to the writings of two scholars—one a sociologist, the other a political scientist. I group them together here because the work has really grown in tandem, even though they never worked in direct collaboration with one another. But both were equally inspired by a kind of vision of civil society and civic virtue, a vision whose roots can be traced back to the writings of Durkheim and Tocqueville.

The beginnings of the perspective are to be found in the work of James S. Coleman, a most brilliant sociologist. Shortly before his death, Coleman completed a massive work, *The Foundations of Social Theory*.[42] In it he proposed a general social theory of action that was intended to rival the works of the great masters of sociology, like Karl Marx and Max Weber. Although it remains to be seen whether the work will have that sort of lasting influence, there is one critical idea that has proven quite fruitful and provocative to recent scholars. Coleman suggested that people possess something he called *social capital*. Social capital, he claimed, refers to the social resources that individuals possess and on which they can draw in making critical decisions and taking critical action. (Glenn Loury, who originally advanced the concept, had intended it to refer to the family and its network of relations in explaining the economic accomplishments of individuals.)[43] Coleman intended for the concept to refer both to the social relations of people and to the sense of underlying trust and confidence they have in one another.

Coleman illustrates his conception of social capital with various examples. He refers, for instance, to the idea of the "rotating credit association," an association made famous by an article by the cultural anthropologist Clifford Geertz.[44] The rotating credit association is a form of cooperative economic venture practiced among people in Southeast Asian societies. By joining together in a common venture, people can pool their meager resources, and then they can rotate in drawing on the general fund of credit created by the collective pool. The method provides a means for coping with circumstances in which no single individual has enough funds to begin an economic enterprise. Once a person draws on the collective pool of funds, he is required to pay them back from the earnings of his venture. And so the process continues. Moreover, it is found not only in Southeast Asian societies, where Geertz uncovered it, but also among Korean immigrant entrepreneurs in Los Angeles, where it has been used to explain their economic success compared to their African American counterparts.[45]

Coleman insisted that there are many such examples of social trust and cooperation evident in the larger world. They are to be found in extended families and in small groups. They also may be discovered in urban areas, and in the differences between them. Thus, for instance, he notes that a mother who moved to Jerusalem felt more comfortable in allowing her children to play unattended there than in Detroit precisely because she felt a greater sense of trust in the residents living in Jerusalem. In brief, then, Coleman argues that social capital consists of the networks and relations among individuals as well as in the deep sense of trust and comfort people feel in some cultures and locales as compared to others. Moreover, it provides an important resource on which they can draw in making important decisions and choices in their lives.

Coleman died before he was able to explore the various ramifications of his rich concept of social capital. Fortunately for him—and for us—it was an idea that prompted later pathbreaking research by the political scientist Robert Putnam, who acknowledges his deep debt to Coleman as well as to the sociologist Mark Granovetter.[46] Putnam, along with his colleagues Robert Leonardi and Raffaella Nanetti, was able to study the formation of new regional governments in Italy from the moment of their birth in the early 1970s.[47] The Italian government had decided to embark on a major effort to break out of the inertia of its national programs and to create new governments that could cover policy arenas and also work more closely with local citizens. It was an historic venture for Italy, one that Putnam and his colleagues were asked to evaluate. In the end, their assessment covered a period of a quarter of a century, during which a major evolution took place in the regional governments.

Putnam and his colleagues studied the regional governments by doing periodic surveys with the local officials as well as local citizens. They examined, among other things, the citizens' reactions to and sense of satisfaction with the work done by the local governments. In addition, Putnam and his colleagues also measured the effectiveness and performance of the regional governments. They quantified such performance along twelve different dimensions of the workings of the regional government, including: reform legislation; daycare centers; housing and urban development; legislative innovation; cabinet stability; bureaucratic responsiveness; and budget promptness. Each of the twelve dimensions was put into quantitative form, and each covered somewhat different time periods over the course of the entire life span of the regional governments. The investigators finally created an overall index of institutional performance; as it turned out, each of the measures was related to one another although the degree of such a relationship was not always strong.

The three social scientists then proceeded to put their data together. They looked for and discovered variations in the institutional performance of each of the twelve regional governments; they also uncovered important variations in the satisfaction of citizens with the effectiveness of each government's performance. As it turned out, citizens were more satisfied with those regional governments that performed better, thus satisfying both the Italian authorities and the investigators. Then the research turned more interesting.

Putnam, who assumed responsibility for the argument seeking sources of the effectiveness of the regional governments, embarked on his theoretical excursion as an advocate of the kind of argument put forth by Alexis de Tocqueville. He assumed that something like civic traditions, or habits of the heart, are present among people, and that they could account for democracy, in general, and for the link between the effectiveness of government and the satisfaction of citizens. He put his claims to the test. He showed, for instance, that variations in the institutional effectiveness of the regional governments could not be explained by variations in the level of their local wealth. This constituted both a test, and a disproof, of the hypothesis linking wealth and democracy provided by Seymour Martin Lipset. Next he turned to see whether the civic trust and traditions of a region were at all linked to institutional effectiveness, creating an index comprised of measures of voting turnout, and associational involvement by local citizens, among other things. An examination, then, of the correspondence between his measure of the civic community and institutional performance provided overwhelming confirmation of his argument: where the local civic community was strong, there, too, institutional performance was the most effective by the regional governments. Indeed, the correlation was on the order of +0.90, surprisingly strong evidence of correspondence in the social sciences.[48]

Not content to let his case rest simply on this evidence, Putnam considers alternative explanations, finding all of them wanting. He also expands on the argument about the civic community, an argument he links directly to the work of Tocqueville on American democracy. He finds that the civic community is something that can be linked to the Italian past, in particular, that stronger communities grew in the Italian north as early as the Middle Ages, whereas the south was weaker in such traditions. The difference between the north and south of Italy is also parallel to the difference between those regions where the regional governments were ineffective and effective, respectively. To ground his case firmly, he then expands on the theory of the civic community, noting the importance of social networks and social trust, drawing explicitly on the work of Coleman and Granovetter.

Putnam's work has won him much praise and several awards, and it is the strongest evidence yet of the continuing importance of civic traditions, and of civil society, for the grounding and development of democratic politics. More over, as we shall discover in Chapter 9, he has extended the thesis of social capi-tal and democracy even further, landing it on the shores of modern America.

Conclusion

Over the past few years, civil society has emerged among sociologists and, to a lesser degree, among political scientists, as the place to turn for interesting explanations of everything from democracy to revolution. There has been a virtual explosion of interest in the form and nature of civil society, much of it springing from works like Robert Putnam's *Making Democracy Work*. Though not all observers agree with Putnam—and many are now searching more care-fully for evidence on such things as voluntary associations and social networks—most agree that Putnam has reinvigorated this long-neglected paradigm.

The interest in Putnam and civil society represents a return to the kinds of arguments and explanations offered a century ago by Emile Durkheim and, especially, Alexis de Tocqueville. The appeal of these arguments is quite sim-ple. People are now searching for ways both to understand and to create, if not restore, democracies in the world. Neither Karl Marx, with his emphasis on social classes and the illusion of state power, nor Max Weber, with his concern about the actions of aggressive states, offer nearly as much hope for those wish-ing to establish and create new democracies. Moreover, many analysts find in the notion of civil society a way of understanding how the collapse of older regimes, like that of Poland, came about. Timothy Garton Ash, one of the ear-liest commentators on the collapse of communism in Eastern Europe, used the notion of civil society to portray the efforts of the Solidarity movement to rise up against the communist regime and to succeed. Ash argued that the success of Solidarity lay precisely in the fact that it had helped to create new associations in civil society, which were able to replace those of communism once it was over-thrown.[49] It is likely that as long as our world remains in some turmoil, with the collapse of old regimes and efforts to create new ones, there will also continue to be a strong interest in understanding how the institutions of civil society work and, more than that, how they shape the workings of government.

NOTES

1. Emile Durkheim, *The Rules of Sociological Method*, 8th ed., translated by Sarah A. Solovay and John H. Mueller and edited by George E. G. Catlin (New York: the Free Press of Glencoe), 2–3.

2. Ralf Dahrendorf, *Class and Class Conflict in Industrial Society* (Stanford, CA: Stanford University Press, 1959).
3. On the origins of the distinction, see *Hegel's Philosophy of Right*, translated with note by T. M. Knox (London: Oxford University Press, 1952; 1967), especially subsections 2 and 3 on civil society and the state, respectively.
4. Durkheim, *Rules of the Sociological Method*, lvi.
5. Emile Durkheim, *Suicide: A Study in Sociology*, translated by John A. Spaulding and George Simpson; edited with an introduction by George Simpson (Glencoe, IL: The Free Press, 1951).
6. Immanuel Kant, *The Critique of Pure Reason*, translated by Norman Kemp Smith (New York: St. Martin's Press, 1929; 1965).
7. Emile Durkheim, *The Elementary Forms of the Religious Life*, Joseph Ward Swain, trans. (New York: Collier Books, 1961).
8. Emile Durkheim, *The Division of Labor in Society*, translated by George Simpson (New York: Free Press, 1964), 408–09.
9. Emile Durkheim, *Moral Education: A Study in the theory and Application of the Sociology of Education*, Everett K. Wilson and Herman Schnurer, trans. (New York: The Free Press of Glencoe, 1961).
10. Durkheim, *The Division of Labor in Society*.
11. Ibid.
12. *Elementary Forms of the Religious Life*, Book I.
13. Ibid.
14. Ibid., 432.
15. Ibid., 388.
16. *The Division of Labor in Society*, 268.
17. See, for example, *Suicide*.
18. Ibid., 380.
19. Alexis de Tocqueville, *The Old Regime and the Revolution*, edited and with an introduction and critical appraisal by Francois Furet and Francoise Melonio; translated by Alan S. Kahan (Chicago: University of Chicago Press, 1998).
20. Louis Hartz, *The Liberal Tradition in America: An Interpretation of American Political Thought Since the Revolution* (New York: Harcourt Brace Jovanovich, Inc., 1955).
21. Alexis de Tocqueville, *Democracy in America*, the Henry Reeve text with notes and bibliographies by Phillips Bradley (New York: Vintage Books), volume I, 4.
22. Ibid., 48.
23. Tocqueville, *Democracy in America*, II, 127.
24. Op. cit., *Democracy in America*, I, 203.
25. Op. cit., *Democracy in America*, II, 373.
26. Gunnar Myrdal, with the assistance of Richard Sterner and Arnold Rose, *An American Dilemma: the Negro Problem and Modern Democracy* (New York: Harper, 1944).
27. Tocqueville, *Democracy in America*, II, 171.
28. Op. cit., *Democracy in America*, I, 270–71.
29. Seymour Martin Lipset, *Political Man: The Social Bases of Politics* (Garden City, NY: Doubleday & Company, 1959).

30. Seymour Martin Lipset, *Agrarian Socialism*, updated edition (Garden City, NY: Doubleday, 1968).
31. Seymour Martin Lipset, Martin A. Trow, and James S. Coleman, *Union Democracy: The Internal Politics of the International Typographical Union* (Garden City, NY: Doubleday Anchor, 1962).
32. Ibid., p. 442.
33. Seymour Martin Lipset, "Some Social Requisites of Democracy," *American Political Science Review*, vol. 53 (March 1959), 69–105.
34. *Class, Status and Power*, Seymour Martin Lipset and Reinhard Bendix, eds. (New York: Free Press, 1966).
35. Robert N. Bellah, *Beyond Belief: Essays on Religion in a Post-Traditional World* (New York: Harper & Row, 1970).
36. Emile Durkheim, *Elementary Forms of the Religious Life*, 475.
37. Bellah, op. cit., 171.
38. See Robert Bellah, *The Broken Covenant: American Civil Religion in a Time of Trial* (New York: Seabury Press, 1975).
39. Robert N. Bellah, Richard Madsen, William M. Sullivan, Ann Swidler, and Steven M. Tipton, *Habits of the Heart: Individualism and Commitment in American Life*, Updated Edition with a New Introduction (Berkeley: University of California Press, 1996).
40. Letter from Tocqueville to Corcelle, September 1853; as quoted in Tocqueville, *The Old Regime and the French Revolution*, volume 1, op. cit., 10.
41. *Habits of the Heart*, 218.
42. James S. Coleman, *Foundations of Social Theory* (Cambridge, MA: The Belknap Press of Harvard University Press, 1990).
43. Glenn Loury, "Why Should We Care About Group Inequality?" *Social Philosophy and Policy*, 1987, 5, 249–71.
44. Clifford Geertz, "The Rotating Credit Association: A 'Middle Rung' in Development," *Economic Development and Cultural Change* , 1962, 10, 240–63.
45. Ivan Light, *Ethnic Enterprise in America: Business and Welfare Among Chinese, Japanese and Blacks* (Berkeley: University of California Press, 1972).
46. Mark Granovetter, "Economic Action and Social Structure: The Problem of Embeddedness," *American Sociological Review*, volume 91 (November 1985), 481–510.
47. Robert D. Putnam, with Robert Leonardi and Raffaella Y. Nanetti, *Making Democracy Work: Civic Traditions in Modern Italy* (Princeton, NJ: Princeton University Press, 1993).
48. Ibid., p. 98.
49. Timothy Garton Ash, *The Uses of Adversity: Essays on the Fate of Central Europe* (New York: Random House, 1989).

Chapter 5

On the Politics, Law, and Morality of Markets

Karl Polanyi

[T]he behavior of liberals themselves proved that the maintenance of freedom of trade—in our terms, of a self-regulating market—far from excluding intervention, in effect, demanded such action, and that liberals themselves regularly called for compulsory action on the part of the state as in the case of trade union law and anti-trust laws. Thus nothing could be more decisive than the evidence of history that as to which of the two contending interpretations of the double movement was correct: that of the economic liberal who maintained that his policy never had a chance, but was strangled by shortsighted trade unionists, Marxist intellectuals, greedy manufacturers, and reactionary landlords; or that of his critics, who can point to the universal 'collectivist' reaction against the expansion of market economy in the second half of the nineteenth century as conclusive proof of the peril to society inherent in the utopian principle of a self-regulating market.[1]

Globalization has been a central topic of debate during the post–Cold War period. Neo-liberals since Ronald Reagan and Margaret Thatcher have insisted that "there is no alternative" to integration within a single global economy through international trade and finance modeled on free market capitalism and that resistance is futile. A variety of movements around the world have challenged this vision of globalization from very different perspectives, ranging from transnational revolutionary movements like al-Qa'ida, which use terrorist tactics, to transnational social movements seeking to democratically reform global financial institutions through nonviolent tactics. Those on all sides of the debate have much to learn from the political sociology of Karl Polanyi and his analysis of the failed projects of economic globalization in the past.

The Essential Polanyi[1]

Karl Polanyi was born in Vienna in 1886 and raised in Budapest. He founded the radical Club Galilei while at the University of Budapest and actively engaged other leftist thinkers, such as Georg Lukács and Karl Mannheim. Later, he co-founded the Hungarian Radical Party. He earned his Ph.D. in 1908, and graduated in law in 1912.

Polanyi returned to Vienna to work as a journalist writing economic and political commentary during the period leading up to the Great Depression and the rise of fascism. With Hitler's ascent to power in 1933, Polanyi left for England and worked as a lecturer for the Universities of Oxford and London. He taught as an adjunct professor at Columbia University in New York from 1947 to 1953.

Polanyi's book *The Great Transformation: The Political and Economic Origins of Our Time* (1944) received immediate acclaim and is now widely recognized as a classic of sociological thought. It remains influential because of its powerful critique of market liberalism, or "neo-liberalism" (the belief that national societies and the global economy can and should be organized through self-regulating markets).[2] He challenged the arguments of Ludwig von Mises and Friedrich Hayek, whose work, associated with the Austrian School of Economics, restored the intellectual legitimacy of market liberalism in the United States and United Kingdom after the Second World War.

In Chapter 2 we learned how Karl Marx's concept of the "mode of production" challenged market liberalism to the extent that it asserted that social inequalities emerge from the natural course of production, rather than having anything to do with the nature of human beings themselves. This challenges Adam Smith's still popular understanding of markets, which posits that their attendant inequalities exist prior to production in humans' natural propensity to truck, barter, and exchange one thing for another. In contrast, Polanyi argued that both market liberalism and Marx had failed to denaturalize markets, and instead shared the belief that markets were capable of self-regulating at a global level, albeit with very different understandings of the consequences for humans.

Polanyi wrote that the entire tradition of modern economic thought rested on a faulty concept of the economy as an interlocking system of markets that automatically adjusts supply and demand through the price mechanism. He maintained that this concept sharply differs from the reality of human societies and that the human economy has always been and remains *embedded* in society and subordinated to politics, law, morality, and social relations. According to Polanyi, the classical economists' goal of a disembedded, fully self-regulating market economy was a utopian project that could not exist for any length of time without physically destroying humans and transforming their surroundings into a wilderness.

Fictitious Commodities: Land, Labor, and Money

Polanyi, like Marx before him, continually criticized the classical economists for their tendency to assume that the economic patterns that they had identified would exist for all time. Marx's analysis of the fetishism of commodities was a direct attack on a naturalized view of economic arrangements. He recognized that within capitalism, the social relations among human beings become reified, as when people are reduced to their labor power, or when abstract market forces are perceived as determining prices. He stressed that this tendency made it harder to change existing arrangements because people forget that economic institutions are social creations that could be recreated in different ways.

Polanyi advanced a similar proposition in elaborating his concept of *fictitious commodities*. In contrast to Marx's emphasis on the general "overabundance of commodities"—i.e., a surplus that exceeded the capacity of the world market to absorb it—Polanyi instead emphasized particular commodities (land, labor, and money) that he argued were "fictitious"—i.e., not originally produced to be sold on a market. Land is subdivided nature. Labor is human activity. The supply of money and credit is necessarily shaped by governmental policies. To treat these as real commodities—as just any other "widgets"—without setting protective limits on the degree to which they can be commodified is detrimental to human society and ultimately points to the seeds of a would-be disembedded market's inevitable destruction.

Polanyi's argument is in part a moral one: markets must be embedded in morality. Environmental degradation and slavery are immoral. Nature and human beings should not be subordinated to the needs of the market, rather the market should ultimately be subordinated to the needs of nature and human beings.

State Action is Inherent to Market Formation

But his argument also seeks to show how markets are embedded in politics. The state plays a fundamental role in managing land (e.g., food supply, land-use regulation), labor (e.g., unemployment, education for the workforce, migration flows), and money (e.g., avoiding inflation or deflation). As Block explains:

> [T]he role of managing fictitious commodities places the state inside three of the most important markets; it becomes utterly impossible to sustain market liberalism's view that the state is 'outside' of the economy....It often takes *greater* state efforts to assure that these groups will bear these increased costs without engaging in disruptive political actions. This is part of what Polanyi means by his claim that '*laissez-faire* was planned'; it requires statecraft and repression to impose the logic of the market and its attendant risks on ordinary people.[3]

Markets come into being through the activity of political organizations and, in the modern period, specifically through the actions of states. In short, markets are neither natural nor self-regulating. Markets do not arise spontaneously from our natural inclinations to "truck and trade," but instead through consciously planned, political actions and choices. For Polanyi, the free market is a utopian conception. All markets are regulated in the sense that their parameters are established by state institutions.

Yet, unlike Marx, Polanyi did not think that capitalist society necessarily contained the seeds of its own destruction. Marx's effort to identify the essential dynamics of the capitalist mode of production meant that he, like the many classical economists that he criticized, created a theoretical framework insufficiently sensitive to its own historical limitations. In seeking to identify the "laws of motion" of the capitalist economy, i.e., a transhistorical essence to capitalism that will continue to exist regardless of changes in the specific institutional arrangements of the economy, he ended up naturalizing what he sought to criticize. By contrast, Polanyi does not equate globalization with the logic of either capitalism or modernity per se, but rather sees it as one possibility for a modern capitalist society, the realization of which requires conditions that are both contingent and political.[4]

It is also worth contrasting how economic ideology plays a different role in the work of Marx than in that of Poalnyi. For Marx (as we saw in Chapter 2), ideology is a central feature of capitalism's "superstructure," representing a form of "false consciousness" insofar as the ideas of capitalism were not those that served the best interests of the workers, but rather those that served the best interests of the capitalists and modern capitalism itself. But for Marx, at a deeper level, it is the features of the system itself that are self-sustaining. For Polanyi, however, it is this belief held by Marx—that the features of the system are self-sustaining—which represents the false ideology of the self-regulating market and which Marxists as well as neo-liberals sustain.

The Interwar Years[5]

The interwar years (1919–1938) are important to international social science because they raise one of the most challenging puzzles for students of globalization: Why did the prolonged period of relative peace and prosperity in Europe, from 1815 to 1914, give way to a world war followed by an economic collapse, the rise of fascism and socialism, and then another world war? This period saw the emergence of new international political bodies, the rise of the human rights framework, and *attempts to construct a self-regulating global market*, all of which came crashing down. Polanyi offers an answer to this historical puzzle that still has relevance for students of contemporary globalization.

Internationalists pursued global peace through two mechanisms which failed in the short term, but which left lasting impacts on social, political, and economic systems today. One mechanism was the creation of the League of Nations, an international organization that generated extraordinary expectations among millions of people around the world with its promise of a new style of diplomacy, global approaches to common problems, and the institutionalization of human rights and humanitarian law. The other mechanism was the restoration of the gold standard for fixing currency exchange rates and regulating prices in the international monetary system. It is the struggle over the latter, for Polanyi, that is key to understanding the internationalists' failure to secure global peace.

With the Westphalian balance of power in ruins, American President Woodrow Wilson promoted the League of Nations to be the primary body of a new style of international relations. Based on the cooperation of the nations of the world, he hoped that the United States would play a central role in European and world politics through the League. Anti-internationalist opposition within the United States destroyed this vision and weakened the institution. The League of Nations, which first met in November 1920, initially represented forty-two nations. Germany, Russia, and the United States were notably absent. Germany was initially barred from membership for having instigated World War 1 (although it was eventually admitted in 1926). Russia was not invited due to the radical policies of its new communist government (although it was invited to join in 1935). Embarrassingly for Wilson, the United States Senate voted in 1919 against membership in the League and never joined. This marked the beginning of a period of relative isolationism for the United States, which kept the nation effectively out of European political affairs for most of the interwar years.

While refusing to participate in international political bodies such as the League, the United States remained involved in the economic affairs of Europe. Throughout the 1920s, the United States insisted upon repayment of the loans made to Britain, France, and other allies during the War. Fueling American refusal to reconsider the war debts was fear that American public opinion would not stand for a writing-off of war debts—particularly since many Americans felt that the Great War had not been their war. France and Britain, in turn, insisted that Germany pay to them the enormous reparations agreed to at Versailles. But the strain on the German economy of paying reparations threatened to disrupt the German political and economic order and weaken European stability in general.

American internationalists turned to a series of ad hoc arrangements that kept the United States involved in European affairs. The Dawes Plan in 1924 and the Young Plan in 1929 both refinanced international loans to Germany to help them with their reparation payments. Huge amounts of direct and portfolio capital flowed from the United States into Germany. But toward the end of

1929, when the New York stock market boom absorbed all available funds for foreign investment (much of which was highly speculative) and stemmed the capital flow to Germany, it placed severe pressure on a German economy that had become dependent on this flow. In addition to still heavy reparation obligations, Germany now had sizable debt to American bondholders.

But, as Polanyi explains, other internationalists promoted a return to the gold standard. One of the central organizing tenets of this transnational network of elites was that if individuals and firms are given maximum freedom to pursue their economic self-interest, the global marketplace will make everyone better off. Reaching far beyond this elite network was a common faith in the idea that banknotes have value because they represent gold. Beginning in the 1870s up until the start of World War I, market liberals created a financial mechanism called the gold standard to extend the scope of markets internationally by enabling people in different countries with different currencies to freely engage in transactions with each other.

In short, the idea was that if every country adhered to three basic rules, the global marketplace would have a mechanism for global self-regulation: First, set the value of your nation's currency in relation to a fixed amount of gold and commit to buying and selling gold at that price; Second, base your domestic money supply on the quantity of gold that your nation is holding in its reserves, and your circulating currency will be backed by gold; Third, try to give your residents maximum freedom to engage in international economic transactions.[6]

Where some historians suggest the gold standard ultimately served to intensify the importance of the nation as a unified entity and imposed austerity measures on people that were literally unbearable, in part contributing to World War I, Polanyi observes in addition that market liberals of the day perceived the monetary crisis leading up to the War as further evidence that Europe desperately needed the strict discipline of the gold standard and fixed exchange rates. Efforts to restore the gold standard and an open world economy after World War I failed to reestablish the stability of the prewar period. The openness of the international economy had only served to transmit deflationary pressures from one country to another after 1929 and had acted as an obstacle to national recovery programs in the early 1930s.

In the United States, the Federal Reserve Board refused to manage the economy according to the gold standard, acting instead to neutralize the expansionary effects of large gold imports into the United States. This prevented a domestic price rise and attendant weakening of the American competitive position internationally, which would have stemmed the inflow of gold. Most of the gold flowing into the United States was the result of capital flight from unstable conditions in Europe. Thus, by keeping prices artificially stable, the United States placed an even greater burden of adjustment on European economies already facing severe economic problems. Despite the United States' contributions to the structural weakness of the interwar gold standard, it was not until the American stock market crashed and the onset of the Great Depression that internationalists abandoned their experiment with restoring the gold standard:

> Nineteenth-century civilization was not destroyed by the external or internal attack of barbarians; its vitality was not sapped by the devastations of World War I nor by the revolt of a socialist proletariat or a fascist lower middle class. Its failure was not the outcome of some alleged laws of economics such as that of the falling rate of profit or of underconsumption or overproduction. It disintegrated as the result of an entirely different set of causes: the measures which society adopted in order not to be, in its turn, annihilated by the action o the self-regulating market.[7]

Protectionist Countermovement

Polanyi's analysis of the interwar years highlights another of his key propositions: society must contain the space in which markets operate "freely" in order to protect itself. Unless communities protectively restrict and regulate markets in an effort to stem their socially disruptive effects, they will either collapse altogether or else develop authoritarian tendencies for the purpose of resisting the market's effects upon communities.

Looking at the rise of national markets, Polanyi argued that the socially unsustainable character of "self-regulating" markets generated a natural "protective" reaction on the part of a variety of social groups, including a portion of the elite. Unfortunately, in Polanyi's analysis this protective reaction was overwhelmed by the inability of the same protective reaction to prevail at the international level.[8]

Polanyi's point was *not* that a self-regulating market destroyed the peace. Rather, it was the countermovements of society—under the banners of Fascism and Nazism—that destroyed civil society, ironically, in their effort to protect themselves from the destructive pressures of the gold standard system. Nor was Polanyi suggesting that only countermovements destructive of civil society are the *necessary* result of efforts to construct a global self-regulating market. He *does* posit that some kind of protectionist countermovement must emerge in response, but these can be democratic countermovements that protect and enhance civil society as well. As Fred Block points out in a new introduction to the 2001 edition of *The Great Transformation*, Polanyi thought that the cycle of international conflict could be broken:

> The key step was to overturn the belief that social life should be subordinated to the market mechanism. Once free of this 'obsolete market mentality,' the path would be open to subordinate both national economies and the global economy to

democratic politics. Polanyi saw Roosevelt's New Deal as a model of these future possibilities. Roosevelt's reforms meant that the U.S. economy continued to be organized around markets and market activity, but a new set of regulatory mechanisms now made it possible to buffer both human beings and nature from the pressures of market forces.[9]

Thus, in contrast to Lenin, who argued against the reformist efforts that had occurred within various camps of socialists (see Chapter 2), Polanyi advocated reform over revolution. Polanyi cautioned that civil society had to defend itself against the twin dangers of an overly powerful market as well as an overly powerful state. He emphasized the degree of the market's social embeddedness—overly "free" or overly "planned" markets both lead to destructive results for society.

A Global "Free Market" is Impossible

Polanyi assumed that his generation was in a position to wish a final "good riddance" to this failed political economic experiment. However, the global rules, discourses, and networks currently being constructed around the interests of transnational corporations would suggest otherwise. Nevertheless, Polanyi's words seem prescient for contemporary transnational neo-liberal political coalitions and their challengers:

> This, indeed, is the last remaining argument of economic liberalism today. Its apologists are repeating in endless variations that but for the policies advocated by its critics, liberalism would have delivered the goods; that not the competitive system and the self-regulating market, but interference with that system and interventions with that market are responsible for our ills. And this argument does not find support in innumerable recent infringements of economic freedom only, but also in the indubitable fact that the movement to spread the system of self-regulating markets was met in the second half of the nineteenth century by a persistent countermove obstructing the free working of such an economy.... Liberal leaders never weary of repeating that the tragedy of the nineteenth century sprang from the incapacity of man to remain faithful to the inspiration of the early liberals; that the generous initiative of our ancestors was frustrated...above all by the blindness of the working people to the ultimate beneficence of unrestricted economic freedom to all human interests, including their own.[10]

Polanyi's work contributes to contemporary debates on globalization because he presents a direct challenge to the neo-liberal market ideology that a fully self-regulating market free of government interference will make everyone better off. By emphasizing the centrality of the laws and rules that govern the global economy, Polanyi provides an alternative to the dominant "law and economics" school, which holds that free markets create the most efficient distribution of property. Polanyi's work provides a model for legal scholars who wish to show that economics, law, and the rules of global governance cannot exist autonomously in a vacuum (contrary to the propositions of neo-liberalism), but that they instead must remain embedded in a complex structure of social relations.

Polanyi's propositions remain relevant to what might be called the "second free market utopia," or a single global market as it is conceived by contemporary neo-liberalism.[11] There are at least two implications of these propositions for analyzing contemporary globalization. First, neo-liberalism is a cultural structure that enables (and constrains) state responses to markets. The human economy is enmeshed in historically contingent institutions, both economic and noneconomic. For Polanyi, "[i]nstitutions are embodiments of human meaning and purpose."[12] Inclusion of the noneconomic is vital. Ideas, including the cultural dimensions of political structures that generate resources and constraints, are a constitutive source of globalization. Second, globalization necessarily remains a contested and ultimately unrealizable project.

The "free trade" discourse presents itself as a neutral diagnosis rather than as a powerful contributor to the emergence of the very conditions it purports to analyze.[13] The "free trade" discourse has been successful because many politicians (and voters) have been persuaded that it is economic development that causes the political response of deregulation. Yet, as Alan Scott contends:

> [I]t is precisely the belief of key political and economic actors, even those who oppose its effects, that globalization is inevitable which contributes to its political puissance. The question for social scientists then becomes to what extent are we contributing to the same inevitabilist logic...."[14]

Future Prospects

Polanyi's work has experienced something of a revival with the resurgence of policy discourse hailing market liberalism since the 1980s. In academia, it was the quickly emerging field of economic sociology that first began calling attention to the relevance of Polanyi for comparing "neo-liberal" globalization to the earlier historical period of globalization, from the later half of the nineteenth century through World War I. The purpose has been to show how markets are always embedded in politics, law, and morality.

More recently, however, anthropologists of development politics have been drawing upon Polanyi's ideas to ethnographically explore global financial institutions (e.g., the World Trade Organization, the International Monetary Fund, and the World Bank) that are managed by actors who are not democratically elected and whose decisions shape the rules and regulations of international trade and finance. Obviously, these actors have a significant affect on our lives. But precisely how? To what extent are these powerful institutional actors' decisions shaped by neo-liberal economic thought, and to what extent by other ideas and principles? What might our anthropological research uncover about the politics of influence over these key actors shaping the future direction of globalization?

One other important area of contemporary research on globalization that draws upon the work of Polanyi focuses on transnational social movements. While some of these movements may be accurately depicted as "antiglobalization movements," many actually seek to democratize globalization—not to derail it altogether. One of the hallmarks of these movements is that their targets are not always primarily states. For example, as we will see in Chapter 11, many of these movements target transnational corporations or global financial institutions. As a result, social movement researchers have been turning from traditional state-centered approaches to state decentered approaches. Polanyi's emphasis on the cultural dimensions of the state that impinge directly on its effort to construct a transnational regulatory framework for a global market makes his view of the state more compatible with these state decentered approaches that are developing in contemporary political sociology.

NOTES

1. Karl Polanyi, *The Great Transformation: The Political and Economic Origins of Our Time*, 2nd Beacon paperback ed., with a foreword by Joseph E. Stiglitz and new introduction by Fred Block (Boston: Beacon Press, [1944] 2001), 157.
2. The biographical sketch provided here can be found in John Dale, "Karl Polanyi," In David S. Clark, ed., *Encyclopedia of Law & Society: American and Global Perspectives* (Thousand Oaks, CA: Sage Publications, 2007). For a more detailed biography, see Kari Polanyi-Levitt, ed., *Life and Work of Karl Polanyi* (Montreal: Black Rose Press, 1990).
3. Fred Block, "Introduction," in Karl Polanyi, *The Great Transformation: The Political and Economic Origins of Our Time*, 2nd Beacon paperback ed., with a foreword by Joseph E. Stiglitz and new introduction by Fred Block (Boston: Beacon Press, [1944] 2001); Fred Block, "Karl Polanyi and the Writing of the Great Transformation," *Theory and Society*, 2003, 32(3),275–306; and Kenneth McRobbie and Kari Polanyi-Levitt, eds., *Karl Polanyi in Vienna: The Contemporary Significance of the Great Transformation*(Montreal: Black Rose Press, 2000).
4. Fred Block, "Introduction," in Karl Polanyi, *The Great Transformation: The Political and Economic Origins of Our Time*, 2nd Beacon paperback ed., with a foreword by Joseph E. Stiglitz and new introduction by Fred Block (Boston: Beacon Press, [1944] 2001) xxvi and xxvii.

5. Fred Block and Margaret R. Somers, "Beyond the Economistic Fallacy: The Holistic Social Science of Karl Polanyi," in Theda Skocpol, *Vision and Method in Historical Sociology* (New York: Cambridge University Press, 1984); Alan Scott,"Introduction— Globalization: Social Process or Political Rhetoric," in Alan Scott, ed., *The Limits of Globalization. Cases and Arguments* (New York: Routledge, 1997).

6. Large portions of this description of the interwar years comes from John Dale, "The Interwar Years," in William A. Darity, ed., *International Encyclopedia for the Social Sciences*, 2nd ed. (Farmington Hills, MI: Macmillan Reference USA). (Forthcoming, 2008).

7. Fred L. Block, *The Origins of International Economic Disorder: A Study of United States International Monetary Policy from World War II to the Present* (Berkeley: University of California Press, 1977), Chapter 2.

8. Karl Polanyi, *The Great Transformation: The Political and Economic Origins of Our Time*, 2nd Beacon paperback ed., with a foreword by Joseph E. Stiglitz and new introduction by Fred Block (Boston: Beacon Press, [1944] 2001), 257.

9. Fred L. Block, *The Origins of International Economic Disorder: A Study of United States International Monetary Policy from World War II to the Present* (Berkeley and Los Angeles: University of California Press, 1977); Peter Evans, "Fighting Marginalization with Transnational Networks: Counter-Hegemonic Globalization," *Contemporary Sociology*, 2000, 29(1), 230–41.

10. Fred Block, "Introduction," in Karl Polanyi, *The Great Transformation: The Political and Economic Origins of Our Time*, 2nd Beacon paperback ed., with a foreword by Joseph E. Stiglitz and new introduction by Fred Block (Boston: Beacon Press, [1944] 2001), xxxv.

11. Karl Polanyi, *The Great Transformation: The Political and Economic Origins of Our Time*, 2nd Beacon paperback ed., with a foreword by Joseph E. Stiglitz and new introduction by Fred Block (Boston: Beacon Press, [1944] 2001), 150–51.

12. Fred L. Block, *Postindustrial Possibilities. A Critique of Economic Discourse* (Berkeley: University of California Press, 1990); Fred L. Block, *The Vampire State. And Other Myths and Fallacies About the U.S. Economy* (New York: The New Press, 1996); Philip McMichael, *Development and Social Change. A Global Perspective*, 2nd ed. (Thousand Oaks, CA: Pine Forge Press, 2000); Alan Scott, "Introduction—Globalization: Social Process or Political Rhetoric," in Alan Scott, ed., *The Limits of Globalization. Cases and Arguments* (New York: Routledge, 1997); Michael Peter Smith, "Transnationalism and the City: From Global Cities to Transnational Urbanism," in *The Urban Moment*, edited by Sophie Body-Gendrot and Robert A. Beauregard (Thousand Oaks, CA: Sage, 1998); Peter Evans, "Fighting Marginalization with Transnational Networks: Counter-Hegemonic Globalization," *Contemporary Sociology*, 2000, 29(1), 30–241; Marc Edelman and Angelique Haugerud, eds., *The Anthropology of Development and Globalization: From Classical Political Economy to Contemporary Neoliberalism.* (New York: Wiley, 2004), 1–52.

13. Karl Polanyi, *The Great Transformation: The Political and Economic Origins of Our Time*, 2nd Beacon paperback ed., with a foreword by Joseph E. Stiglitz and new introduction by Fred Block (Boston: Beacon Press, [1944] 2001), 262.

14. See Michael Peter Smith, *Transnational Urbanism. Locating Globalization* (Oxford: Blackwell, 2001), Chapter 3; J. K. Gibson-Graham, *The End of Capitalism (As We Knew It). A Feminist Critique of Political Economy* (Malden, MA and Oxford: Blackwell Publishers, 1996), Chapters 5 and 6.
15. Alan Scott, "Introduction—Globalization: Social Process or Political Rhetoric," in Alan Scott, ed., *The Limits of Globalization. Cases and Arguments.* (New York: Routledge, 1997), 2.

Chapter 6

Basic Forms of Political Authority

If there were a people of gods, it would govern itself democratically. Such a perfect government is not suited to men.

Jean Jacques Rousseau, *The Social Contract*

So a prince need not have all the…good qualities, but it is most essential that he appear to have them. Indeed, I should go so far as to say that having them and always practising them is harmful, while seeming to have them is useful. It is good to appear clement, trustworthy, humane, religious and honest, and also to be so, but always with the mind so disposed that, when the occasion arises not to be so, you can become the opposite. It must be understood that a prince and particularly a new prince cannot practice all the virtues for which men are accounted good, for the necessity of preserving the state often compels him to take actions which are opposed to loyalty, charity, humanity, and religion. Hence he must have a spirit ready to adapt itself as the varying winds of fortune command him. As I have said, so far as he is able a prince should stick to the path of good, but, if the necessity arises, he should know how to follow evil.

Niccolo Machiavelli, *The Prince*

The theorists who have shaped the foundations of political sociology—in particular, Karl Marx, Max Weber, Emile Durkheim, and Alexis de Tocqueville—all were broadly concerned with how to explain the nature of the social world. Except for Tocqueville, who devoted a great deal of thought to examining the nature and foundations of modern democracy, they also were more concerned with understanding the nature of social forces than they were with exploring the nature of political ones. Today, however, we realize that there are critical variations among the types of governments, or political regimes, in the modern world and that these differences have significant consequences for the lives of citizens. Thus it is no longer sufficient simply to mull over the broad relationship between society and politics. We must do more; we must dig deeper. We must also seek to understand the important variations that exist from one government to another one as well as the sources of these differences.

In this chapter we discuss important basic variations that exist from one type of political regime to another. We shall ground our discussion in the classical conceptions of these notions—the Greek ideas of democracy and oligarchy. We then shall move on to expand our sense of governments and to consider in somewhat greater detail the differences among regimes.

Our discussion in this chapter, we should note, will simply furnish the broad outlines of these ideas. In later chapters we shall take these notions even further, showing how, for example, modern democracy is dependent upon a host of different decisions and key social conditions.

Basic Types of Political Rule: The Classical Greek Conceptions

Aristotle's conception of the Greek body politic, the polis, rested on two features: the qualities of its residents and the nature of its rules.[1] First, the polis was made up only of the body of citizens in a city-state; citizens were those who were governed and who could exercise the privilege of governance. Lower classes, including mechanics, artisans, and the large number of slaves, were not included among the people who qualified as citizens and hence as members of the polis. Second, the rules of the polis consisted of the laws and traditions of the Greek city-state; the laws were for Aristotle the most sovereign feature of the city-state. The governance of the citizens of the polis meant the "rightly constituted laws...and personal rule, whether it be exercised by a single person or a body of persons, should be sovereign only in those matters on which law is unable, owing to the difficulty of framing general rules for all contingencies, to make an exact pronouncement."[2]

There were, Aristotle further thought, two broad sets of political arenas: those in which men achieved all the prime moral values—wisdom, goodness, beauty, justice—and those in which men lived in more debased, in not more "real" circumstances.[3] Within each of these two sets were three subsets of polis: the moral set contained kingship, aristocracy, and polity; the other comprised tyranny, oligarchy, and democracy. Each of the three also possessed its counterpart in the other set. Thus, kingship had tyranny as its counterpart, aristocracy had oligarchy as its counterpart, and polity possessed democracy as its counterpart. The chief element that the three pairs held in common was the number of rulers in the polis; in kingship and tyranny there was only a single ruler, in aristocracy and oligarchy there existed several rulers, and in polity and democracy the large majority of citizens were their own rulers. There were other differences among the several forms, but Aristotle reserved most of his attention for democracy, oligarchy, and polity.

Oligarchy was thought to represent the perversion of the aristocratic form of rule. Aristotle believed that under the rule of oligarchy those individuals who held property—a minority of the population—limited the exercise of governance to themselves and ruled in ways that would advance their interests exclusively. Democracy represented the perversion of rule in polity—a polis in which the large majority of people had become sovereign but in so doing violated the rights of the minority, the property holders. Each of the two forms violated the sense of justice that should prevail in the ideal community. Instead of adhering to the principle of distributive justice—the contribution of an individual to a society's well-being is rewarded in an amount commensurate to his contribution—democracy and oligarchy rewarded citizens on the basis of special qualities having nothing to do with their contributions to the vitality of the community. Hence, a democracy held all citizens to be equal although not all of them contributed equally to the well-being of the polis; an oligarchy insisted that all citizens are unequal although such inequality existed only by virtue of their disproportionate property holdings, not by the degree of their contribution to the well-being of the polis.[4]

In contrast to Plato, Aristotle maintained that in principle a democracy could possess certain desirable traits. For one thing, he believed the people as a whole possessed a better combination of qualities of judgment and good sense than any small number of individuals. "Each of the [people]," he wrote, "may not be of good . . . quality; but when they all come together it is possible that they may surpass—collectively and as a body, although not individually—the quality of the few best."[5] He further claimed that the governance of the polis by the people, or by their elected magistrates, could be justified on the grounds that the people represent the best judges of their own interests.

Polity and tyranny appeared to him as the best and the worst of political arenas. Although at first polity seemed to be only the virtuous counterpart of democracy, on further analysis it appeared as a mixed form of government, incorporating features of democracy and oligarchy. Citing the examples of Sparta, Aristotle claimed that polity ought to be construed by some observers as an oligarchy, by others as a democracy. He remarked:

> There are many who would describe [Sparta] as a democracy, on the ground that its organization has a number of democratic features. In the first place, and so far as concerns the bringing up of the young, the children of the rich have the same fare as the children of the poor, and they are educated on a standard which the children of the poor can also attain. . . . No difference is made between the rich and the poor: the food at the common mess is the same for all, and the dress of the rich is such as any of the poor could also provide for themselves. . . . A second ground for describing Sparta as a democracy is the right of the people to elect to one of the two great institutions, the Senate, and to be eligible themselves for the other, the Ephorate. On the other hand there are some who describe the Spartan constitution as an oligarchy, on the ground that it has many oligarchical factors.

> For example, the magistrates are all appointed by vote, and none by log; again, the power of inflicting the penalty of death or banishment rests in the hands of a few persons; and there are many other similar features. *A properly mixed "polity" should look as if it contained both democratic and oligarchic elements—and as if it contained neither.*[6] (italics added)

Moreover, polity, if properly planned, corrected for the extremes of democracy, the rule by the many, and of oligarchy, rules by the few, by basing its form of rule upon the majority, the middle class. Asserting his preference for moderation in all things, Aristotle argued that polity, being based upon a large middle class, assisted in eliminating the conflicts and tensions evident in democracies and in oligarchies. Yet, he noted, the establishment of polities was unlikely, for in most Greek city-states the middle class was very small and disputes inevitably arose between the very rich and the very poor. Tyranny, in contrast to polity, represented the very worst sort of government. It was a base type of rule because it benefited the smallest possible number citizens in a polis. Also, it represented a form of government in which the rule of the person replaced the rule of law; lawlessness for Aristotle was the most perverse form of governance.

To complete this brief portrait of the Greek view of politics, we should remind ourselves that in actual practice the constitutional orders of ancient Greece comprised many different features, including magistrates, councils, and sometimes assemblies of the entire body politic. Still, the differences between democracy and oligarchy pervaded the entire polis. Leonard Whibley, a close student of the Aristotelian conceptions of the polis and of the actual practices of the ancient Greek constitutional orders, summarily observed some of these differences between the two types of polis:

> In the fully developed democracy the people wanted to exercise their powers directly, they were jealous of all institutions in the state other than the assembly, and both council and magistrates were rendered in every way subordinate agents of the popular power. The duties of government were divided amongst a great number of magistrates whose authority was restricted as far as possible: the lot secured that ordinary men would be chosen (so that it was impossible to leave much to their discretion): their tenure was short, reelection was usually forbidden, offices were intended to rotate and all who exercised the smallest authority did so with a full responsibility to the governing body. In the oligarchies almost every one of these conditions is reversed. The functions of government were not so thoroughly divided, the magistrates had larger independent powers, they were appointed by and from a small privileged body, the same men might be reelected.[6]

In sum, the basic principles that Aristotle revealed through his analysis of the nature of democracies—in particular, the size of the ruling group, their social foundations in property, and the interests on behalf of which their leaders ruled—were in practice found to be operating down to the very smallest details in the Greek city-states.

How useful are these ideas to the analysis of contemporary political orders? Can we transport them across 2,500 years of time and use them to illuminate the features of current political realities? In fact, we think they are useful in isolating some of the basic outlines of the political order and some of the fundamental differences that exist among such orders. But there are at least two reasons why they cannot be transplanted unchanged from Aristotle and the Greek world to the contemporary world. First, the Aristotelian conceptions are useful primarily for the study of social groups no larger than the common city-states of ancient Greece—communities typically numbering in the tens of thousands. Many twenty-first-century nations number in the tens, if not hundreds, of millions of people; simply by virtue of the difference in magnitude of population there is a less than perfect fit between the Aristotelian notions and contemporary circumstances.[7] Second, the revolution in industry and technology that in the eighteenth and nineteenth centuries helped to lay the economic foundations for the modern world brought about a number of changes of great political consequence—changes in our conception of citizenship, changes in our sense of the legitimate boundaries between public concerns and private interests, and transformations in the technical means that rulers may employ in cultivating the obedience of those whom they rule. One simple reflection of this feature of the modern world is that both Karl Marx and Max Weber wrote of bourgeois or capitalist democracies, not simply democracies, suggesting that to them this form represented something unique. Thus, it is insufficient to apply the Aristotelian conceptions to social and economic circumstances that are so very different from those of 2,500 years ago. The classical Greek conceptions must simply be seen as broad guidelines on the nature of the significant features of current political orders.

Types of Political Rule in the Modern World

In recent history there have been two almost opposite forms of political rule. First, there is *modern democracy,* a form that retains the ancient name because it shares certain features with the Greek polis of the same description—for instance, an emphasis upon widespread and voluntary citizen involvement in public life. Second, there is a new form, one that has elements of the ancient tyranny to which Aristotle referred but that also has a number of unique features; this is *totalitarianism,* represented in its purest respects in the former Soviet Union and in Germany under the rule of Adolf Hitler. Today its closest empirical counterpart is that of the People's Republic of China, although China is becoming something of a hybrid regime. A third form, which is somewhat different from both democracy and totalitarianism, is that of *authoritarianism*. We shall discuss all three forms below, with the greatest emphasis on democratic and totalitarian regimes.

Democracy: The Moral Vision and the Empirical Reality

There are two different sets of ideas about modern democracy. Scholars sometimes refer to the difference as that between substantive democracy, or how democracy really is intended to work, and formal democracy, or that which characterizes many of the so-called democratic nations in the world today. Here we shall refer to the two types as the *moral vision* of democracy and the *empirical view* of it. The first, similar to that of the ancient Greeks, envisions the shape of democratic rule in utopian terms and thus seeks the very best and the most just form of political rule under which citizens may live. In somewhat different fashion, this view of a democratic society was shaped by political philosophers such as Jean Jacques Rousseau, John Locke, Montesquieu, and John Stuart Mill in the eighteenth and nineteenth centuries and assisted by the writings of John Dewey and Robert MacIver, among others, early in the twentieth century.[8]

The Moral Vision. At heart, the moral vision of a democratic society claims that individuals are the best judges of their own interests. Eschewing a society sustained by a small number of rulers—a group of oligarchs in other words—this vision insists that individuals can exercise the faculties of sound judgment and wisdom required to maintain the well-being of the body politic. The authors of these ideas, moreover, believe that the political capacities of individuals, their skills as well as their actual comprehension of the mechanics of politics, are capable of improvement through self-governance. Even those individuals without sound judgment on politics benefit from engagement in the institutions and processes of the political arena. These premises suggest to some of the authors of the moral view that all persons should be permitted an equal opportunity to participate in politics and to secure protection from political institutions. "The very fact of natural and psychological inequity," Dewey wrote, "is all the more reason for establishment by law of equality of opportunity, since otherwise the former becomes a means of oppression of the less gifted."[9]

The moral vision of a democratic society also insists that the very involvement of individuals in the process of self-governance is a desirable goal in and of itself. Writing of the American experiment in democracy begun at the end of the eighteenth century, Hannah Arendt observed that the fundamental assumption underlying popular political participation "was that no one could be called happy without his share in public happiness, that no one could be called free without his experience in public freedom, and that no one could be called either happy or free without participating, and having a share, in public power."[10]

Contemporary theorists continue to mull over and modify the moral vision of democracy as articulated by such theorists as Dewey and Arendt. In a widely read work, political scientist Benjamin Barber argues on behalf of a vision of strong democracy as compared to the weaker, liberal—or thin—version.[11] Barber insists that democratic nations such as the United States or Great Britain do not represent true democracies. Instead, he believes that true democracy

> in the participatory mode resolves conflict in the absence of an independent ground through a participatory process of ongoing, proximate self-legislation and the creation of a political community capable of transforming dependent private individuals into free citizens and partial and private interests into public goods.[12]

Strong democracy demands that citizens be active in the political process and that they engage with one another in dealing with and resolving disputes among themselves. It also means that there are opportunities and facilities through which individuals, even in large-scale societies like the United States, are able to proceed with their engagement. "Strong democracy requires unmediated self-government by an engaged citizenry," Barber writes, "[and] institutions that will involve individuals at both the neighborhood and the national level in common talk, common decision-making and political judgment, and common action."[13] Like Arendt and Dewey before him, Barber was unsatisfied with modern arrangements, such as representative government, believing that individuals, engaged with one another, can create for themselves the best form of democratic action.

More recently, the political philosopher Joshua Cohen has argued on behalf of what he calls *deliberative democracy*.[14] To Cohen the essential feature of democratic governance is that there exists a forum through which individuals can engage in continuous deliberation over issues of common concern to them. *Deliberation* is the central concept. It requires continuity on the part of the participants as well as their trust in one another's capacity to engage and discuss issues in with one another. It demands a complete faith and trust in the process of deliberation as a principle and requires that no other grounds be chosen to arrive at a common choice among participants. In essence, it goes back to the very earliest meanings of democracy, yet it appends to them modern concerns—owing, in particular, to theorists like Jürgen Habermas—with the importance of public settings and debate and negotiation over the issues of common concern to participants.[15] Finally, as Cohen notes, it is a pluralist configuration of actors rather than people of uniform faith or constitution. "The members (of the association)," he writes, "have diverse preferences, convictions, and ideals concerning the conduct of their own lives. While sharing a commitment to the deliberative resolution of problems of collective choice, they also have divergent aims."[16]

These latest versions and reworkings of the moral vision of democracy reflect much of the contemporary debate over the root meaning of democracy, especially in light of the collapse of the older totalitarian regimes of Eastern Europe. Many theorists struggle to define the essence of democracy, an essence that could comfortably fit such circumstances as large global economy and the development of postindustrial societies. Obviously, they also find unsatisfying the notion that nations like the Unites States, which call themselves democracies, actually reach anywhere near the ideal, or moral vision. And in any case, they are a far cry from the empirical view of democracy today.

THE EMPIRICAL VIEW

There is a second body of thought that considers the nature of modern democratic societies; it seeks the creation of a theory of democracy inductively, based upon the study of current political realities. It is this stream of scholarship that furnishes many of the ideas and facts for the discussion in this book; this theory, for instance, in one way or another incorporates views described in the chapters on power in the United States, power in communities, and citizen participation in politics. The general set of notions embodied in this empirical view of democracy are found in some of the writings of Bernard Berelson, Robert A. Dahl, Giovanni Sartori, and Joseph Schumpeter, among many others.[17]

At its root the empirical conception of democracy shifts attention from the qualities of individual citizens and their fundamental rights of self-government to the rulers and the public competition that has brought them into office. In particular, this conception lays claim to the premise that modern democracy consists of institutions that furnish contenders for public office; typically, if not invariably, these institutions are political parties. The empirical theory holds, moreover, that there usually exist rival claimants for the opportunity to occupy the highest public offices. It incorporates the notion of citizen into its purview by asserting that citizens have the right to select among the rival sets of leaders those who they believe best represent their interests. A now classic quotation from Joseph Schumpeter succinctly serves to portray these features of the empirical theory by asserting that the democratic method is "that institutional arrangement for arriving at political decisions in which individuals acquire the power to decide by means of a competitive struggle for the people's vote."[18]

Having transferred the emphasis from citizens to leaders in democratic societies, the empirical theory further reduces the necessary role of citizens in their own self-governance. It asserts that in order for a society to lay claim to the label "democratic," its leaders merely need to be responsive to the wishes of the majority of citizens. This is accomplished in two ways: first, through the medium of elections—if the candidates for public office fail to respond to the wishes of the majority of citizens, the candidates would fail to be elected; and second, through the development of policies in office that are supposed to anticipate the wishes of the citizens. In other words, it is not necessary for citizens to engage actively in the process of politics. In fact, the widespread active and continuous engagement of the citizenry in the body politic constitutes for some empirical theorists a greater danger than benefit to a democracy—a claim that echoes Alexis de Tocqueville's fear of the "tyranny of the majority" (see Chapter 4). Berelson, for example, makes the following observation:

> How would a mass democracy work if all the people were deeply involved in politics? Lack of interest by some people is not without some benefits, too. True, the highly interested voters vote more, and know more about the campaign, and read and listen more, and participate more; however, they are also less open to persuasion and less likely to change [sic]. Extreme interest goes with extreme fanaticism that could destroy democratic processes if generalized throughout the community ... [whereas low] interest provides maneuvering room for political shifts necessary for a complex society in a period of rapid change.[19]

Thus, the empirical conception virtually transforms the root meaning of democracy—whether defined in Aristotelian terms as rule by many citizens or in those of the modern political philosophers. Democracy is no longer a body politic in which the engagement of citizens exists as its *sine qua non*, but one in which active involvement may be unnecessary, even undesirable.

Since these two perspectives, the moral vision and the empirical theory, exist as countervailing views of the nature of modern democratic societies, one must carefully scrutinize and compare them to search for similarities as well as the advantages and disadvantages of each. The moral vision is founded upon both ancient and modern ideals and represents a set of prescriptive statements about the conditions necessary for the working of a democratic society. The empirical theory, on the other hand, is grounded in a set of facts uncovered in societies conventionally thought to be democratic and constitutes a set of descriptive statements about the actual conditions of governments. One obvious danger in the facile adoption of the moral vision is that one might fail to understand the actual workings of a democracy by not attending to their realities. The dangers of an easy acceptance of the empirical theory might prove more harmful, however. First, the empirical view too readily accepts the conventional definitions of societies as "democratic"; this definition is sometimes more myth than reality. After a review of many facts, it remains possible to draw the conclusion that the United States more nearly resembles an oligarchy than a democracy (see Chapter 7). Second, adoption of the empirical theory can lead to an ideological justification of existing political forms. Berelson's previously cited observations, for instance, are couched within a broader analysis that implies not only that democracy actually performs in a certain manner, but also that it should perform in this fashion. Last, by abandoning a commitment to the utopian ideal of widespread citizen participation in the body politic, the empirical view dismisses, perhaps unwittingly, a rich heritage of political thought and tradition; more importantly, it relinquishes a position it could serve in the modern world of revealing how modern democratic societies could be refashioned in ways to approximate more closely the ancient ideal of a democratic society.

Regardless of this dispute—one likely to remain unresolved—we want to provide here a few of the more salient empirical details of modern democratic societies. These introduce the nature of these societies as well as provide a benchmark for a comparison with totalitarian orders.

Constitutional and Procedural Foundations. Democratic societies are invariably based upon a tradition of law with an emphasis on broad civil rights for the citizens, including, among others, the right of dissent. There is a separation of functions among the various branches of government, producing three separate organs: an executive, a legislative, and a judicial branch; the actual functions of each of these vary from one democratic society to another. The process of governance is carried out through a system of representatives; the institution in which the representatives serve is variously called the parliament or the congress. Suffrage is widespread, and elections occur frequently. The occupants of the executive branch are either elected directly, as in the presidential democracy of the United States, or indirectly, as in the parliamentary democracy in Great Britain.[20]

In the twentieth century these constitutional and procedural foundations have been supplemented through the continued or new growth of a large bureaucratic apparatus. The scope of the operations of this bureaucracy, initially designed to aid and to protect the constitutional rights of the citizenry, has begun to encroach seriously upon these rights in places such as the United States.

Ideological Foundations. Modern democracies are founded upon beliefs in the equality of individual citizens, in widespread public liberties, and in the desirability of citizen involvement in politics.

Social Foundations. Fundamental to the social foundations of modern democratic societies is a widespread plurality of groups and diversity of interests. A large number of voluntary organizations have been developed for citizen membership and involvement and serve as an infrastructure or a buffer zone between the lives of individual citizens and the political control exercised by the rulers. Chief among these many groups are political parties and factions within a single party that serve, among other things, as means for organizing and expressing citizen concerns and for attaining the constitutional right to exercise power.

Economic Foundations. Modern democratic societies, such as Great Britain and the United States, developed concomitantly with the growth of capitalist institutions. Thus, their fate became inextricably linked to the fate of these institutions. General conditions of affluence seem to have been most favorable to the growth of democratic governments, as in the United States, and the governments themselves have acted in important ways to further the conditions of affluence. However, even in settings of pervasive poverty, as in India, modified forms of democracy exist or have existed. In the twentieth century especially, the institutions of the state increasingly assumed widespread welfare responsibilities for the citizenry; the extent of such responsibilities varied from extensive, as in Sweden, to only moderate, as in the United States.

This description of the principal features of modern democratic societies should provide at least a general impression of them; details of their composition are etched more sharply in later chapters. In addition, this capsule portrait helps to distinguish between democratic and nondemocratic societies in the modern world.[21]

TOTALITARIANISM

The idea of totalitarianism, or totalitarian dictatorship, is meant to convey the absolute domination of a nation and its people by a single political party as well as by those who control the party.[22] Totalitarian rule seeks to obliterate the social ties and groups typical of democratic societies, for instance, the ties of the nuclear family, and to substitute for them new forms of social ties that are intended to absorb the individual completely as a member of the society. Between the party and its leaders, no groups or individuals are permitted to intervene and to replace the party as the single object of the individual's loyalty and commitment. The concept has been used primarily to describe two different historical regimes in the twentieth century: the former Soviet Union, especially under the rule of Joseph Stalin, and Nazi Germany. The combination of these two historical forms under a single rubric overshadows certain differences between them, in particular the distinction between the nature of communism and of Nazism. Some observers, however, regard the dissimilarities between the two to be more substantial than their common features.[23]

Carl J. Friedrich and Zbigniew K. Brzezinski, two scholars who have contributed greatly to our understanding of totalitarian societies, claim that such societies can be singled out for six distinctive qualities: (1) an elaborate ideology that covers each and every phase of an individual's life; (2) a single political party that typically is led by one individual, the "dictator"; (3) a widespread system of terror, channeled through both state and party institutions and directed alike against external and internal enemies of the regime; (4) virtually complete control of the apparatus of mass communication that is unique because of its technological sophistication and complexity; (5) a monopoly over the weaponry and persons associated with the armed forces; and (6) the direction of the entire economy, or at least its most significant sectors, by the state bureaucracy.[24] Alone, however, these six characteristics of totalitarian societies do not sufficiently convey the true nature of such regimes. Thus, as a counterpart tp the capsule analysis of modern democratic societies, the features of totalitarian ones are briefly elaborated. Nazi Germany is discussed in particular, but many of the same features describe equally well the general characteristics of the former Soviet Union.

Constitutional and Procedural Foundations. One of the principal features of Germany under the reign of Adolf Hitler and the National Socialist Party was the absence of constitutional and legal foundations; the only procedural foundations were those established through the auspices of the party. To all outward appearances, however, Nazi Germany seemed to constitute an extension of the government inaugurated as the Weimar Republic in 1918. Actually the National Socialist Party committed a legal revolution, overturning the Weimar Constitution by employing that constitution's very own provisions. Among the means used to achieve this end were a series of decrees and enabling acts passed in 1933 and 1934 that placed all power in the hands of Hitler as Chancellor and, later, President of Germany. In addition, the regime represented a virtual morass of offices and rules; Hitler fashioned a system in which the National Socialist Party and the state bureaucracy seemed to share equal power—though the party and Hitler ultimately were dominant—and in which for each office in the state bureaucracy there existed a parallel and competing one in the National Socialist Party. From Hitler's point of view, of course, the result of this morass was to create rule through divide et impera; the competition among occupants of parallel offices secured the effectiveness of his own leadership. Apart from Hitler, only key members of his immediate coterie—most notably Martin Bormann, Joseph Goebbels, and Heinrich Himmler—were able to exercise reasonably free and unrestrained rule; yet even they were not entirely free, for they remained in positions of unquestioning obedience to the commands of Hitler. During the early years of the Third Reich, there was also a façade of apparently democratic procedures that were consistent with the provisions of the Weimar Constitution. Thus, for example, there were several nationwide elections, but despite the large turnout of voters and the overwhelming support for the National Socialist Party, these elections were thoroughly manipulated by Hitler and his staff through their exclusive command of the radio and most newspapers and their ability to assemble at a moment's notice large rallies of supporters.

An important part of the Nazi regime in Germany was the organs of the party and the state that were designed to combat internal enemies; these agencies included the Gestapo, or secret police, and the Schutzstaffel (SS) troops under the authority of Heinrich Himmler. Both agencies were employed as means for combating dissent and for eliminating the "enemies of the state," particularly Jews. The SS troops, in particular, assumed responsibility for the administration of the death camps.

Ideological Foundations. One of the most visible and unique features of Hitler's totalitarian dictatorship was its ideology, an assortment of myths that were transplanted, in toto, from the declarations Hitler had earlier set out in his autobiography, *Mein Kampf.* Hitler and the National Socialists dispensed a doctrine of racial and national dogma that established the myth of the Aryan race as world saviors and made Jews appear as the scum of the earth; moreover, they sought and gained widespread popular acceptance of this doctrine. After 1938 these principles became transformed into actual practices of the Nazi regime, first through random terror committed against Jews inside Germany—as, for example, during Kristallnacht—and later through the terror organized under the auspices of the concentration camps and the wartime hostilities undertaken against many nations.

Social Foundations. In their effort to secure total commitment and obedience from the people, totalitarian regimes literally seek to declassify citizens. Upon their accession to the positions of leadership in the German government, for example, the National Socialist Party leaders, through their practices of terror, tried to eliminate the many diverse social groups that existed during the Weimar Republic. Trade unions, for one, were eliminated and replaced by the Labor Front, which simply became an organized means for the National Socialist Party to manipulate the interests and lives of workers. Except in a few instances, independent news media were either destroyed or taken over by the party. The churches remained more or less institutionally intact, but priests became the object of intense and unremitting attacks by members of the Nazi regime. In place of older organizations, new ones arose under the management of the National Socialist Party; thus, for instance, Nazi youth groups designed to socialize young Germans in the new, official system of thought were developed in large numbers. Symbolic of this gigantic program to design German society anew were the mass rallies that took place in the early years of the Third Reich; in those that occurred in Nuremberg, for example, thousands of people were arrayed across the floor on the arena—attentive, obedient, and absolutely mesmerized by Hitler.

Economic Foundations. Many analysts characterize the totalitarian economy as a command economy, noting such particulars about its structure as the regular plans for its expansion—five-year programs in the Soviet Union, four-year plans in Nazi Germany—the regimentation of the labor force, the special organization of the industrial plants, and the centralized form of planning concerning the budget and industrial output. These characteristics, like others, matured more fully in the former Soviet Union than they did in Nazi Germany; moreover, it is difficult to know precisely how the German economy might have performed under extended peacetime circumstances, since Germany went to war in 1939, only six years after the inception of Nazi rule. During its brief existence, however, the German economy actually comprised two different sectors: the command sector that was controlled through the National Socialist Party and state administrations and the large private sector that comprised many cartels in manufacturing and other forms of industry.[25]

This brief description naturally cannot do full justice to the range and the depth of the features of different totalitarian societies; hence, I urge you to consult other materials on Nazi Germany as well as various discussions in later chapters of such nations as the former Soviet Union. Nonetheless, the overview here helps to introduce two of the most prominent features of totalitarian regimes—the elimination of all autonomous institutions of the civil society, thus leaving the distinction between the public and private realms absolutely meaningless, and the genuine dominance of the party, its leaders and ideology, over all other institutions of the society. This last point, in particular, seems to render Marxist interpretations of Nazi Germany fundamentally incorrect; Hitler's dictatorship effectively supplanted all of the conventional features and processes of a capitalist economy with an administration less driven by economic doctrines than by national and racial dogma. These latter doctrines represented the motive force behind the establishment and short-lived reign of the Third Reich.

There is one nation today that most closely fits the defining features of totalitarian regimes, that of the People's Republic of China. China appears to fit most of the features associated with the concept—for example, a complete and total control of the country by the Communist Party, including all major institutions, ranging from the educational to the religious. However, at the same time China today is engaged in a massive experiment designed to discover whether a country tightly controlled by its leadership from the top can also become open to the introduction of major economic reforms from below. In the past three decades there have been major reforms in the economy, resulting in the introduction of many foreign companies. In addition, the government has engaged in an effort to produce massive investment in its Special Economic Zones, a range of regions on the southeastern border of the country that includes Hong Kong. Whether, and how, these economic transformations can influence the control of the Party remains to be seen. So far, however, the Party seems to have effectively walked the tightrope between its economic reform measures, which have loosened its control over industries and even over regions, and the demand mainly from abroad for more democracy and freedom at home for its citizens.

AUTHORITARIANISM

One of the problems that now confront analysts of political rule is how to depict regimes that are neither totalitarian, in the classic sense of the Soviet Union or Nazi Germany, nor democratic, in the sense of the United States or Great Britain. There are many such forms of political rule today, and many seem to resemble nothing so much as the rule of absolute dictators. Examples easily come to mind. Consider the case of Muammar Khadaffi in Libya. He rules his country with an iron fist, controls and is backed by a loyal military, and has the admiration of most of his countrymen. Then of course there was the more notorious case of Saddam Hussein in Iraq. He obviously did not preside over a democratic society, was in firm control of the military, and also appeared to have secured, somehow, the loyalty of many of his fellow citizens. In both instances the rulers exercised their power as virtual dictators, but their regimes also lacked critical features of totalitarian rule, such as the reign of continuous terror against their enemies and the absence of a single political party in which authority and power actually are lodged. There are countless other examples— governments that are clearly not totalitarian but lack the features of democratic regimes, such as regular elections and widespread civil liberties.

Scholars have puzzled over these different forms of rule for years and have tried to capture their most essential features, especially as compared to democratic and totalitarian regimes. Years ago, the sociologist Edward Shils wrote about different kinds of oligarchies, drawing on the classic Greek distinction.[26] He suggested that in many of the developing nations of the world there was a tendency for the leadership to rule in a very authoritative fashion, in part because such nations, if they were to advance economically, almost required absolute political control by their leaders. Identifying such forms of rule as oligarchies, Shils distinguished among different types. These included tutelary democracies, in which there is both a concentration of power among the leaders and representative parliaments, and traditional oligarchies, characteristic of many African nations, in which leadership is run through tribal councils and there are very few of the elements of either advanced democratic countries or totalitarian ones.

Shils' distinctions draw attention to two special features of many of the regimes in the developing countries of the world: (1) the tendency for leaders to govern in an almost dictatorial fashion and (2) the effort by these same leaders to promote the economic development of their countries. It is precisely these two features that have prompted today's scholars to conceive of a third form of political rule, one they believe lies somewhere between that of democratic and totalitarian regimes. It is called *authoritarianism*, and in the original words of the inventor of the concept, Juan Linz, it refers to

> ...limited, not responsible, political pluralism—without elaborate and guiding ideology (but with distinctive mentalities); without intensive nor extensive political mobilization (except at some points in their development); and in which the leader (or occasionally a small group) exercises power within formally ill-defined limits but actually quite predictable ones.[27]

Linz developed the concept especially to apply to the regime of General Francisco Franco in Spain, for he believed that the regime was certainly not democratic, but that it also did not exhibit many of the excesses of the totalitarian governments of Hitler or Stalin.

Since Linz offered his original definition, the concept of authoritarianism has become further refined. Analysts point out, for example, that there are authoritarian regimes that are deeply populist: they cultivate the sentiments of and are much admired by the mass of citizens. An example would be the government of Juan Perón in Argentina—perhaps even that of Saddam Hussein would qualify for such a description. In a recent study of the links between capitalism and the development of different kinds of political regimes, Dietrich Rueschemeyer, Evelyne Stephens, and John Stephens refine the notion of authoritarianism. They take it to mean, in general, those regimes that lack regular, free, and fair elections of representatives with universal and equal suffrage, and a state apparatus which is responsible to an elected parliament.[28]

Over the past two decades, the most widely used conception of an authoritarian regime has been that of Guillermo O'Donnell. He developed a concept of what he called a *bureaucratic authoritarian* regime.[29] He included in the term the following elements: (1) the exercise of political rule by a small group of leaders, often backed by the military; (2) the reliance of the political rulers on a large group of technical personnel (technocrats), who exercise much of the day-to-day control over the operations of the society; (3) an effort to promote the economic growth of the society, in part as a response to a period of economic stagnation; and (4) the extensive repression of the various classes in the society, especially the rising and expanding middle class. O'Donnell invented the term to depict a situation he had witnessed during the 1960s and 1970s both in Argentina and in Brazil—countries that had experienced rapid economic growth but in which the political leadership, rather than promoting and developing the institutions of civil society, sought to repress them.

The notion of bureaucratic authoritarianism, while useful in depicting the often unstable governments in a number of advanced Latin American countries, has also been applied to nations outside of Latin America. Some have perceived somewhat similar tendencies in the great economic advances made by the nations of Taiwan, South Korea, Singapore, and Hong Kong—the "four little dragons."[30] Like Brazil and Argentina, these countries had experienced considerable economic success, but did so at the expense of civil liberties and exercise of freedom by their citizens. In fact, while there was great improvement in the economic fortunes of these countries as a whole, there was also considerable economic inequality, with the lower classes and poor citizens suffering immense hardship while the wealthy accumulated much of the gains.[31]

Regardless of which precise term one uses, it is plainly evident that a number of the governments in today's nations are run by leaders who seek to exercise a very tight control over both over the direction of governmental policy and the expression of opinions by citizens. In many cases, such control is justified by leaders who claim they want to advance the fortunes of their country and that the only way to do so is to have absolute power, free from the interference of meddling parliaments or citizens. What remains to be seen is whether such regimes can endure over a long period of time. Like the charisma of authority, the success of authoritarian regimes pretty much depends on the success of their individual leaders and their allies. Once Franco died, for example, Spain became a more open and resilient political system. And since the late 1980s, the exercise of authority in South Korea has also become more democratic.

The other, equally pressing, issue is whether such regimes might make a transition to more democratic forms of rule, as in Spain or South Korea, or whether they will swing in the opposite direction, becoming more totalitarian. This is the difficult question facing many of the regimes in Eastern Europe and the former Soviet Union. What may decide the outcome in the end is the health and success of their economies—always a decisive factor. If the Eastern European countries achieve growth and prosperity, this could reduce the tendency to revert to the totalitarian governments of the past half-century or more, thus promoting more open and democratic governments. And yet, as the cases of Argentina and Brazil both illustrate, such success may in fact require an ever-tighter control on both the citizenry and the economy from the top, a kind of control that is only a short step from the long arm of totalitarianism.

Conclusion

In the coming decades one issue will face many of the world's nations—whether they will make a successful transition from an authoritarian regime to either a democratic or totalitarian one. Authoritarian systems, it seems clear, are both intermediate forms and transitional ones. They tend not to be stable over the long run. Even within the span of a single regime, as in the case of Argentina, authoritarianism can become transformed into a ruthless purge and search for the regime's enemies. The most glaring and horrendous example of such a regime in recent memory is that of Pol Pot in Cambodia in the 1970s, the scourge which became known as "the killing fields."

As we have pointed out, there are many pitfalls and quandaries facing the developing nations of the world. Most regimes want to make the great economic leap forward, but it almost is impossible to do so unless there is some considerable concentration of power among the leadership of the country. But once such power becomes concentrated, there can be a tendency for those who hold it to stay in office; power does not necessarily always corrupt, but it is nevertheless a very seductive force for many officials. The problems become even more difficult as the global economy expands. Firms wish to deploy their capital funds in ways that will be most profitable, and many will search to invest them in the developing markets of the world. But if the regimes in those markets are unstable, then the very volatility of the market itself can further destabilize the regimes.

Francis Fukayama, in his famous thesis about the "end of history," suggested that with the collapse of communism, capitalism was on the way to achieving its hegemony as the reigning economic system of the world.[32] Fukayama may have been premature. It is one thing for communism to collapse, and quite another for it to be replaced by a stable democratic system. Indeed, it is likely that the pressures for the developing economies to swing back to some form of authoritative regime—authoritarian or totalitarian—will be great in coming years. The recent chaos in Russia, as well as in other Eastern European nations, provides evidence of such pressures. And similar pressures are likely to be found in Southeast Asia as well as in many Latin American nations.

NOTES

1. Aristotle, *The Politics of Aristotle*, trans. Ernest Barker (London: Oxford University Press, 1975), III, IV, and V.
2. Aristotle, *Politics*, 127.
3. The reader must remember that Aristotle, like other Greek philosophers, did not make a distinction between idealized visions for the purposes of realizing a certain moral aim and idealized visions constructed to achieve certain analytical goals. In other words, Aristotle drew a distinction only between the ideal and the real, whereas today we distinguish between the ideal in moral terms, the ideal in analytical terms—for instance, Weber's notion of the Protestant ethic and Marx's notion of capitalism—and the real. Thus, when Aristotle wrote of the ideal set of constitutional orders, he wrote of a moral vision; when he described the debased set, he spoke both of an unjust and a more realistic portrait of their character. This may explain why Aristotle spent so much more of his effort in *Politics* writing of the non-ideal polities; he simply meant to concede that they represented those forms more likely to achieve realization in ancient Greece.
4. Aristotle, *Politics*, II, Chapter 9.
5. Ibid., 123.
6. Leonard Whibley, *Greek Oligarchies: Their Character and Organization* (New York: G.P. Putnam's Sons, 1896), 144.
7. For interesting observations on the matter of size and the character of the body politic, see Robert A. Dahl and Edward R. Tufte, *Size and Democracy* (Stanford, CA: Stanford University Press, 1973).
8. For writings that illustrate these themes, see Jean Jacques Rousseau, "The Social Contract," in *The Essential Rousseau*, trans. Lowell Bair (New York: New American Library, 1974), 1–124; and John Stuart Mill, "On Liberty" and "Representative Government," in *Utilitarianism, Liberty, and Representative Government* (New York: E.P. Dutton and Co., 1951), 81–229, 231–532.
9. John Dewey, "Democracy as a Way of Life," in *Frontiers of Democratic Theory*, ed. Henry Kariel (New York: Random House, Inc., 1970), 15.
10. Hannah Arendt, "On Public Happiness," in *The Frontiers of Democratic Theory*, ed. Kariel, 5. This very short condensation of the utopian vision, in addition to having been based upon the writings of Rousseau and Mill, was aided in its formulation by several important secondary analyses of these matters. In particular, the reader is urged to examine the following excellent studies: Graeme Duncan and Steven Lukes, "The New Democracy," *Political Studies*, II (1963), 156–77; Lane Davis, "The Cost of Realism: Contemporary Restatements of Democracy," *Western Political Quarterly*, 17 (1964), 37–46; Kariel, *The Frontiers of Democratic Theory*; Carole Pateman, *Participation and Democratic Theory* (Cambridge, UK: Cambridge University Press, 1970), Chapter 2 especially; and Dennis F. Thompson, *The Democratic Citizen* (Cambridge, UK: Cambridge University Press, 1970).
11. Benjamin R. Barber, *Strong Democracy: Participatory Politics for a New Age* (Berkeley: University of California Press, 1984).

12. Ibid., 151.

13. Ibid., 261.

14. Joshua Cohen, "Deliberation and Democratic Legitimacy," in *Deliberative Democracy: Essays on Reason and Politics*, eds. James Bohman and William Rehg (Cambridge, MA: MIT Press, 1997). See also the various other illuminating essays in this original and thoughtful work.

15. See, for example, Jürgen Habermas, *Between Facts and Norms: Contributions to a Discourse Theory of Law and Democracy*, trans. W. Rehg (Cambridge, MA: MIT Press, 1996).

16. Cohen, op. cit., 72.

17. Bernard Berelson, "Democratic Practice and Democratic Theory," in *Voting*, ed. Bernard Berelson, Paul Lazarsfeld, and William McPhee (Chicago: University of Chicago Press, 1954), 305–23; Robert A. Dahl, *Who Governs? Democracy and Power in an American City* (New Haven, CT: Yale University Press, 1971); Robert A. Dahl, *Polyarchy: Participation and Opposition* (New Haven, CT: Yale University Press, 1971), Chapter 1; Giovanni Sartori, *Democratic Theory* (New York: Frederick A. Praeger, 1965); and Joseph Schumpeter, *Capitalism, Socialism and Democracy*, 3rd ed. (New York: Harper & Row Publishers, 1962), 21.

18. Schumpeter, *Capitalism, Socialism, and Democracy*, 3rd ed., 269.

19. Berelson et al., 318–19.

20. There has been a good deal of recent discussion among scholars about the comparative strengths and weaknesses of parliamentary and presidential democracies. Much of the discussion was stimulated by an article by Juan Linz in which he argues that parliamentary democracies have decided advantages over presidential ones. Among other things, he observes, presidential democracies can result in a stalemate of power if the president and the congress are from different political parties; parliamentary democracies can more easily resolve differences because the leader of the victorious party also becomes the prime minister, and head of government. See Juan Linz

21. This portrait of democratic societies is based upon a large number and wide variety of materials—too many, in fact, to be able to cite here. Some of the broader treatments that figured in this presentation include: Robert A. Dahl (ed.), *Political Oppositions in Western Democracies* (New Haven, CT: Yale University Press, 1966); Robert A. Dahl, *Polyarchy: Participation and Opposition*; Leon D. Epstein, *Political Parties in Western Democracies* (New York: Frederick A. Praeger, Publishers, 1967), Chapters 1–4; and Edward Shils, *Political Development in New States* (The Hague: Mouton, 1962).

22. For somewhat different definitions of this concept, compare the following works: Hannah Arendt, *The Origins of Totalitarianism* (Cleveland, OH: World Publishing Co., 1958); Benjamin R. Barber, "Conceptual Foundations of Totalitarianism," in *Totalitarianism in Perspective: Three Views*, ed. Carl J. Friedrich, Michael Curtis, and Benjamin R. Barber (New York: Praeger Publishers, 1969), 3–39; and Carl J. Friedrich and Zbigniew K. Brzezinski, *Totalitarian Dictatorship and Autocracy*, 2nd ed. rev., by Carl J. Friedrich (Cambridge, MA: Harvard University Press, 1965), Chapter 1 especially.

23. For one observer who found the difference to be highly significant, see Barrington Moore, Jr., *Social Origins of Dictatorship and Democracy: Lord and Peasant in the Making of the Modern World* (Boston: Beacon Press, 1975), Chapters 7–9 especially.
24. Friedrich and Brzezinski, *Totalitarian Dictatorship and Autocracy*, Chapter 2.
25. This portrait of totalitarian regimes, with special attention to the Third Reich, is based upon the following sources: Hannah Arendt, *The Origins of Totalitarianism*, part 3 especially; Lucy S. Dawidowicz, *The War Against the Jews: 1933–1945* (New York: Holt, Rinehart and Winston, 1975), part 1; Joachim C. Fest, *Hitler*, trans. Richard and Clara Winston (New York: Avon Books, 1971), parts 5–8 especially; Carl J. Friedrich and Zbigniew K. Brzezinski, *Totalitarian Dictatorship and Autocracy*; Adolf Hitler, *Mein Kampf*, trans. Ralph Manheim (Boston: Houghton Mifflin Company, 1971), vol. 1, Chapter 11 especially; Helmut Krausnick et al., *Anatomy of the SS State*, trans. Richard Barry et al. (London: Collins, 1968), especially Chapters 2–3; Franz Neumann, *Behemoth* (New York: Oxford University Press, 1952); and Albert Speer, *Inside the Third Reich*, trans. Richard and Clara Winston (New York: Avon Books, 1971), parts 2–3 especially.
26. Edward Shils, *Political Development in New States*, op. cit.
27. Juan J. Linz, "An Authoritarian Regime: Spain," in *Cleavages, Ideologies and Party Systems: Contributions to Comparative Political Sociology*, ed. Erik Allardt and Yrjo Littunen (Helsinki: the Academic Bookstore, 1964), 297.
28. Dietrich Rueschemeyer, Evelyne Huber Stephens, and John D. Stephens, *Capitalist Development & Democracy* (Chicago: University of Chicago Press, 1992), 43–44.
29. Guillermo O'Donnell, *Modernization and Bureaucratic-Authoritarianism: Studies in South American Politics* (Berkeley: Institute of International Studies, University of California, 1973; 1979). Also see his more recent excellent collection of essays, *Counterpoints: Selected Essays on Authoritarianism and Democratization* (Notre Dame, IN: University of Notre Dame Press, 1999).
30. Ezra F. Vogel, *The Four Little Dragons: the Spread of Industrialization in East Asia* (Cambridge, MA: Harvard University Press, 1991).
31. Frederic C. Deyo, *Beneath the Miracle: Labor Subordination in the New Asian Industrialism* (Berkeley: University of California Press, 1989).
32. Francis Fukuyama, *The End of History and the Last Man* (New York: Harper Perennial, 1993).

Chapter 7

Power and Authority in America

The business of America is business.
Calvin Coolidge

W riting in the nineteenth century, Karl Marx offered us the first view of how power might operate in a large and growing industrial society. He insisted that capitalism was the foundation of the growth and development of modern societies and that the arm of the state under capitalism served mainly to promote the interests of capitalists, that is, of business and industry. The capitalists had become a ruling class; they not only controlled the operations of the economy, but they also controlled those of the state. Thus, they, or their agents, made policies and decisions that, in the long run, would benefit their interests and secure their dominance over the rest of society.

Marx's view has a strong ring of truth to it, so much so that even today, a century and a half later, many still believe this is the way the world of power and politics operates. But not everyone does. And what we, as students of politics, must do is to consider the evidence about power with great care and to decide whether the view of Marx, or someone else, might be correct. The object of political sociology, here as elsewhere, must be to develop empirically grounded theory and then to subject it to careful and thorough empirical scrutiny.

In this chapter we will review the evidence we have today about the nature and operation of power in America. Thirty years ago, when the first edition of this book appeared, this chapter looked very different from the one you are about to read. At a minimum, it is clear, the research and hard work of political sociologists in this most debated of intellectual terrain has come far and made some clear advances. This chapter will consider the following themes: (1) the nature of the government, or state as we shall call it, and some of the important variations among states; (2) the nature of the modern economy, particularly the modern corporation, and its power; and (3) issues of economic inequality and political equality in contemporary America.

At the end, we hope you will ask yourself: Is there an answer to the question of who holds and exercises power in America? We believe there is one, but it is a bit complicated, like all such matters. What we hope to show you is that while America clearly possesses a democratic state of the form we discussed at length in the last chapter, such a state operates in ways that run counter to our general sense of what an ideal democracy is all about.

Prologue

At the risk of complicating a fluent narrative about power in America, we shall make a brief detour here at the start. In particular, we want to provide you with a short history of the key debates and issues that have surrounded the study of power in America. Our rendition will show you where the field has come as well as how it has gotten here. Moreover, this tale also is essential to understanding how political sociologists approach the study of power in America today, in particular, what issues remain alive for them and what issues no longer are relevant. Some of their concerns, you will see, draw freely on the writings and ideas of Karl Marx, Max Weber, and Alexis de Tocqueville.

For as long as Americans have thought and written about power, there have been debates about what it looks like and how it operates. Many scholars— and members of the lay public, too—prefer to take American democracy at its word. They emphasize the underlying values of American democracy, and how the processes and debates of politics actually favor the workings of democratic government. Democracy is rooted, they argue, in the very nature of a system of checks and balances, the design of government that was created by the framers of the U.S. Constitution. Three different branches of government exist—executive, legislative, and judicial—and each pursues a separate task of governance—to make policy, to debate policy, and to make judgments about the implementation of policy.

Still, there always have been dissenters from the dominant view of American democracy. There have been those who do not take the system at its word, and who believe that there are forces that operate behind the scenes. Some dissenters, for instance, have drawn explicitly, or implicitly, on the writings of Karl Marx. One such dissenter was the famous economic historian Charles Beard, who believed that the economic foundations of American society actually held the key to the operations of government. Beard pursued this thesis in a number of ways, including a famous book in which he insisted that the Constitution of the United States was a flawed and biased document precisely because most of the framers of the Constitution were themselves wealthy plantation owners and businessmen.[1] How, then, he asked, could they possibly create a government that would be impartial to their interests?

The debates over the nature of American democracy continued beyond Beard, but the dominant view always remained more or less intact. Democratic politics was to be taken at its face value. It was a matter of give and take, negotiations, the workings of the different branches of government each pursuing its own task, until, in the end, the process resulted in policies and actions that favored the interests of the majority of Americans.

Roughly mid-twentieth century, the intensity of the debate heated up. Fresh from a victory over Germany, Japan, and Italy in World War II, Americans returned home and began to work hard at moving themselves ahead. Work was on their minds, but politics was, too. Although America and its allies had won the war, important new political alliances and divisions had been created. The most important development was the rise of the Soviet Union and Communist China to new roles as players in world politics. "An iron curtain" had been dropped across part of the world, in Winston Churchill's famous words delivered in 1948, one that would not only divide nations, but also Americans one against another. In America at the end of the 1940s, a new movement began, McCarthyism, led by Congressman Joe McCarthy of Wisconsin, which was intended to root out Communists, and other fellow-travelers, in the United States. It would divide Americans against one another and result in the tragic and premature end to the careers of many highly successful people. The effect was not only to destroy the careers of many Americans, but also to stifle dissent in the United States.

It did anything but stifle dissent. Among social scientists two different views came to prevail about the nature of American democracy. One, authored by the political scientist Robert Dahl, insisted that the nature of American democracy was such that every dominant group played a role in the game of politics and that the rules of the game permitted and sustained an equal participation of their roles. Dahl's view, which came to be known as the pluralist view of American politics, articulated the dominant, mainstream interpretation of politics for Americans. It was a view that was elegantly expressed and that, as a result of the research by Dahl and his assistants, was supported by evidence showing, among other things, that on different political issues, different parties came to the table to play, with no one party being more dominant than another.[2]

At about the same time, yet another, very different, perspective was offered on the nature of American politics. Although various forms of Marxist analyses of American democracy had been around ever since Beard, and even before, the new view represented a radical departure from the past. This view was advanced by C. Wright Mills, a young sociologist from Texas, who would die prematurely at the age of 46 in 1961. Mills argued, in effect, that American democracy was something of a sham.[3] Politics did not allow everyone an equal opportunity to participate. Some people possessed and exercised much more power than others; they, in effect, were the ones who made decisions that controlled and directed the lives of other Americans. And there was little Americans could do about such matters, in large part because of the origins and positions of those in power. There were three critical axes to this new coalition of power: (1) "the power elite"—big business, or corporations, (2) the leading military officials, especially members of the Joint Chiefs of Staff of the military, and (3) the members of the executive branch of government. Americans could only choose one part of this "power elite," the figure who sat in the White House. They certainly could not determine the people who ran the corporations, nor could they select the high-ranking members of the military.

Mills' view was to become as popular, if not more popular, among younger Americans, especially those just off to college. Just as Dahl's view possessed a *prima facie* element of truth, so, too, did that of Mills. The President of the United States, after all, was a great military hero, Dwight D. Eisenhower, who had led the American troops during World War II. Many of the men who served in his Cabinet had been members of leading business firms and corporations prior to their service in government. Moreover, it also appeared true, as Mills argued, that power had moved from Main Street to Wall Street and to 1600 Pennsylvania Avenue—and, in particular, that it was the federal government, both under the New Deal administration of Franklin Delano Roosevelt and then Eisenhower, that was making the key decisions about the lives of Americans. For many Americans, these were important issues, yet for the great majority such issues did not matter, as they worked hard to support young families and to furnish their new homes in the suburbs.

To sociologists, the debate raged on between the proponents of the Dahl, or pluralist, view of American politics and the proponents of the Mills, or elitist, view of American politics. Each camp was able to assemble an arsenal of evidence to support its own view. Over the course of the late 1950s and early 1960s, the Dahl camp was able to assemble evidence that showed how different groups came to play prominent roles in urban politics. Using research studies from work in New Haven, New York, and Chicago, among other cities, the pluralists gradually accumulated a great deal of evidence to support their perspective.[4] The adherents of the Mills view also accumulated evidence, plus a great deal of new enthusiasm for the work by a number of younger sociologists who, locked in their own debate with government about the War in Vietnam, came to believe deeply and firmly in the truth of Mills' view.

By the early 1970s, the debate had become something of a stalemate, each side claiming a kind of intellectual victory. But then the grounds of the debate began to shift, and new angles emerged on the matter of power in America. A version of the Mills thesis began to circulate that insisted that America was run not merely by the power elite, but by a ruling class. Advanced by the sociologist Ralph Miliband (see Chapter 2), it argued that those people who held high political office in America represented, in effect, agents of the ruling class, or capitalists. Therefore, it could be expected that their views and decisions over policy would ultimately advantage business in America—as clearly they seemed to do based upon the various government policies made over the course of the 1950s, 1960s, and 1970s. Another neo-Marxist view at the time was that of the economists Paul Baran and Paul Sweezy.[5] They argued that America had reached a new phase in its development, that of "monopoly capitalism." Among other things, this meant that the structure of the country was designed to favor the interests of the dominant corporate monopolies, and to do so by engaging in wars abroad to promote and extend the economic power of these corporations.

One other view also emerged, representing yet a different twist on the nature of politics. It was the view of the French sociologist Nicos Poulantzas (see Chapter 2). He insisted that the structures of the state actually had, in effect, taken on a life of their own, thus becoming "relatively autonomous" from control by members of the ruling class, or capitalists. The state advanced the interests of the capitalists, or businesspeople, in America in a way that did not require continuous, or even periodic, oversight by the capitalists themselves. In other words, it no longer mattered who held office on Pennsylvania Avenue, because it was the office, not the occupant, that mattered. What gave Poulantzas' argument a special appeal to sociologists was that his view accorded with the deepest dictates of the discipline—it was the institution and the office, *not the individual occupant*, that mattered in the long-term operations of all institutions, whether they be political, business, or otherwise.

We thus arrive at today's platform from which to view power in America. The debate between the pluralists and the elitists has become transformed in important respects. Although there are elements of the pluralist view that still have a ring of truth to them, for example, that there are different players in politics in America, there is very little evidence today to support the main tenets of this view. Granted that the broad legal and historic outlines of the American state remain democratic, almost all political sociologists seem to agree that some players are simply much more powerful in the game of politics than other players, though they disagree on the precise reasons for their power. The federal government is a key player in the structure of American power, many agree, if only because of the resources it controls and can manipulate. In addition, major corporations remain key players in American politics, again because of the resources they control. In general, there also has been a shift away from identifying individuals as the loci of the exercise of power to viewing organizations and broad institutions as the loci of such power. This shift is in keeping with the growing emphasis among sociologists on the significance of the concepts of social networks and institutions.

Three specific views today dominate the writings of students of power in America. The first is what we might call the *dominant*, or *ruling*, *class* view, a variant on the original conception of Karl Marx.[6] It claims that the critical decisions in America are more or less made and dominated by an upper class of people who serve on the boards of major corporations, intermarry with one another, go to school with one another, and the like. The second is what has been called an *institutional elite* model, so coined by the sociologist G. William Domhoff. It argues that it is the people who occupy the positions of great authority in major institutions in America that control the dominant decisions of the society, and that such institutions include both those in the federal government and in major corporations. The third is the *state-centered* view of American politics, which originated with the important work of sociologist Theda Skocpol (see Chapter 3). It argues that the state is actually the main locus of power and that the individuals who occupy the major positions in the state, such as the president and his advisors, act in decisive and deliberate fashion to further the interests of the state, not those of capitalists *per se*.[7] In matters of power, in the game of politics, within America and in dealings with other nations, it is the decisions of those who are in the government that really matter, according to Skocpol, not those of the members of the upper class. Such decisions, Skocpol appears to suggest, spring not from the class or other background interests of those in government, but from the immediate organizational dictates and broad policies of the state, itself.

Our discussion, then, about matters of power in America today will be guided by the general focus provided by these three views and by the evidence, much of it quite sophisticated, assembled by their proponents. As to which of the views is most correct, that is another matter. But let us first review the evidence on the main lines of the arguments below, and then return at various points in the chapter to reassess the key questions of power, and of democracy, in modern America.

The Power of the American State

The American state, as compared to other states, is defined as a weak system.[8] By this analysts mean that American government lacks the same degree of centralization of authority and decision making so characteristic of European democracies. In England, for example, the authority of the government is concentrated in the hands of the national government at Westminster. The national government makes decisions about the most important matters of taxation and revenues, schooling and public buildings, whereas local governments have a limited authority to spend and disburse funds for such matters as local public housing. In France, too, the authority is concentrated in the hands of the national government, and provincial governments exercise only limited authority over issues of concern to the public. The centralization of authority in the governments of these nations, and in those of other European countries as well, has roots in the far distant past, dating back to the seventeenth century.

The American state, by comparison, has, from its founding and in the terms of the Constitution, been one in which the authority to make policy is divided and dispersed among different agencies and branches. There is, first, the system of checks and balances produced by the three different branches of government. In addition, and equally important, power also is dispersed among different levels of government—the federal government in Washington, the state governments of the fifty states, and the local governments of the many municipalities. Such a system of federated government has resulted in a kind of dilution of central power, purposefully limiting throughout much of its history the ability of the federal government to exercise authority over the lives of American citizens. On matters of school funding, for example, both state and local authorities make the critical decisions. On issues of public spending for parks and for police and fire departments, it also is the local and state authorities that have the final say. This dispersal of authority is written into the very nature of the American Constitution, and thus sets limits on what the federal government can and cannot do.

Yet while the rules and regulations produce considerable dispersion of authority among different agencies and across different levels of government, there has been a *de facto* growth over time of authority in the hands of the federal government. Local governments began as the real centers of authority in America, creating a kind of system that can best be described as a *bottom-up* rather than a *top-down* democracy. The achievements and accomplishments that were made by government, especially in nineteenth-century America, often were the achievements of local, or state, governments. Critical decisions were made about such matters as schools or railroads, or other modes of transportation, and such decisions frequently were made by local and state officials, and had the force of binding authority. But as the nineteenth century unfolded, the character and locus of power began to shif, from the local levels to the state and then to the federal government.

The political scientist Stephen Skowronek, in a masterful work, characterizes this period in the development of the American state not as one of weakness, but as one in which the "courts and parties" exercised great control.⁹ Such a state, he finds, had its beginnings in the nineteenth century when both the judiciary and the political parties were the dominant players in the law making and decisions taken by the federal government. Even after the Pendleton Act of 1883, for example, which would make merit the primary qualification for the holding of a civil service appointment, political parties continued to play a central role in helping to determine who the potential occupants for such offices would be. The courts likewise exercised a great influence over the manner of federal policy making, not merely helping to interpret the law, but also acting as active arbiters in establishing the substantive nature of law itself. The American state, in Skowronek's view, ultimately came to represent a special historical/cultural mix of tendencies built into the Constitution and of the needs for an expanding society to provide governmental decisions over a brand range of issues and a wide expanse of territory. It was not so much a weak state, in his view, as a state whose hands were tied by the penetration of the forces on behalf of courts and parties into its innermost workings. Moreover, as America was buffeted by the winds of industrialization, winds that would demand a centralization of authority, the state changed in ways that continued to reveal the deep imprint left on it by the power both of the courts and of the two dominant political parties.

The most dramatic period in the centralization and concentration of authority in the hands of the federal government (what Skowronek refers to as the national state) took place during the course of the Roosevelt administration from 1933 to 1945. Stimulated largely by the economic devastation of the Great Depression and, then, by entrance into World War II, the Roosevelt administration was able to develop a degree of authority unmatched by any other presidential administration. Here we shall review a few details about Roosevelt and the power of the executive branch of government in America in general. In addition, we shall also consider several other key agencies of the federal government: the military, the Central Intelligence Agency (CIA), and the Federal Bureau of Investigation (FBI). This review will bring us all up to date on some of the key episodes in the growth of power of the federal government. Moreover, it will introduce us to a central, if not *the* central, aspect of the federal government—the state as a war maker.

THE AMERICAN STATE AS A WAR-MAKING STATE

The Executive Branch. Franklin Delano Roosevelt was a figure of enormous charisma and equally unbounded ambition. He and his administration managed during his tenure in office to initiate a number of federal programs that eventually served to reshape the links between the federal government, the world of business, and the broader public. During his administration, for example, there came into existence the Social Security Program in 1935, the Tennessee Valley Authority in 1933, and a host of general welfare programs designed to extricate the United States from the depths of the Great Depression. Under Roosevelt, too, because of both the circumstances of the Depression as well as World War II, Congress seemed to become less and less an equal partner in the operations of the federal government. Because of his special gifts for communication, Roosevelt's influence extended well beyond the confines of 1600 Pennsylvania Avenue. Thus, during the 1930s he managed to fashion a structure of partisan loyalties and identities in the United States that would not disappear for at least another thirty years.

Yet Roosevelt was only the first of several presidents to have succeeded in expanding the power and influence of the presidency, though he surely was one of the most skillful. Partly as a result of the more aggressive role the United States sought in world affairs during as well as after World War II, the incumbents of the presidency came increasingly to make decisions that had worldwide, not to say historic, significance. Harry Truman made the decision to drop the atomic bombs on both Hiroshima and Nagasaki, acts that set into motion an entirely new understanding of the meaning of war and human violence. John Foster Dulles, Dwight Eisenhower's Secretary of State, made decisions that reshaped the nature of the balance of power in the Middle East, and with it the relations between the United States and the Soviet Union.

During the administrations of Kennedy, Johnson, and Nixon, the power of the presidency truly came into its own. During this period, beginning with the Kennedy administration in 1960, the U.S. government sought to extend its influence abroad, creating new alliances in Asia, Africa, and Latin America. In 1960, for example, the Organization of American States (OAS) was created under the initiative of the Kennedy administration. Ostensibly designed to furnish American aid to Latin American countries and to solidify the American alliance in the north and south, may observers saw the OAS in truth merely as a device to extend and to protect American political and economic interests in Latin America.[10] The Peace Corps, too, was an innovation of the Kennedy administration, apparently created to furnish aid to citizens of other countries with no strings attached; yet, once more, from another angle observers saw it as simply a means of extending the hegemony of American political power abroad. In addition, there was the famous abortive Bay of Pigs invasion of 1962, taken under the initiative of the Kennedy administration. It was carried out with the cooperation of the CIA and marked still another attempt by an American president and his counselors to extend American influence beyond the shores of the United States.

The event that decisively contributed to the growth in the power and influence of the president and his counselors, to the development, in the words of

Arthur Schlesinger, Jr., of an "Imperial Presidency," was the Vietnam War.[11] To all outward appearances, the United States government should have had little, if any, interest in Vietnam. Here, after all, was a country in the midst of an internal conflict, a war that had only a decade earlier led to the humiliating defeat of France. It was a country thousands of miles from the shores of the United States; yet, for some reason only later to be clarified, the president and his counselors believed it necessary to introduce American troops into the struggle. Hence, in 1963 the United States started to increase aid to the tottering Diem regime in South Vietnam. With the assassination of President Kennedy, and after winning election on a platform in which he condemned his opponent for his trigger-happy intentions in Vietnam, Lyndon Johnson presided over a major escalation of the U.S. effort. He did so, moreover, through actions, such as the Gulf of Tonkin incident in 1965, that seemed to be strategically designed to force the United States into ever-greater participation, and he did so, most significantly, without the free and ready advice and consent of the American Congress.

Why should the United States have become involved in such a war? And why did the president and his advisors, particularly the members of the National Security Council under the leadership of Walt Rostow and McGeorge Bundy, seek to assert American influence in this far-flung region of the world? Those who have studied documents that bear the imprint of these officials argue that American advisors believed that the national interest was at stake, in fact that the Communist nations posed a major threat to American democracy. Hence, they reasoned, it was important for the United States to put up an aggressive front, in the words of Richard Barnet, to display a "macho and aggressive style" as a means of protecting the national interests of the United States. If Vietnam fell, it was assumed in terms of the so-called domino theory, so, too, would other nations in the region, leading eventually to the dominance of the Communists in that part of the world and thereby shifting the balance of power between the Communist and non-Communist countries.[12] Such an event, the Kennedy and Johnson administrations both believed, must be avoided, and thus they engaged in almost reckless use, and sacrifice, of American troops and weaponry.

The end of the War in Vietnam in 1975, coupled with the resignation of President Nixon following the Watergate fiasco, helped restore Congress to a more powerful role in the workings of the federal government by diminishing the power of the presidency. Nevertheless, the administration of President Ronald Reagan should be credited, in part, for helping to bring about the demise of the Soviet Union and its Communist allies throughout Eastern Europe. Though Reagan was a decidedly uncomplicated man, he was a powerful opponent of the Soviet Union, insisting that the Communist menace must be wiped out. In his administration, the United States government, for example, continued to put pressure on the Soviet Union. Although there were a number of internal problems and issues that helped to bring about the collapse of Communism, many observers also believe that the policies of the Reagan presidency assisted as well.

The end of Soviet-style Communism created a vast new and uncertain terrain for world politics and economics. The administration of President William Jefferson Clinton was more notable for its attempts to promote a range of important domestic policies, especially with regard to redesigning elements of the welfare state, than for its appreciation of the new dynamics of the world after the end of Soviet Communism. Apart from the NATO action against Kosovo, the United States was not involved in a major war effort during the Clinton administration. Moreover, both Clinton's enemies and his own missteps limited the power that he might have exercised in office. Indeed, the failure of his effort to create a major national health plan, one that would have been a revolutionary effort to help many millions of Americans, might well be regarded, in retrospect, as the decisive turning point in his administration. In addition, the election in 1994 of a Republican Congress spelled further doom for the Clinton presidency and for the ability of Clinton to take decisive new steps in reshaping America.

Yet another turning point in the power of the presidency happened during the tenure of George W. Bush as President from 2000 to 2008. The historic moment, of course, took place on September 11, 2001, when a group of terrorists destroyed the World Trade Center in New York as well as causing major damage to the Pentagon in Washington, DC. Thereafter, Bush assumed the mantle of the "wartime president," someone who saw the mission for his time in office as eliminating the elements of terror, especially Osama bin Laden and al-Qa'ida, as a threat to the world. The Bush administration unleashed two specific actions: military action in Afghanistan to eliminate the Taliban and Al-Qa'ida the War in Iraq. Both actions would once again promote a kind of "Imperial Presidency," something that had not been seen in the United States since the War in Vietnam.

Both Afghanistan operation and the War in Iraq have dragged on for a period of years. Many Americans were initially strongly behind the effort in Iraq with the vast majority supporting the president's plan to topple the regime of Saddam Hussein and establish a new democratic government in its place. But Bush had employed faulty intelligence, arguing that America had to get rid of Hussein because he had weapons of mass destruction. As it turned out, no such weapons were ever found, nor, in fact, as reports would later show, did they exist in 2003. Yet it is highly likely that Bush would still have gone to war in Iraq because a number of his key advisors, including Vice President Dick Cheney, Secretary of Defense Donald Rumsfeld, and Deputy Defense Secretary Paul

Wolfowitz, were convinced that regime change in Iraq would ultimately promote democracy across the Middle East.[13]

In fact, as of this writing nothing of the sort has happened. Nor is it likely to happen in the near future. Indeed, the presence of U.S. forces in Iraq has promoted a widespread insurgency against the United States, drawing in elements from across the region, not simply from Iraq. The United States has also taken a severe beating in public opinion across the world, and, as the presidency of George W. Bush comes to end, those who have sought to create an Imperial President once again have come up short. Moreover, they have left the United States entangled in a quagmire in Iraq much like the quagmire that once existed in Vietnam. It will be up to the next president to seek an effective solution to this tangle of affairs and to wrestle with the question of a vision for the United States in the new global order of the twenty-first century.

The Military, CIA, and the FBI. C. Wright Mills insisted that much of the authority wielded by the federal government lay in the role of the military and its capacity to control resources. Mills argued that the military principals of the government had come to assume an enormous impact on the making of public policy after the end of World War II. In fact, individuals with experience in the American military have come to occupy high positions in the government over the course of the past five decades. A favorite example for Mills was Dwight Eisenhower, who moved from being the Commander of Allied Forces in Europe to becoming president for two terms, beginning in 1952. Other military figures who have become important in the shaping of American foreign and domestic policies in the years since the close of World War II include General Maxwell Taylor, who during the Vietnam War furnished key advice to the Kennedy and Johnson administrations.

Although the power of the military to influence American policy has declined in recent decades, even during the 1980s military figures exercised power in the federal government. Consider the case of General Alexander Haig. Haig first rose to prominence as chairman of the Joint Chiefs of Staff of the armed forces, later became a personal and controversial counselor to Richard Nixon, and, it was said, played a large role in the final days of Nixon's presidency.[14] In the administration of Ronald Reagan, Haig achieved the penultimate position, perhaps, for a military figure, apart from the presidency itself, serving as Secretary of State. His influence undoubtedly was part of the reason for the Reagan administration's highly aggressive stance on foreign policy, not to say the recommended increases for spending on defense. Moreover, Haig entered the 1988 presidential campaign, vying for the highest office himself. Other prominent military officers continue to play a role in the policy making of the federal government, including General Colin Powell, who served as the Commander of the Joint Chiefs of Staff during the administration of George W. Bush.

Over this same period of time, spending on the defense budget also revealed the extent to which the United States relied on the military, and defense, for its policies and directions. In 1970, for example, while the United States was still in the midst of the War in Vietnam, the federal budget targeted $78.7 billion for defense, fully 40 percent of the entire federal budget at the time.[15] In 1980, a figure of $130.4 billion was directed to the Department of Defense, about one quarter of the national budget. By 1999 the portion of the federal budget devoted to military expenditures had risen somewhat, to 32 percent, still quite a bit lower than it was during the 1970s.

Besides the military, other agencies of the federal government have, since the end of World War II, exercised considerable influence over American foreign and domestic policies. The two most significant have been the CIA and FBI. The CIA came into being as a result of the National Security Act of 1947, the same act that created the Department of Defense and established the National Security Council.[16] Originally it had been the intention of its creators that the CIA remain under the control of the National Security Council and that it operate explicitly to gather intelligence overseas. But after its establishment, and particularly under the leadership of Allen Dulles, brother of Eisenhower's Secretary of State, the role of the CIA expanded considerably. It funded a wide variety of clandestine activities abroad, among them efforts to overthrow governments perceived to be unsympathetic to American national interests. Ever since the enlargement of its role under the tutelage of Dulles, the CIA has acted in important ways to shape and to direct American foreign policy.

There have been countless instances of foreign conflicts and episodes in which the CIA somehow has been involved, including of course the major fiasco, the Bay of Pigs, in which the CIA virtually sponsored an effort to oust Fidel Castro and his regime. There also was the famous U-2 spy plane incident of 1960, when Francis Gary Powers was shot down while flying over Russia. Later it was discovered that his mission was under the supervision of the CIA. The CIA also participated in the overthrow of the Guatemalan regime in 1954, another government claimed to be unfriendly to American interests, and it provided funds and personnel to help undermine the Marxist government of Premier Salvador Allende in Chile in 1973. The Reagan presidency was itself implicated in scandal involving the CIA. As the Iran-Contra hearings during the summer of 1987 revealed, there were deep machinations and plots involving administration officials, from William Casey in the CIA to Oliver North on the staff of the National Security Council, perhaps even to Vice President George Bush—although he denied any active involvement. The plans involved a complicated exchange of people and goods, with American captives in Lebanon

freed and aid shipped surreptitiously and illegally to support the antigovern-
ment Contra effort in Nicaragua. At the center of this plot were the CIA and its
former director, William Casey.

To the chagrin of many people, officials and public alike, the CIA has not
overstepped the tacit limits of national sovereignty on foreign soil exclusively. In
the early 1970s, for instance, it was learned that the CIA had for a period of time
provided considerable financial support to certain members of the National
Student Association in return for their help in collecting information on
alleged radical students. Elsewhere on campuses and in research laboratories
throughout the United States, it has been reported, the CIA has also provided
financial support to people willing to inform on the activities of their colleagues
and friends. All such acts, and many other foreign engagements abroad, have
been done in complete secrecy, conceived and produced by an inner council within the CIA known as the Special Group. Moreover, the budget of the
CIA, although artfully disguised from the curious eyes of wary congressmen,
is reported to have rivaled in size that of its Russian counterpart, the KGB. As
David Wise and Thomas Ross tersely claim in their important analysis, the CIA
has during the years of its existence operated almost as an "invisible government" within the United States.

Nevertheless, the CIA has had as many failures as successes during its existence. Those who know the CIA well, including former directors, claim that
while the agency has done a good job of assembling and collecting intelligence
for purposes of espionage, it has not done a very good job of analyzing these
data or of sharing them with other branches of the federal government. Its most
notable failure occurred during the run-up to the War in Iraq. It was the CIA
and its director, George Tenet, that claimed that Saddam Hussein possessed
weapons of mass destruction, yet on closer inspection such intelligence was
based on dubious sources, at best. Indeed, the recent intelligence failures of
the CIA led President Bush to reorganize the security and intelligence services
of the federal government, effectively diminishing the once-powerful status of
the CIA.[17]

With the death of J. Edgar Hoover in 1970, the influence of the FBI
declined in importance, aided in no small part by investigations of its activities
by the Congress. Yet during the reign of Hoover the FBI represented a very
powerful agency of the federal government; presidents themselves even occasionally seemed to reverse the constitutional relationship between the president
and his subordinates, showing enormous respect and deference toward Hoover.
Over the years the FBI has limited its own intelligence work to American soil,
but it has ranged far and wide in the pursuit of information on alleged dis-
sidents. During the late 1940s into the 1950s, the FBI played a major part in
collecting information on so-called Communist agents or sympathizers in the

United States, helping to feed American political paranoia in that decade.[18] Where the FBI began to overstep itself, in terms simply of gathering intelligence, was in the fabrication of information that could be used to discredit otherwise important and respected Americans.[19] For instance, it has been reported that the FBI fabricated stories about alleged sexual liaisons of the Reverend Martin Luther King, Jr., during the mid-1960s in an attempt to diminish his influence as a spokesman for civil rights. And, even more controversial, in 1980 the FBI undertook the ABSCAM effort, an intelligence operation in which an FBI agent posing as an Arab oil magnate tried to bribe various congressmen. Defense attorneys for several of the congressmen indicted for accepting such bribes have tried to show that the FBI did not merely "gather" information, as is its mandate from the government, but tried to create it instead.

The American State as a Welfare State

The power of the executive branch of government to make critical decisions about war, coupled with the authority of the military, the CIA, and the FBI, all represent one side of the operations of the state—the *war-making*, or social control side, of state policy. But there is another, equally important side to the exercise of power by the federal government, which we can call the *welfare* side of state policy. It was during the course of the Roosevelt administration that major measures were taken to promote the well-being of American citizens, including the Social Security Act of 1935. It is this side of the state that has come to be seen increasingly as a crucial feature—which can promote the well-being of its citizens.

The welfare state, in general terms, came into being during the course of the twentieth century.[20] Various nations of Western Europe introduced a number of policies and measures designed to improve the well-being of their residents. Such measures included provisions for the cost of general healthcare, pensions for the elderly, aid to orphans and widows, and other such benefits. Some nations became exemplary for the broad array of benefits they furnished for their citizens. The Scandanavian countries, including Sweden and Norway, stand out among all Western nations for the level of benefits they provided.

Compared to other nations, the United States has provided far less for its citizens, creating "safety nets" that are less secure and comprehensive. Although the United States has provided pensions, through the Social Security Act, such benefits are not nearly as comprehensive as those of other countries. In addition, though the United States provided funds to cover the costs for young children of single parent families, those funds, too, were fairly meager. The economist Gosta Esping-Andersen (Table 7.1) speaks about three different kinds of welfare systems. There are those of the Scandinavian countries, which he refers

TABLE 7.1. Public Social Security and Health
Expenditures as a Percentage of Gross
Domestic Product in Selected Countries,
1980–1990

OECD Countries[a]	1980	1990
Canada[b]	17.3	18.8
Denmark	26.0	27.8
France	23.9	26.5
Germany	25.4	23.5
Netherlands	27.2	28.8
Norway	21.4	28.7
Sweden	32.4	33.1
United Kingdom	21.3	22.3
United States	14.1	14.6
Other Countries[c]	**1975**	**1986**
Czechoslovakia	17.2	21.5
Hungary	14.9	16.2
Ukraine	13.8	17.3
USSR	13.6	15.5
Autralia	10.3	9.2
New Zealand	14.5	17.9
Japan	8.9	12.2
Argentina	6.8	6.1
Brazil	5.2	5.0
Chile	11.0	13.1
Costa Rica	5.1	7.3

[a] These figures are based on OECD definitions which are not comparable with the ILO's (International Labor Organization).
[b] Data for Canada refer to 1982 and 1990.
[c] ILO-based data. For the ex-communist nations, spending calculated in
terms of net material product.
SOURCES: OECD, *Employment Outlook*, Paris, 1994, Table 4.7; ILO, *The Cost
of Social Security*, Geneva, 1991. Reprinted by permission of Sage Publications
Ltd. from Gosta Esping-Andersen, *Welfare States in Transition: National
Adaptations in Global Economies* (London: Sage Publishers, 1996), 11.

to as social democratic welfare systems: these furnish the most comprehensive
benefits to the largest number of citizens. Then there are the welfare systems
of countries like Germany, which he refers to as corporativist welfare systems.
They provide benefits for workers' compensation and unemployment, but their
provisions are tied to a worker's previous earnings and are not nearly as generous
as those of the Scandinavian countries. Finally, there are what Esping-Andersen

refers to as the "residualist" welfare states. Such nations provide benefits, but these benefits are limited and cover only specific areas of welfare. The United States is an example of this more limited kind of welfare state.

Since the mid-1970s there have been general changes in the nature of the welfare state. Most nations were forced to reconsider the amounts of money they provided in benefits to their citizens primarily because of a financial crunch they experienced after the worldwide oil crisis of 1973–74. When the welfare state first came into being, it was argued by such key figures as William Beveridge in Great Britain that the state could afford to be generous in the monies it provided citizens so long as unemployment remained low. With low rates of unemployment, there would be plenty of cash reserves, secured by taxes from employed citizens, to provide benefits for the small number of people who were unemployed and for other items, such as pensions for the elderly and healthcare aid. But by the early 1970s unemployment rates had increased world-wide, and pressures began to build to find ways to solve the problem.

For a number of nations, especially European ones, the solution was to be found not in increasing employment, but in reducing the amounts of expenditures on welfare items.[21] Prime Minister Margaret Thatcher of England led the way, arguing the radical position that the state should no longer provide welfare in the amounts it had. She insisted that the welfare programs created after World War II in England were a bad idea and that people had to become more responsible for their own lives. The Thatcher Revolution, as it was called, resulted in a change of attitude, and eventually a change of policy, in Great Britain, signaling a change that would happen in other nations as well. In Great Britain, for example, public housing, which had been a guarantee for poor families for several decades, changed, and the Council houses were put up for sale and rent. This was only one of the measures instituted in changing the course of the welfare state.

Other nations have not made as many dramatic reductions in their welfare policies, but all countries have been compelled to reconsider the nature of their benefits. In the absence of full employment, it becomes difficult to provide government funding for the array of measures and benefits previously guaranteed to all citizens. Even in the generous welfare states of Scandinavia, for example, important rethinking has been done about the nature of the benefits to be provided.[22] In the United States, which has lacked the generous benefits of the Scandinavian countries, the reduction in the size of the safety net happened not simply through a cutback of benefits but also because of an unparalleled degree of economic expansion over the course of the 1990s. In fact, from 1991 through 1999, economic growth continued rapidly, and rates of unemployment rose to levels not seen in more than thirty years. The effect was to provide the foundations for a sea change in the limited American welfare state, creating new workfare programs that provided jobs for many people, often single mothers, previously on the welfare rolls. As of 2008, the revolution in the nature of welfare in America seemed to be doing better than even the most vigorous critics had believed, with thousands of Americans now working rather than living off welfare benefits such as unemployment insurance or monies for families with young children. But the jury still remains out on whether the economic boom really helped the most impoverished families in America.

SOCIOLOGICAL PERSPECTIVES ON THE POWER OF THE STATE TODAY

Much of the controversy among political sociologists in recent years has been over the nature of the state not as a war-making but as a welfare-providing state. While all observers agree that the American welfare state operates in a less generous fashion than others, there remain questions about the reasons for its different character. Theda Skocpol, for example, has argued that American welfare policy is the result of "polity-initiated decisions," a number of which took place before the actual policies developed and implemented by the Roosevelt administration (see Chapter 3).[23] She insists that the United States was on a course to create strong welfare measures, such as pensions for widows and Civil War veterans, but that such decisions came to nothing because of the political efforts directed against them early in the twentieth century. For her, the source and origins of the American welfare state, however limited it might be, lay in the efforts of political associations and state managers to develop coherent policies. Central to her argument is that such policies were being fashioned well before the years of the Great Depression and the material misery suffered by many Americans. Hence, she concludes, it was state officials, and a broader body of political figures, who were responsible in the end for the welfare measures adopted during the 1930s. The timing of the development and adoption of the measures is critical for her argument.

G. William Domhoff counters her view by insisting that the origins, and limits, of welfare policy in America can be traced directly to the actions not of the state and its managers, but rather of its business groups and the corporate community.[24] Domhoff argues, for example, that the Social Security Act of 1935 was a product not of the Roosevelt administration per se but rather of self-interested business figures in the administration and business organizations in the United States. He writes about old-age pensions that

> the experts who wrote it were direct employees of one of the most powerful upper-class families of the day, the Rockefellers;...several top executives supported the plan;...the level of benefits was tied to salary level, thus preserving the values established in the labor market; there were no government contributions from

general taxes, an exclusion that business leaders insisted on; (and) there were both employer and employee contributions to old-age pensions, which business leaders insisted on.[25]

A variant of this view is that of sociologist Jill Quadagno, who insists that it was class-related issues that produced limits to the welfare policies of the United States government. Quadagno argues that "the struggle for old age pensions (in the United States) was part of a broader process of class struggle, shaped first within the marketplace and later within the electoral-representative political system."[26]

This is one of those important debates that is difficult to resolve on the basis of the available evidence because each view uses somewhat different evidence to furnish support for its argument. Domhoff emphasizes the immediate business backgrounds of state officials who helped to draw up the old age pension plan as part of the Social Security Act, whereas Skocpol emphasizes the policies and ideas about pensions developed well before the Roosevelt administration took office. Skocpol also argues that the limited character of the American welfare state springs not from the power of business, but from the political contests early in the twentieth century. These were contests won by the political parties and organizations that opposed, for a variety of reasons, benefits such as workers' pensions.

In this debate we have our own preference—the state-centered view. One important reason is quite simple and basic. People who occupy the major offices of the government are bound, by the nature of their office, to promote the interests of the government, or state. Their tenure, indeed their success, rests on their ability to do promote these interests. Granted, many such officials come from the business community, as in the case of the very effective former Secretary of the Treasury, Robert Rubin, a former Wall Street banker. Such officials are compelled to take a view of the state as a player in world politics and the world economy. They act, in effect, to further the interests of the state. If they did not, they, and their associates, would quickly be out of office.

Yet we also would argue that the power of the American state, and its officials, is indeed constrained, limited by its own history and structure and by contending powers in America. The institution of the American state does not exercise near the power of the state wielded by the People's Republic of China or by the various authoritarian regimes throughout the world. Business has a far greater presence in America than in many other nations. Nevertheless, while the business community can limit what the state can do, it cannot initiate and pursue new policies and actions. Those remain the prerogatives of the state.

Moreover, the power of the state compared to that of business can vary from one time period to another. Clearly during the 1930s the American state exercised great power over the nation; it was responsible in large part for bringing the country out of the depths of the Great Depression. During the economic prosperity of the 1990s, however, the business community grew more forceful and prominent in American politics than ever—far more than during the years of the Cold War when state officials were forced to exercise much greater authority. Just how important the business community has been, and may become, is the issue we take up in our next section.

The Power of Business and Corporations

When Alexis de Tocqueville wrote of the nature of equality in America, he identified three major features of the society that could pose threats to such equality (see Chapter 4). One, of course, was the element of race. Though white Americans, especially males, enjoyed unparalleled freedom, especially as compared to their counterparts in Europe, black Americans and Native Americans, alike, suffered at the hands of the whites. Another possible threat was that of the *tyranny of the majority*, a threat that lay in the fact that in a society where everyone was deemed equal, decisions would rest with the majority opinion, which, by definition, carried the most weight. But the major threat, in Tocqueville's eyes, lurked in the form of business. Business and great industry posed a potential threat to equality because, like social class in Europe, they held the potential to undermine democracy through the unequal distribution of material wealth. Tocqueville may have been a great believer in democracy, but he also was a practical enough thinker to realize that there were no real barriers to preventing wealth from exercising its influence over politics.

Many observers have come to realize that great wealth can, and has influenced, the course of politics in America. The historian, David Potter, for instance, acknowledged that one of the features that enabled the American political system to run as well as it has, and to survive many obstacles over the course of two hundred years, has been its history of affluence and wealth.[27] America has had more than its share of natural resources on which to draw, including an abundance of land and territory, and it has been able to make its way, relying as much on domestic markets as on its success in invading markets abroad. Even today, America stands out for its prosperity, able to withstand the difficulties of a global economy even as other nations struggle abroad.

But prosperity and wealth are not equally divided among Americans, nor have they been. By the early part of the twentieth century, it had become clear that large business organizations would furnish the direction to the American economy, and that they would do so based upon their ability to accumulate and invest financial resources. The pioneering work to identify that trend was the singular book by Adolf Berle, Jr. and Gardiner Means, entitled *The Modern*

Corporation and Private Property.[28] Berle and Means took note of a startling fact—that much of the business conducted in the American marketplace was done at the time by very large firms. In fact, they observed that a comparatively small number of such firms actually controlled a disproportionate amount of the assets in each of several fields. For instance, in 1929, shortly before the crash on Wall Street that resulted in the Great Depression, 130 of 573 companies that did business on the New York Stock Exchange could be classified as corporations. Furthermore, these 130 companies controlled fully 80 percent of the assets in the market. In fact, it appears from research done by sociologist William Roy that the tendency for corporations to become the real players in the American economy had begun decades before, as a number of corporations began to accumulate large amounts of resources and to overshadow the wealth of other businesses.[29] Today virtually all sociologists take for granted that the dominant players in the modern economy are not people, but rather large corporations and, among them, those corporations that control the greatest amount of assets.

The lopsided distribution of resources, which Berle and Means uncovered in the 1920s, continues to be a prominent part of the American economy. In the early 1980s, for example, there were about 260,000 manufacturing firms in the United States. Only a handful of them, 657, actually controlled 80 percent of the assets of all manufacturing firms. Likewise, there were about 15,000 commercial banks at the time, of which 478 held 63 percent of the assets of all banks. Moreover, the concentration of resources has grown over the decades: in 1950, the 200 largest manufacturing firms held 48 percent of the assets of all such firms, but by the early 1980s, the 200 largest firms held 61 percent of the assets of all firms.[30] In the prosperous 1990s, the trends continued in the same direction: although the economy boomed and jobs were abundant, large corporations continued to control most of the assets and resources.

Able to control such resources, it is the large corporations, everyone agrees, that can exercise the most clout in the American market. But even if they do exercise control over assets and wealth, it is the nature of the market, so the argument goes, that such corporations are in competition with one another. Berle and Means, having exposed the vast wealth of a few large corporations, went on to make another startling argument—that control of corporations had moved out of the hands of a few rich families, like the DuPonts and the Rockefellers, into the hands of managers and shareholders. It was the managers of the corporations, Berle and Means claimed, who actually now controlled the destiny of corporate wealth in America.

But are managers, working more or less in competition and in isolation from one another, controlling the destiny of the large firms? It is in answer to this and related questions that sociologists have reached some of their most important discoveries in recent years.

THE CORPORATE COMMUNITY

The largest corporations in America today not only control a vast amount of
wealth and resources, but they also are part of what G. William Domhoff calls a
"corporate community."[31] This community has taken form because of the social
networks that bind one large corporation to another. Sometimes such networks
happen as a result of friendships between or schools and clubs attended by members of the larger corporations. But most often the networks occur at the highest
decision-making level of the corporation—the board of directors. Various studies by sociologists over the past two decades document these networks, or what
are called "interlocking directorates."[32]

In a recent version of his writings on power and authority in America,
Domhoff studied the corporate interlocks among the top 1,029 corporations
in America, based upon the level of their assets. Among these wealthy corporations, including General Motors, Coca-Cola, and Kmart, Domhoff found a
surprisingly large number of overlapping memberships among individuals. For
example, people who sat on the board of the Chase Manhattan Bank held 48
similar positions among the top corporations. Altogether, about 20 percent of
the top firms had extensive ties with other firms by virtue of the interlocking
memberships on their boards of directors.[33]

Even within the corporate community, some players may be more significant to the activities of the market than others. There is an old argument, which
can be traced back to the writings of Rudolf Hilferding, that says as modern
capitalism grows and develops, financial capital will be more important than
other kinds (see Chapter 10).[34] Hilferding argued that financial capital helps to
open new markets abroad for domestic firms, and that even in domestic markets
it plays a key role in promoting the development of new firms. Domhoff's study
reveals that a number of banks were among the most connected of corporations, including Chase Manhattan, Bank of America, and Wells Fargo.

Sociologist Richard Ratcliff was among the first sociologists to document
Hilferding's general thesis in a series of important studies of firms in the St.
Louis area. Ratcliff found, for example, that while many local manufacturing
firms began to decline during the 1970s and 1980s, local financial firms continued to flourish, largely because of the investments they were able to make in
new markets and developments outside of St. Louis. He notes that the

> evidence thus suggests that Saint Louis, despite its image as a declining older
> industrial metropolis, was actually producing a net capital surplus that was depos-
> ited in the major banks and then exported for investment elsewhere, presumably to
> the Sunbelt and other high growth areas.[35]

Sociologists Michael Schwartz and Beth Mintz have also uncovered similar evidence of the key role of financial institutions among American corporations. They found that banks and savings and loan associations appear to stand at the center of corporate interlocks among corporations, though their power is limited by market forces and by the autonomy of various industries. Yet they concluded that the "portrait that emerges is that of a loosely structured system which follows the dictates of the market but under the leadership of the money market commercial banks."[36]

THE CORPORATE INNER CIRCLE

The significance of the corporate community in America and its actions received its most sophisticated and sustained attention by the sociologist Michael Useem. In research among corporations and their leaders in the United States and Great Britain, Useem uncovered evidence of several forms of corporate community. He relied on interviews with members of various boards of directors, conducted in 1979 and 1980, and on data about the largest corporations.[37]

Useem's main discovery was of an *inner circle* among the members of the boards of directors—a kind of core group or central elite. The inner circle members were those who were at the center of the social and business networks. They also possessed a decidedly different view of the business and political world than their contemporaries. Thinking not of their own particular corporate or business interests, they sought to view the "bigger picture" of the world, taking what Useem refers to as a *classwide* scan. This meant that they thought in broader and more general terms about politics than other directors. Moreover, Useem adds that developing the inner circle is a crowing moment in the development of modern capitalism. At the end of the nineteenth century, families like the Rockefellers were in control of firms. Then came the managerial revolution, identified by Berle and Means, and managerial capitalism. At the close of the twentieth century, Useem sees an emergent form of *institutional capitalism*, a form in which business institutions have become dominant and the members of their boards of directors the leading force on behalf of a unified, classwide view of the world.

MULTINATIONAL CORPORATIONS AND THE GROWTH OF THE GLOBAL ECONOMY

In the early 1960s, long before there was talk of a global economy, there was talk of something else—the multinational corporation whose power extended beyond the boundaries of nation-states.

These firms, variously called transnational, multinational, or even global, corporations, exemplified especially by firms like Exxon, General Motors

Corporation (GM), International Telephone and Telegraph (IT&T), and International Business Machines Corporation (IBM), introduced an even more novel phenomenon, but one entirely consistent with the forecast by Berle and Means. Operating in more than one nation, they not only rivaled the economic resources of some nation-states, but it seems they could operate free of any meaningful sanctions or penalties by the nation-states themselves. Richard Barnet and Ronald Müller, co-authors of the definitive treatment of these organizations, quote the president of the IBM World Trade Corporation, who declared:

> For business purposes the boundaries that separate one nation from another are no more real than the equator. They are merely convenient demarcations of ethnic, linguistic, and cultural entities. They do not define business requirements or consumer trends. Once management understands and accepts this world economy, its view of the marketplace—and its planning—necessarily expand.

The same author concludes by remarking that the "world outside the home country is no longer viewed as a series of disconnected customers and prospects for its products, but as an extension of a single market."[38]

With the collapse of the Soviet Union and the opening of new democracies like South Africa, the large multinational corporations now exercise considerable influence throughout the world. Such corporations include IBM, McDonalds, and a wide variety of firms that now seek to make profits in worldwide markets. Such firms act as the spearheads of capitalism and penetrate new markets easily. Many such corporations, moreover, are financial ones that invest in the new markets abroad. In fact, it is their investments, or the withdrawal of them, that may have helped to account for the financial collapse of a number of the Asian economies over the past decade.[39]

DOES AMERICA POSSESS A RULING CLASS—OR EVEN A DOMINANT CLASS?

Recall Marx's image of the ruling class. It is a class of capitalists who exercise power not only over markets, but also over the running of the state. The state rules on its behalf. The state makes policies that further the interests of the capitalists. Such policies would include minimal capital gains taxes, providing only a small dent in the earnings of people of great wealth. They would also include policies that exercise limited control over the business dealings of corporations.

But there are all sorts of questions that arise in trying to determine the existence of a ruling class that, in effect, runs the machinery of state. How does the ruling class operate? It certainly does not operate as it would in the early days of the "robber barons," when the wealthy moguls of America seemed to control the fate of its citizens. If the corporate community lies at its center, how does the community make its influence felt? Moreover, if there is a ruling class at work, why do large corporate chieftains, like Microsoft boss Bill Gates, get called to Washington to defend the practices of their companies against the charge of monopoly? These are the kinds of questions that must be asked, and for which the evidence must be uncovered, to prove that America is run by a ruling class.

Several methods of inquiry have been developed to try to learn whether such a ruling class exists. One method for discovery, on which G. William Domhoff relies, is to find evidence of some kind of social networks that link the corporate chieftains to the rulers of state.[40] Presumably, if there are such networks, of the same kind found at the highest levels of the largest corporations, this provides *prima facie* evidence of a community of interest, even if it does tell us how the influence flows—whether from the corporate leaders to the leaders of state, or in the other direction. The best work along these lines has been furnished by sociologist Gwen Moore.[41] Moore and her associates conducted a survey of the leaders of a number of different institutional sectors, including the federal government, in 1971–72. The results showed evidence of communication among a number of leaders in each sector, along with the presence of over thirty social cliques, consisting of 227 men and women, all of whom possessed relationships with one another, as well as crucial links to other cliques. This inner group, drawn largely from the members of Congress, political appointments, and business circles, possessed not only common social ties to one another, Moore found, but in some cases certain of its members belonged to the same social clubs, thereby further contributing to a common sense of purpose.

Another method is to inquire whether the corporate community also acts in concert on matters of state and politics. This is the method that sociologist Mark Mizruchi pursued in his fine analysis of the structure of corporate power in America.[42] Examining a number of top corporations, Mizruchi made a series of inquiries about the nature of the corporate interlocks and the unity on political matters among corporations. He found clear evidence that the largest corporations not only possessed important interlocks but that they also acted in common to make sizable contributions to political campaigns, to provide testimony on business issues to Congress, and to exercise a kind of unified voice in politics. His research, he notes, tends to support the view of Michael Useem about the existence of an inner circle among America's corporations, one that acts in concert in politics.

There is yet additional evidence of a more indirect and circumstantial nature that suggests that the corporate community can exercise great power over the actions of the state. Political action committees, for example, have been the subject of study by sociologists.[43] This research reveals that such committees are very careful about the funds they disburse to candidates and that such funds can make a large impact 0n the course of a campaign. In fact, the financial contributions that the corporate community can make to the political campaigns of different candidates can make a major difference in who runs and who wins—a difference that seems to be increasing rather than diminishing in its effect.

Such is the piecemeal and diverse evidence to suggest that, via social networks and such key elements as campaign contributions, the corporate community can make its great influence felt in the design of American politics. But does it act as a cohesive and coherent ruling class? The evidence at this point is circumstantial but suggestive. From his research on the directors of the top business organizations in the United States and Great Britain, here is the way Useem sums it up:

> The rise of institutional capitalism in the U.S. and U.K. contributed to the rise of more conservative political climates in the early 1980s. Though the new corporate political activity was not decisive, its significance should not be underestimated. A central objective of the business political mobilization on both sides of the Atlantic was to restore company profits to levels of an earlier decade.... The electoral success and political thrust of the Thatcher and Reagan governments were in no small part products of this business venture into politics.... [T]he rise of the new conservative forces that were among the pillars of the Republican and Conservative governments was a product of the formation on both sides of the Atlantic of informal and formal organizational networks linking together most large corporations.[44]

In other words, business represented a substantial force in shaping government policy even in the 1980s.

Our own view of the matter can finally be summed up like this: big business does play a role in American politics, but that role is not as the captain of the ship of state. A more apt image is this: think of the large corporate interests as the winds that fill the sails on the ship of state. State officials steer the ship across the seas, but the corporate community can affect the course that is sailed. Ultimately, however, it is the skill of the sailors, i.e., state officials, and the durability of the ship, i.e., the state, not the winds, that determine where the ship of state will head and where it will land.

Equality and Inequality in Modern America

Any assessment of the nature and structure of power in modern America must come to grips with the prevailing inequalities among individuals in the society. Wealth is not distributed equally, as we have seen in the case of corporate power, nor has it ever been. And in the past decade or so, during a period of record high employment rates during peacetime, the differences between the wealthy families and the poorest families have been increasing rather than diminishing.

ECONOMIC INEQUALITY

In a society in which capitalism is the dominant force in the economy, economic inequalities are likely to arise. In the early years of modern industrial capitalism in America, the inequalities were sharp and deep. Certain families, founders of great corporations like Standard Oil or the plutocrats like Andrew Carnegie and J. Pierpont Morgan, held a tremendous amount of wealth. This wealth gave them an ability to exercise influence over both the economy and the polity that was not available to the average American. Most Americans held jobs as members of the working class, many employed in factories or firms engaged in various forms of manual labor.

But as America developed it appeared that the distribution of wealth had evened out. More and more families were now able to move up the ladder of wealth and to join the ranks, if not of the upper classes, surely of the middle classes. By the middle part of the twentieth century, many observers were hailing America not simply as the land of opportunity, but as a land where the middle class had become dominant, thereby making political democracy a reality.[45] The kind of imagery which Alexis de Tocqueville had imagined—of America as a land of equality and freedom for all—seemed to have become a reality just after the close of World War II. Many Americans now were able to move to the suburbs and secure their dream homes. Granted, not all were able to do so. Black Americans, in particular, still suffered from inequality in America, even after slavery had ended.[46] But if the fortunes of blacks could be improved, it appeared that, even in the midst of some inequality, the fortunes of the great majority of Americans were prospering, giving rise to the image of America as an "affluent society."[47]

The corporate wealth of the 1990s should silence those who parade America as a land of equality. For just as corporate wealth has become concentrated in the hands of fewer and fewer large corporations, so, too, there are dangerous signs of a growing economic inequality in America—between the very rich and the very poor.[48] Since the 1970s, America has become home to a large "underclass," in the words of William Julius Wilson, a noted sociologist.[49] The underclass is made up of black Americans who live in the inner cities of the major metropolitan areas of the United States. These are people, often unmarried women with young children, who over a period of several decades became part of a large group of people dependent on the state for their resources. Many were people who simply did not have the skills to work, but most, particularly the men, were unemployed because jobs had left the American city. There developed a growing class of the unemployed, left inside the American city, with little access, either because of education or residence, to the new fortunes that had grown up on the fringe areas, in the edge cities, of the American metropolis (see also Chapter 8.)

The early indications are that, with high rates of employment, many of the members of the underclass are now securing jobs, able to support their families in ways they were not able to do so before. Special programs, in the states of Wisconsin and Pennsylvania, reveal that with intensive help and aid, many of the underclass who previously lived off the state now have joined the workforce and are able to bring home salary checks. But many of their jobs tend to be temporary. While work has provided such people with a new sense of self-esteem, the tenure of their employment still remains in question.

In addition, even while the underclass has seen improvements, there is a growing concentration of wealth at the very top of American society—a disparity that is growing between the wealth of the richest Americans and that of the poorest. A 1999 report by the Center on Budget and Policy Priorities, a nonprofit organization in Washington, DC, finds that the "gap between rich and poor has grown into an economic chasm so wide that this year the richest 2.7 million Americans, the top 1 percent, will have as many after-tax dollars to spend as the bottom 100 million."[50] Even more significantly, just as the American welfare state has been less generous than that of other welfare states in the twentieth century, so, too, the economic inequality in America is more pronounced today than that of other Western nations. Edward N. Wolff, an economics professor at New York University, notes that the United States is "the most unequal industrialized country, in terms of income and wealth, and we're growing more unequal faster than the other industrialized nations."[51]

America thus is not a society of economic equals, where wealth is evenly distributed. And as the inequality increases, what will happen to the society as a whole? Will a growing number of Americans become disenchanted with the society? Or will they simply be content to live with the economic disparities? It was such inequalities, you will recall, that Marx believed would cause the end of modern capitalism. But they have not, and one of the reasons they have not is because of the other key feature of American society. This is the opportunity to be able to exercise a kind of freedom and voice in politics that, however imperfect, is a far cry from the oppression of people under other regimes, particularly totalitarian ones.

POLITICAL EQUALITY

One of the crucial facts about the nature of Western democracies over the course of the twentieth century is this: citizenship, the very essence of democratic rights, has been extended to an ever-growing number of people and groups. One of the most famous arguments along these lines is that of T. H. Marshall.[52] His argument has been seen as the underlying rationale and groundwork for the development of the welfare state in the twentieth century. He proposed that there were three sets of rights: civil rights, or the rights of individuals under the law; economic rights, or the rights of individuals to labor and to work; and social rights, or the rights of individuals to be entitled as citizens to support and benefits provided by the state. He further claimed that these rights gradually became granted by the state over the course of three centuries, culminating in the provision of social rights during the course of the twentieth century. Although there are those who take issue with some of his claims, Marshall's key insight is that as Western democracies have developed, citizenship rights have been expanded and extended, both in terms of what individuals can expect as citizens and in terms of the broad array of groups covered under the terms of citizenship. A similar argument has been made by the sociologist Michael Schudson. Countering the view of many sociologists, Schudson argues that America has become increasingly a rights-based nation, one in which rights have been extended over time to more and more groups of people.[53] It is this rights-based society that, from my point of view, provides the foundations that limit the impact of economic inequalities on the lives of average Americans. Sharp economic differences are critical to the lives of people, but if people also believe they have the freedom to move ahead, the inequalities will never appear as sharp or sting as much.

The meaning of citizenship in the United States has almost from the very first been defined in terms of equality. The Declaration of Independence proclaimed that all men are created equal and that they are by nature free to pursue ends of their own chose. Decades later, Alexis de Tocqueville declared that Americans seemed to feel themselves the social equal of one another, and this had come about, he further suggested, because America avoided the obstacles inherited from a feudal past. That very same theme was articulated a century later by the great Swedish economist Gunnar Myrdal. He claimed that the central foundations of American society had been erected on the fundamental notion that all people were created equal. Yet he went on to observe that while true in principle, in fact there was considerable inequality in the United States, particularly between the races.[54]

Myrdal in some sense turned out to be the more accurate observer. Even while Tocqueville was claiming evidence for the presence of considerable social and political equality in the United States, many people did not share in it. In the mid–nineteenth century slavery still remained widespread, and only men could exercise the principal right of citizenship, that of suffrage. Not until the twentieth century did the idea of equality come to be extended to the great majority of people, and it happened because they were claimed to be citizens, thereby entitled to exercise certain basis constitutional rights.

Citizenship in the twentieth century has become expanded in the first instance through the extension of certain fundamental rights to ever larger and more varied types of people. The passage in 1918, for example, of the Nineteenth Amendment to the Constitution meant the guarantee that women now could exercise the right to voteand thus join their male counterparts after being deprived for almost one hundred and fifty years. In 1948, the armed forces became integrated by a presidential order, putting black and white combat troops on an equal social footing for the first time in American history. Yet the major breakthrough so far as the extension of citizenship rights was concerned took place with the Supreme Court decision in the case of *Brown v. Topeka* in 1954, the famous ruling on school desegregation. Under the guiding hand of Earl Warren, the Court decided that no black American should be denied the right to an education equivalent of that of whites, and it thus declared that public schools should become desegregated "with all deliberate speed."

The decision of the Court proved historic in more than one sense, for by overturning the earlier ruling in the case of *Plessy v. Ferguson*, the case in which the Court decided in 1896 that Plessy, a black man, was not entitled to travel in the same public accommodations as whites, it proclaimed that black Americans were entitled to equal treatment before the law *simply* and *primarily* because they were citizens of the United States. That legal interpretation, together with subsequent congressional decisions in the Civil Rights Acts of 1964 and 1965, served to shore up the extension of citizenship to black Americans. At the same time, the implications of those actions were that no citizens could be deprived of equal and fair treatment in education, politics, or even in such public domains as housing and public accommodations on the basis of their race, color, or creed. By implication, then, other non-Anglo groups, such as Hispanic Americans and Native Americans, fell under the rule of these new laws and the new interpretation of the Constitution; thus, like blacks, they too came to benefit from the extension of citizenship to all.

Soon, the movements inspired by these historic legal and congressional decisions worked to the advantage of the largest minority group in America— women. Working hard and long hours, many women together with their male supporters managed to get an Equal Rights Amendment passed by the Congress. This further ensured that the rights of citizenship would be extended to women much along the same lines they had been expanded for religious and racial minorities; that women, too, could not be subject to any type of occupational discrimination based simply upon their sex. Yet, the battle for full and complete citizenship for women is likely to be the longest and most difficult; this became clear when the necessary number of state legislatures failed to ratify the Equal Rights Amendment, and thus it did not become law. On balance, however, a greater variety of people, including women, can enjoy the benefits of citizenship and the implementation of the constitutional provisions for equal treatment and opportunity than in times past.

The extension of citizenship in the twentieth century took another, more profound turn. Until the 1954 Supreme Court decision, citizenship only included the most minimal kinds of rights. In the case of women, for example, it only meant the right to vote; even in the case of black Americans, until the 1954 Court ruling, citizenship only covered, in a limited fashion, suffrage. The more significant meaning, then, of the 1954 decision was that citizenship now came to take on a new meaning—people regarded as citizens of the United States were now to be further guaranteed, as part of their constitutional heritage, a right to receive the same education as one another. The philosophy of "separate but equal" claimed legitimate in 1896 now was deemed to be invalid; true citizenship meant the full and complete implementation of the notion of equality, taking in the widest possible spectrum of the social domain. In light of this reinterpretation, and fundamental extension, of the meaning of citizenship, it only could be a matter of time until citizenship actually took on a more substantial form. It is in this regard, then, that the congressional acts of the 1960s served simply to secure the 1954 Supreme Court ruling. Moreover, this very same period of the 1950s and 1960s witnessed additional elaboration upon the basic redefinition of the meaning of citizenship. Thus, with the passage of the various welfare measures in the 1960s, the Johnson administration was not merely creating a dependent population, as some social critics have claimed.[55] In fact, the administration was saying, in effect, that citizenship in the United States now not only furnished a person the chance to live, to work, and to be educated—by themselves an extraordinary extension of rights—but it also guaranteed a certain minimum standard of living to those people, who, for whatever reasons, were unable to secure one for themselves.

The effort to extend the rights of citizens to larger and larger segments of the American community continues apace. Over the course of the following three decades new policies were effected that were intended to secure and protect the rights of citizens. Such measures included the American Disabilities Act of 1991, new policies to protect women against sexual harassment in the workplace, and a number of other new policies. A very minimal interpretation, thus, of citizenship at the beginning of the twentieth century has, since that time, turned out to be an extraordinarily broad one.

But all is not rosy for the rights of citizenship in America. Two portentous signs on the horizon involve efforts designed to counter the extension of the liberal ethos in America. One is the controversy that has arisen about the matter of affirmative action. In the 1970s new guidelines came down from the federal government designed to protect the rights of groups that were historic minorities in America. In particular, they were guidelines designed to enable black Americans to secure opportunity in arenas that were denied them in the past, especially in terms of entrance to forms of higher education. Many colleges and universities adopted such guidelines and proceeded to admit black applicants when the qualifications of such applicants were roughly comparable to those of white applicants. Litigation was brought against such affirmative action guidelines that challenged the principle, in particular, the famous challenge offered in the case of Allan Bakke in 1978. Bakke had been denied admission to the Medical School of the University of California at Davis, even though his credentials were as good as those of a number of minority applicants who were admitted ahead of him. In their ruling on this case, the Supreme Court argued that the Davis Medical School could not, in effect, discriminate against Bakke by admitting minority applicants less qualified than him, and therefore ruled that he had to be admitted. Nevertheless, the case did not establish a clear rejection of the general affirmative action guidelines; later federal laws even managed to sustain the intent of affirmative action policies.

By the mid-1990s there were serious challenges to affirmative action, however. A federal court ruled, for example, that the University of Texas could no longer provide special consideration of blacks and Hispanics in the admission to law school. The effect initially was quite dramatic, resulting in many fewer applications and admissions. In California, an action by the Board of Regents also had the same chilling effect: applications and admissions from minority candidates were down. The controversy continues, however. And there is no end in sight. Affirmative action was a set of policies designed to extend the rights of citizens in ways previously denied them. Challenges to affirmative action are seen as challenges to the whole extension of citizenship. Moreover, recent efforts in California to limit the benefits available to recent immigrants, particularly undocumented immigrants, further reveal the challenge that now exists in the United States in a century that has become known as the century of citizenship—through the welfare state and other such measures.

America, like many other Western countries, now finds itself at a turning point. Immigration, for example, will continue, and probably increase as various barriers to immigration come down. Since 1965, and the initiation of the new immigration law in the United States, millions of immigrants have come to this country. Their very presence here poses some fundamental challenges and issues for the coming century. Will citizenship rights be rolled back, and will they become limited to only certain groups of immigrants? How will America as a whole deal with the vast new groups of immigrants? What will happen in the process to the situation of black Americans, the largest minority group now, but by the year 2050 second to the Hispanic population?

The presence of the new immigrants, coupled with the continuing economic troubles of black Americans, will once again test the fundamental tenet of American democracy, that of the breadth and depth of equality. Will equality be limited, as it was during de Tocqueville's time, only to certain groups? Or will it be extended to greater and greater numbers of people? This is *the* American dilemma: and it is one that cannot be avoided.

Conclusion

America has been seen as both the land of economic opportunity and the site of great corporate giants, organizational plutocrats of the twentieth century. It is a place where citizens are free to exercise their rights to vote, to engage in free speech, and to assemble for peaceful purposes, but it also is a country in which the modern state can exercise great, even decisive, power over the course of world events.

Different sociological observers treat different features of American society and history as though they were the only features. Neo-Marxists, and even those who are not, such as G. William Domhoff, believe there is a dominant class, a group of corporate powers that more or less run the country. Theda Skocpol and her followers maintain in contrast that the modern American state is the essential locus of power and the agency that drives the country forward, particularly during times of great national crisis. Alexis de Tocqueville, and those who have adopted his point of view, including Gunnar Myrdal, point to the essence of America in the emphasis on equality and equality of opportunity for all people. Such opportunity, even if imperfectly granted, clearly expanded over the course of the twentieth century.

Each view can find some support and comfort for itself in the actual empirical evidence we have at hand. And perhaps that is the main point. As a large and massive international force at the beginning of the twenty-first century, America is complex. Its laws insist on equality and guard against infringements on the rights of others; but many of the forces that drive it are forces of considerable resources that aim to gain for themselves and not for the larger public. Capitalist democracy, even in a nation known as the best in an imperfect world, is not a simple matter.

NOTES

1. Charles A. Beard, *An Economic Interpretation of the Constitution of the United States* (New York: Free Press, 1935; 1965).

2. Robert A. Dahl, *Who Governs? Democracy and Power in an American City* (New Haven, CT: Yale University Press, 1961).

3. C. Wright Mills, *The Power Elite* (New York: Oxford University Press, 1959).

4. Edward Banfield, *Political Influence* (New York: Free Press, 1961); Wallace S. Sayre and Herbert Kaufman, *Governing New York City* (New York: Russell Sage Foundation, 1961).

5. Paul Baran and Paul Sweezy, *Monopoly Capitalism: An Essay on the American Economic and Social Order* (New York: Monthly Review Press, 1968).

6. G. William Domhoff, in his book, *Who Rules America?*, insists on a distinction between the ruling class and the dominant class (his version) about power in America. The chief difference, as I understand it, is that his view insists on a looser coordination among the components of the class view. That is, there is not a close and intimate correspondence between the interests and dominance of the class and the actions by political leaders. But the difference is only one of degree; his argument, for all intents and purposes, is closely similar to the argument advanced by Marx in the last century.

7. See, for example, Peter Evans, Dietrich Rueschemeyer, and Theda Skocpol (eds.), *Bringing the State Back In* (Cambridge, MA: Cambridge University Press, 1985).

8. Bertrand Badie and Pierre Birnbaum, *The Sociology of the State* (Chicago: University of Chicago Press, 1983).

9. Stephen Skowronek, *Building a New American State: The Expansion of National Administrative Capacities 1877–1920* (Cambridge, UK: Cambridge University Press, 1982).

10. See Julio Cotler and Richard R. Fagen, eds., *Latin America and the United States: The Changing Political Realities* (Stanford, CA: Stanford University Press, 1974).

11. Arthur M. Schlesinger, Jr., *The Imperial Presidency* (New York: Popular Library, 1974).

12. Richard J. Barnett, *Roots of War* (Baltimore, MD: Penguin Books, 1972).

13. This most recent history of the American presidency as a war-making machine is based upon the following sources: Peter W. Galbraith, *The End of Iraq: How American Incompetence Created a War Without End* (New York: Simon & Schuster Paperbacks, 2006); Michael Isikoff and David Corn, *Hubris: The Inside Story of Spin, Scandal, and the Selling of the Iraq War* (New York: Three Rivers Press, 2006, 2007); Kenneth M. Pollack, *The Threatening Storm: The United States and Iraq: The Crisis, the Strategy, and the Prospects After Saddam* (New York: Random House, 2002); and Thomas E. Ricks, *Fiasco: The American Military Adventure in Iraq* (New York: Penquin Books, 2006, 2007). While all these books are very informative, the most thoughtful and intelligent treatment is that by Hicks.

14. Bob Woodward and Carl Bernstein, *The Final Days* (New York: Simon & Schuster, 1976).

15. *Statistical Abstract of the United States*, 1980, Tables 432 and 436.

16. David Wise and Thomas B. Ross, *The Invisible Government* (New York: Random House, 1974); Bob Woodward, *Veil: The Secret Wars of the CIA, 1981–87* (New York: Simon & Schuster, 1987); Scott D. Breckinridge, *CIA and the Cold War* (Westport, CT: Praeger Publishers, 1993).

17. The best and most comprehensive examination of the history of the CIA is to be found in the recent book *Legacy of Ashes: The History of the CIA* (New York: Doubleday, 2007), by Tim Weiner. Weiner provides a detailed account of the workings of the CIA from its origins in the 1940s to its most recent activities. All the many clandestine operations of the CIA are detailed therein, the evidence coming from a variety of internal CIA reports as well as other government documents that only became available in the past several years.

18. See, for example, Gary T. Marx, "Thoughts on a Neglected Category of Social Movement Participants: The Agent Provocateur and the Informant," *American Journal of Sociology*, 80 (September 1974), 402–421; and James Rule, Douglas McAdam, Linda Stearns, and David Uglow, *The Politics of Privacy* (New York: New American Library, 1980).

19. Gary Marx, "The Agent Provocateur and the Informant;" also see more generally, Gary T. Marx, *Undercover: Police Surveillance in America* (Berkeley, CA: University of California Press, 1988).

20. For some recent discussion, see Rodney Lowe, *The Welfare State in Britain Since 1945* (London: Macmillan, 1993); John Brown, *The British Welfare State: A Critical History* (Oxford: Basil Blackwell, 1995); Gosta Esping-Andersen (ed.), *Welfare States in Transition: National Adaptations in Global Economies* (London: Sage Publishers, 1996).

21. Gosta Esping-Andersen, "After the Golden Age? Welfare State Dilemmas in a Global Economy," in Esping-Andersen, ibid., 1–31.

22. John P. Stephens, "The Scandanavian Welfare States: Achievements, Crisis and Prospects," in Esping-Andersen, ibid., 32–65.

23. Theda Skocpol, *Protecting Soldiers and Mothers: The Political Origins of Social Policy in the United States* (Cambridge, MA: The Belknap Press of Harvard University Press, 1992).

24. G. William Domhoff, *Who Rules America? Power and Politics in the Year 2000*, 3rd ed. (Mountain View, CA: Mayfield Publishing Company, 1998).

25. Ibid., p. 272.

26. Jill Quadagno, *The Transformation of Old Age Security: Class and Politics in the American Welfare State* (Chicago: University of Chicago Press, 1988), 189.

27. David M. Potter, *People of Plenty: Economic Abundance and the American Character* (Chicago: University of Chicago Press, 1954).

28. Adolph A. Berle and Gardiner C. Means, *The Modern Corporation and Private Property*, revised edition (New York: Harcourt Brace Jovanovich, 1968).

29. William Roy, *Socializing Capital: The Rise of the Large Industrial Corporation in America* (Princeton, NJ: Princeton University Press, 1997).

30. *Statistical Abstract of the United States*, 1986, Tables 821 and 893.

31. Domhoff, *Who Rules America?*, Chapter 2.

32. On important early work, see Michael Patrick Allen, "The Structure of Interorganizational Elite Co-optation: Interlocking Corporate Directorates," *American Sociological Review*, 39 (June 1974), 393–406; Michael Patrick Allen, "Management Control in the Large Corporation: Comment on Zeitlin," *American Journal of Sociology*, 81 (January 1976), 885–94; Maurice Zeitlin, "Corporate Ownership and Control: The

Large Corporation and the Capitalist Class," *American Journal of Sociology*, 79 (March 1974), 1073–119; and Maurice Zeitlin, "On Class Theory of the Large Corporation: Response to Allen," *American Journal of Sociology*, 81 (January 1976), 894–903. On somewhat later work see Michael Schwartz (ed.), *The Structure of Power in America: The Corporate Elite As a Ruling Class* (New York: Holmes and Meier, 1987), Part I; and Mark S. Mizruchi and Michael Schwartz (eds.), *Intercorporate Relations: The Structural Analysis of Business* (Cambridge, MA: Cambridge University Press, 1987).

For a careful assessment of network interlocks in the corporate sphere, see Mark S. Mizruchi, "What Do Interlocks Do? An Analysis, Critique and Assessment of Research on Interlocking Directorates," *Annual Review of Sociology* (1996), Volume 22, 271–98.

33. Domhoff, *Who Rules America?*, 36 ff.
34. Rudolf Hilferding, *Das Finanzkapital* (Vienna: I. Brand, 1910).
35. Richard Ratcliff, "The Inner Circle and Bank Lending Policy," in Schwartz (ed.), *The Structure of Power in America*, 154.
36. Beth Mintz and Michael Schwartz, "Corporate Interlocks, Financial Hegemony, and Intercorporate Coordination," in Schwartz, ibid., 34–47.
37. Michael Useem, *The Inner Circle: Large Corporations and the Rise of Business Political Activity in the U.S. and U.K.* (New York: Oxford University Press, 1984).
38. Richard J. Barnet and Ronald E. Muller, *Global Reach and the Power of the Multinational Corporations* (New York: Simon & Schuster, 1974), 14–15.
39. James Bearden, "Financial Hegemony, Social Capital and Bank Boards of Directors," in Schwartz (ed.), *The Structure of Power in America*, 48–59.
40. G. William Domhoff, *Who Rules America?*, Chapter 2.
41. Gwen Moore, "The Structure of a National Elite Network," *American Sociological Review*, 44 (October 1979), 673–92.
42. Mark S. Mizruchi, *The Structure of Corporate Political Action: Interfirm Relations and Their Consequences* (Cambridge, MA.: Harvard University Press, 1992).
43. Dan Clawson, Alan Neustadtl, and Denise Scott, *Money Talks: Corporate PACs and Political Influence* (New York: Basic Books, 1992).
44. Michael Useem, *The Inner Circle*, op. cit., 192.
45. Essentially this is the interpretation taken by Seymour Martin Lipset. See Seymour Martin Lipset, "Some Social Requisites of Democracy," *American Political Science Review*, vol. 53 (March 1959), 69–105.
46. See, for example, Gunnar Myrdal, *An American Dilemma: The Negro in A White Nation*, Volumes I and II (New York: McGraw-Hill, 1944; 1962).
47. John Kenneth Galbraith, *The Affluent Society* (Boston: Houghton Mifflin 1958).
48. Edward N. Wolff, *Top Heavy: A Study of the Increasing Inequality of Wealth in America* (New York: Twentieth Century Fund Press, 1995).
49. William Julius Wilson, *The Truly Disadvantaged: The Inner City, the Underclass, and Public Policy* (Chicago: University of Chicago Press, 1987).
50. David Cay Johnston, "Gap Between Rich and Poor Found Substantially Wider," *The New York Times*, Sunday, September 5, 1999, 14Y.
51. As quoted in *The New York Times*, Monday, April 17, 1995, A1, C4. For other recent data on the inequality of wealth in the United States and other nations, see Denny

Braun, *The Rich Get Richer: The Rise of Income Inequality in the U.S. and the World* (Chicago: Nelson Hall, 1997), and the United Nations Human Development Report, 1999.

52. T. H. Marshall, "Citizenship and Social Class," in T. H. Marshall and Tom Bottomore, *Citizenship and Social Class* (London: Pluto Press, 1950; 1992).
53. Michael Schudson, *The Good Citizen: A History of American Civic Life* (New York: The Free Press, 1998).
54. Gunnar Myrdal, *An American Dilemma*, Vol. 1, Chapter 1.
55. Frances Fox Piven and Richard A. Cloward, *Regulating the Poor* (New York: Pantheon, 1971).

Chapter 8

Power and Authority
in the Metropolis

Today, as the world becomes a smaller place, it would seem that many older institutions and structures might lose their influence over our lives. Nation-states, for instance, no longer seem to be such a powerful force. New alliances have formed, erasing old divisions and creating the basis for new, more broad-ranging policies in the future. Consider the case of Western Europe. Here are nations that are several centuries old, with long divisions and conflicts with one another, about to embark on a great economic and political experiment—the European Union. Or consider the case of cities. Once, in the fifteenth and sixteenth centuries, cities wielded great power over the world. Recall the city-states of Venice and Florence. These were medieval empires with their own navies and armies, and they acted like the nation-states of today. But for all their strength and magnificence, they have disappeared, replaced by nations, and today by transnational alliances.

In this chapter we shall ask about the nature of cities and the ways in which they remain important to our lives. We shall argue that cities do, indeed, play an important part in our lives and that the ways they wield power—and we as citizens who live within them wield power—remain significant features of the contemporary world. In some countries, particularly the United States, cities retain a great deal of their power, largely because of the federal structure of the

American government and the local autonomy in the rule of municipalities over many of their own affairs. In other countries the power of the locality is more limited. In Great Britain, for example, the national government controls much of the funding for local communities, and the exercise of politics and power, while quaintly seated in local councils, is really fought out in the House of Commons. But things change. In just the past two decades, for example, the People's Republic of China has witnessed a major shift of control in cities. Special economic zones (SEZs) have been created in which the role of local leaders and businessmen is larger than ever before. In cities like Shanghai, the role of local officials has become ever more important, a startling change from the pre-1978 period under the rule of Mao Zedong.

This chapter will consider the following prominent themes: (1) the nature of the city in American history and how historical changes are reflected in the nature of its politics; (2) the varying and competing theoretical perspectives on cities and politics; and (3) the changing fortunes of cities as the effects of a global economy make themselves ever more present in the lives of citizens living in cities, particularly in the largest cities of the world.

The Metropolis in American History

We begin with a short historical review of cities and American history, furnishing you with a few historical facts before we move into a discussion of theories and analyses of the city. To begin with, the American city has not always been the same, of course. As the structure and institutions of American society have changed, so has the city itself. In part, the changes of the city reflect the changing circumstances of the United States. For example, as the Industrial Revolution of the nineteenth century emerged and swept across America, it naturally influenced cities and their residents. But other changes have taken place in cities, particularly with regard to the uses and abuses of power that are more than simple reflections of broad historical changes. These elements as well as others will be highlighted in our survey of the city in American history.

The Rise and Decline of the Industrial Metropolis

In American history there have been several different forms of the city. In the eighteenth century there was the *mercantilist city*. This was a city in which commerce and local business played a prominent role. The economic philosophy of the day was mercantilism, a philosophy that emphasized the limited role of government and the central significance of commerce to the fortunes of

the city. It was a city of limited size, and even more limited growth. Local government did matter to the fortunes of local residents. It was a city that the historian
Sam Bass Warner, Jr. would characterize as a "walking city."[1] Distances meant
nothing to travel. The city, especially the central part, was small. Residents
could walk anywhere and visit one another often. They came to be neighborly
and to know one another intimately. It was the kind of city that the nineteenth-
century sociologist Ferdinand Toennies and the twentieth-century urbanist
Louis Wirth would commend for its qualities of *Gemeinschaft*, or community:
small, friendly, commercial, sociable.[2] Early Boston and early Philadelphia
represent examples of such a city.

By the middle part of the nineteenth century, however, the nature of
many American cities began to change. They changed under the weight of
the Industrial Revolution, the great revolution that brought about such fundamental transformation to the way business and commerce were conducted
in America and the American city, in particular. Over the course of the next
century, the American city would become, in effect, an industrial city. And the
nature and fortunes of industry would leave their mark deeply etched on the
character of this city.[3]

We can trace the growth and development of the industrial city in terms of
a series of stages. Four stages are evident: (1) a *preindustrial stage* that represents
the early origins of many such cities; (2) an *early industrial stage* in which the
city becomes radically transformed; (3) a *mature industrial stage*, in which the
rapid growth declines and the nature of the city also becomes altered; and (4)
a *stage of incipient decline*, when industry begins to depart the city, looking for
more profits elsewhere, and when the city—and local citizens—begin to face
substantial crises. Each stage has become associated with a different form and
type of politics and governance. In fact, because the stages also are associated
with differences in the form of internal politics, they may also help to explain
why there can be differences among cities at the same point in time.[4]

THE REIGN OF LOCAL NOTABLES AND THE
ENGAGEMENT OF ORDINARY CITIZENS

The first stage of the industrial city was for many the stage of their origins. It
was a time when certain fairly small groups of men dominated the life of the
city. In particular, those people who specialized in the purchase and sale of
land for the city exercised dominance over its business and political life. They
were men who were among the founders of the city. They were the city's earliest
businessmen, and often the most successful. In part, because of their importance to the commerce of the city, their fellow citizens often selected them
to become the first public officials of the city. Thus, in the city of Milwaukee,

Wisconsin, for instance, Byron Kilbourn and Solomon Juneau, among the city's founders, were also among the city's earliest first mayors, but the same pattern—founders and early mayors—characterized other cities at a similar period in their development.[5] Moreover, because the nature of government was primitive and undeveloped—essentially there was no local government—many local citizens became engaged in the activities of the time, giving a sense of genuine commitment to and involvement in the local community. It was at this stage, in the 1830s and 1840s, that Alexis de Tocqueville would come to America, observing what for him was a defining characteristic, the extensive and active participation by Americans in its many forms of associations and politics.[6]

THE INDUSTRIAL REVOLUTION AND RISE OF THE CAPITALIST CLASS

Almost overnight the character of the preindustrial, or commercial, city changed. In many older American cities, this took place in the 1860s and 1870s.[7] There was a great industrial boom, brought about by the steam engine and other inventions that made work go more easily. Manual labor was replaced by the labor of machines. One invention after another piled up, resulting in a whole range of new implements, from farm equipment to new forms of leather and leather manufacture. New industry meant a plethora of new jobs and job opportunities as well. This was a time when many immigrants came to America from abroad because of the opportunities they found here. Within the city itself, the nature of politics changed as well. The early entrepreneurs, who had specialized in the sale and purchase of land, now were overtaken by new businessmen who were making fortunes hand over fist. Industry, in general, came to drive the overall expansion of the city, replacing the earlier forms of commerce.[8]

This stage also witnessed the rise of a new capitalist class in the city, in general, those whose wealth came from profits and fortunes in the industrial sector. Though much remains to be learned about the precise nature of this class, in cities like Milwaukee there is clear evidence that not only was the power at this time lodged in the hands of individuals of great wealth, but such individuals came to form, along with others, a tight-knit class.[9] At the same time there emerged in many American cities a class of laborers who themselves came to form an opposition to the capitalist class. Moreover, their organization often took the form of unions, or radical politics, providing a wedge and division from the capitalists.

Government in this phase remained small and comparatively primitive, showing only small signs of the kind of expansion and dominance that came to highlight business and industry. If there were, in contemporary terms, a growth machine, it was not government, at all, but industry—hard, heavy industry that brought in many workers from abroad and drove the expansion of the city forward.[10]

THE MATURE INDUSTRIAL CITY: GOVERNMENT EMERGES AS DO POLITICAL DIVISIONS

By the turn of the century, many of America's new industrial cities had changed dramatically from only two or three decades earlier. They were substantially larger cities, many having grown by the hundreds of thousands. The city of Chicago, for instance, grew from a city of 109,260 in 1860 to a city of 1,698,575 in 1900. But more than the growth of the local population was involved.

There also came to be a new configuration of forces and structures that characterized and drove the fortunes of the city. In Milwaukee, Wisconsin, for example, local government had risen to prominence by the end of the century. New departments came into being, including the police and fire departments. Professional staffs ran them; they had hired numbers of new employees.[11] Compensation was now offered for the services of individuals, whereas earlier volunteer citizens had maintained such forces. The overall structure of local government had increased immeasurably by 1900—if not rivaling the value of local industry, at least approximating its worth.

The effect of the growth of government, and the consolidation of local business, was to transform government from being merely a kind of hand-maiden to the work of business to becoming a rival for power in the city. Again, Milwaukee provides an illustration of how this happened.[12] In Milwaukee, local businessmen had long been strong supporters of local government. In fact, there was something of an alliance between the two groups: business supported the work of government, and government supported the work of business. But as the powers of government grew, in terms of new departments, a profession-alization of the staff, and the very value of local political structures, a divi-sion also emerged between local government and local business. Government demanded more resources for the needs of local citizens. Businessmen began to resist. In Milwaukee, the division was fueled because the Social Democrats had come to assume such strong power in the city.

This was a period for many cities when the institution of government had grown so much in its authority over the life of local citizens that some figures came to office and were corrupted by the power they experienced. It was, in a sense, the historical heyday both of local government and of local mayors who could use the power of local government. For most of the older American industrial cities this stage took place in the early 1900s, when the power of local government provided a platform for ambitious officials to exercise and wield their dominance over the urban arena.[13]

THE DECLINE OF THE INDUSTRIAL CITY: THE LOSS OF INDUSTRY, LOCAL CLOUT AND THE EMERGENCE OF ETHNIC/RACIAL CONFLICTS

By the 1930s, many local governments would reach the pinnacle of their power. Local mayors were critical to the success of local cities. This was as true of cities like Philadelphia as it was of cities like Boston or Chicago. The great financial collapse caused by the Depression soon changed the fortunes of cities and their local officials.[14] Many cities were again transformed, but now from bustling local business empires to places that could no longer meet the needs of their citizens. As businesses failed, more was asked of government, especially local government. Early welfare measures happened, such as local relief efforts to provide food and clothing. But the main responsibility was shifted to the federal government. Only in a few places, like Milwaukee, did the local officials manage to work so effectively that they actually had surplus monies in their coffers by the end of the fiscal year. Most cities were virtually bankrupt.[15]

The decline of the American industrial city that had begun in the 1930s would let up briefly during the period of World War II, but accelerate once again in the 1960s and 1970s. This truly was a time when the industrial city came to experience substantial decline and misfortune. Several events happened that would change the city once more. Many businesses began to depart the central city, leaving either for places in the South and Southwest or for abroad. They were lured to their new surroundings by one simple fact: bigger profits. In the South they could expect to find few, if any, taxes; abroad, wage labor was far cheaper than in the United States. The net effect, however, was to leave many of the industrial cities in deep financial trouble.[16] Lacking the monies they secured from local businesses, by way of local taxes and by way of the wealth spent in the city, local governments now were left bereft of funds and resources.[17]

The American industrial city was thus left looking like a shell of its former self. Cities like Cleveland, Pittsburgh, and Detroit were in great physical disrepair. Old manufacturing plants stood as the relics of a rich and flourishing past. Parts of Detroit at the time resembled nothing so much as a kind of urban concentration camp, old buildings having been boarded up, ringed by barbed wire fences to prevent people from getting in—or perhaps getting out. The loss of business and the inability of local governments to survive successfully especially hurt certain populations of people. Older residents were hurt—those in their fifties and sixties who were fired by the departing businesses. Many such employees not only were left without a job, but also without pensions to cover their old age. Ethnic minority populations, in particular African Americans as well as Latinos, were left to become an underclass in the American city, particularly hard hit by the loss of industries.[18]

What is especially tragic is the way that the decline of the industrial city helped to fuel the tensions between different racial and ethnic groups. Blacks and Hispanics were hit particularly hard by the decline.[19] Black populations expanded in certain cities just as the jobs they sought left. Many such populations also became prey to the machinations of local businesses and industries. Certain areas of cities in which blacks lived became areas in which local banks and savings and loans refused to provide money for the purchase of homes.[20] The suburbs, which began to grow after World War II, also made the situation doubly difficult because many such places, if they did not actively discourage minority residents, certainly did not welcome them with open arms.

This last stage of the American industrial city is one from which many cities are just now emerging. It is a stage when both local industry and local government have been shown to be incredibly vulnerable, subject to the whims and vagaries of broader national as well as global events. It is a stage when the federal government came to assume a great deal of the responsibility for helping the needs of the elderly and the black underclass but, in recent years, has shifted that responsibility back to state governments.

CONCLUDING OBSERVATIONS

The American city has changed greatly over the past two centuries. Initially a small settlement of relatively minor numbers of people, it has grown to be a vast expanse of institutions and structures that stretch across wide expanses of the American landscape. The city and its residents have faced a number of crises in its history, none more significant than those of the past several decades. As industries left the cities for greener pastures they left behind thousands of employees, many of them older, many of them members of minorities. The effect was not only to abandon the city but also to abandon people. And local institutions, local government in particular, was left with the responsibility for saving the city. Nevertheless, today there are efforts all across America to revitalize and revamp the city. Look around and you will see those efforts: new parks and tourist attractions in downtown, new housing for residents moving back into the city—these and other innovations are beginning to restore many cities and to set them on a new course for the future. Though the industrial city has died, new kinds of cities are now emerging to replace it. Local governments still must have revenues to provide services to their residents, and so they seek various ways to replace the industries that have left them. Many cities today, for example, have turned to tourism as a means of reviving themselves. Thus, Cleveland built the Rock and Roll Hall of Fame; Milwaukee engaged the services of a world-renowned architect to add a new, breathtaking beautiful wing to its art museum; and Chicago, in the grandest and most expensive gesture of all, built Millenium Park, a public park that cost hundreds of millions of dollars but which, in a very short space of time, has brought thousands of visitors to the city.

American cities as well as European cities, especially the old industrial centers like Barcelona, Spain, or Manchester, England, have had to reinvent themselves in a short space of time. They have turned to various devices in order to provide their residents with a new and prosperous future. Whether they survive, however, no longer simply depends on their capacity to attract big industries with jobs. That was the solution of the nineteenth and twentieth centuries. Today cities must do more. They must not merely furnish jobs, they also must furnish their residents with a lifestyle that is comfortable and attractive. As one urban sociologist has put it, amenities, not industry, have become the way to attract and retain new urban residents.[21]

The Politics of the Contemporary American City

THE CONTENTIOUS POLITICS OF THE AMERICAN METROPOLIS: CENTRAL CITIES, SUBURBS, AND EDGE CITIES

One of the principal features of the American city, and the larger metropolis, that emerged at roughly the same time as the industrial city was a deepening division between the central city and the suburbs.[22] The historian Kenneth Jackson traces the history of American suburbs in considerable detail, noting that many of them began in the nineteenth century in an effort on the part of Americans to capture their bucolic past.[23] Many of the more wealthy residents of the city were able to move to its outer fringes, especially as facilities for transportation became available. Soon this began to leave the city looking somewhat like its growing class divisions—the poorer, laboring class living in the central parts, near work, while the richer residents were able to take advantage of the outer fringes, either for recreational housing or for year-round living.[24]

As time went by, the effect became very marked. By the early part of the twentieth century, many suburbs were incorporating themselves separately from the central cities.[25] Part of the effort was fueled by the growing class differences in their residents, but part was simply facilitated by the ability of small American municipalities to incorporate them. Thus began the deep, and continuing, division between the central cities and the suburbs of the American metropolis. The split was made more or less real, and legal, by key court decisions, such as

that in the case of St. Louis in 1875. This decision said that localities were creatures of the state and that the state had jurisdiction over such localities. It also
gave permission to small local areas, like villages and burgeoning suburbs, to
split off from the central cities. Cities like St. Louis, for example, soon became
ringed by sets of small villages and suburbs, a fringe area that would eventually
become a refuge for the city's wealthier residents.[26]

In some metropolitan areas, like Milwaukee, the spatial division became
accentuated by the effort of local industrial suburbs to remain strictly autonomous of the city. West Allis, for instance, a suburban area that housed the
Allis-Chalmers manufacturing firm, refused to become incorporated as part
of Milwaukee largely because it wished to control the its own resources. In
Cleveland, new housing developments wee built in suburban areas, and, for their
own reasons, they, too, sought and secured legal and political independence
from the city of Cleveland. When cities sought to annex, or to consolidate with
such suburban regimes, suburbs generally successfully fought off such attempts,
supported by both the courts and rural-dominated state legislatures.[27]

As many older industrial cities entered the declining phase of their development, in the 1960s and 1970s, the central-city suburban split came back to haunt
them. What had begun as an effort by suburbanites to protect their affluent
lifestyle now became the device that would further deepen the economic woes
of many central cities. The highways and expressways built after World War II
had accelerated the move to the suburbs. By the early 1960s, suburban areas
accounted for a growing percentage of the American metropolitan population.
The suburbs not only had robbed central cities of residents, they had robbed
them of their wealthier residents. And because local taxes were secured from
local residents, the gap in the financial resources of the central cities and the
suburbs widened considerably. Cities like New York and Cleveland went into
default in large part because they no longer housed the residents able to provide
the tax monies for their budgets.[28]

Such facts, historical and cultural in nature, provide the framework
for understanding both the politics and the varied successes and failures of
American cities over the past couple of decades. Recent research by David
Rusk, former mayor of Albuquerque, New Mexico, suggests that metropolises
that have been able to expand and to incorporate their suburban regions generally have done better surviving the industrial decline than those that have
not.[29] Such expandable, or elastic, cities are ones that somehow managed to
escape the deep splits and financial hardships of many other industrial cities.
In addition, Minnesota state legislator Myron Orfield has demonstrated that
the blight and problems of inner cities have begun to move into the first ring
of suburban areas of certain metropolises like Minneapolis. Building on these
discoveries, Orfield has argued that metropolitan areas must make an effort to

create metropolitan solutions for themselves, thereby overcoming the historic divisions between cities and suburbs. Orfield, among others, has become a proponent of "regionalism," a movement that urges more cooperative programs between the cities and suburbs of the American metropolis.[30] It is likely that this movement, and this program, will in the near future become a more visible feature of the politics of American cities.

A corollary to the growth of the regionalism movement on behalf of American cities is the recent emergence of *edge cities*.[31] Such cities are found on the fringe areas of the American metropolis, their growth often stimulated by the interstate highway system. Generally speaking, they consist of a cluster of businesses and malls, along with nearby housing developments. Such edge cities have flourished in recent years, springing up almost everywhere in America. Like the earlier suburbs, they are separate and autonomous from the central cities of the metropolis, governed, in the words of Joel Garreau, by small "shadow governments" that exercise considerable control and regulation over the lives of their firms and residents. Moreover, they are also the sites where many of the new jobs are now available in American cities, and thus they only make worse the problems that members of the underclass face in the inner city as they try to find new job opportunities.[32]

As edge cities increase, and as suburbs come to house more and more of America's residents—rather than the central city—the fulcrum of American urban politics also has begun to shift. In the past, the suburbs represented the heart of the Republican strength of the American city, but recent signs suggest that the Republican Party can no longer take the suburbs for granted. Nevertheless, the social composition and political inclinations of the suburbs are vastly different from their counterparts in the inner cities, thus accentuating the longstanding divisions. How politicians deal with these differences will, along with regionalism, represent some of the key political issues of the near future for the American city.

SUNBELT CITIES AND METROPOLITAN FRAGMENTATION

Just as the interstate highway system accelerated the movement of Americans to the suburbs, so it aided the development of cities beyond the pale of industrial America. Virtually all of the industrial cities developed in the Northeast and Midwest in places like Boston, New York, Pittsburgh, and Detroit. But as the decline of these cities took place, many industries and firms began to relocate where they would not face taxes—in places like Atlanta, Dallas, and Phoenix. Spurred also by the growth of the defense industry during World War II, a tremendous urban boom happened in the so-called Sunbelt, its first signs evident in the 1960s.[33]

Sunbelt or postindustrial cities seem to be very different in their form and politics from the older industrial cities, although their pattern of underlying development seems much the same.[34] Most have avoided the deep political divisions evident between central cities and suburbs. Some have managed to avoid them simply because they learned from the experience of these older cities; others have managed because they are in states in which home rule exists, and in which many localities exercise more control over their own affairs than in the older industrial Midwest or Northeast. Sunbelt cities as a result have grown massive in terms of both the number of residents and spatial dimensions. Cities like Phoenix or Tucson, Arizona, have exploded in size over the past several decades, far outdistancing older places like Pittsburgh and Milwaukee. Many have become the refuge for older residents, migrating from the North to the Sunbelt. And of course, one effect of their expansion has been to shift the political weight of America somewhat from the North to the South.

Because of the rapidity of their growth, and because they are seen as lying on the frontier edges of America, such cities have become the central locale for deep conflicts and confrontations over the wisdom of unfettered growth and expansion. It is in such cities as these, which have mushroomed so quickly, that the divisions are not so much over material and economic issues, in the older sense, or between the Republicans and Democrats, as between the pro-growth and anti-growth forces.[35] States like Florida or Georgia are where these issues are fought out in urban areas.

Some such Sunbelt cities also provide evidence of virtually no governmental controls over the place of urban expansion. Sprawl, which has become the fashionable epithet for those who oppose such expansion today, is evident in many such metropolitan areas, including Dallas, Atlanta, and Tucson, among others. Houston, Texas, is the site of almost massive sprawl. Houston has virtually no zoning controls over its growth. Because of this, real estate developers have been able to exercise their dominance over Houston. Sociologist Joe Feagin refers to Houston as a "free enterprise city," a place where the business community exercises its power almost at will.[36] Real estate developers have been able to create various residential tracts almost free of any kind of zoning regulations. Moreover, Feagin suggests that the absence of such controls has created decided disadvantages, including greater pollution of the atmosphere and uneven growth in the metropolis.

Many other Sunbelt cities have taken on a similar character. The earliest such example is that of Los Angeles, described by the urban historian Robert Fogelson as "the fragmented metropolis."[37] Los Angeles, unlike the cities of the north, did not possess a large industrial empire to drive its growth and expansion. As a result, it came to lack the spatial character of many northern cities: there was no industrial core downtown to act as a magnet for the new immigrants to the city. Instead, the city became the site of countless new housing developments, each searching for its new area on the fringe for a kind of "suburban dream." Key developers played a role in this process, among them Henry Huntington, Jr. Moreover, such businessmen exercised considerable power in the city, partly because municipal authority was relatively weak and they were able to fuel the drive outward from the center of the city. New industries were located not in the center but on the outskirts and the fringes. Finally, the failure to develop a comprehensive and effective municipal system of railways, brought about by the limited railways developed to expedite travel to individual housing developments, spurred the growth of the highway system and the attraction of the automobile. Los Angeles came to be the epitome of the new Sunbelt city—deconcentrated, laced with an extensive system of overlapping highways, and housing countless numbers of local governments and municipal bodies.

Interpreting the City

As one might expect, there are different theories with which political sociologists approach the city. These theories owe something to the broad theoretical platforms of political sociology—to the writings, in particular, of Karl Max and Max Weber as well as Alexis de Toqueville. One such theory emphasizes the significance of varying social formations and groups in the city as they attempt to secure advantage and power for themselves. This view, the pluralist view, assumes, as Max Weber did, that modern society is composed of a variety of different and competing social groups. Drawing also on the theoretical insights of Alexis de Tocqueville, this theory emphasizes the consensual nature of American democracy in the sense that even though groups engage in conflict, they remain bound by the same democratic rules and values.

A second view, the view of the city as a growth machine, owes its inspiration in part to the ideas of Karl Marx. It argues, in contrast to the pluralist view of the city, that power is held unequally among the social groups and organizations within the city. Some groups—in particular, the alliance of leading officials, real estate investors and local media personnel—are able to control and manipulate the agenda of local politics to their advantage. These parties, united by a common interest in growth and its benefits, are often able to have their way on the local scene, in part because of the effectiveness with which they can manipulate the media and local politics to promote the growth of the city.

We shall also consider here a third view—the view of the city in terms of its creative energies and resources. This perspective, while not directly connected to any of political sociology's main platforms, has taken local officials as well as urban scholars by storm. Indeed, its creator, Richard Florida, spends much of his time on the road nowadays, advising local officials both in the United States and in Europe about ways to revive the energies and fortunes of their cities.

POLITICAL PLURALISM IN THE CITY: CIVIL SOCIETY AND THE DISPERSAL OF POWER

Though pluralism has a long and rich history in American political thought, it was only with the writings and theory of the political scientist Robert A. Dahl that pluralism shifted from a rough paradigm to a full-fledged theory of urban politics.[38] Dahl's argument was cast very broadly, and though he spoke of an urban polity, he really intended his general view to be applicable more broadly to the making of modern democracies. His is a view that grows out of the general notion that the institutions of the civil society of a society, or place, are very significant to the politics of that society.

Dahl's view is based on an analysis and interpretation of politics in the city of New Haven, Connecticut, in the early 1960s. He begins by insisting that life in New Haven, like that in the rest of America, can best be seen in terms of dominant institutional sectors—the economic, political, the arts, and the religious. Within each of these major institutional sectors, special organizations and groups produce and demand the special talents of members of the general public. Next, he claims that the ongoing character of each of the institutional sectors and, of course, the organizations within them operates through the accumulation and investment of basic resources. Moreover, the operations of each sphere tend to require specialized forms of resources; the economic sphere deals in the accumulation and investment of material wealth, the sphere of high society in the accumulation and investment of prestige, and the political sphere in the accumulation and investment of political power. Here, of course, he follows Max Weber in specifying, in effect, the crucial differences among class, status, and parties (see Chapter 3).

In addition, he argues that most people do not care much about politics. There are those who are active and concerned in a regular fashion about politics, including mainly political officials but also some citizens, but most citizens are subject to inertia and do not care what happens in the political world. Nevertheless, the world still operates well in Dahl's pluralist universe, primarily because the leaders always seek *to anticipate* the wishes and desires of the citizens—that, of course, is the essence of the democratic electoral process—and because all citizens, leaders and lay citizens alike, share the same common values and goals. Finally, Dahl actually put his theory to a test and, with the aid of several key research assistants, closely examined the process of decision making over the period of a year. And he more or less confirmed his expectations: power was dispersed widely among the public; on different issues, such as schools and parties, alternative groups came into play; and the most powerful or influential figure in the city was the mayor, Richard Lee.

A number of important studies in the 1960s generally confirmed and supported Dahl's pluralist portrait of the city, including important work by Wallace Sayre and Herbert Kaufman on New York City.[39] Indeed, for a time the pluralist view was the most widely accepted view of the way politics operates in the cities and communities of America. Even today, there is much to recommend the notion that different groups can exercise their will over the nature of urban politics, depending on the particular kinds of issues up for discussion. But there also are important reservations about the pluralist view. And they come from camps based more centrally on a neo-Marxist, or political economy, rendering of the city.

THE CITY AS A GROWTH MACHINE: THE POLITICAL ECONOMY OF THE CITY

In the early 1970s, the pluralist view of the urban polity came under heavy fire. In part, there was criticism that the pluralists did not possess an objective view of politics, but rather a view that had become entrenched as the American ideology.[40] In part, the criticism came from the other school of urban sociology, the elitists, who believed that the pluralists failed to understand how much power the rich and wealthy exercised in many American communities. But the main criticism of the pluralist view was leveled by the sociologist who, as it so happened, provided a new interpretation of the urban arena—Harvey Molotch.

The pluralists had argued that essentially all policies and groups were equal in the urban polity. Everyone had a voice; every group could exercise power; only political officials seemed to exercise more of it. Molotch, trained at the University of Chicago, argued that the pluralist view was mistaken. Not all issues count the same; not all voices are equal. In fact, the main emphasis of cities, and communities, Molotch insisted, is that of growth. Growth is the driving force of the city; all other issues and principles are subordinate to it.[41]

The city, Molotch writes, is like a growth machine. It churns out policies that favor and promote its growth. This is, in effect, its *raison d'être*:

> [T]he political and economic essence of virtually any given locality in the present American context, is *growth*. . . . [The] desire for growth provides the key operative motivation toward consensus for members of politically mobilized local elites. [This] growth imperative is the most important constraint upon available options for local initiative in social and economic reform . . . [Thus] the very essence of a locality is its operation as a growth machine.[42]

The very nature of the American city is to expand and to grow. Real estate brokers and entrepreneurs are growth's main proponents. They play a large role, transforming the land and space of the city into commodities. But other actors in the city also profit from growth. Political officials, Molotch argues, stand to gain from growth because the greater the number of residents and territory over which they rule, the greater their power. Eventually a kind of unholy alliance emerges in the city—of real estate entrepreneurs, bankers, political officials, even the media brokers—all of whom generally favor and sponsor growth because they benefit from it.

In a sequel to Molotch's article, he and John Logan expand on the theory of the urban arena.[43] Drawing from some important other work, such as that of the geographer David Harvey, they argue that cities, like other forms of property under capitalism, are subject to two kinds of valuation.[44] One is valuation based on the market, otherwise known as *exchange value*; the other is valuation based on the use to which residents put their property, otherwise known as *use value*. The distinction is one first introduced by Karl Marx to explain the nature and emergence of *commodities* under modern capitalism. Logan and Molotch go on to argue that urban land and space, themselves, become subject to an eventful history of *commodification*.

The political struggles and tensions of cities are waged over how, and whether, land and space will become commodities. They write: "[the] legal creation and regulation of places have been primarily under the domination of those searching, albeit sometimes in the face of use-value counter-demands, for exchange value gains."[45] Citizens have their own preferences for land, particularly for their own land and land in their neighborhoods. As Logan and Molotch observe, there are several different use values evident among property owners and their neighbors. They include "the daily round" that residents make about their neighborhood, the sense of identity connected to a place, and the presence of social support networks.[46] When the purposes of real estate brokers and entrepreneurs come into conflict with those of local residents, essentially over the nature of the values for land and space, then major political battles break out, often visible in the contentious politics of city hall.

Orum points out, in his research on a Sunbelt city, that there can be deep cultural differences between those who view the land of these areas in terms of the profit they can gain from them and those who view the land for its main value for them. In Austin, Texas, and other cities across the Sunbelt, the main use value lay in terms of the broader environmental meaning that the land held for main people. Orum writes:

> On the one hand, there are those people who today define the land purely and simply in terms of modern-day capitalism, that is, as a commodity. To them, the land in and around Austin has meaning only insofar as it can be sold, and it can bring them a profit, perhaps of considerable proportions....On the other hand, there exists another group of people, who possess an entirely different conception of the land. To them, humans and nature possess a special kind of relationship, one of balance, a harmony that must not be based by the senseless abuse of land. To this

group of people, the land is to be preserved as much as possible in its natural, primitive state, and equally as much to be used for the enjoyment of the broad public rather than simply the large-scale developer, or even the private landowner.[47]

Indeed, the sense that nature possesses a value in and of itself has come to characterize many of the more rural areas subject to development and growth now in America, a part of the broader effort to implant environmentalism as a new and important American value.

Other research has also emphasized the role of real estate entrepreneurs and developers in the urban arena. Sociologists Joe Feagin and Mark Gottdiener argue that real estate entrepreneurs play a major role in shaping the city and that their power often acts invisibly to determine the choices that cities make.[48] Other urban scholars, like Susan Fainstein, make similar points.[49]

The growth machine view of the city, and of urban politics, has become immensely popular over the past twenty years—certainly the most widely cited interpretation of urban politics. While many voices often can, and are, heard, it is clear that in early twenty-first-century America, urban growth continues to be a central issue, and those who advocate it frequently represent an unholy alliance of actors on its behalf.

THE CITY AND THE CREATIVE CLASS: REVIVING THE METROPOLIS TODAY

Obviously the most pressing problem for most, if not all, American cities today is that of figuring out how to revive their earlier vitality. Cities like Milwaukee, Cleveland, and St. Louis, for example, were once proud and booming urban empires, places that attracted tens of thousands of new residents from abroad as well as from the American countryside. These and many other cities now seek a way out of their industrial doldrums, and they do so, in part, by casting an eye to the great growth centers of today, such as Phoenix or Tucson, Arizona, San Francisco, California, or even Austin, Texas. What is it, the officials of the older cities ask, that makes these other cities such magnets for new residents? How have they become so vital? And what must we do to turn our fortunes around?

Several years ago an answer to these questions was proposed by the regional economist Richard Florida.[50] Florida began by taking on the work and theory of Robert Putnam, whose ideas about social capital and politics we examined earlier in this book. Putnam is wrong, Florida argued: it is not social capital that provides the germ of vitality and prosperity in twenty-first-century America, but rather it is "creative capital." Creative capital consists of those resources and attributes of individuals that allow them to be creative. It includes such things as one's level of education but also one's interest and tolerance for social diversity. Where creative capital is concentrated, moreover, there, too, will be tremendous growth and vitality. Creative people like to be with other creative people. Thus, cities that are able to attract musicians or artists, for example, are also likely to be the cities that will attract economic entrepreneurs who are interested in starting and developing new business ventures.

Where, then, are such urban concentrations of creative capital to be found? Cities like San Francisco, Seattle, and Austin are examples of cities where there is a high concentration of creative people. They are sites, as one knows, of considerable economic innovation and expansion over the past three decades—recall, for example, that the technology giant Hewlett-Packard had its origins in a garage near the campus of Stanford University—but also sites of great creative energy in general. Austin, for instance, has become a leading center of country music in the United States, while Seattle gave birth to Kurt Cobain. The key element about such places is, Florida argues, that there is a kind of synergy that develops among the various creative types in the city, and this synergy promotes ever-greater expansion. Once the stories of these cities are known, moreover, they become the places where other creative people, especially young people, will want to live.

Florida's theory of cities and creative capital has become immensely popular in a short space of time. It is, as one might imagine, particularly attractive to local officials of the older, diminished industrial cities in America. Florida is routinely invited to come to those cities and speak to the Chambers of Commerce. But he also has made the rounds of many European cities as well, furnishing officials in England and France with his vision of how to restore the energies of older cities.

CONCLUDING OBSERVATIONS

Each of the three theories we discussed in this section were all at one time or another the most compelling story of the American city. Dahl's view of the city as an arena of diverse and equal powers was most popular during the period of the mid–twentieth century. But its popularity receded, especially as the forces on behalf of urban growth took over in a number of cities. Dahl believed that there were various and different interests in the city, but the Logan-Molotch view of the city as a growth machine simply made much more sense out of the politics and conflicts for the last few decades of the twentieth century. Though that view still remains important today, it fails to provide a way to address the matter of how declined cities can be restored.And that is precisely the issue that Richard Florida addresses in his new theory of the city and the creative class.Instead of becoming embroiled in old controversies over power, Florida provides an answer to those city forces—which include not only the leading officials and other powerful agents, but also those people interested in improving the conditions of the poor—that want to move beyond the old arguments.

Remaking the American City

One of the features that characterized the recent period of decline of older industrial American cities is the fact that some cities emerged from this period more quickly and more successfully than others. They managed to make decisions that helped them escape the ravages of decline, including the recruitment of new industry; some even made decisions that provided clear benefits for the large majority of their residents. In particular, cities like Minneapolis–St. Paul were successful in escaping the deep decline of Detroit, while Pittsburgh did much better than Milwaukee in remaking itself from a city known worldwide for its steel industry to a city that began to be known for its educational institutions and high-technology industries.

Why, then, did some older industrial cities escape decline more quickly? Orum and Gramlich argue that there is a feature common to all cities, something they call *civic capital*.[51] They further suggest that civic capital consists of four basic components: a *vision*, or general plan and direction for the city, one that provides a map for the future of the city; a *strong commitment* to the city, or place, shared generally by the majority of residents, and especially by the leading figures and class; *alliances* between the leading political and economic figures of the city, which helped to furnish a concentration of power at the top; and, finally, and most significantly, *bridges* that link the alliances of the city to its citizens through such intermediary factors as neighborhood organizations, local voluntary associations, even trade unions. Together these four elements constitute the civic capital of a city. And cities appear to vary in their civic capital, which, in turn, makes a difference in their capacity to make decisions that will benefit the majority of their residents.

Consider the recent stories of three separate cities, all of which experienced the growth of industry early in the twentieth century. The Twin Cities of Minnesota have managed to make critical decisions to move themselves forward. The most important was the creation of the Metropolitan Council in 1967. The Council was designed to make decisions that would aid the residents of the entire metropolitan region, not simply the central cities. It has helped to provide a means for making policies about regional resource sharing on matters such as water and sewage treatment. It also provides the current framework for helping to attack more fundamental issues, such as local crime and problems in the local schools.

The city of Pittsburgh is equally notable for some of its advances. Though hit hard by the decline of the 1960s and 1970s, and suffering the loss of many thousands of residents, Pittsburgh has bounced back much more quickly than some other cities. It has managed to create a first-rate set of universities, including Carnegie-Mellon University, and has been able to attract new industries. It also has managed to remake its downtown area, the Triangle, creating a beautiful park and area for residents to enjoy.

In contrast to both the Twin Cities and Pittsburgh, the city of Milwaukee has lagged far behind in its effort to move beyond industrialization. Until recently, Milwaukee was unable to attract much in the way of new industry; what industry has come to the region has settled on its fringes. It also had had great difficulty making a decision about the future of its local baseball club, the Milwaukee Brewers. And it remains a city that is very segregated—racism was cited by the local newspaper as a major problem in the 1990s.

Three very different cities, three very different stories of success in climbing beyond industry. Orum and Gramlich argue that the differences can be explained by differences in the amount of civic capital available to the cities. The Twin Cities area, which stands above both Pittsburgh and Milwaukee in its success in making decisions on behalf of its residents, seems to have the most. It possesses a strong vision, nurtured by many community leaders; it possesses a strong commitment to place on the part of its residents, also fostered by such things as immense local philanthropy by its leading businessmen and businesswomen; it has a history of strong alliances between the leading political and business figures, evident in the work they did in the early 1950s to sponsor urban renewal downtown; and there is evidence of bridges that link the alliances to local citizens' groups. Pittsburgh has almost as much civic capital as the Twin Cities: in fact, it is noteworthy for the alliances and the vision developed in the 1940s for its future by its key political and business leaders, such as H. J. Heinz and David Lawrence. What it may lack are the solid bridges linking the alliances of the city to its citizens groups. Milwaukee, one should not be surprised to learn, is the weakest in terms of its civic capital. In fact, based upon my own research, it appears that the only element that has been evident in Milwaukee, at least until recently, is that of alliances. On the matter of commitment to place, vision, and bridges, the city of Milwaukee has been notably lacking.

In brief, then, a comparison of the three cities suggests that where there is more civic capital, cities will be better able to make decisions that benefit the majority of their citizens. This conclusion awaits further research, but is highly suggestive.

Cities and the New Global Economy

One of the great transformations of our age is the development of the new global economy. Aided by the creation of vast new information technology, people and firms are now more closely connected and intertwined with one another than ever before. The effects are felt everywhere, including in metropolitan areas and among their residents. How these effects will play out in the future remains unknown, but there has been interesting speculation in the past few years, to which we now shall turn.[52]

GLOBAL CITIES

The sociologist/urban planner Saskia Sassen has advanced the most arresting argument about global forces.[53] She argues that three cities, in particular, have become global cities: Tokyo, London, and New York. What has happened in these cities, she suggests, is that the economy has moved beyond the dominance of heavy industries to the dominance of new sectors: finance, real estate, and information technology. Within these sectors there has been a considerable increase in employment and generation of great wealth. In New York City, certain real estate magnates like Donald Trump have risen to the top of the wealth hierarchy, and the financial sector on Wall Street has made immense profits and fortunes over the past decade. Information technology firms also make a difference, and there has been a rapid increase and growth of such businesses—not only in New York, of course, though it has come to be one home to these new firms.

In this postindustrial phase of the world economy, other important tendencies also have become apparent. Sassen argues that there has been a tendency toward an increasing inequality of wealth based upon the nature of these new businesses and the nature of the metropolises themselves. In effect, there has been a growing sector of the very rich, and a growing sector of the very poor. The rich hold the professional and managerial positions in the new industries, while the poor are located at the bottom rung of the occupational ladder, holding the poorly paying positions in the service industries. Moreover, as these positions have opened up, they also have become available to the many new immigrants who have come into these major metropolises, thereby providing them employment, though only at low wages. Sassen suggests that these tendencies can eventually have a real impact on the politics of the cities, heightening poverty, for example, and with it the need to make clear policies to aid the new urban poor.[54]

Moreover, Sassen argues that the new global cities have become a world unto themselves. Their economic and political players have become attuned to the actions of one another rather than to the actions within their countries. Financial managers in London, for instance, are more apt to be attentive to the actions of financial managers in Tokyo or New York than to their fellow financial figures elsewhere in their own home countries. In effect, new business empires are being established that transcend national boundaries and divisions. The argument is an extension of an earlier argument, treated in Chapter 6, by Richard Barnett and Ronald Muller on the emergence and development of multinational corporations. Sassen, in effect, has extended the argument to examine the nature of these three metropolises and the important consequences, such as the polarization of income and wealth.

Sassen's view of these three modern areas also relegates other cities, in America as well as Japan and England, to lower rungs on the hierarchy of dominance. Ecologists have for a long time argued that cities exist in terms of a hierarchy of dominance based on their flow of goods and traffic, and Sassen now suggests a new kind of dominance based on the emergence of the global economy. But, while elegant and attractive, much of Sassen's argument remains at this point speculation. Economists argue that the polarization of wealth we see may be due to other forces and factors. In addition, it remains to be seen whether the other large metropolitan areas will be propelled automatically into the new arena of global cities, or whether, in fact, they will continue to be shaped and modified by the culture and politics of their own countries.

OTHER POSTINDUSTRIAL CITIES

One of the real questions raised by the analysis of Sassen, and by the changing nature of the world's economy, is the extent to which cities will become like one another or remain uniquely bound to the culture of their own nations. Some analysts have argued on behalf of a convergence thesis, claiming that cities around the world are becoming more and more similar. Such is the analysis of Michael A. Cohen, who insists:

> [W]hile the causes of urban unemployment in the (Northern and Southern hemispheres) are certainly different, their manifestations and consequences are similar, if not identical. Increasing numbers of low-income earners, working in the service sector, face rising prices for many needed urban services and the satisfaction of basic needs. Homelessness, youth unemployment, and growing social problems of the poor, including crime and drugs, are evident in both northern and southern cities.[55]

But the problem with such an analysis is that it completely ignores the history and culture of individual countries and their places and, by ignoring different causes of similar outcomes, cannot provide coherent policies.

What is clear is that many of the older industrial cities around the world are taking political actions to improve themselves and their fortunes that tend to be very similar. In a powerful and insightful analysis, Weiping Wu, a professor of urban studies and planning at Virginia Commonwealth University, finds both important similarities and critical differences in the postindustrial development of several cities in very different parts of the world: New York, Barcelona, and Santiago.[56] Drawing on the work of Sassen, she notes the major transformations in New York, especially the loss of manufacturing jobs, and the growing income disparities between the very poor and the very rich. Such inequality, she observes, could ultimately prove to have serious political consequences.

But she also observes the ways in which the city has managed to overcome such inequalities, and how it is taking measures to improve the lives of the poor.[57]

Barcelona, a city once built on an important manufacturing base, has been able to overcome its loss of industry and other factors of decline because it stimulated "competitive economic development by establishing visions for the city, building public consensus, and encouraging public-private cooperation."[58] Moreover, public officials in Barcelona took important steps to promote its fortunes, creating, among other things, municipal funds that would help the city recover from the loss of so many manufacturing positions. Santiago, by contrast, is an entirely different story. Like many other Latin American cities, it houses many impoverished residents who have been unemployed for years. It also has serious problems of pollution, great traffic congestion, and much physical decay. But the Chilean government shifted many resources to the city in the mid-1970s, and the city itself managed to attract much new industry. Thus, it, too, met its challenges and managed to overcome them, unlike many other older industrial cities in the world. In brief, Wu finds that while cities may differ, and many may face the challenges of the loss of jobs and growing poverty, cities like New York, Barcelona, and Santiago are able to overcome these challenges by the ways in which both the national and local governments develop modes of cooperation and, especially, by the shifting of more autonomy and resources to the cities themselves.

REGIONAL AND URBAN EXPERIMENTS OF MAJOR DEVELOPING NATIONS: CHINA, SOUTH KOREA, AND TAIWAN

One of the most important experiments of our current era is that which is taking place in the People's Republic of China. Since the end of the Cultural Revolution in 1978, and under the reforms of Deng Xiaoping, the Chinese government has sought to wed two seemingly different forces—control by a dominant political party and its figures—with the introduction of new economic reforms. Some of the most imaginative steps, in fact, have been taken with regard to the developments of China's urban areas, in particular, cities like Shanghai. The Chinese government has granted to these new areas—indeed, to entire regions—an autonomy they previously did not possess in the hopes of stimulating and expanding the local economy and, eventually, the regional economies.

Several different developing nations have experimented with new regional economic zones. In China such zones have become known as Special Economic Zones (SEZs), whereas in Taiwan and South Korea they are known as Free Economic Zones. The purpose of such zones is to stimulate both the local and the national economies by providing special kinds of incentives to foreign investors. Incentives include such things as lower rates of taxation on profits and fewer trade restrictions. In Taiwan such zones were first established in the mid-1960s, in Korea in 1970, and in China in 1979, just at the end of the Cultural Revolution. So far the results have confirmed the hopes of officials.[59] In each country these zones have stimulated considerable investment by foreign enterprises: Japan has invested heavily in Taiwan and South Korea, while Macao and Hong Kong were the major investors in Shenzhen in China until 1990. Each of the zones also has grown rapidly in terms of population. China's experiment may be the most promising of all. Between 1979, when Shenzhen was begun, and 1990, the number of firms in the zone grew from 224 to 2,470. There was a great growth of the labor force, and it has emerged as one of the most modern and attractive of China's cities. Moreover, the pace of investment in the city has not only contributed to the wealth of the local population, but appears to have generated wealth across the region—which was the original intention.

Such zones represent new kinds of economic experiments for developing nations of the world. The hope is that the economic development they engender will both provide direct benefits to the nation and serve as models of what other cities and businesses might achieve. In China the experiment is the most unusual, for although the city represents a kind of free economic zone intended to encourage foreign investment, the entire experiment is controlled and regulated by the Chinese State Council. Shenzhen thus represents in model form the effort of China to try to marry a socialist government with a free market economy. Besides the innovations of the SEZs, the Chinese government has also permitted local metropolitan officials, like those in Shanghai, to exercise more authority over local decisions.[60] Such decisions involve both the political administration and the economic decisions for their areas. In Shanghai there are also new zones, for example Pudong, in which an effort is being made to foster new strength in both foreign industry as well as the financial sector.

The question raised by the greater autonomy now permitted by the Chinese government over localities is whether the economic payoff will be great enough to offset any disadvantages. In particular, if polarization of wealth and income should happen in the SEZs, or in Shanghai, what are the likely political consequences of such outcomes? And how much leeway will the government permit, especially if the resistance to it increases? These are intriguing and important questions, and they could pose serious threats to China's new experiment, a strong socialist government that seeks to encourage deep reforms in its economy.

Conclusion

Over the course of the past thirty years there have been tremendous changes in the world economy and in the nature and configuration of nation-states. Such changes have made themselves felt in a number of ways. In this chapter we have considered both the local configuration of metropolitan governments in America and the impact that the world situation has had upon the local American scene. In addition, we also have considered the nature of cities in the new global economy and some of the new forms, in the form of global cities, that have appeared.

Metropolitan life and politics in the United States as well as elsewhere have changed dramatically in just a short period of time. What remains the same is the effort by cities and their citizens to carve out a decent and successful life in a world undergoing profound and rapid change. Although the problems seem most challenging in the older industrial cities, there are equally vexing issues in the rapidly growing cities of the world, especially those of Asia.

NOTES

1. Sam Bass Warner, Jr., *The Private City: Philadelphia in Three Periods of Its Growth* (Philadelphia: University of Pennsylvania Press, 1968).
2. Louis Wirth, "Urbanism as a Way of Life," *American Journal of Sociology*, 44 (July 1938), 1–24.
3. Raymond Mohl, Jr., *The Making of Urban America*, 2nd ed. (Wilmington, DE: Scholarly Resources, 1997); Raymond A. Mohl and Neil Betten, eds., *Urban America in Historical Perspective* (New York: Weybright and Talley, 1970); Dennis R. Judd and Todd Swanstrom, *Private Power and Public Policy* (New York: HarperCollins, 1994), Chapters 2–7; Bayrd Still, "Patterns of Mid-Nineteenth Century Urbanization in the Middle West," *Mississippi Valley Historical Review*, 28 (September 1941), 187–206; and Charles N. Glaab and A. Theodore Brown, *A History of Urban America* (New York: The Macmillan Company, 1967).
4. Much of the general framework in the discussion below is drawn from my own work, but it is generally supported by the historical literature as noted above. See Anthony M. Orum, *City-Building in America* (Boulder, CO: Westview Press, 1995).
5. Ibid., Chapter 3.
6. Also see Robert A. Dahl, *Who Governs?*
7. Mohl and Betten, op. cit., Part IV.
8. Dahl, op. cit.
9. Orum, op. cit., 91–95.
10. Ibid., Chapter 4; Mohl, op. cit.
11. Orum, op. cit., Chapter 5. Also see these important works on a similar theme: Eric Monkonnen, *America Becomes Urban: The Development of U.S. Cities and Towns, 1780–1980* (Berkeley: University of California Press, 1988); and Jon Teaford, *The Unheralded Triumph: City Government in America, 1870–1900* (Baltimore, MD: The Johns Hopkins University Press, 1984).
12. Orum, ibid., Chapter 5.
13. Judd and Swanstrom, op. cit., Chapter 3.
14. Ibid., Chapters 5–7.
15. Orum, op. cit., Chapter 5; also Mohl, Jr., *The Making of Urban America*.

16. See, for example, Todd Swanstrom, *The Crisis of Growth Politics: Cleveland, Kucinich and the Challenge of Urban Populism* (Philadelphia: Temple University Press, 1985).
17. Peterson, *City Limits*, Chapter 10; Orum, op. cit., Chapters 6 and 7; Judd and Swanstrom, *Private Power and Public Policy*, Chapter 7.
18. William Julius Wilson, *The Truly Disadvantaged: Public Policy and the Making of an Underclass* (Chicago: University of Chicago Press, 1987).
19. Ibid.; and Orum, op. cit., Chapter 7.
20. Gregory D. Squires, *Capital and Communities in Black and White* (Albany, NY: State University of New York Press, 1994).
21. This point of view has been stressed again and again by the urban sociologist, Terry Clark.
22. See, especially, Jon Teaford, *City and Suburb: the Political Fragmentation of Metropolitan America, 1850–1970* (Baltimore, MD: The Johns Hopkins University Press, 1979).
23. Kenneth Jackson, *Crabgrass Frontier: The Suburbanization of the United States* (New York: Oxford University Press, 1985).
24. Orum, op. cit., Chapter 4.
25. Teaford, *city and Suburb*, Chapter 2.
26. Teaford, op. cit., *infra*.
27. Ibid., Chapters 2 and 3.
28. Swanstrom, op. cit.; Peterson, op. cit.
29. David Rusk, *Cities Without Suburbs* (Baltimore, MD: The Johns Hopkins University Press, 1993).
30. Myron Orfield, *Metropolitics: A Regional Agenda for Community and Stability* (Washington, DC: The Brookings Institution, 1997).
31. Joel Garreau, *Edge City: Life on the New Frontier* (New York: Doubleday, 1991).
32. For a number of fine articles on these spatial changes, see *Interwoven Destinies: Cities and Nation*, Henry G. Cisneros, ed. (New York: W.W. Norton, 1993).
33. Carl Abbott, *the New Urban America: Growth and Politics in Sunbelt Cities* (Chapel Hill: University of North Carolina Press, 1987); and *Sunbelt Cities: Politics and Growth Since World War II*, Richard M. Bernard and Bradley M. Rice, eds. (Austin, TX: University of Texas Press, 1983).
34. Orum, *City-Building in America*.
35. Mark Baldassare, *The Growth Dilemma* (Berkeley: University of California Press, 1981); *The Politics of San Antonio: Community, Progress and Power* (Lincoln, NE: University of Nebraska Press, 1983); and Orum, *Power, Money and the People*.
36. Joe R. Feagin, *Free Enterprise City: Houston in Political and Economic Perspective* (New Brunswick, NJ: Rutgers University Press, 1988).
37. Robert M. Fogelson, *The Fragmented Metropolis: Los Angeles, 1850–1930* (Berkeley: University of California Press, 1967; 1993 reissued).
38. Robert A. Dahl, *Who Governs? Democracy and Power in an American City* (New Haven, CT: Yale University Press, 1961).
39. Wallace S. Sayre and Herbert Kaufman, *Governing New York City* (New York: The Russell Sage Foundation, 1960); Edward Banfield, *Political Influence* (New York: Free Press, 1961).

40. Theodore J. Lowi, *The End of Liberalism: the Second Republic of the United States* (New York: W.W. Norton, 1969; 1979).
41. Harvey Molotch, "The City as a Growth Machine," *American Journal of Sociology*, 82 (September 1976), 309–32.
42. Ibid., 310.
43. John Logan and Harvey Molotch, *Urban Fortunes: the Political Economy of Place* (Berkeley: University of California Press, 1987).
44. David Harvey, *Social Justice and the City* (Oxford: Basil Blackwell, 1973; 1988).
45. Logan and Molotch, *Urban Fortunes*, op. cit., 37.
46. Ibid., 103–110.
47. Anthony M. Orum, *Power, Money and the People: the Making of Modern Austin* (Austin, TX: Texas Monthly Press, 1987), 309.
48. Mark Gottdiener and Joe R. Feagin, "The Paradigm Shift in Urban Sociology," *Urban Affairs Quarterly*, 24 (December 1988), 163–87.
49. Susan S. Fainstein, *The City Builders: Property, Politics, and Planning in London and New York* (Oxford: Basil Blackwell, 1994).
50. Richard Florida, *Cities and the Creative Class* (New York: Routledge, 2005).
51. Anthony M. Orum and James Gramlich, "Civic Capital and the Construction (and Reconstruction) of Cities," *Colloqui: Cornell Journal of Planning and Urban Issues*, XIV, 1999, 45–54.
52. H. V. Savitch, *Post-Industrial Cities: Politics and Planning in New York, Paris and London* (Princeton, NJ: Princeton University Press, 1988); *Preparing for the Urban Future: Global Pressures and Local Forces*, Michael A. Cohen, Blair A. Ruble, Joseph S. Tulchin, and Allison M. Garland, eds. (Washington, DC: Woodrow Wilson Center Press, 1996).
53. Saskia Sassen, *The Global City: New York, London, Tokyo* (Princeton, NJ: Princeton University Press, 1991); Saskia Sassen, *Cities in a World Economy* (Thousand Oaks, CA: Pine Forge Press, 1994).
54. See also *Dual City: Restructuring New York*, John H. Mollenkopf and Manuel Castells, eds. (New York: The Russell Sage Foundation, 1991).
55. Cohen, "The Hypothesis of Urban Convergence," in *Preparing for the Urban Future*, op. cit., 29.
56. Weiping Wu, "Economic Competition and Resource Mobilization," in *Preparing for the Urban Future*, ibid., 123–54.
57. Roger A. Waldinger, *Still the Promised City: African-Americans and New Immigrants in Postindustrial New York* (Cambridge, MA: Harvard University Press, 1996).
58. Wu, op. cit., 134.
59. Xiangming Chen, "The Changing Roles of Free Economic Zones in Development: A Comparative Analysis of Capitalist and Socialist Cases in East Asia," *Studies in Comparative International Development*, 29 (Fall 1994), 3–25.
60. Xiangming Chen, "Urban History as Contemporary City (Re)Building: Shenzhen's Rise and Shanghai's Renaissance in Post-Mao China." Paper presented to the 55th Annual Meeting of the Midwest Political Science Association, Chicago, April 10–12, 1997.

Chapter 9

Political Parties

In the 2004 American presidential election, there was a great deal of discussion about the political geography of the United States. Observers talked about "blue" states and "red" states, the former being those states that favored the Democrats and lay primarily on the American coasts, the latter those states that favored the Republicans and basically occupied the center of the United States. This political division led political pundits to rail on about the deep divisions in America today in terms of parties: the Republican Party and its supporters were viewed as the heartland of America, representing the best of conservative ideals, whereas the Democratic Party and its supporters were viewed as liberal, progressive, and, above all else, deeply skeptical about the Bush administration and its War in Iraq. If all this discussion were to be believed, America was no longer a country united by a deep faith in its ideals of freedom and democracy, but rather one deeply divided along party lines. Indeed, while Republicans were almost uniformly happy about the direction of the country, Democrats seemed to be very angry and almost uniformly disaffected from the directions taken by president and his administration.

Whatever the ultimate outcome of these divisions, it is clear today that political parties play a very important part in the workings of the American republic. Party officials take very different views of the future of America, and they manage to stir up the passions of their supporters in seemingly deep and countless ways.[1] Even though most people are only active in the workings of the party system at election time, the parties themselves nonetheless play a major role in the working of everyday life in America—especially now, in a world in which we hear almost every day about new acts of terrorism, the failures of the American efforts in Iraq and Afghanistan, and the looming problems with nations like North Korea and Iran.

In this chapter we consider the nature of political parties from the perspective of political sociology. We want to ask a series of key questions: Why have political parties come about? Do they serve special purposes that other organizations fail to fulfill? How have they managed to escape the efforts of politicians who wished to prevent their rise to power? These and other questions will serve as the main agenda for this chapter. Specifically, we shall consider the following topics: the nature and origins of modern political parties, variations in the organizational structure both of modern and older political parties, the politics internal to party organizations, and the nature and development of parties, and political partisanship, mainly in contemporary American politics.

The Nature of Modern Political Parties

Modern political parties first arose in the nineteenth century. In the United States, their birthplace, parties surfaced just prior to the presidential election of 1800, but the complete trappings of the modern party—the strength of organization and the involvement of the public—did not fully appear until the 1820s and 1830s. In Great Britain, political clubs and cliques existed long before the advent of nineteenth-century politics, but only after the passage of the electoral reforms of 1832 and especially of 1867 did parties develop into something akin to contemporary institutions in the United States. Elsewhere, in Europe, modern parties were somewhat slower to develop; in the Scandinavian countries, for instance, they did not emerge until the turn of the twentieth century.[2]

As the parties in the United States and Britain evolved over time, they became transformed, eventually assuming many of the special features we now associate with the modern political party. William Nisbet Chambers, in his definitive analysis of the early American parties—the Federalists of Hamilton and Washington, the Republicans of Jefferson—identifies the several unique qualities of the modern parties through a comparison with their predecessors, the cliques and factions.[3] Chambers observes, first of all, that the modern political party involves an active leadership group committed to goals that advance the party rather than individual personalities. The club or clique, in contrast, is typically a temporary alliance of individuals. It is not identified by specific party labels, and members are more concerned with their own personal advancement than that of the group to which they belong. In addition, Chambers notes, the modern party has developed specific practices designed to further its own expansion and to allow it to work within the government. They include the practices of electioneering for campaigns, the techniques of nominating candidates for office, and the special arts of compromise required to maintain a hold over high political office. To clubs and cliques of politicians, such practices appear quite foreign. The party, moreover, also encompasses a wide variety of interests and supporters, each of which attempts to shape the opinions of party leaders; in contrast, the club is only based on a narrow range of concerns. Coherent programs, or ideologies, flow from the structure and activities developed by the modern parties, partly as a means of further securing its continuity both in and out of government, while clubs or factions rarely, if ever, advance programs or statements of principle. Last, Chambers notes, modern political parties rely heavily upon the support of the public to remain in office and thus seek to solicit and mold opinion among the public, whereas factions or cliques, which are highly self-contained groups, manifest little concern, or need, for broad public support.

Such are the principal features of modern political parties. We should see them as representing a kind of Weberian ideal type, an abstraction that is created from a number of similar features of modern parties everywhere.[4] There is, however, considerable diversity among modern parties, as we shall see shortly. First, however, let us consider the origins of political parties.

The Birth of Modern Political Parties

There are a number of reasonably good theories and accounts of the origins of modern political parties.[5] Some take a specifically historical tack, attempting to locate the origins of parties in the special circumstances and setting of a nation.[6] Others take a broad, comparative stance, identifying the origins of modern parties in features common to many nations.[7]

One of the most fascinating and interesting accounts about the origins of political parties comes from a political scientist, John Aldrich.[8] Earlier in this book we discussed rational actor, or rational choice, theories of political behavior. These theories are now very popular among political scientists and are attracting more and more attention from political sociologists.[9] Such theories assume that people choose to participate in politics for motives and reasons that are strictly self-interested. That is, if you to choose to vote or to participate in a specific political organization, you do so because you believe you will gain some specific benefit from that activity. Aldrich develops a theory about the origins of political parties that is based on the principles of rational choice theory.

Let's consider an example here of how such theories work and the problems to which they are applied. Suppose that you are concerned about the trash on the streets in your neighborhood. A group of you and your neighbors decide that you want to get the streets cleaned up in order to improve your local area. So you form an organization, the neighbors come together, and you demand that your local government do a better job of cleaning up the trash in the neighborhood. Seen from the perspective of rational choice theory, the formation of your neighborhood organization is a rational response to a problem that you and your neighbors perceived. All of you obviously saw a benefit to be gained, and you decided that the benefit was greater than the costs involved, such as time or even money that you and your neighbors had to spend in order to put the organization together and go to the local city hall to demand that the work be done.

Aldrich applies a similar kind of logic to the formation of political parties in the United States. Parties, he argues, should be seen as organizations that are invented and used by ambitious politicians and party officials who seek office and power, nothing more, nothing less. They do not simply originate because of certain passing historical circumstances, but rather because they help politicians to solve recurring problems in a rational manner. Office seekers, for example, must mobilize and persuade people to vote for them. Parties become the means whereby such office seekers can effectively reach the electorate. Parties have the organizational apparatus as well as financial resources that assist office seekers, and they have the means to routinely tap into and persuade people how to vote. They are employed, in general, in ways that will maximize the benefits that figures, such as party officials, gain but also minimize their costs of participation. And they are also used in different ways, depending on whether the party operates in government or to secure the vote of the electorate.

Now you might think this is a rather simple-minded way of viewing the origins of political parties. It seems to neglect history, for example, as well as how outside forces and institutions can influence the life of political parties. But Aldrich insists that we can still think of parties in terms of rational choice theory if, on the one hand, we see the party as an institution that also changes in response to changes in government or in the circumstances of the electorate, and, on the other hand, the office seeker as someone who alters his self-interested behavior in response to such changes. For example, when the modern political party—of conventions, rallies, parades, and dedicated professionals—came into existence in the 1830s, it did so in order to reach a broader electorate. Office seekers and party officials realized that in order to win office the party had to campaign and effectively reach out to an expanding electorate. They thus changed the elements of the party organization so as to reach a large number of voters and convince them to vote for the party. Likewise, Aldrich argues, the party organizations of today have changed in important ways as well, in part because the candidates for office now can rely on other devices, such as television, to reach the voters. The party organization in some respects remains as strong today as ever, but, he insists, it is now used in different ways by self-interested politicians and party officials who seek to win office and gain power in government.

Aldrich's theory is an extremely interesting and compelling account of the origin and workings of political parties in America in particular. With a few basic principles, derived from rational choice theory, he is able to explain a great deal of behavior of both party officials and voters. Although his view might be seen as very different from those of political sociology's founding figures, in certain respects it is not. Like Max Weber, who also wrote about political parties, Aldrich takes the political party very seriously as an actor in modern society that can shape political action. But rather than focusing very broadly on historical or comparative circumstances as Weber did, Aldrich focuses explicitly on the ends of political parties and how self-interested actors use those parties to secure and maintain power in the modern world.

Variations in Modern Political Parties: Highlights of Current and Former Patterns

The notion of modern political parties we introduced at the outset of this chapter should serve as a guide to help us sort out and to better understand the real world. Like all such abstractions, however, it represents a composite of many common, yet subtly different, forms; it advances our understanding by showing us what apparently disparate groups hold in common, and yet it prevents an even deeper appreciation by downplaying important differences. In this section we consider some of these differences by looking at some of the contemporary and earlier variations.

CURRENT PATTERNS

The most illuminating discussion of differences among current parties can be found in the analyses of Maurice Duverger in *Political Parties: Their Organization and Activity in the Modern State*. Duverger provides an exhaustive taxonomy of party structures; two criteria he uses to distinguish among parties—their constituent units and their form of membership—are of special interest.[10]

Constituent Units. According to Duverger, there are three principal forms of the constituent units of modern parties: the caucus, the cell, and the branch.

By closely examining the structure and activities of these units, Duverger suggests, one is better able to understand the nature and relative effectiveness of the political parties that employ them.

The caucus, which, for example, is characteristic of the Democratic and Republican parties in parts of the United States, is fairly limited as an organization. Its number of full-time members is small, and it seeks only the most minimal expansion of its membership in the public. It rarely engages in efforts to generate much enthusiasm and support in the broader society because it wishes to remain a closed and, to a large extent, select organization. Moreover, it incorporates a wide expanse of geographical territory; American caucuses cover such large units as counties and municipalities. Consonant with its limited aims for expansion, the caucus operates only on an intermittent basis, becoming active just at election times.

At the lower levels of organization, caucus leaders are typically precinct captains and other agents whose responsibility is to see that the voters turn out for the party's candidates at election time. The precinct captains also have the responsibility of disseminating information and generating enthusiasm among party members for the nominating conventions, those few occasions when party adherents gather together for the purpose of electing people to run for office. The membership, however, rarely plays a part in the selection of candidates; the primary tasks of choosing candidates are left up to the major party figures.[11]

Duverger regards the caucus with no little disdain, especially as compared with the cell and the branch forms. He notes, for instance, that in European countries the caucus is on the decline and is generally being replaced by the cell or the branch. Duverger observes that the caucus remains a viable organization only in the United States, largely because it appears to be more compatible with special features of the U.S. historical setting, particularly the strength of individualism and the absence of a sense of class-consciousness.[12] Among other things, he notes that "caucuses are an archaic type of political party structure [sic]. . . . In their composition as well as in their structure [weak collective organization, predominance of individual considerations] they represent the influence of the upper and lower middle class. . . . The greater efficiency of recruiting techniques directly adapted to the masses [for example, the system of branches] has usually brought about the decline of the caucus."[13]

The branch, which is characteristic of most Socialist parties in Europe, is in most respects fundamentally different from the caucus as a form of party organization. In general, the branch represents a highly centralized form of organization in which the membership is tightly locked through an intricate division of labor and in which there is a clear emphasis on control from above. It incorporates a fairly large number of members, is ever after new ones, and attempts to establish for itself a broad base among the public. It generally seeks an open stance with regard to the broader society, hoping thereby to establish itself as a permanent and broad point of reference and to be able to mobilize people for a variety of purposes.

One of the striking features of the branch is that it exists for more than simply the election of candidates to high political office. This explains, for example, why the branch takes an expansionist approach among the public. This also accounts for the regularity and intensity of the branch's activities; the leaders of the branch attempt to keep in constant communication with their membership and to encourage informal ties among the members. The branches of the Socialist parties, for example, generally hold meetings twice a month at which they provide a broad form of political education in addition to the more routine forms of information pertaining to elections.

Comparing the branch and the caucus, it is evident that Duverger far prefers the former type of organization, partly because he believes that it enables all people to play a much more prominent role in the internal affairs of the party and, hence, that it is fundamentally more democratic: "There is no doubt the caucus is undemocratic...; this small closed group, composed of semi coopted, well-known figures, is obviously oligarchic in character. The branch, on the other hand, which is open to all, and in which the leaders are elected by the members (at least in theory), corresponds to the requirements of political democracy."[14]

The third, and last, principal form of constituent unit of modern parties is that of the cell, a form similar in most respects to the branch. Like the branch, for example, the cell is always seeking to expand its membership base among the public and actively searches for new members through regular meetings and extensive propaganda. The cell, an invention of the Communist parties of Europe, also possesses two features that make it an even more tightly knit and cohesive unit than the branch. First, the cell is based on the occupational locus of individuals rather that the residential one—it is found not in the commune or district as is the branch, but instead in the factory of the office. Naturally this provides the cell with an unusually firm and vivid presence among its membership and thereby secures its psychological hold upon the loyalties of members. Second, the size of the cell is smaller than that of the branch; whereas the branch typically has more than one hundred members, the cell rarely achieves this size. Its comparatively smaller membership provides the cell with an additional basis for creating an intense solidarity and loyalty on the part of its members.

The cell, Duverger further suggests, represents a profound change in the conception of a political party. Whereas the caucus is organized principally for electoral victory and the branch for establishing a broad base of adherents among the public in addition to electoral victory, the cell is organized as a means of overthrowing the established governmental order. He observes, moreover, that "instead of a body intended for the winning of votes, for grouping the representatives, and for maintaining contact between them and their electors, the political party [under the cell] becomes an instrument of agitation, of propaganda, of discipline, and if necessary, of clandestine action, for which elections and parliamentary debates are only one of several means of action, and a secondary means at that. The importance of this change cannot be overemphasized. It marks a breach between the political regime and the organizations it has produced to ensure its working."[15]

Form of Membership. A second means of illuminating the differences among modern parties and thus cast light on their relative advantages and disadvantages, Duverger claims, is through classification on the basis of form of membership. There are two broad types of party based upon this criterion: the *cadre* party and the *mass* party. The cadre party, which most closely resembles American political parties, is a limited enterprise that restricts membership to very few people and attempts to attract important and familiar faces that provide the party with a blue-ribbon image. It is a party that is loosely knit in its organization and that rarely maintains a high level of control over its organizational bases in society. The cadre party, moreover, seeks only to prepare itself for the electoral battles. Therefore its leaders are principally interested in maintaining their contacts with candidates; in stirring up the public, members and nonmembers, just for electoral campaigns; and in winning the allegiance of voters, not of citizens per se. Duverger further asserts that the cadre party is generally on the decline—at least in Western countries—having been replaced in most areas at the end of the nineteenth century and the beginning of the twentieth century by the *mass* party.

The mass party, which is a creation essentially of the broad modern extension of suffrage and most characteristic of the branch-cell–based European Socialist and Communist parties, is interested in gaining converts to its cause as well as in generating votes at the polls. Thus it attempts to create widespread as well as intense support among members of the public. As it is primarily interested in attracting adherents, it creates sophisticated machinery for the recruitment and enrollment of large numbers of dues-paying members. Moreover, it is necessary to differentiate clearly between degrees or levels of membership in the mass party. These are the categories: supporters, who simply pay dues and infrequently attend the meetings of the party; militants, who are the active members and the ones upon whom the success of the party chiefly depends; and the inner circle, or core group, that exercises complete control over every facet of the party's structure.

Although these, and other, taxonomic devices employed by Duverger have been criticized, they still remain highly illuminating and useful.[16] Duverger, for instance, draws attention to the fact that the cadre, caucus-based political parties, like those in the United States, tended to develop historically from within the legislature; in his view, this may explain why they have also retained an emphasis on limited membership of the public and an elitist quality. In contrast, the branch- or cell-based mass parties, like the Communist and Socialist parties in Europe, developed outside the legislature; this may account for their greater responsiveness to the participation of the public and for their more frequent attempts to promote rank-and-file members to posts of leadership.

Candidate Campaign Organizations. In recent years there have been some noticeable changes in the structure of political parties, particularly in the United States. The most important has been the development of candidate campaign organizations, especially of candidates for major political offices. These campaign organizations rely heavily upon the appeal of the specific candidate and are also responsible for creating large war chests of funds for the rigors of the campaign itself. They also become the means through which large amounts of money are funneled to the candidates, often well in advance of the actual election campaign. By the fall of 1999, for example, George W. Bush had already assembled more than $50 million for his race, even though the election was more than a year away. It was the largest amount of campaign money ever assembled by any presidential candidate in American history. Moreover, the presidential campaigns of George Bush and John Kerry in 2004 cost the two candidates more than $250 million combined!

The effect of these new candidate campaign organizations, which essentially are run independently of the party, has been to limit the impact of the political party even more in the United States and to place a greater emphasis upon the strengths of the individual political candidate. But this has been a long-term tendency in the nature of American political parties, noted years ago by V. O. Key in his seminal analysis of American parties. In Europe, by contrast, the political party continues to be a strong component of any political campaign, providing an important structural and ideological integrity to the character of political races and contests often lacking in the United States.

Electoral Laws. The history of politics and political organization provides one key to understanding the nature of parties in general and to the differences between parties in Europe and the United States. Another, even more crucial, key lies in the nature of electoral laws themselves.[17]

The electoral system of most continental European nations has been based upon what is called the system of *proportional representation*, or some variation of it. This is a method that awards seats in the legislature on the basis of the proportion of votes gained by a candidate in the electoral contest itself. For example, if there are 100 seats up for election, those seats will be awarded to parties based upon the proportion of the vote they secure. If Party A secures 35 percent of the vote, then it will also secure 35 of the seats in the contest; likewise, if Party C secures 10 percent of the vote, it will also secure 10 seats. Through this method, which is the most common method of election throughout democratic countries, a variety of political parties can be represented in a nation's legislature.[18]

The method of election in the United States is much different. Here there is a *winner-take-all*, or plurality, system of election. Victors are determined on the basis of who secures the majority of votes in a single election or a single district. The long-term effect has been to produce the two major party contestants in America, the Republicans and the Democrats. Other political parties, because they cannot secure any form of representation based upon their overall share of the electoral vote, get tossed aside.

There are several obvious and not-so-obvious consequences of the differences in the form of electoral laws. One is that the electoral system in the United States has made it virtually impossible for third party candidates to secure any continuing form of representation in the legislature, either state or national. Over the course of American history, various third party candidates have run for office. They include Theodore Roosevelt, who won as the Progressive candidate in 1912; Strom Thurmond, who ran for president as a rump Dixiecrat candidate in 1948; and most recently, Ross Perot, who ran for president under the banner of the Independent Party in 1992 and 1996. Perot did better as a third party candidate than other figure in recent memory, securing almost 20 percent of the vote. The effect of his popularity was to give the presidency to Bill Clinton on a mere plurality, not a majority, of the popular vote cast. Perot's candidacy took its toll—it cost him many millions of dollars from his own personal fortune for the campaign—and he failed to gain nearly the same popular vote in 1996. In 1998, Jesse "the body/mind" Ventura ran successfully as the Independent Party candidate for Governor of Minnesota, the first such third party victory for gubernatorial office since Robert LaFollette ran and won on the Progressive Party ticket in Wisconsin.

Another important consequence of the different form of electoral laws in Europe and the United States is that the parties in Europe have been based more heavily on a strong ideological platform and appeal than in America. Proportional representation allows parties to run on the basis of particular ideological platforms and appeals as they seek to gain a share of the overall vote for themselves. In general, it favors the representation of minorities.[19] This method was clearly helpful in the rise of the Green Party in Europe as it sought to campaign based on important environmental issues. In general, proportional representation helps to encourage the development and success of even small

parties. In comparison, the winner-take-all system in America has forced parties to appeal to the sympathies of the large group of middle-of-the-road voters,
people who generally do not take strong ideological positions on any issue but
are necessary to electoral victory. It is the vote of these citizens that will determine who wins a particular contest. The effect, observers note, has been to
diminish the distinctive ideological character of both American parties as they
seek to gain the vote of the great middling sector of the electorate.

EARLY PATTERNS: THE POLITICAL MACHINE OF URBAN AMERICA

Party machines dominated the political life of many large American cities for a
number of years.[20] The rise of the machine roughly corresponded to the waves
of European immigrants in American cities; in New York City, large numbers of
immigrants arrived in the 1840s and 1850s, and the political machine showed a
parallel rise in strength. In most cities, the machine was run by the Democrats,
but in a few cities, like Philadelphia, it was run by the Republicans. Control of
the machine was typically in the hands of members of distinct ethnic groups.
In Boston, for example, it was the Irish—most notably Boss Curley—who found
their way into the positions of control over the machine; while in New York
City, it was the Irish and later the Italians who controlled the party machine. As
the case of New York City illustrated, it was not simply that the reins of power
were held by distinct ethnic groups, but also that these reins were transferred
over time from one ethnic group to another.[21]

What did the party machine look like? How did it wield power? The
machine seemed to have both the structure and the internal discipline of an
army and often worked as effectively. Typically at its top was a single leader,
a boss, who exercised principal control over the operations and inner structure of the machine.[22] Slightly lower in the hierarchy were his associates or
lieutenants whom he relied upon for information and for the successful implementation of his commands. The social ties between the boss and his lieutenants often began in childhood, as Mike Royko's insightful analysis of Richard
Daley's Democratic machine in Chicago reveals; these were hardened through
the years by common political battles and enemies.[23] Beneath this top echelon
there were further niches in the machine's structure, including those of various
party functionaries.

The principal goals of the machine were electoral victories and, through
such victories, the control of the privileges and reward of public office in the
city. Insofar as the winning of political office was concerned, the strength of the
machine lay far down in the recesses of the organization—in the vast networks
that punctuated the many wards and precincts of cities. In each precinct there

was a captain, beneath him were lieutenants, and further beneath them were other functionaries; it was these officials who helped to keep the wheels of the machine greased and upon whose shoulders rested the fate of the machine's candidates at the polls. The men of the machine knew the members of their district, and when the time came to get them to the polls, these men had carefully laid the foundations for a large, and sometimes overwhelming, victory of the machine. The classic revelations of how the local members of the machine performed their tasks are found in the discourse on practical politics offered by George Washington Plunkitt. Plunkitt was a member of the Tammany Machine in New York City at the height of its power in the late nineteenth and early twentieth centuries. Consider just a few of his pearls of practical political wisdom:

> What tells in holdin' your grip on your district is to go right down among the poor families and help them in the different ways they need help. I've got a regular system for this. If there's a fire in Ninth, Tenth, or Eleventh Avenue, for example, any hour of the day or night, I'm usually there with some of my election district captains as soon as the fire engines. If a family is burned out I don't ask whether they are Republicans or Democrats, and I don't refer them to the Charity Organization Society, which would investigate their case in a month or two and decide they were worthy of help about the time they are dead from starvation. I just get quarters for them, buy clothes for them if their clothes were burned up, and put them up till they get things runnin' again. It's philanthropy, but its politics, too—mighty good politics. Who can tell how many votes one of these fires brings me? The poor are the most grateful people in the world, and let me tell you, they have more friends in their neighborhoods than the rich have in theirs.
>
> If there's a family in my district in want I know it before the charitable societies do, and me and my men are first on the ground. I have a special corps to look up such cases. The consequence is that the poor look up to George W. Plunkitt as a father, come to him in trouble—and don't forget him on election.
>
> Another thing, I can always get a job for a deservin' man. I make it a point to keep on the track of jobs, and it seldom happens that I don't have a few up my sleeve ready for use. I know every big employer in the district and in the whole city, for that matter, and they ain't in the habit of sayin' no to me when I ask them for a job.
>
> And the children—the little roses of the district. Do I forget them? Oh, no! They know me, every one of them, and they know that a sight of Uncle George and candy means the same thing. Some of them are the best kind of vote getters. I'll tell you a case. Last year a little Eleventh Avenue rosebud, whose father is a Republican, caught hold of his whiskers on election day and said she wouldn't let go till he's promised to vote for me. And she didn't.[24]

For a long time, the machines of political parties exercised a tight control over municipal governments and the political arena generally in many urban settings. They did so because they were able to provide the needy and dependent immigrants with material inducements not available elsewhere.[25] The machines provided jobs to recently arrived immigrants who could not otherwise secure positions. The machine provided general forms of welfare, including money and clothing, again to those people who could not otherwise secure the basic necessities of life. These, plus other benefits, served as inducements and enabled the machine to secure the compliance of voters on election day—a rather minor request after all was said and done.

The Power and Politics of Modern Political Parties

Although the modern political party is recognized for a number of distinctive and innovative features, the scope and vitality of its organization—the neatly defined hierarchies, the vast network of communications, and the overriding commitments of leaders to organizational goals and growth—rank as the characteristics of singular historic significance. Many writers have drawn special attention to them.[26] One of the most persuasive was Moise Ostrogorski, the first and possibly still the most brilliant analyst of modern parties.[27] Writing at the close of the nineteenth century, Ostrogorski took special note of the political organizations formed by the Jacksonian Democrats in the United States and of the Liberal Party's Birmingham Caucus in England. Painting his analysis with a good deal of cynicism and moral condemnation, Ostrogorski emphasized the ways in which the organizational strength of the Democrats in the United States and the Liberals in England enabled their leaders to manipulate the sentiments of the electorate. Ostrogorski feared, moreover, that the strength of these party organizations might grow so considerable that citizens could be deprived of their right to choose political representatives free from party interference and that party leadership could dominate the public representatives in the legislature.[28]

ROBERT MICHELS' IRON LAW OF OLIGARCHY

Among political sociologists, the seminal analysis of the organizational features and internal processes of modern parties is that of Robert Michels, a German-born scholar.[29] Michels' analysis principally concerns the German Social Democratic Party at the turn of the twentieth century, but it deals as well with trade unions and other parties both in Europe and in the United States. He considers why seemingly fluid democratic organizations like parties become transformed into highly ossified structures with members robbed of rights to participate in decisions and leaders granted inordinate power. His examination, known chiefly by its identification of an "iron law of oligarchy," is so important that it is worth dwelling on at some length.

To begin with, Michels asserts that the members of the working classes, and by implication those of the mass public, can only achieve privileges for themselves by combining their numbers into organizations. Adopting a position roughly equivalent to that of V. I. Lenin—though apparently unaware of Lenin's own analysis—Michels maintains that the "principle of organization is an absolutely essential condition for the political struggle of the masses."[30] Nevertheless, he claims, once a party organization has been formed by the masses, the reins of power inevitably fall into the hands of an oligarchy. Psychological factors contribute to the inability of the masses to retain control of the organization. These include their suggestibility to orators and propaganda in general and their willingness to submit to the commands of leaders.[31] Besides these there are also technical factors that produce organizational incompetence on the part of the masses. For instance, once the representatives of the membership of the organization have been elected, Michels avers, they achieve a level of expertise and a degree of control over the means of communication that individual members of the rank and file could not even hope to attain.

There are also qualities of the positions of leadership, however, that enhance the tendencies for oligarchies to emerge in party organizations. The attainment of expertise by the leaders falsely encourages them to believe that they are indispensable to the life of the party. The financial benefits that accompany office in the organization provide an incentive for leaders to retain their positions, particularly if their prior positions in the organization were as impoverished as those of other members of the rank and file. Michels writes:

> When the leaders are not persons of means and when they have no other source of income, they hold firmly to their positions for economic reasons, coming to regard the functions they exercise as theirs by inalienable right. Especially is this true of manual workers, who, since becoming leaders, have lost their aptitude for their former occupation. For the loss of their positions would be a financial disaster, and in most cases it would be altogether impossible for them to return to their old way of life.[32]

Ultimately those who serve as leaders become so enamored of the power and privileges of their positions that they seek to retain the positions indefinitely. Among other things, they try to coopt future leaders from among the rank-and-file members and, thus, to prevent members' free choice in the selection of their future leaders. They also create further positions within the leadership ranks, multiplying the benefits that can be obtained from holding office and simultaneously further insulating themselves from contact with and influence by the rank and file.

Michels is fully aware that leaders cannot dominate the membership of party organizations indefinitely, even by using such ploys as cooptation.

To explain the change that occurs in the leadership of party organization, he adopts a form of explanation similar to that which Vilfredo Pareto used to explain the changes in the composition of the governing class in society.[33] Michels argues that there never is a clear break between the composition of the old leadership group and that of the new one. Instead of *circulation des elites*, there is *reunion des elites*, that is, an amalgam of elements from the old leadership group with elements drawn from the new one. Change in leadership through amalgamation is coupled with change through decentralization, Michels further observes, with smaller and smaller oligarchies emerging from the original large one. Nonetheless, the acts of amalgamation and decentralization do not detract from the one essential fact of every party organization—oligarchy—or the concentration of power at the top of the party organization and the resulting loss of power incurred by members of the rank and file.

Michels' thesis about the accumulation and concentration of power at the top of party organizations might as easily be called the "ironic law of oligarchy." It is nothing short of a major irony that socialist parties, such as the German Social Democratic Party, which preached the end of class rule and the equal dispersion of power and privilege among all people in society, displayed vast internal inequities in the distribution of power and wealth. The irony in the discovery further convinced Michels that he had uncovered an eternal verity about party organizations, in particular, and perhaps even about mass organizations, in general.

Other researchers have followed up on Michels' leads. Maurice Duverger, for example, found evidence of oligarchical structures in many different political parties, especially the Communist parties in Europe that introduced systematic methods for recruiting and training new leaders.[34] He observes that even in presumably democratically administered parties, oligarchical leadership seems to surface: "In theory, the principle of election should prevent the formation of an oligarchy; in fact, it seems rather to favour it. The masses are naturally conservative; they become attached to their old leaders, they are suspicious of new faces."[35]

Renate Mayntz and Samuel Eldersveld find reasons for making revisions in Michel's iron law. Mayntz, in a study of a district unit of the Christian Democratic Union in West Berlin, uncovered some signs of oligarchy. She found, in particular, that new leaders often received their positions through the influence of older members of the leadership group, and the rank and file hardly exercised much power at all in the selection of new leaders.[36] Yet the leadership was not oligarchic in the sense portrayed by Michels; the leaders did not deliberately attempt to maintain themselves in office through the devices to which Michels pointed—for example, control of communications and monopoly of organizational skills. Instead, certain features of the party organization contributed to a high degree of autonomy on the part of the leadership. Such autonomy included an election process that prevented the rank and file from exercising much choice over the selection of leaders, a strict hierarchy in the organization that prevented the rank-and-file from easily evaluating the performance of the leadership, and an absence of regular channels that would permit the rank-and-file members to participate in the formulation of party policies. Mayntz concludes that while this party organization, at least, may not strictly conform to the pattern and sources of oligarchy noted by Michels, it is also a far cry from the achievement of a democratic process in which leaders and followers freely interact with and influence one another. Eldersveld, basing his ideas on his observations of local party organizations in Michigan, argues that the current political party is best conceived as a special kind of organization. It is one in which command does not clearly flow down from the top, but rather is diffusely partitioned among several layers of the organization, resulting in a very loosely coordinated structure.[37] Furthermore, he claims, the cohesiveness of the elite groups at the top of the political party organizations is less real than apparent; instead of a single oligarchy, Eldersveld believes that there are several different suboligarchies that are only loosely coordinated and only infrequently in contact with one another.

Among the efforts to reexamine Michel's thesis, there is none that ranks as more imaginative and thorough than the analysis of Seymour Martin Lipset, Martin Trow, and James Coleman.[38] Recognizing considerable truth in Michels' iron law, Lipset and colleagues set out to discover the conditions under which oligarchies fail to arise in large organizations. The site of their study was a trade union, not a political party, but the choice was propitious nonetheless, since trade unions, like parties, are often as vulnerable (if not more so) to the growth of oligarchic leadership. Moreover, the particular union they examined, the International Typographical Union (ITU), represented the single trade union in the United States that had a long history of democratic politics. There were two political parties that regularly competed for union offices and that just as consistently alternated in the control of the offices. Inasmuch as all other unions were run by oligarchies, the specific question for Lipset, Trow, and Coleman became: Why does the ITU have democratic (competitive) rule instead of oligarchic control?

There were, as Lipset and his colleagues found, both historic and structural reasons for the presence of democracy, or absence of oligarchy, in the ITU. First, at the founding of the ITU, the printers revealed a strong identification and commitment to their craft; this loyalty became transformed into an interest and concern about their union. As a result, they were less apt to fall into the trap of membership passivity that Michels thought assisted the rise of oligarchies. Second, the ITU was somewhat notable among unions for the autonomy of the local branches; instead of having been created from the top down, it had been created as a federation of autonomous units. This fact played an important part in the subsequent politics of the union, facilitating as well as sustaining dissent against established practices and policies in the union. Third, among blue-collar workers, printing carries high prestige and also considerable financial rewards. These attributes perhaps serve to reinforce the printers' commitment to their craft, and they also create less of a disparity between the job of union leader and that of rank-and-file worker. Hence, the incentive for a leader to retain his office for its special perquisites was notably absent in the ITU. Fourth, as a result of their general concern and participation in the union, the printers as a group seemed to be especially skilled in the informal and formal ways of politics. Such skills on the part of the rank and file further encouraged engagement in union politics, even enabling some rank-and-file members to achieve high office in the union. These, too, are qualities that Michels did not find in the membership of the oligarchic parties and unions he observed.

The study of the ITU, in short, was instructive for the lessons it may provide to political parties—and other organizations—wishing to avoid oligarchy. The following qualities are especially important to achieve democracy within parties: encourage commitment to the party, foster participation by the rank and file, create a climate receptive to dissent and innovation, and breed social and political skills in the rank and file.

The nature of the internal structure of political parties will remain an interesting matter of study as long as parties remain important institutions. Michels' analysis provides an important insight into the basic character of these organizations; its essential truth seems hard to disprove even now, many decades after its initial declaration. Moreover, his insight raises intriguing and difficult questions about the relative advantages and disadvantages of parties that exhibit oligarchic tendencies over those that exhibit democratic ones. A true democrat may believe that any form of oligarchy is reprehensible and to be avoided at all costs. However, organizations that permit competition and dissent to arise among factions are often so debilitated by the internal conflicts that they are incapable of attaining their goals in the larger society. Those, by comparison, that insist on unity within the ranks and manifest cohesive leadership, perhaps even oligarchy, frequently are more successful in attaining the broader goals.[39] Which should one prefer—democracy within the ranks or victory outside the ranks? That is a question we all are left to ponder.

Political Partisanship: Contemporary Patterns and Trends in the United States

To what degree are people actually motivated by the actions of political parties and their leaders? To what degree do they identify with parties, for example?

And are such identities maintained over time? These are the sorts of questions we shall examine here. We shall limit our analysis, for the sake of brevity, to the national level of politics, to presidential or congressional elections, as well as to related phenomena at this level.

THE BREADTH OF POLITICAL PARTISANSHIP

We can study political partisanship in different ways. One is by looking at how people identify with political parties, if they do so at all. Party identification, it turns out, is a very important dimension of how people think and act in politics.[40] Generally, people who adopt a particular party identification will vote for that party in national elections. But over the course of the past several decades there have been some profound changes in the nature and impact of party identification among American voters.

When studies of voting behavior and party identification were first done in the 1950s, there were some fairly clear empirical patterns. About one of every two voters identified as a Democrat, another three of every ten identified as Republicans, and the remainder—twenty percent—claimed they were Independents, with no regular party identification.[41] Those who identified with the Democrats tended to vote Democratic in national elections, whereas those who identified with the Republicans tended to vote Republican. Independents, as you might expect, were a kind of free-floating electorate that would vary in their choice of actual candidates from one election to another.

This pattern of party identification and voting remained more or less descriptive of the American electorate for about fifteen years, until the late 1960s. Then the pattern began to crumble and important new shifts began to appear. In particular, there was a growing number of Independents to be found among the party identifiers and a smaller number of people who identified themselves as Democratic partisans. These changes began to appear just after the election of Richard Nixon, a Republican, in 1968. When Nixon was reelected in 1972, the shift to Independents became somewhat more marked.[42]

Tables 9.1 and 9.2 provide a closer look at these patterns. The data come from the National Election Studies. These are surveys of a sample of the American electorate done every two years that provide a glimpse of how people are voting and how they identify in terms of the two major political parties. If you examine the data in Table 9.1 you will see the broad changes in the nature of the American electorate from 1952 through 2004. Among other things, note the growth in the overall proportion of people who claim to be Independents, which includes the three main rows listed as Independents: it rose from 23 percent in 1952 to 39 percent in 2004. Another way of seeing roughly the same thing is shown in Table 9.2. Note that the partisan voters, including both weak and strong partisans, declined from 74 percent in 1952 to 61 percent 2004.

TABLE 9.1. Party Identification 7-Point Scale, 1952–2004

QUESTION TEXT:
"Generally speaking, do you usually think of yourself as a Republican, a Democrat, an Independent, or what?" (IF REPUBLICAN OR DEMOCRAT) "Would you call yourself a strong (REPUBLICAN/DEMOCRAT) or a not very strong (REPUBLICAN/DEMOCRAT)?" (IF INDEPENDENT, OTHER [1966 and later: OR NO PREFERENCE]:) "Do you think of yourself as closer to the Republican or Democratic part?"

	'52	'54	'56	'58	'60	'62	'64	'66	'68	'70	'72	'74	'76	'78	'80	'82	'84	'86	'88	'90	'92	'94	'96	'98	'00	'02	'04
Strong Democrat	22	22	21	27	20	23	27	18	20	20	15	17	15	15	18	20	17	18	17	20	18	15	18	19	19	17	17
Weak Democrat	25	25	23	22	25	23	25	28	25	24	26	21	25	24	23	24	20	22	18	19	18	19	19	18	15	17	16
Independent Democrat	10	9	6	7	6	7	9	9	10	10	11	13	12	14	11	11	11	10	12	12	14	13	14	14	15	15	17
Independent Independent	6	7	9	7	10	8	8	12	11	13	13	15	15	14	13	11	11	12	11	10	12	11	9	11	12	8	10
Independent Republican	7	6	8	5	7	6	6	7	9	8	10	9	10	10	10	8	12	11	13	12	12	12	12	11	13	13	12
Weak Republican	14	14	14	16	14	16	14	15	15	15	13	14	14	13	14	14	15	15	14	15	14	15	15	16	12	16	12
Strong Republican	14	13	15	11	16	12	11	10	10	9	10	8	9	8	9	10	12	10	14	10	11	15	12	10	12	14	16
Apolitical	3	4	4	4	2	4	1	1	1	1	1	3	1	3	2	2	2	2	2	2	1	1	1	2	1	1	0
N	1784	1130	1757	1808	1911	1287	1550	1278	1553	1501	2694	2505	2850	2283	1612	1411	2236	2166	2032	1966	2474	1787	1710	1276	1797	1488	1197

SOURCE: The American National Election Studies, University of Michigan, Ann Arbor.

TABLE 9.2. Strength of Partisanship, 1952–2004

QUESTION TEXT:
"Generally speaking, do you usually think of yourself as a Republican, a Democrat, an Independent, or what?" (IF REPUBLICAN OR DEMOCRAT) "Would you call yourself a strong (REPUBLICAN/DEMOCRAT) or a not very strong (REPUBLICAN/DEMOCRAT)?" (IF INDEPENDENT, OTHER [1966 and later: OR NO PREFERENCE]): "Do you think of yourself as closer to the Republican or Democratic part?"

	'52	'54	'56	'58	'60	'62	'64	'66	'68	'70	'72	'74	'76	'78	'80	'82	'84	'86	'88	'90	'92	'94	'96	'98	'00	'02	'04
Independent or Apolitical	9	11	13	11	12	12	9	13	12	14	15	18	15	16	15	13	13	14	12	12	13	12	10	12	13	9	10
Leaning Independent	17	15	15	12	13	13	15	16	19	18	22	22	22	24	22	19	23	21	25	24	27	25	26	24	28	28	29
Weak Partisan	39	40	37	39	39	40	38	43	40	39	39	35	39	37	37	38	35	37	32	34	32	33	34	34	27	33	28
Strong Partisan	35	35	36	38	36	35	38	28	30	29	25	26	24	23	26	30	29	28	31	30	29	30	30	29	31	31	33
N	1784	1130	1757	1808	1911	1287	1550	1278	1553	1501	2694	2505	2850	2283	1612	1411	2236	2166	2032	1966	2474	1787	1710	1276	1797	1488	1197

SOURCE: The American National Election Studies, University of Michigan, Ann Arbor.

What is evident in these overall patterns in the American electorate is that the old New Deal Democratic coalition, created under the administration of Franklin Delano Roosevelt, had begun to come apart by the early 1970s. The elections of Dwight Eisenhower, another Republican presidential candidate in the 1950s, were among the first signs of the demise of the Democratic coalition; Nixon's two victories cemented the change. By the time of Ronald Reagan's second presidential victory in 1988, only 35 percent of Americans considered themselves Democrats compared with 45 percent in 1960 when John Kennedy was elected president.

The Theory of Realignment. The appearance of more and more Independents among voters, coupled with the elections of Republicans Nixon and Reagan, forced observers of American politics to rethink the structure of the American electorate. For years, the Democrats had been the majority party in America, but now the Republicans were challenging their dominance. Did this change signal something more profound?

Among scholars seeking a deeper explanation of the changing partisan patterns, there was one theory that attracted much attention: the theory of "realignment" of the electorate, proposed by the prominent political scientist V. O. Key, Jr.[43] Key proposed that American electoral history had seen a series of almost different party systems, each with its own dominant party and with its own pattern of alignment of segments of the population supporting the majority and the minority parties. One important system had come into being in the presidential contest of 1896. The Republican won this contest, which pitted the great Democratic orator William Jennings Bryan against the Republican William McKinley. Over the course of the next generation, the Republicans would remain the dominant national Party, winning more often than not. But Key discovered something even more important. The social alignments of the two parties remained more or less the same over the course of the period: the Democratic voter was apt to come from a rural agrarian background, whereas the Republican voter tended to come from an affluent urban setting.

With the election of 1932, a new majority power and a new alignment of the electorate took effect. The Democrats became the majority party of the nation as they would win the p presidency consistently from 1932 to 1968, losing only to Eisenhower in 1952 and 1956. Moreover, Roosevelt's victory in 1932 brought about a "critical rep-alignment" in the electorate: the Democrats now became the party of the city, the Republicans the party of rural America. The Democratic voter tended to be a working-class ethnic American, whereas the Republican voter tended to be a white rural or small-town resident.

Key argued that such realignments in the American electorate were a product of generational shifts in the sympathies of voters and in the appeal of candidates. Once their loyalties were formed, voters tended to remain attached to a particular party over the course of their voting lifetime. As they aged, and as world events changed, something of a seismic shift began to occur that resulted in a new majority party and a new configuration of social groups behind both the majority and the minority parties.

If Key's theory was correct, it appeared that 1968 signaled the end, more or less, of the dominance of the Democratic Party. The Nixon victories, together with the growing number of Independent partisans, seemed to be the first real signs of the major partisan shift about to occur in America. But were they?

Partisan Realignment—or Dealignment?. One of the great debates today among students of voting is whether America has actually witnessed a critical realignment of the form predicted by Key's theory, or whether something different has happened. In one sense there seems to have been something resembling a realignment. Out of the last ten presidential elections, dating back to 1968, the Republicans have won the majority of the contests—seven. In the previous ten Presidential elections they had won only two. Moreover, Clinton's victory in 1992 was won with just a plurality—43 percent of the vote—not a majority, owing to the large number of votes that went to Ross Perot.

But appearances can be deceiving, especially in this case. One of the main features of a period of critical realignment, according to Key's theory, is that there is a major shift in the sympathies of specific social and economic segments of the electorate. Thus, in 1932, the shift took place as urban voters began to flock to the Democrats, replacing rural America as the main force behind the Democrats. But no such shift seems to have taken place during the past couple of decades, and certainly not in 1968 as might have been expected. Instead, what observers find is a growing number of people who identify themselves as Independents, thus neither Democrats nor Republicans.

The growth in the proportion of Independents in the American electorate began in the late 1960s. Over the course of this period, the proportion of the electorate that identified itself as Independents was on the order of about 12 to 15 percent.[44] Including Independents who leaned toward the Democrats and Independents who leaned toward the Republicans, it actually came to about 1 of every three voters at its peak. In 1952, when the New Deal coalition was still in place, only 1 of every 4 voters identified as an Independent. By the mid-1980s, the shift toward Independents had leveled off. And by 1996, the proportion of people who identified themselves as pure Independents had diminished to only 8 percent of the electorate.[45]

Some analysts, such as political scientist Everett Carll Ladd, Jr., argue that we are in the midst not of a realignment but of a *dealignment* of the voters.[46] Voters have not shifted away from the Democrats to the Republicans on a regular basis so much as they are simply refusing to identify with either of the major parties on a consistent basis. In part, this new era may be a product of two different demographic trends among citizens. One is the growth in the education of the electorate, signaling that voters are bringing more of their knowledge to bear on their electoral choices. The other is that many of the new Independents are younger voters, hence they share few of the entrenched political loyalties of their parents.[47]

And yet not everyone agrees with this particular assessment. There is some evidence to suggest that some kind of partial realignment has taken place. Sociologists Clem Brooks and Jeff Manza argue that there is evidence that more professional workers, like lawyers and doctors, are now drawn to the Democratic Party than in the past.[48] They suggest that this disproportionate strength of the Democrats among the professions represents a sign of the actual realignment. Brooks and Manza, however, are the only social scientists thus far to detect such a trend of this sort.

VALUES AND PARTISANSHIP

There is yet another way to think about the partisan views of the electorate—in terms of the values that people hold. Although there is a good deal of evidence to suggest that there is a limited degree of ideological thinking among voters, especially in America, there may be values held by voters that escape the usual net of partisan loyalties and identification. This is the line of analysis that has been pursued by political scientist Ronald Inglehart.[49]

Inglehart argues that over the course of the last three decades there has been a growing shift in the values held by citizens living in Western industrial democracies. We can think of the values held by people, he suggests, in terms of whether they reflect a concern with issues of safety and defense, or whether they reflect a concern with the environment and matters of equality. The first orientation is what he terms a *materialist* view of the world, whereas the second is a *postmaterialist view.* He theorizes that since the late 1960s there has been a shift in the value orientations of citizens from a materialist to a postmaterialist view of the world. Those holding to a materialist view still remain in the majority, but the postmaterialists are becoming a larger percentage of the population. The shift is associated with other structural changes in the economies of Western industrialized countries, including a shift away from primary manufacturing to high technology.[50]

Inglehart and his colleagues have done a number of studies to confirm and identify the various dimensions of the materialist and postmaterialist view of the world. As Figure 9.1 reveals, between 1970 and 1994 there was a noticeable increase in the proportion of people who held postmaterialist orientations.

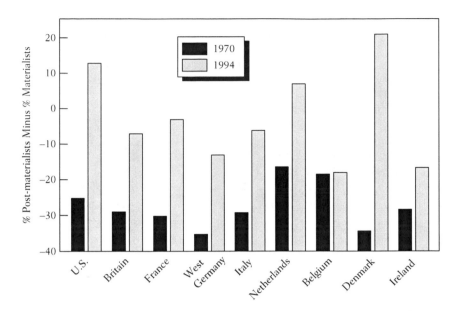

FIGURE 9.1 The shift toward postmaterialist values among the publics of nine Western societies, 1970–1994. (From Terry Nichols Clark and Michael Rempel, eds., *Citizen Politics in Post-Industrial Societies* [Boulder, CO: Westview Press, 1997], 65.)

One important implication of this work is that the difference between the materialists and postmaterialists influences their partisan attachments and preferences at the voting booth. Political scientist Russell Dalton, in a study of value orientations among citizens in four nations, shows that postmaterialists clearly prefer more left-wing parties, while materialists prefer more right-wing parties. In the early 1990s, 67 percent of the postmaterialists preferred the Democrats compared to only 50 percent of those holding materialist values. In Great Britain the link between value orientations and party preferences was even more pronounced. Seventy percent of the postmaterialists preferred the left-wing Labour Party, while 70 percent of the materialists preferred the right-wing Conservative Party.[51]

One can speculate that if the industrialized nations continue to move in the direction of great technological development and expansion, there is apt to be a corresponding increase in the proportion of citizens who hold to postmaterialist values.

THE SOCIAL BASES OF PARTISANSHIP

Social Class. The earliest studies of political parties, especially in the United States, revealed a very consistent set of findings.[52] Upper-class voters were apt to support the Republicans, while lower- and working-class voters tended to support the Democrats. The differences often were quite striking among the major sources of variation to be found in the kinds of people who divided along party lines. The most important and interesting research on the matter is a classic work on stratification and partisanship by sociologist Robert Alford.[53]

In research conducted in the early 1960s, Alford compared the impact of social class, measured in occupational terms, on voting for left- or right-oriented parties in four countries: Australia, Canada, Great Britain, and the United States.[54] He found that class voting—by which he means the relative degree of support provided by manual and nonmanual workers for each party—was considerably lower in the United States than it is in either Great Britain or Australia. Even in Great Britain, class voting, which Alford expected to be strong, was comparatively weak. This pattern remained consistent from about 1940 to 1965.

National elections in recent years reveal, however, that the pattern of class differences in voting has become less marked. Working-class citizens no longer prefer the Democrats in large numbers, nor do upper-class citizens regularly prefer the Republicans. As noted above, for example, sociologists Clem Brooks and Jeff Manza find a growing number of professional workers shifting to the Democratic Party in America over the period of 1972 to 1992.[55] Other studies reveal a similar decline in class voting in America. Sociologist Norval Glenn, for instance, found that in nonsouthern areas of the United States there has been a decline in the degree to which members of the different classes vote for the Republican presidential candidates. In 1936 there was a difference of almost 23 percent in the rate of support provided by blue-collar and white-collar workers for the candidacy of Alf Landon[c], whereas in 1968 there was a difference of only 11 percent between the classes in their support for the candidacy of Richard Nixon.[56] Political scientist Paul Abramson found somewhat similar results in an analysis of patterns of party voting during recent presidential contests. He observes, moreover, that the decline in the level of class voting can be attributed to a greater proportion of Democratic partisans among members of the post-World War II middle class as compared with the pre-World War II middle class.[57]

In the most recent presidential elections, there continued to be a decline of class-linked voting in the United States. Abramson and colleagues found that in the 1996 presidential election, Bill Clinton supporters were more likely to come from the middle class than from the working and lower classes, and the traditional differences in class backgrounds of the Democrats and Republicans continued to weaken.[58]

What is even more interesting is that the differences in social class backgrounds of left-wing parties, like the Democrats and the Labour Party in Great Britain, and right-wing parties, like the Republicans and the Conservative Party

[c]The Republican running against Democrat Franklin Roosevelt

in Great Britain, are diminishing in other industrial democracies as well. This seems to be part of a general shift on the part of a number of political parties across nations to broaden their appeal to the middle classes, much like the Democrats did in America in the 1990s.[59]

Social Networks. Some of the earliest studies of partisanship in the mass electorate, notably those by Berelson, Lazarsfeld, and their colleagues, reflect a central concern for the impact of primary group influences. Because of the early development of party preferences, it becomes somewhat difficult to assess the manner in which primary groups influence the voting behavior of adults; that is, it is uncertain whether primary groups mold opinions or whether they are self-selected by the individual. Nevertheless, two findings from this early research stand out as particularly interesting. First, Berelson, Lazarsfeld, and McPhee report that the greater the homogeneity in the opinions of the members of one's primary groups—family and friends—the greater the support of the individual for a particular political candidate. Specifically, if one's friends and family all intended to vote for or prefer the Republican candidate for president, then one would have a stronger conviction for that Republican candidate than he or she would if such persons were divided in their opinions. The second major finding of this early research emerges as a corollary to the first; people who are subject to conflicting opinions from the members of their primary groups are apt to behave reluctantly and uncertainly. For example, either they tend to put off making their decision about whom to support until the end of the campaign, or they fail to vote at all. Such a pattern became characterized as one of "cross-pressures" and, in various forms, became the basis for a considerable amount of later theoretical and empirical work.[60]

The importance of social networks and social context continues to be underscored by recent research. Political scientists Robert Huckfeldt and John Sprague find that people construct social networks that will tend to reinforce their own political preferences during electoral campaigns. Moreover, these same networks may work to supply people with a continuing flow of political information, some of which is incorrect and may be misperceived by its recipients. Huckfeldt and Sprague argue that, in general, such social contexts today play a very important part in the transmission and reception of political information.[61]

The Past and Future of Modern Political Parties: The Case of the United States

The halcyon days of the political parties in the United States were those in the last quarter of the nineteenth century. The party organizations performed with an efficiency, a discipline, and an intensity since unmatched; as Richard Jensen notes, political campaigns at this time were carried out with the vigor and precision of military campaigns.[62] The feelings engendered among the voters were also more intense than in recent years; Ostrogorski provides a most vivid description of the party feelings at the time:

> The name of the party is its own justification, in the eyes of millions of electors. They say, with a well-known politician, an ex-Senator of New York, "I am a Democrat" (or "I am a Republican," as the case may be), just as a believer says, to explain and justify his faith, "I am a Christian!" The reader knows how, and through what political sentiment all the world over, has been intensified in the United States and raised to the level of dogma—the dogma of "regularity," which makes the party creed consist in voting the "straight party ticket," whatever it may be. The sins against the religion of the party are sins against the ticket.[63]

Turnout among voters for presidential, state, and local elections was considerably higher then than it has been recently. It reached an average near 80 percent, while in the past several presidential elections it has declined steadily, from 63 percent in 1960 to slightly over 50 percent in 1996.[64] The competition between political parties for elective office was also considerably keener than it is now. In short, the party organizations were unusually vigorous at the end of the nineteenth century in the United States and were in some respects considerably stronger than at present. Inasmuch as this change appears to represent a more or less continuous decline that has been interrupted only occasionally, what might have brought it about?

Observers point to a number of sources. Perhaps the most significant one is the Progressive movement that developed in the 1890s and was largely organized and advanced by white middle-class Protestant Americans who saw party organizations and their adherents as threats to their own values and lifestyles. The tensions between the Progressives and their opponents grew out of a clash of many different interests and beliefs: the genteel and impersonal outlook of the indigenous Americans against the rough and personal orientations of the ethnics; the Protestantism of the indigenous Americans against the Catholicism of the ethnics; the wealth of middle-class Americans against the poverty of the ethnics; and so on.[65] The specific results of the Progressive movement, though designed ostensibly to promote greater participation in politics by the public, were really intended to deprive the ethnic groups of control of the party organizations that were their one hold on and source of satisfaction in American life. As the reformers intended, the ethnics ultimately lost control of the party organizations, but this loss resulted in serious and permanently crippling blows to the vitality of the party organizations.

Several products of the Progressive movement undercut the party organizations; the most prominent one was the establishment of direct primary elections, which took the nomination of candidates away from parties and their leaders and gave it to the public. Having lost their right to nominate candidates, parties eventually lost their ability to establish and to enforce a firm party line among their candidates. Fights eventually came to prevail more between the personal factions within political parties than between the parties themselves. The actual candidacy of people for office came to rest less on their loyalty to the party beliefs and hierarchy than on their capacity to generate funds for the political contests. In short, the direct primary stripped the political parties of an important function of identifying and nominating candidates for office; thus, it assisted in the decline of the party organizations in the United States. (One could justify the party's loss as the public's gain, but apparently the public does not see it that way, for it turns out for primary elections in even smaller numbers than for regular elections.)

Two other circumstances that made their first appearance at the end of the nineteenth century also contributed to a decline in the vitality of party organizations. One was the loss of patronage that was one of the mainstays of the political party. The Pendleton Act passed in 1883 opened civil service positions to competition on the basis of merit; initially, it covered only 10 percent of the civil service positions in government, but it now covers 90 percent. The loss of patronage meant that the parties could no longer provide the attractive inducements that secured a large and loyal staff of workers; the absence of other attractive substitutes was another crippling low to party organizations. The other circumstance was the introduction in the early twentieth century of a new style of campaigning/advertising. Partly a consequence of the diminishing strength of the party organization and partly a cause for diminishing it even further, advertising as a mode of campaigning was adopted by candidates as an easy and efficient way to communicate with voters. The earlier style of campaigning, the militarist, in the words of Richard Jensen, relied heavily on precinct workers and various other party staff members to draw out the vote for candidates. Advertising relies upon the media to appeal to voters. In recent years, advertising has become even more heavily relied upon at the expense of party workers; television now makes the house-to-house rounds among voters. The effect of this new mode of campaigning, of course, is to rob the party of yet another of its principal functions and to further contribute to the demise of the organization.

One last important historical fact working against party organizations has been a trend we noted previously about the United States—that is, the gradual concentration of financial resources in the federal government and the use of these resources to provide welfare monies to the impoverished and disabled. The party organizations in urban areas relied upon their provision of funds as a means of securing services in precincts of poor immigrants—for a little cash, one could easily drum up a few more voters in a ward. During the Roosevelt administration, the federal government began to provide these funds in the form of unemployment compensation and countless other programs, and party organizations lost their exclusive appeal. The poor could now turn to the federal government for money, and the parties had nowhere else to turn for staff replacements.

So what will become of party organizations in the future? Are they necessary and important to the survival of American democracy? Or are they, in fact, organizations whose importance has run its course, and which may now be scattered among the various ashes of political history? What is clear is that such organizations are vastly different than their nineteenth—indeed, even mid–twentieth-century—counterparts. They no longer wield the power for their bosses in urban areas, nor do their leaders exercise the kind of power they once held. They work very well to provide a medium through which voters can express preferences, but obviously far from perfectly. The rise to prominence of the Independent Party in the 1990s suggests that third parties still provide a choice to voters, even in some specific local circumstances, but, given the nature of American electoral laws, it is unlikely that the Independent Party will ever become a dominant force.

Instead, Americans seem to live with parties, but when they do political work it is often through other forums—through local groups, civic organizations, and similar instruments. Whether America can survive with the limited involvement of the public in the activities of parties, and even of voluntary associations, is a question that, as we have seen, has prompted a good deal of recent speculation by such figures as Robert Putnam, among many others. As long as the economy is booming in America, it is likely that such questions will be postponed. But what will happen if the economy turns sour? How will people express their voice and their dissatisfaction? If they have become unaccustomed to working and talking in the forum of public affairs, how will they know how to reengage in such activities?

Problems like these will remain on the agenda for political sociologists and political scientists to explore in the near future. The great irony is that America is held up as a model of an effective democracy for many of the emerging nation-states just at a time when a number of social scientists are voicing their concerns over the diminishing level of civic commitment and interest on the part of American citizens. Is it possible that democratic nations can reach the point where they continue to work effectively, even in the absence of a vigorous party system?

NOTES

1. There are some astute analysts who argue that the current vitriolic debate between the Democrats and Republicans is primarily one between the party officials and

politicians rather than members of the public at large. See Morris P. Fiorina with Samuel J. Abrams and Jeremy C. Pope, *Culture War? The Myth of a Polarized America* (New York: Pearson, 2005).

2. A number of good general treatments of the history of parties in different countries can be found in Sigmund Neumann, *Modern Political Parties: Approaches to Comparative Politics* (Chicago: University of Chicago Press, 1956).

3. William Nisbet Chambers, *Political Parties in a New Nation: The American Experience 1776–1809* (New York: Oxford University Press, 1963), Chapters 1 and 2, especially 45–49.

4. Max Weber, *The Methodology of the Social Sciences*, translated and edited by Edward A. Shils and Henry A. Finch, with a Foreword by Edward A. Shils (New York: The Free Press, 1949), 80.

5. See, for instance, Hans Daalder, "Parties, Elites, and Political Development in Western Europe," in *Mass Politics in Industrial Societies: A Reader in Comparative Politics*, ed. Giuseppe Di Palma (Chicago: Markham Publishing Company, 1972), 4–36; Maurice Duverger, *Political Parties: Their Organization and Activity in the Modern State*, rev. ed., trans. Barbara and Robert North (New York: John Wiley & Sons, Inc., 1959).

6. Along these lines, for example, see Neumann, *Modern Political Parties*.

7. One of the most common explanations of this form is that which traces the rise of parties in both the United States and Western Europe to the extension of suffrage in the nineteenth century. See, for instance, Leon D. Epstein, *Political Parties in Western Democracies* (New York: Frederick A. Praeger, 1967), 19–26.

8. John H. Aldrich, *Why Parties? The Origin and Transformation of Political Parties in America* (Chicago: University of Chicago Press, 1995). Also see John H. Aldrich, "Rational Choice and Turnout," *American Journal of Political Science*, Vol. 37, No. 1 (February 1993), 246–78.

9. In *The Handbook of Political Sociology*, a collection of articles that depicts the current state of political sociology, the editors describe rational choice theory as one of two major perspectives that now challenge some of the major principles and elements of a political sociological view of the world. See Thomas Janoski, Robert R. Alford, Alexandere M. Hicks, and Mildred A. Schwartz, eds., *Handbook of Political Sociology* (Cambridge, UK: Cambridge University Press, 2005).

10. Duverger, *Political Parties*, rev. ed.

11. Epstein, *Political Parties in Western Democracies*, Chapter 8.

12. Duverger, *Political Parties*, 22–23. Duverger, of course, is not the only observer of U.S. history to point to the salience of these features for its institutions.

13. Duverger, *Political Parties*, 20–21.

14. Ibid., 26.

15. Ibid., 35–36.

16. For criticism, see, for example, Aaron Wildavsky, "A Methodological Critique of Duverger's *Political Parties*," *Journal of Politics*, 21 (May 1959), 303–18; Epstein, *Political Parties in Western Democracies*, Chapters 2 and 4.

17. For two excellent works on electoral laws and their impact on party politics, see Douglas W. Rae, *The Political Consequences of Electoral Laws* (New Haven, CT: Yale University Press, 1967); Arend Lijphart, *Electoral Systems and Party Systems: A Study of Twenty-Seven Democracies 1945–1990* (Oxford, UK: Oxford University Press, 1998).
18. Actually the method of representation is more complicated than this simple explanation suggests. There are different methods for determining the actual proportion of a party's representatives to be awarded seats. The Hare system most closely approximates the form given in my explanation; other methods determine the outcomes in a slightly different manner. See Lijphart, ibid., Appendix A.
19. Ibid., Chapter 7.
20. The seminal work on the party machines in the United States during their early rise to power remains M. Ostrogosrski, *Democracy and the Organization of Political Parties*, vol. II, trans. Frederick Clarke (New York: Macmillan & Co., Ltd., 1902).
21. For an interesting analysis of this phenomenon, see Robert Dahl, *Who Governs?* (New Haven, CT: Yale University Press, 1961), Chapter 4.
22. The following analysis is based principally on Mike Royko, *Boss: Richard J. Daley of Chicago* (New York: New American Library, 1971).
23. Ibid., Chapter 2 especially.
24. William L. Riordon, *Plunkitt of Tammany Hall: A Series of Plain Talks on Very Practical Politics* (New York: E. P. Dutton and Co., Inc., 1963), 27–28.
25. For the analysis in this paragraph, see Fred I. Greenstein, "The Changing Pattern of Urban Politics," *Annals of the American Academy of Political and Social Science*, 353 (May 1964), 1–13. Also see Fred I. Greenstein, *The American Party System and the American People*, 2nd ed. (Englewood Cliffs, NJ: Prentice-Hall, Inc., 1970), Chapter 4. For the relationship between power and inducements, see the discussion of the notion of power at the beginning of Chapter 6 in this book. An insightful analysis and updating of the nature of political machines is to be found in Thomas M. Guterbock, *Machine Politics in Transition: Party and Community in Chicago* (Chicago: University of Chicago Press, 1980).
26. See, for example, Duverger, *Political Parties*; Philip Selznick, *The Organizational Weapon: The Study of Bolshevik Strategies and Tactics* (Glencoe, IL: The Free Press, 1960).
27. M. Ostrogorski, *Democracy and the Organization of Political Parties*, I and II.
28. On the first point, Ostrogorski's fear may have been well founded, even though he exaggerated them; on the second point, his fear turns out to have been less sound, as later scholarship on British parties reveals. See R. T. McKenzie, *British Political Parties: The Distribution of Power Within the Conservative and Labour Parties*, 2nd ed. (New York: Frederick A. Praeger, Publishers, 1964), 642–49.
29. Robert Michels, *Political Parties: A Sociological Study of the Oligarchical Tendencies of Modern Democracy* (New York: Collier Books, 1962).
30. Ibid., p. 61.
31. Somewhat prophetically, given the rise of Hitler and the Nazi regime only decades later, Michels believed that the need for submission to a leader's will was possibly

peculiar to the German people and the residue of a long tradition and of the recent leadership of Bismarck.

32. Michels, *Political Parties*, 207.

33. Vilfredo Pareto, *The Mind and Society* (London: Jonathan Cape, 1935) III, 1427–31.

34. Duverger, *Political Parties*, 116–68.

35. Ibid., 135.

36. Renate Mayntz, "Oligarchic Problems in a German Party District," in *Political Decision Makers*, ed. Dwaine Marvick (Glencoe, IL: The Free Press, 1961), 138–92.

37. Samuel J. Eldersveld, *Political Parties: A Behavioral Analysis* (Chicago: Rand McNally & Company, 1964), 1–13.

38. Seymour Martin Lipset, Martin Trow, and James Coleman, *Union Democracy: The Internal Politics of the International Typographers Union* (Garden City, NY: Anchor Books, 1962).

39. For relevant evidence on this matter, see William A. Gamson, *The Strategy of Social Protest*, 2nd ed. (Belmont, CA.: Wadsworth Press, 1990).

40. Angus Campbell et al., *The American Voter* (New York: John Wiley & Sons, Inc. 1960), and, more recently, Paul R. Abramson, John H. Aldrich, and David W. Rohde, *Change and Continuity in the 1996 Elections* (Washington, DC: CQ Press, 1998).

41. Campbell et al., ibid.

42. See, for instance, Norval D. Glenn, "Sources of the Shift to Political Independence: Some Evidence from A Cohort Analysis," *Social Science Quarterly*, 53 (December 1972), 494–519.

43. V. O. Key, Jr., "A Theory of Critical Elections," *Journal of Politics*, 17 (February 1955): 3–18.

44. Abramson et al., op. cit., Chapter 8.

45. Ibid., 167.

46. See, for example, Everett Carll Ladd, Jr., "The Shifting Party Coalitions—From the 1930s to the 1970s," in Seymour Martin Lipset, ed., *Party Coalitions in the 1980s* (San Francisco: Institute for Contemporary Studies, 1981), 127–49.

47. Paul R. Abramson, "Generational Change in American Electoral Behavior," *American Political Science Review*, 68 (March 1974), 93–105.

48. Clem Brooks and Jeff Manza, "The Social and Ideological Bases of Middle-Class Political Realignment in the United States, 1972–1992," *American Sociological Review*, 62 (April 1997), 191–208.

49. See, for example, Ronald Inglehart, *Culture Shift in Advanced Industrial Society* (Princeton, NJ: Princeton University Press, 1990).

50. Ronald Inglehart, "The Trend Toward Postmaterialist Values Continues," in Terry Nichols Clark and Michael Rempel, eds., *Citizen Politics in Post-Industrial Societies* (Boulder, CO: Westview Press, 1997), 57–66.

51. Russell J. Dalton, *Citizen Politics: Public Opinion and Political Parties in Advanced Industrial Democracies* (Chatham, NJ: Chatham House Publishers, 1996), 189.

52. Paul F. Lazarsfeld, Bernard Berelson, and Hazel Gaudet, *The People's Choice* (New York: Duell, Sloan and Pearce, 1944); also Campbell et al., op. cit.

53. Robert Alford, *Party and Society* (Chicago: Rand McNally, 1963).
54. Alford, *Party and Society*, and Alford, "Class Voting in the Anglo-American Democracies, in *Mass Politics in Industrial Societies*, Di Palma, 166–99.
55. Brooks and Manza, op. cit.
56. Norval Glenn, "Class and Party Support in the United States: Recent and Emerging Trends" *Public Opinion Quarterly*, 37 (Spring 1973), 1–20.
57. Paul R. Abramson, "Generational Change in American Electoral Behavior," *American Political Science Review*, 68 (March 1974), 93–105.
58. Abramson et al., op. cit., Chapter 5.
59. Dalton, op. cit., 175.
60. Careful examination of the results in *Voting* reveals that the authors believed cross-pressures characterized situations of conflicting social statuses, among many others; hence, their research in a way can be directly connected to the large amount of work on the effects of status inconsistency. Moreover, their research also figured quite prominently in the development of cognitive dissonance theory by psychologist Leon Festinger.
61. Robert Huckfeldt and John Sprague, "Networks in Context: The Social Flow of Political Information," *American Political Science Review*, Volume 81 (December 1987), 1197–216. For a recent and excellent treatment of these issues, see the various articles in Alan S. Zuckerman, ed., *The Social Logics of Politics: Personal Networks as Contexts for Political Behavior* (Philadelphia: Temple University Press, 2005).
62. Richard Jensen, "American Election Campaigns: A Theoretical and Historical Typology," in Walter Dean Burnham, *Critical Elections and the Mainsprings of American Politics* (New York: W.W. Norton and Company, Inc., 1970), 72.
63. Ostrogorski, ibid., 353–54.
64. William Nisbet Chambers, "Party Development and the American Mainstream," in William Nisbet Chambers and Walter Dean Burnham, eds., *The American Party System* (New York: Oxford University Press, 1967), 14.
65. Richard Hofstadter, *The Age of Reform* (New York: Vintage Books, 1960), Chapter 6.

Chapter 10

Social Movements
Basic Perspectives

It is typically movements outside the political system that force insiders to recognize
new fears and desires.... [W]hile formal organizations are the main source of technical
change, they are rarely a source of change in values, in social arrangements.[1]

T he success of social movements on the level of civil society should be conceived not in terms of the achievement of certain substantive goals or the
perpetuation of the movement, but rather in terms of the democratization of
values, norms, and institutions that are rooted ultimately in a political culture.
Such a development cannot make a given organization or movement permanent, but it can secure the movement form as a normal component of self-
democratizing civil societies.[2]

Introduction

People do not always pursue power or change through regular institutional
channels. Instead, they may engage in a form of contentious politics that is
called *collective action*. People seek forms of power outside of existing political structures for many reasons. For example, they may believe that the electoral process is too heavily weighted in favor of those who already have power.
Violent or nonviolent, collective action is one way to compensate for the disparity in power between people or groups of people and stronger opponents.
What is often difficult, however, is finding ways to act collectively that are not
already dominated by states or transnational governmental networks. Social

216

movements, then, have to search for ways of creating disruption, forcing a halt or even a change in everyday routines and business-as-usual attitudes that sustain and reproduce social relations of inequality and domination.

A call for collective action is not necessarily a call for revolution. *Revolutionary movements* are a particular kind of social movement that is sustained by organizations or networks and their supporters for the purpose of fundamentally transforming the political, or possibly the socioeconomic, order—typically by means of overthrowing one or more governments or states.[3] On the other hand, other social movements may be self-limiting and reform oriented. They may emphasize a single issue, press for the political inclusion of people with a collective identity (such members of a race or gender), or defend a right that has been taken away or never granted. Any of these goals might produce significant social change or reform that is short of a revolution.

"Taking it to the streets" seems today an obvious course of action for disgruntled citizens. However, social movement scholars caution us that the fact that we take for granted the idea of public protest or civil disobedience reflects that we live in what they call a "movement society." Contentious politics that relies on collective action once was seen as unpredictable, disruptive, and taking place outside of acceptable society. But strikes, sit-ins, and marches are now actually institutionalized in societies: they have become repeatable and self-sustaining processes. Like voting, calling your local school board, or lobbying Congress, some forms of collective action have become politics as usual.

What we are seeing, some social movement scholars suggest, is an increase in the institutionalization of movement activity itself.[4] The majority of today's movement activity (at least in Western democratic societies) takes the form of peaceful and orderly routines that break no laws and violate no spaces.[5] What does it mean when the politics of disruption are so normal and routine that they are no longer actually disruptive?

After September 11, 2001, this claim may seem incongruous and the question irrelevant. Certainly terrorist tactics qualify as disruptive politics that states have not institutionalized or rendered predictable and routine. After living with print, broadcast, and online media dominated by competing stories and discourse concerning the "global war on terror," it is reasonable to ask what the relationship is between nonviolent forms of contentious collective action and the violent ones deployed by terrorist organizations? Are antiwar protesters who are calling for the United States to end its occupation in Iraq aiding the terrorists? Are members of al-Qa'ida participants in a social movement? And if so, how do we make sense of it in relationship to movements that members of the public and the state view as positive and even inevitable, such as the Civil Rights Movement in the United States during the 1960s?

As we will see, social movement scholars offer competing answers to these questions. Appreciation for the variety in their answers begins with understanding how they conceptualize social movements differently in the first place. So let us first turn to the task of defining a social movement.

The Nature of Social Movements

We often think of social movements as identical with the groups and organizations that participate in them, as though human rights groups, like Amnesty International and Human Rights Watch, make up the human rights movement or, similarly, as if environmentalist groups, like Greenpeace and Friends of the Earth, define the environmental movement. The logic is that these organizations—working together on a cause—comprise a complex form of organization that pursues collective goals, controls its own performance, and has a boundary separating it from other social movements, other aspects of *civil society*, and the political sphere.

Civil society refers to both the private and public spheres of association and conversation that fall outside the direct control of the state. It encompasses the dialogue and interaction through which political views take shape and through which groups construct and negotiate their interests in relation to each other and to the state and other authorities. Civil society includes, for example, voluntary associations, friendship networks, religious groups, and independent media. From a normative point of view, it is in these spaces that we learn to compromise, "put ourselves in another's shoes," value diversity, understand and redefine community identity, mobilize ourselves to act collectively, assert new rights, and determine what it is about ourselves—our practices and traditions—that we want to preserve or change. It is a space that is not reducible to the market, bourgeois society, or the state. It is in part constituted by rights to assemble, communicate, and associate. However, it is a space that must be actively defended if it is to avoid the twin threats of the modern state and the market economy. It is, in short, the space from which we initiate social movements.

Thinking about social movements in this way should raise a series of questions for the social movement scholar. First, what distinguishes a social movement from a political party, aside from the latter's successful incorporation into *political society* (i.e., the state and its institutions and political parties and their organizations)?[6] Does Michels' "iron law of oligarchy" (discussed in the previous chapter) apply to movements? And, if so, can collective actors in civil society influence those in political society, short of selling out or being coopted (an outcome that would better describe political society's influence on civil society rather than the other way around)? In other words, are the actors of civil society whom we imagine to populate our contemporary social movements capable of changing the discourse and action of the actors engaged in politics? Or has political society conditioned civil society to organize and collectively act in ways that this political society sanctions? Is it true that only hierarchically (that is to say, undemocratically) organized bureaucracies can get anything accomplished politically—even when the goal is to effect democratic change?

In this chapter we will address these questions. But we will start with a fundamentally special conception of a social movement. Political sociologists disagree about how best to understand contemporary movements, yet the vast majority has come to follow this piece of advice from Charles Tilly: avoid thinking of social movements as groups and, instead, think of a movement as consisting of a *sustained series of interactions*.[7] As Tilly explains:

> Indeed, it is a mistake to think of a social movement as a group of any kind. Instead, the term *social movement* applies most usefully to a sustained *interaction* between a specific set of authorities and various spokespersons for a given challenge to those authorities. The interaction is a coherent, bounded unit in roughly the same sense that a war or a political campaign is a unit. Such interactions have occurred from time to time ever since their authorities of any kind. The broadest sense of the term *social movement* includes all such challenges.[8]

Political sociologists generally agree that a movement is not some unitary actor, despite the efforts of both its participants and opponents to portray it as such. Rather it is a *process* created by a collective, organized, sustained, and noninstitutional challenge to some target whether it be a state, corporation, religious institution, global financial institution, civil society, or some combination of any or all of the above. In fact, the target need not even be an authoritative or powerful actor, or even an actor per se. A social movement may also target laws or cultural beliefs and practices.

Political sociological theories of contemporary social movements must attempt to grapple with some of the following questions:

1. When, why, and where do social movements occur? In what kinds of societies or social spaces do movements emerge? Are they more prone to emerge in democratic than in authoritarian states? Do they emerge more frequently today than in the past? In more rather than less "globalized" societies? In more rather than less "privatized" societies?

2. To what extent do contemporary movements represent a break with the past? Are contemporary movements organized differently than in the past? Are their targets and scope of action substantially different? And if they are substantially new in terms of their organization and scope, to what extent do resources like collective memory of past conflict or institutionalized

gains for civil society secured through "traditional" movement action play a part in contemporary movements?

3. What institutions are contemporary social movements capable of influencing, and how much? How do states, markets, and mass media influence movements? What is their relationship to civil society, law, or rights (both civil and human)? What changes do movements bring about?

4. What is at stake politically for contemporary social movements? How does a movement's use of violence (such as the violence employed by transnational terrorist movements or radical environmentalists) affect those stakes for contemporary social movements in general?

5. What can collective actors realistically hope to achieve by participating in social movements today? How is the political influence of social movements facilitated and constrained by globalization?

These are the sorts of issues and questions that we shall address and hope to answer in this chapter on social movements.

Collective Behavior vs. Collective Action

Most of us living in Western democratic states tend to think that social movements are commonplace, normal, and a healthy part of a democracy. As common sense as it might seem to us today, this view is a new one. Before the 1960s, most people feared social movements, including the scholars in Western democratic states who studied them. Throughout the preceding century, students of social movements thought of them as irrational crowds, or worse, dangerous mobs spontaneously aroused and drawn by extremist firebrands and rabble-rousers or charismatic agitators.[9]

The sociological psychology tradition of the Chicago School, also known as the collective behavior approach, was the dominant theoretical paradigm of social movement scholarship until the late 1960s and early 1970s.[10] Social movement scholars also paid serious attention to variants, such as Neil Smelser's structural-functionalist model of collective behavior and William Kornhauser's "mass society" theory.[11] These approaches all assume that social movements are operating within a political system characterized by "free and fair" elections. They also presume that the political system includes freely competing interest groups and political parties that include minorities. From this perspective, any "extra-institutional" collective action by definition signals a threat to the democratic consensus that underlies the institutions of a civil society. Crudely put, the collective behavior approach views collective action as inherently undemocratic.

The masses in an industrializing West typically demanded better working conditions and the right to vote. Scholars then, like many politicians or television newscasters today, asserted that these crowds or mobs possessed a herd mentality that rendered the otherwise rational individuals comprising them temporarily insane or irrational.[12] They understood any collective action of social movements not as something that might be fueled by a shared sense of injustice deriving from a violation of social norms, but rather as deviant behavior spontaneously generated by emotions incited by and somehow disseminated among the crowd itself.

This attitude toward extra-institutional political action changed radically in the late 1960s and early 1970s when large-scale social movements emerged in the United States and Europe. In this era, for one of the first times in history, members of the elite (namely college students) allied with less privileged people of color to demand what people had been demanding in other forms of protest over the previous century: better working conditions and the right to participate in a meaningful way in electoral politics. Sociologist Doug McAdam describes how thousands of students, mostly northern whites, involved themselves and risked, in some cases, even lost, their lives to help black people in Mississippi register to vote.[13] Although they were demanding a stake in the political process, the activists of the civil rights movement often acted outside of it.

Social scientists found themselves forced to rethink and to reframe the way they spoke of such social movements and, in particular, the motivations of people to participate in them. It became harder to dismiss civil rights demonstrators—or the emerging voices of the feminist movement or the socialist "New Left"—as misguided, immature, or irrational. The actions of participations did not lack a moral dimension at all. It represented instead clearly articulated alternative norms, specific goals, and rational strategies for pursuing them. These movements emerged within democratic polities with diverse voluntary associations and thriving public and private spheres. The social movement scholars espousing the collective behavior paradigm were unable to point to clear examples of normative or institutional breakdown. And the collective behavior paradigm could not offer an explanation to account for the timing or emergence of these movements. The social movements, in fact, were far more complex than irrational mobs roiled by demagoguery or driven by hunger.

New Paradigms for the Study of Social Movements

Social movement theory has developed significantly over the past thirty years. Social movement theorists would not today depict college students in the United

States involved in civil rights struggles, such as the post–Hurricane Katrina recovery efforts in New Orleans or the mass demonstrations for immigrants' rights, as spontaneously organized, irrational, or dangerous. Conservative news analysts or law enforcement might portray them as such, but they would be doing so without an understanding of contemporary social movement theory.

In the 1960s, two significant paradigms arose in social movement scholarship to fill the theoretical hole that collective behavior theories could not fill. In the United States, social movement scholars developed the "resource mobilization" paradigm. In Western Europe, scholars developed the "new social movements" paradigm. Both approaches, which we discuss in detail below, directly challenge the collective behavior paradigm by emphasizing (1) the preexisting social ties and organization and (2) the rationality of collective conflict. In short, serious observers of social movements could no longer assume that institutionalized political channels were the sole or even primary political space of rational collective action. Serious, thoughtful, creative, and well-organized politics take place "in the streets" routinely. Social movement scholarship was forced to account for how and why this kind of collective action can be a normal and strategic political response to perceived injustices. Ironically, the term "collective action" is, today, typically used exclusively to connote extra-institutional activity.

THE RESOURCE MOBILIZATION PARADIGM

The *resource mobilization* theory of collective action reveals the economic dimension of what was for so long understood to be an exclusively social-psychological phenomenon. Table 10.1 contrasts the predominant assumptions of each of these theoretical approaches.

Resource mobilization theory focuses on two key points. The first is that sustaining a social movement requires more than an irrational mob. It requires, in particular, resources: money, personnel, even if volunteer, and space to work. Movement organizers today—even those operating on a shoestring budget out of the director's garage—typically need at least phones, Internet access, computers, printers, and software.

Large-scale movements that rely on formal organizations typically require a steady flow of capital for renting office space; employing full-time staff; paying utility bills, transportation costs, janitorial services, and lobbyists; purchasing telephones, answering machines, desktop computers and desks, heavy-duty printers and/or printing services, photocopiers, office supplies, art supplies (including, e.g., pickets, masks, costumes, floats, and spray paint), letterhead, envelopes, business cards, postage; securing weapons and training (in the case of more violent movements); and, of course, raising more funding and recruiting

TABLE 10.1. Collective Behavior vs. Resource Mobilization: A Comparison of the Key Assumptions Underlying Each Theory

COLLECTIVE BEHAVIOR THEORY	RESOURCE MOBILIZATION THEORY
There are two kinds of action: (1) Institutionalized (conventional); and (2) Noninstitutionalized (collective).	Social movements must be understood within a conflict theory of collective action.
Noninstitutionalized, collective action is not shaped by social norms and forms in response to or to address "undefined" or unstructured situations.	There is no fundamental difference between institutional and noninstitutional collective action.
It assumes that these situations result from structural change and represent a "breakdown" in civil society's existing social institutions and/or norms—due either to insufficient social control or to inadequate normative integration.	Both entail conflicts of interest built into institutionalized power relations.
Normative breakdown results in "strains" (or discontent, frustration, and aggression) that lead individuals to engage in collective behavior.	Collective action involves the rational pursuit of interests by groups.
The *crowd* is the smallest unit of analysis in the theory's explanation of collective behavior.	The rational actor (individual and collective) using strategic and instrumental reasoning replaces the crowd as the central referent for the analysis of collective action.
Noninstitutional collective behavior follows a "life cycle" that moves from spontaneous crowd action to the formation of social movements.	Goals and grievances are permanent products of power relations and cannot account for the formation of social movements.
Movements in this cycle emerge and grow through crude processes of communication (contagion, rumor, circular reaction, diffusion, etc.).	Movements form because of changes in resources, organization, and opportunities for collective action.
It emphasizes psychological reactions to breakdown, crude modes of communication, and volatile goals that reflect an implicit bias toward regarding collective behavior as an irrational response to change.	Mobilization involves large-scale, special purpose, bureaucratic formal organizations. Success involves the recognition of the group as a political actor or increased material benefits.

SOURCE: Adapted from Jean Cohen L. and Andrew Arato, *Civil Society and Political Theory* (Cambridge, MA: MIT Press, 1992)

more supporters. Activists spend a great deal of their time mobilizing and organizing these resources in ways that enable them to develop and communicate their ideas—among themselves and, outside, to potential recruits, authorities, and other targets.

The second key point is that resource mobilization theorists have shown that sophisticated organizing and communicating among "rational actors"—not social contagion or emotional diffusion among "the crowd"—contribute to the *mobilization* that produces the kind of large-scale collective action from which social movements develop. That is, while social strains or unjust conditions are *necessary* for a movement to develop, they are *not sufficient* to explain the emergence of social movements. In fact, there are many repressive or seemingly unbearable situations in which protests do not emerge. People collectively starving in the deserts of Africa might continue to do so, and not be able to protest their conditions, if they lack resources to mobilize or if they remain too disorganized to mobilize the resources that they do have.

Organization, interests, resources, strategies, as well as some combination of repression and opportunity, form the building blocks of sustained social movements. Resource mobilization theorists posit that collective action involves the rational pursuit of interests by groups. The *rational actor*, using strategic and instrumental reasoning, replaces the mob as the central referent for the analysis of collective action. Goals and grievances are permanent products of power relations and cannot account for the formation of social movements. In this paradigm, movements form because of changes in resources, organization, and opportunities for collective action. Also, mobilization involves large-scale, special purpose bureaucratic formal organizations. Success under this paradigm is usually defined as the recognition of the group as a political actor or increased material benefits.

Sociologists John McCarthy and Mayer Zald proposed one of the earliest and more influential arguments of this kind.[14] They introduced the economic metaphor of an "industry" to describe the "work" of social movements. The core of this social movement industry, they argued, is comprised of formal organizations, or social movement organizations (SMOs), that act very similarly to "firms"—the iconic form of rational organization—for their survival. They accumulate money, power, and other resources, employ a staff of workers organized within a hierarchical command structure who engage in specialized tasks, and sell their ideas in order to generate funds and support. Additionally, they compete with other SMOs for scarce resources and "market share."

Recently, Clifford Bob has extended this line of analysis to show how social movement actors in the developing world, including violent protest or secessionist movements, jockey among a vast array of competing movement causes—on an uneven playing field—for the relatively scarce resources and the political

legitimacy that nongovernmental organizations (NGOs) provide.[15] He also documents for us the ways in which these same NGOs engage in "the business" of
venue shopping, strategically choosing to support certain movement "clients"
over others and marketing the cause in which they invest.

As a result, movements often alter their characteristics, or their representations of their collective identity, to meet the expectations of potential NGO
patrons. This theory posits that the most successful movements are those that
learn to promote themselves abroad and pigeonhole themselves into categories
of protest that NGOs perceive as acceptable, or at least risk worthy. Bob uses
the market language of "supply and demand" to describe this relationship, but
he is quick to point out that it is one wrought with organizational inequality.
The supply side is comprised of a few influential NGOs looking for some reason
to choose one needy group or movement cause over another. On the demand
side are many local groups who seek what their international connection to
NGOs provides them: the improved resources and clout that can transform
their domestic conflicts. Yet, "demand" in this model is not a function of the
local groups' need per se. Rather it is a function of a group's willingness to sell
out or at least compromise and often dramatically redefine within their patrons'
standards of acceptability the very claims and identity upon which the collective grievance was initially based.

Some social movement scholars today argue that the resource mobilization
paradigm left several key factors unexamined. For example, some charge that
the emphasis on rational economic action goes too far in exorcizing the psychological dimensions of social movement actors, at both a cognitive and an
emotional level of analysis. For example, one's fear at the emotional level might
well inhibit one's decision to protest, despite agreeing at the cognitive level that
protest is the correct course of action.

Moreover, as Jeff Goodwin and James Jasper argue, the weakness of social
movement approaches that emphasize formal organizations like SMOs and
NGOs is in their depiction of protesters as invariably self-interested, despite
the many emotional and cognitive processes that shape the construction of any
movement's goals. They claim, in particular, that,

> having rejected the psychology of older traditions, these scholars inadvertently
> embedded the assumptions of neoclassical economics in their models: people
> were rational pursuers of their own narrow interests. These scholars ignored one
> of the central issues of social movements: how people come to perceive a shared
> grievance or interest, especially in something remote from their daily lives, such as
> global warming, nuclear energy, or human rights in distant lands.[16]

Other critics have focused on how the resource mobilization theory fails
to link collective action to its origins in cultural beliefs about legitimate rights.

For all of its emphasis on how collective action is a rational and organized response to collectively perceived *injustice*, most of the work in resource mobilization theory merely identifies a conflict between preexisting moral traditions. It does not explain how people come to view a lack of a specific right or resource as an injustice. Furthermore, the paradigm fails to demonstrate how such rights are differently embedded in contexts of state authority.[17]

Another critical shortcoming of resource mobilization theory is that it does not account for how the social and political terrain creates the conditions for the emergence or success of some modern movements and the stillbirth of others.[18] The paradigm's focus on economic factors and political opportunities fails to account for how those resources or opportunities arise in specific political or historical contexts.

POLITICAL PROCESS VS. IDENTITY POLITICS

Exploration of the social and political terrains became largely separate endeavors within the field of social movement research during the 1980s and early 1990s. Broadly defined opposing camps emerged, resulting in two schools of thought: *political process theory* in the United States and *new social movement theory* in Western Europe. Political process theory grew directly out of the resource mobilization paradigm, yet sought to address its critical weaknesses: its lack of attention to history and to politics. New social movement theory is largely an identity-oriented paradigm that rejected both neo-classical assumptions regarding social actors and the anemic conception of the role of civil society and culture in forging, shaping, and sustaining the "new" social movements that were emerging in the 1960s.

Today we can see that the resource mobilization/political process paradigm and the identity-oriented paradigm each involve a theoretical framework that excludes the main focus of the other. Yet, as Cohen and Arato have brilliantly elucidated, both paradigms rely on key features of modern civil society to identify what is specific to contemporary social movements: "a self-understanding that abandons revolutionary dreams in favor of radical reform that is not necessarily and primarily oriented toward the state."[19]

Political Process Theory. A great deal of social movement research has focused on the question of how to conceptualize the political environments in which movements operate. Political process approaches have dominated this effort, shaping the concepts, discourse, and research agenda of the social movement field. As critics Jeff Goodwin and James Jasper point out, political process theory "...may be criticized, but it cannot be ignored."[20] Before examining the key concepts and assumptions that political process theory proposes, let us first understand how this paradigm emerged from resource mobilization theory. In doing so, we will also explore the environment that political process theorists claim historically has facilitated the emergence of social movements, the nation-state.

Charles Tilly was one of the first and most influential shapers of political process theory (see our lengthy discussion of Tilly in Chapter 3). His work brought to light tha fact that social movements, although they may act outside of institutionalized political channels, are tied to the political process and the political sphere in important ways. Political process theorists fondly assert that states are both the target and fulcrum of social movements, suggesting that social movements not only target their grievances toward, but expect redress to come from, the state. As Goodwin and Jasper (2003) point out, political process theories

> ...have focused on conflict and the external environments of social movements, to the extent that they even explain the emergence of social movements as resulting from 'opportunities' provided by the state (such as a lessening of repression or a division among economic and political elites).[21]

This emphasis on the explicitly political dimension of social movements gradually distinguished political process theories from resource mobilization theories. According to political process theory, the timing and emergence of social movements requires an understanding that goes beyond the mobilization of economic resources and must reach out to understand what are called "political opportunity structures."

In the late 1970s and early 1980s, Tilly developed a comparative historical analysis of violent collective action in Western Europe, especially Britain and France, which allowed him to situate the otherwise unhistorical and utilitarian logic of his own earlier model of resource mobilization.[22] While people have banded together to pursue common ends since the beginning of history, Tilly (1982) explains that it was only in the nineteenth century that the social movement emerges and rises.[23] Tilly demonstrates that the occurrence of a historical shift from local to national structures of power at this time in Western Europe affected the organizational forms as well as the "repertoire of collective action," that is, "the set of means which is effectively available to a given set of people."[24]

Tilly asserts that states are the most powerful actors in modern industrial societies and, based on the perceived interests of the state elites who act on their behalf, are able to selectively repress or promote social movements.[25] The state obviously attempts to repress revolutionary or terrorist movements that directly target its power or policies. At the same time, states also tolerate, and even promote, some social movements to the point where they absorb them into the polity, providing them with routine government access.

Like some collective behavior theorists, he still understands modernization, or large-scale structural change, to affect collective action. But, he effectively argues against breakdown theories that link the timing and rate of urbanization and industrialization directly to economic hardship or political conflict. Instead, he shows how economic transformation, urbanization, state making, and the emergence of the mass media undermine some forms of collective action while simultaneously facilitating the emergence of other forms.

The novelty of Tilly's modernization thesis is that it posited that the impact that structural change has on political conflict is in the long-term reshaping of everyday forms of *solidarity* rather than in the immediate production of stress and or strain. Under conditions of modernization, voluntary associations replace communal solidarities. Collective action becomes increasingly characterized by more formal, deliberately organized meetings of voluntary associations, displacing the more casual, routine gatherings of communal groups, local markets, festivals, or others sanctioned by paternalistic authorities. The more spontaneous food riots and tax rebellions typical of the eighteenth century become gradually repressed and, by the nineteenth century (in Britain and its North American colonies, as well in Italy, Germany, and France), generally superseded by more autonomous forms of organization and protest, such as demonstrations and strikes.[26]

The shift occurred, Tilly explains, because states and capitalists won control over the resources formerly wielded by households, communities, and other small-scale groups.[27] Also, urbanization and the development of mass media reduced the costs of large-scale mobilization for formally organized associations. Finally, Tilly argues, the institution and growth of national elections—and the beginning of popular participation in national politics—promoted the crystallization and spread of the demonstration as a key form of collective action. As he writes, "[I]ts basic form resembles that of the electoral assembly, and . . . it provides an effective means of displaying the strength of a contestant, sometimes of influencing the outcome of an election."[28]

Tilly convincingly demonstrates how key institutions of modern civil society, such as rights to organize, recruit, assemble, solicit, publicize, and demonstrate within nationally organized democracies, provide the fertile terrain for the emergence of the national social movement. Tilly's work also shows that modern collective action presupposes the development of autonomous social and political spaces within civil and political society that are guaranteed by rights and supported by the democratic political culture underlying formal representative political institutions.

However, neither he nor the political process theorists who followed his lead made conceptual room in their models for collective action that targets civil society itself. In the political process theory, only collective action that targets *states* sustains movements. By stressing primarily the political opportunities and strategic implications that state practices have for the emergence of the nineteenth-century collective action repertoire, Tilly looks only at the dimensions of those processes that are relevant for the mobilization of organized groups competing for power.

Critical Concepts: Political Opportunities, Mobilization, and Framing. The work of theorists who followed Charles Tilly's lead in state-centered social movement research developed a set of structural concepts, such as "political opportunity structures," "mobilization networks," and "cultural framing." They developed these concepts largely to explain social movements taking place within Western democratic states during the 1960s and 1970s. As Doug McAdam, John McCarthy, and Mayer Zald put it:

> Most political movements and revolutions are set in motion by social changes that render the established political order more vulnerable or receptive to challenge. But these "political opportunities" are but a necessary prerequisite to action. In the absence of sufficient organization—whether formal or informal—such opportunities are not likely to be seized. Finally, mediating between the structural requirements of opportunity and organization are the emergent meanings and definitions—or frames—shared by the adherents of the burgeoning movement.[29]

The political process model asserts that social movements emerge when people with shared grievances who are organized and perceive that they can successfully redress their concerns seize expanding "political opportunities." But what are political opportunities? There is no stable consensus in the political process literature on the definition of political opportunities, despite the efforts of many theorists. However, a few often-cited examples help to convey the general idea behind the concept. Aggrieved and organized groups will not engage in collective protest until one of the following happens:

1. They have (at least some) access to authorities
2. They perceive a decline in repression
3. Elites outside the movement (socioeconomic and/or administrative) become divided
4. They secure the support of elites or other influential groups

Such changes in the political environment can reduce risks and enhance political influence for protesters. Of course, protesters sometimes throw caution to the wind and take very severe risks—or at least ones unanticipated by their targets— that can create opportunities anew rather than simply reacting or seizing opportunities created by the shifting relations and actions of elites.

Although political process theorists do not agree on a single consistent definition of "mobilizing structures" either, they are primarily social or advocacy networks and formal organizations. They may also include family or work units, voluntary associations, social movement organization forms, or tactical repertoires. The concept is meant to address the dynamic element of social movement emergence, although political process theorists usually view them as preexisting structures rather than as the creation of movement organizers. But as Goodwin and Jasper wryly note, "[t]he concept begs the question of how and when certain of these 'structures,' but not others, actually facilitate collective protest."[30]

In the 1980s, political process theorists began to give more attention to the work that protesters devote to convincing people that they have and share grievances, to creating powerful symbols, and to constructing collective identities. These are the processes by which organizers "frame" their issues and targets to resonate with the beliefs, feelings, and desires of potential recruits and the broader public. Extending Erving Goffman's (1974) concept of "framing",[31] social movement scholars began to demonstrate that this cultural work of making the movement and its message understandable and appealing to would-be recruits was a principal activity for organizers.[32] Goffman used the metaphor of the frame to describe how individuals develop and deploy hermeneutic devices that are social-psychological in nature, to reduce the complexity, and organize the meaning, of their world of experience in everyday life. It is through these frames, Goffman argued, that we literally perceive social reality.

Note that collective vision and will plus action are not enough. State repression can prevent the emergence of a movement. Indeed, sometimes the mere threat of state violence can be enough to thwart the collective action of an aggrieved, well organized group, and thus prevent a movement's emergence. Of course, there are other factors besides a state's ability or willingness to use violent repression to consider when accounting for the timing of a social movement's emergence. For example, states sometimes simply ignore the claims of some groups. Alternatively, states are often successful at framing their challengers and their claims as deviant or undeserving, and thus discountable.

We should also remember that collective actors' shared grievances and organization are often ongoing conditions (or "constants," to invoke the language of research design) and thus are insufficient to account for the timing of a social movement's emergence. In short, for political process theorists, explaining the timing of a movement's emergence requires identifying a structure of political opportunities that are opening or expanding for collective actors. Such opportunities, they tell us, can even be provided by the very state that the collective actors target. The political process model also tells us why movements decline. Political opportunities contract, mobilizing structures weaken, or cultural frames discourage and/or delegitimate collective action.

There remain many questions about and critiques of the concept of political opportunities and the political process theory of which it forms a part. At baseline, how do collective actors know a political opportunity when they see one? Is it possible that an opportunity exists to be seized if collective actors never perceive it in the first place? In other words, can we speak objectively of missed political opportunities?[33]

The focus in political process theory on the goal of inclusion and on the acquisition of power obscures the implications for any "politics of influence" aimed at political society. As we discuss in more detail below, influence is well suited to modern civil societies with public spheres, rights, and representative democratic institutions that are open to discursive processes that inform and potentially transform social norms and political cultures. It is possible for collective actors in civil society to culturally persuade actors in political society— not only to gain power or money, but also to prevent the influence of power and money from threatening the institutions and social relations of civil society. And beyond a protectionist stance, a progressive politics aimed at the cultural persuasion of political society can further democratize the existing institutions and social relations of civil society.

IDENTITY POLITICS AND "NEW" SOCIAL MOVEMENT THEORY

In contrast to the premises of *resource mobilization theory* and *political process theory, new social movement theory* derives some its key assumptions from the writings of Karl Marx (see our extensive discussion of Marx in Chapter 2). Inherent to all societies and driving social change within them are unequal relations of power—oppressors and oppressed. Conflict is presumed to be collective, not something that begins with atomized, or socially disconnected, individuals. Conflicting collectivities produce social movements.

New social movement theorists tend to see the modernization of society as a process that has entailed the state's gradual institutional colonization and domination of civil society. They therefore tend to shun a politics of reform in favor of what they perceive to be the only true course of emancipation: revolution. The aim of a social movement, from the perspective of new social movement theory, is not to influence the political process, but rather to transcend the structural limits of the current system and transform it along more democratic lines.

New social movement theory suggests that movement actors choose political strategies that generate or conform to ways of organizing that nonhierarchical and democratic and that encourage wide participation. The organizational means matters. Undemocratically organized movements will not produce democratic change.

"New" social movements were those (1) for which identity was important, (2) that engaged in new forms of politics (e.g., innovative, direct action tactics), and (3) that contributed to new forms of sociability. Examples include indigenous, ethnic, ecological, gay, women's, and human rights movements. A politics of identity entails a war of interpretation and representation—a struggle to make visible or create space for individual and collective identities, redefine cultural norms and appropriate social roles, and channel or transform discursive practices.

While a shared collective identity is necessary for the mobilization of any social movement, identity can also be a goal of social movement activism: either gaining acceptance for stigmatized identities (e.g., "gay," or "lesbian,"), or deconstructing categories of identities (e.g., "Hispanic" vs. Latino/a or Chicano/a). Collective identities can also be deployed as a political strategy, as Noel Sturgeon's work on EcoFeminists nicely illustrates.[34]

Sturgeon's research explains how one faction of the women's rights movement combines discourses on Motherhood and Mother Nature to proffer and celebrate biological distinctions between men and women—much to the dismay of those women within the movement whose understanding of gender inequality is rooted in a social constructionist perspective. Eventually, these factions learn how to live with their cultural diversity and strategically deploy these contradictory identities depending on the opponents that they target. They learn that each identity has different strengths and weaknesses and that they can strengthen their movement by sustaining a wider repertoire of collective identities and discursive heterogeneity.

For new social movement theorist Alan Touraine, the aim of a progressive social movement is not to strategically compete for inclusion and power in a polity, but instead to struggle, beginning at the grass roots, to extend the field of political activity and to democratize new and existing public spaces outside of the state's dominating reach. Contemporary collective actors consciously struggle over the power to construct new identities, to create democratic spheres within both civil society and the polity for autonomous social action, and to reinterpret norms and to reshape institutions. Viewing civil society as the target as well as the terrain of collective action encourages political sociologists to look into the processes by which collective actors create the identities and solidarities that they defend, to assess the relations between social adversaries and the stakes of their conflicts, and to analyze the structural developments that contribute to the heightened self-reflection of actors. As Touraine notes, "...since we have had the privilege of living several centuries in increasingly civil societies, it is now our duty to seek the great alliance between the liberating struggle against the state and a social conflict to prevent this struggle from being waged only for the profit of the leaders of civil society."[35]

Touraine further suggests that it would be a mistake to embrace the liberal project of defending society against the state only to leave intact the relations of domination and inequality within civil society. As the example of liberal capital-ism in England and the United States shows (see Chapter 5 on Karl Polanyi), this might simply mean the primacy of socioeconomic over administrative elites. In other words, as social movements, contemporary conflicts do not have as their stakes merely the defense and autonomy of civil society against the state. Rather, the issue is *which kind* of civil society social movements should defend.

Beyond Democratic Elitism and Democratic Fundamentalism: The 2008 Presidential Campaign and the Pressures for Social Change

In New Hampshire in 2008, Senator Hillary Rodham Clinton (D-NY), despite vying to become the first female President of the United States, found herself being depicted as a vote for the status quo. Clinton's main rival, Senator Barack Obama (D-IL), portrayed himself as carrying the legacy of the civil rights move-ment and styled himself as the candidate for bringing about that type of real change to the United States. He portrayed Senator Clinton as a vote for the political establishment, which was not only incapable of but uninterested in the kind of change he sensed the American public wanted.

Hillary Clinton responded to the charge by suggesting that civil rights for African Americans were secured in the 1960s not only by the movement led by Dr. Martin Luther King, but also by President Lyndon Johnson, who signed the Civil Rights Acts into law. She elaborated that she was not just "talking about" change (implying that Obama was), but that she had a thirty-year record of "getting change done." The Clinton campaign paid a heavy price for these comments as significant leaders of the African American community cried foul and depicted the comments as racist.

But as political sociologists, there is another question besides which can-didate represents the best hope for change. Another bias is revealed in the comments of Hillary Clinton to which we should attune ourselves—that of the role of democratic elitism. The notion of "democratic elitism" is the idea that changes to promote democratic norms, values, relations, and institutions can come only from the elites who comprise political society. Certainly we have seen how the collective behavior paradigm reflects democratic elitism to the extent that it sees social movements, which operate outside existing institution-alized political channels, as fundamentally undemocratic.

Political process theory and resource mobilization theory also foster demo-cratic elitism. It typically appears in one of two forms: (1) when we think of social movements as capable of affecting significant change only when administrative or socioeconomic elites provide them with an opportunity, or (2) when we think that social movements must sacrifice democratic for more hierarchical and unequal forms of organization in order to gain acknowledgement from political society. In short, democratic elitism does not see social movement actors as *creating* opportunities, but only as seizing those made available to them.

However, paying greater attention to how social movements interact with or attempt to influence civil society can help us to avoid the trap of "democratic elitism." We have seen how paying greater attention to civil society can help us to understand that contemporary social movements concern themselves with not only a politics of inclusion but also a politics of identity. It can also help us to explore the terrain from which contemporary social movements wage their politics of inclusion and to answer questions about how social movement actors accomplish the task of constructing viable, relational social identities on which to base their collective action.

On the other hand, we must also be aware that a myopic focus on civil society, such as that underlying the new social movement theory, can as easily present another trap: "democratic fundamentalism." Democratic fundamentalism is the idea that the only way to build a democratic society is through democratic means, norms, values, institutions, and forms of self-organization. In this view, to bureaucratize, as many social movement organizations have, is not only to compromise democracy but also to reinforce antidemocratic values, and can lead ultimately to only nondemocratic change; it is a different version of the argument that Roberto Michels made about the "iron law of oligarchy." In addition, democratic fundamentalism ultimately promotes a collective retreat from engaging political organizations and the state. All efforts at change remain focused on civil society. It fosters the notion that efforts to influence the state only lead to the domination or cooptation of civil society by the state.

So how might a social movement scholar approach this dilemma? One possible dimension of contemporary collective action that attention to civil society helps us to highlight is a politics of influence. It is this dimension of contemporary movement politics—aimed at maintaining the link between civil and political society—that is missing from both political process theory and new social movement theory and may help us to avoid both the traps of democratic elitism and democratic fundamentalism.

The Politics of Influence

Is it possible for grass-roots actors of civil society to change how our political leaders and corporate lobbyists think and act? Or is a politics of democratic reform from below actually a pipedream? Is real change only possible from below through social revolution? What *is* the relationship between collective actors in civil society and those in political society? And what can this relationship tell us about contemporary social movements?

Political society is that part of the political system which deals with how ideas and interests are aggregated into specific policy proposals. Political sociologists studying states undergoing democratic transitions find the concept useful for addressing the problem of how contending social classes and interest groups are to be connected to the governing process. This space of contention is usually referred to as "political society", i.e. the place where specific political institutions (administrative, legislative, or judicial) attempt to manage public demands. Political society and civil society are often seen as having separate, although not necessarily disconnected, political cultures. Actors from each of these spheres may seek to influence the political culture of the other.

Civil society and political society do not exist in separate vacuums. They coexist in a complex and shifting set of relationships. Political society is comprised of people who manage the state. Members of civil society can attempt at least to influence the discourses and actions of people who are members of political society. When social movements convince members of the political elite to change not just what they think about a specific bill or proposal, but how they think about a given topic, the social movement has altered existing boundaries of political discourse. In the best-case scenario they influence political leaders to create space for new identities, new norms, and new representations of need. Indeed, this attempt by members of civil society to influence members of political society is perhaps the key feature of contemporary social movements.

The further democratization of political and economic institutions is also critical to an effective politics of influence. It is not enough to convince a politician to vote in favor of the interests of a group one time. To effect change that is sustained over time and spreads to the culture at large, the social movement actors must affect a reform of the very centers and structures of power. Without this kind of reform, any gains within civil society would be much more vulnerable to the constantly changing political winds.

Culture, Structure, States

To explore how contemporary social movements exercise political influence, political sociologists are rethinking the relationship between culture, structure, and states. *Culture* is a set of practices, both material and nonmaterial, which constitutes meanings, values, and subjectivities.[36] William Sewell, Jr., in his seminal article, "A Theory of Structure, Duality, Agency, and Transformation," defines *structures* as cultural *schemas* that are invested with and that sustain *resources.* Structures also reflect and reproduce unequal power relations.[37] When structures take the form of discourses, rules, policies, methods, recipes, and the like, we can analyze how they enable or constrain action as subjects both intentionally and unintentionally appropriate and extend them to new contexts.[38] Culture in this sense is a dimension of all institutions—economic, political, and social.

Social movement analysis often dichotomizes "culture" on one side and "political structure," that is, states or political society, on the other. For example, Francesca Polletta points out that political process theory improperly conceptualizes culture as constraining action only when it impedes challengers' capacity to perceive the state's objective vulnerability.[39] In other words, despite the theory's emphasis on cultural framing[40] and how culture enables challengers to represent their grievances as shared, to construct their collective identity as a unified actor, and to perceive an existing political opportunity, the theory only considers culture's power to constrain challengers in cases when they fail to perceive what the theorist claims is an objective political opportunity. Furthermore, culture, in this sense, is only that which is inside the heads of challengers. In contrast, political process theory gives significantly less attention, if any, to culture that is inside the heads of state actors. And, until recently, it has given no attention to the cultural dimensions of political structures.

This happens because the theory implicitly conflates agency and culture, resulting in a conception of culture as easily transformed.[41] Thus, "culture" becomes understood as subjective and malleable, whereas "political structure" becomes understood as objective and durable. "Culture" enables protest, but "political structure" constrains protest. The powerless (or actors in civil society) mobilize "culture" to challenge structure, but the powerful (or actors in political society) monopolize "political structure" to maintain power.

How then might we reconceptualize the relationship between culture and structures so that we better understand the politics of influence? Polletta offers a promising alternative approach when she suggests that "[t]he task is not to abandon an emphasis on 'objective' political structures in favor of potential insurgents' 'subjective' perceptions and valuations of political structures, but to probe the (objective) resources and constraints generated by the cultural dimensions of political structures."[42]

Emirbayer and Goodwin have usefully pointed out that conceiving of the cultural dimensions of structures "as symbolic patterns possessing their own autonomous inner logic" is different than thinking of them as "substantively distinct 'domains' of social life."[43] Conceptually dichotomizing culture and political structures, and then reifying the boundaries between them, is to ultimately miss one of the key insights of contemporary social movements. "Culture is political because meanings are constitutive of processes that, implicitly or explicitly, seek to redefine social power."[44] Political structures are also, though not only, cultural. To reiterate, culture is a dimension of all structures and practices— including political structures and practices.

So, how does the politics of influence function, and why is it important to social movement theorists? The actions of the state are always embedded in culture. The actors of political society, the people who govern states, do not lack culture or morality, despite the tendency of political scientists and international relations theorists to define them as such. State actors are not immune to cultural or moral persuasion that draws upon salient cultural structures. Cultural structures—such as constitutional principles, rules of procedure, cultural traditions, "conventional wisdom," institutional memories, political taboos and rituals like swearing an oath to uphold the political duties one is assuming, economic beliefs about the functioning of markets, understandings of legitimate rights, and moral values—can channel the choices and even imaginations of members of the polity as well as social movement activists. To the extent that these cultural structures become institutionalized in the state, we can begin to analyze them as offering potential opportunities for social movements. Since competing structures are often available, social movements can influence political society by getting their preferred structures "into the mix." Note here that the emphasis is on political influence on the polity rather than political inclusion in the polity.

How does this work in practice? One emerging example drawn from recent social movement activity illuminates this process: the struggle to define the meaning, context, and outcome of globalization. We shall define that process in the next chapter on transnational social movements and global politics.

NOTES

1. Jeff Goodwin and James M. Jasper, eds., *The Social Movements Reader: Cases and Concepts* (Oxford, UK: Blackwell, 2003), 4.
2. Jean L. Cohen and Andrew Arato, *Civil Society and Political Theory* (Cambridge, MA: MIT Press, 1992), 562.
3. See John Foran, *Taking Power: On the Origins of Third World Revolutions* (Cambridge, UK: Cambridge University Press, 2005); Jeff Goodwin and James M. Jasper, eds., *The Social Movements Reader: Cases and Concepts*. (Malden, MA: Blackwell, 2003), 3; and Jeff Goodwin, "A Theory of Categorical Terrorism," *Social Forces*, 2006, 84(4), 2028.
4. Hanspeter Kriesi, Ruud Koopmans, Jan Willem Duyvendak, and Marco G. Giugni, *New Social Movements in Western Europe: A Comparative Analysis* (Minneapolis, MN: University of Minnesota Press, 1995).
5. David S. Meyer and Sidney and Tarrow, "A Movement Society: Contentious Politics for a New Century," in David S. Meyer and Sidney Tarrow, eds., *The Social*

Movement Society: Contentious Politics for a New Century (Lanham, MD: Rowman & Littlefield, 1998).

6. For more on the concept of "political society," see the section titled "The Politics of Influence."

7. Charles Tilly, "Britain Creates the Social Movement," in James Cronin and Jonathan Schneer, *Social Conflict and the Political Order in Modern Britain* (London: Croom-Helm, 1982), 26.

8. Charles Tilly, "Social Movements and National Politics," in Charles Bright and Susan Harding, eds., *Statemaking and Social Movements: Essays in History and Theory* (Ann Arbor: University of Michigan Press, 1984, 305.

9. See, for example, Gustav LeBon, *The Crowd: A Study of the Popular Mind* (Whitefish, MT: Kessinger Publishing, 2004).

10. Ralph H. Turner, ed., *Robert E. Park on Social Control and Collective Behavior: Selected Papers* (Chicago: University of Chicago Press, 1967); Herbert Blumer, "Collective Behavior," in Alfred McClung Lee, ed., *New Outline of the Principles of Sociology* (New York: Barnes & Noble, 1957); R. G. Turner and L. M. Killian, *Collective Behavior* (Englewood Cliffs, NJ: Prentice-Hall, 1957). See also the excellent summary of collective behavior theories in Gary T. Marx and James L. Wood, "Strands of Theory and Research in Collective Behavior," *Annual Review of Sociology*, 1975, 1, 368–428.

11. Neil Smelser, *The Theory of Collective Behavior* (New York: Free Press, 1962); and William Kornhauser, *The Politics of Mass Society* (New York: Free Press, 1959).

12. See, e.g., Eric Hoffer, *The True Believer: Thoughts on the Nature of Mass Movements* (New York: Harper & Row, 1951).

13. Doug McAdam, *Freedom Summer* (New York: Oxford University Press, 1982).

14. John D. McCarthy and Mayer N. Zald, *The Trend of Social Movements in America: Professionalism and Resource Mobilization* (Morristown, NJ: General Learning Press, 1973).

15. Clifford Bob, *The Marketing of Rebellion: Insurgents, Media, and International Activism* (Cambridge: Cambridge University Press, 2005).

16. Jeff Goodwin, and James M. Jasper, eds., *The Social Movements Reader: Cases and Concepts* (Malden, MA: Blackwell, 2003), 166–67.

17. John Walton, *Western Times and Water Wars: State, Culture, and Rebellion in California* (Berkeley: University of California Press, 1992), 317.

18. Jean L. Cohen and Andrew Arato, *Civil Society and Political Theory* (Cambridge, MA: MIT Press, 1992), 499.

19. Jean L. Cohen and Andrew Arato, *Civil Society and Political Theory* (Cambridge, MA: MIT Press, 1992), 493.

20. Jeff Goodwin and James M. Jasper, eds., *The Social Movements Reader: Cases and Concepts* (Malden, MA: Blackwell, 2003), 4.

21. Jeff Goodwin and James M. Jasper, eds., *The Social Movements Reader: Cases and Concepts* (Malden, MA: Blackwell, 2003), 6.

22. Charles Tilly, *From Mobilization to Revolution* (Reading, MA: Addison-Wesley, 1978).

23. Charles Tilly, "Britain Creates the Social Movement," in James Cronin and Jonathan Schneer, *Social Conflict and the Political Order in Modern Britain* (London: Croom-Helm, 1982).

24. Charles Tilly, *Big Structures, Large Processes, and Huge Comparisons* (New York: Russell Sage, 1984), 307.

25. Charles Tilly, *From Mobilization to Revolution* (Reading, MA: Addison-Wesley, 1978).

26. Charles Tilly, Louise Tilly, and Richard Tilly, *The Rebellious Century: 1830–1930* (London: J.M. Dent & Sons Ltd., 1975.)

27. Charles Tilly, *Big Structures, Large Processes, and Huge Comparisons* (New York: Russell Sage, 1984).

28. Charles Tilly, *From Mobilization to Revolution* (Reading, MA: Addison-Wesley, 1978), 168.

29. Doug McAdam, John D. McCarthy, and Mayer N. Zald, eds., *Comparative Perspectives on Social Movements: Political Opportunities, Mobilizing Structures, and Cultural Framings* (New York: Cambridge University Press, 1996), 8.

30. Jeff Goodwin and James M. Jasper, eds., *The Social Movements Reader: Cases and Concepts* (Malden, MA: Blackwell, 2003), 20.

31. Erving Goffman, *Frame Analysis: An Essay on the Organization of Experience* (New York: Harper, 1974).

32. See David Snow, A. E. Burke Rochford, Jr. Steven K. Worden, and Robert D. Benford, "Frame Alignment Processes, Micromobilization, and Movement Participation," *American Sociological Review*, 1986, 51, 464–81; and David A. Snow and Robert D. Benford, "Ideology, Frame Resonance, and Participant Mobilization," *International Social Movement Research* 1988, 1, 197–217.

33. See Jeff Goodwin and James M. Jasper, eds., *The Social Movements Reader: Cases and Concepts* (Malden, MA: U.K. Blackwell, 2003), 12

34. Noël Sturgeon, *Ecofeminst Natures. Race, Gender, Feminist Theory and Political Action* (New York: Routledge, 1997).

35. Alain Touraine, "Triumph or Downfall of Civil Society?", in *Humanities in Review*, vol. 1 (Cambridge, UK: Cambridge University Press, 1983), 138.

36. Glenn Jordan and Chris Weedon, *Cultural Politics: Class, Gender, Race and the Postmodern World* (Oxford: Blackwell, 1995), 8.

37. William H. Sewell, Jr., "A Theory of Structure, Duality, Agency, and Transformation," *American Journal of Sociology*, 1992, 98, 1–29.

38. See Swidler 1986; Zerubavel 1990; Sewell 1992; Kane 1997, 2000; and Hall 1999.

39. Francesca Polletta, "Culture Is Not Just in Your Head," in Jeff Goodwin and James M. Jasper, *Rethinking Social Movements: Structure, Meaning, and Emotion* (Lanham, MD: Rowman & Littlefield, 2004), 99.

40. David A. Snow and Robert D. Benford, "Master Frames and Cycles of Protest," in Aldon D. Morris and Carol McClurg Mueller, eds., *Frontiers in Social Movement Theory* (New Haven, CT: Yale University Press, 1992); Robert D. Benford,"An Insider's Critique of the Social Movement Framing Perspective," *Sociological Inquiry*, 1997, 67, 409–30; Mario Diani, "Linking mobilization Frames and Political

Opportunities: Insights from Regional Populism in Italy," *American Sociological Review*, 1996, 61, 1053–69; Anne E.Kane, "Theorizing Meaning Construction in Social Movements: Symbolic Structures and Interpretation during the Irish Land War, 1879–1882," *Sociological Theory*, 1997, 15(3), 249–76; Bert Klandermans*The Social Psychology of Protest* (Oxford: Blackwell, 1996); Doug McAdam, Culture and Social Movements," in Enrique Laraña, Hank Johnston, and Joseph R. Gusfield, eds., *New Social Movements: From Ideology to Identity* (Philadelphia: Temple University Press, 1994); Doug McAdam, John D. McCarthy, and Mayer N. Zald, eds., *Comparative Perspectives on Social Movements: Political Opportunities, Mobilizing Structures, and Cultural Framings* (New York: Cambridge University Press, 1994); Sidney Tarrow, *Power in Movement: Social Movements, Collective Action, and Politics* (New York: Cambridge University Press, 1998), Chapter 7.

41. See, e.g., Doug McAdam, Culture and Social Movements," in Enrique Laraña, Hank Johnston, and Joseph R. Gusfield, eds., *New Social Movements: From Ideology to Identity* (Philadelphia: Temple University Press, 1994). See also William H.Sewell, Jr. "A Theory of Structure, Duality, Agency, and Transformation," *American Journal of Sociology*, 1992, 98, 1–29; Mustafa Emirbayer and Jeff Goodwin, "Network Analysis, Culture, and the Problem of Agency," *American Journal of Sociology*, 1994, 99(6), 1411–54; Sharon Hays, "Structure and Agency and the Sticky Problem of Culture," *Theory and Society*, 1994, 12, 57–72; and Francesca Polletta, "Culture Is Not Just in Your Head," in Jeff Goodwin and James M. Jasper, *Rethinking Social Movements: Structure, Meaning, and Emotion* (Lanham, MD: Rowman & Littlefield, 2004).

42. Francesca Poletta, "Snarls, Quacks, and Quarrels: Culture and Structure in Political Process Theory," *Sociological Forum*, 1999, 14(1), 64; see also Francesca Polletta, "Culture and Its Discontents: Recent Theorizing on the Cultural Dimensions of Protest," *Sociological Inquiry*, 1997, 67: 431–50; and Mabel Berezin, "Politics and Culture: A Less Fissured Terrain," *Annual Review of Sociology*, 1997, 23, 361–83.

43. Mustafa Emirbayer and Jeff Goodwin, "Network Analysis, Culture, and the Problem of Agency," *American Journal of Sociology*, 1994, 99(6), 1440; contrast, e.g., Allison Brysk, *From Tribal Village to Global Village. Indian Rights and International Relations in Latin America* (Stanford, CA: Stanford University Press, 2000, 42–44.

44. Sonia E. Alvarez, Evelina Dagnino, and Arturo Escobar, Introduction, in *Cultures of Politics, Politics of Cultures: Re-Visioning Latin American Social Movements*, edited by Sonia E. Alvarez, Evelina Dagnino, and Arturo Escobar (Boulder, CO: Westview Press, 1998), 6.

Chapter 11

Transnational Social Movements and Globalization

S ome of the most dynamic social movements today are engaged in the struggle over what globalization will mean for the world. What they are teaching
us is that globalization is not some natural and inevitable force to which local
communities must submit themselves. In this chapter we will examine transnational social movements as well as dominant forces of globalization and how
they have shaped such movements today.

The Multiple Meanings of Globalization

The dominant features of *contemporary globalization*—the reorganization of
production at the global level and the disproportionate growth of trade and
finance that crosses the borders of nation-states—continues the nineteenth-
century process that Karl Polanyi identifies in *The Great Transformation* (see
Chapter 5). They are reinforced by powerful transnational networks of actors,
including corporations, states, social movements, and others (that we discuss
in more detail later), as well as a powerful economic ideology known as *neo-
liberalism*.

The economic concept of "free markets" is the cornerstone of the neo-
liberal vision of the globe as a marketplace in which all trade and other economic

action is "freed" from the "constraints" of law, politics, and morality—in short, freed from governance. The best markets, this discourse asserts, are those that are most efficient, and the most efficient markets are those governed only by the "natural" laws of human competition. Any efforts to embed the global market within the constraints of law, politics, and morality ultimately make the market less competitive and thus "hurt" the economy by reducing its productivity (i.e., growth and profitability) and, in turn, shrinking the overall size of the "economic pie."

Obviously, these processes are not the only ones shaping contemporary globalization. Globalization is a multifaceted set of processes. Equally important to note is that globalization is still "under construction," so to speak. While there are many ways to organize it, globalization still requires rules, policies, regulations, and enforceable contracts. The struggle over their content, working principles of justice and morality, and pragmatic institutionalization comprises a critical aspect of what we call the *politics of globalization*.

The "free market" discourse has been successful because many politicians have been persuaded that economic development *causes* the political response of deregulation, that neo-liberal economic globalization is inevitable, and that states have no choice but to follow its logic or else be marginalized. In this sense, we can speak of neo-liberalism as a cultural structure influencing political society. It is, at this point, an extremely powerful cultural structure, with many adherents. However, social movement actors who disagree with its premises or disapprove of its outcomes can seek to challenge it so that it does not remain dominant. Social movements have started to deploy what Michael Peter Smith calls a "transnationalist discourse" of globalization that presents a different vision of what an increasingly globalized world could look like.

The transnationalist discourse insists that the economy is always embedded in law, politics, and morality. In this discourse, the neo-liberal vision of the self-regulating market, despite current efforts to construct such an elusive arrangement, is not only socially undesirable but—to echo Karl Polanyi—a "utopian impossibility." It is important to note that "transnational" and "transnationalist discourse" do not have the same meaning. "Transnational" refers to that which transcends nation-state boundaries and the *inter*national system of states. The transnationalist discourse challenges the binary distinction between globalization and the nation-state and "insists on the continuing significance of borders, state policies, and national identities even as these are often transgressed by transnational communication circuits and social practices."[1]

Moreover, this discourse does not treat the nation-state and transnational practices and processes as mutually exclusive social phenomena, nor even as binary conceptual categories. The transnationalist discourse depicts nation-states and transnational practices and processes as contributing to the constitution of each other. It sees nation-states not only as being transformed by transnational practices and processes, but also as often participating in and even promoting those that are transforming nation-states. It is worth quoting at length Saskia Sassen's recent description of these transnational phenomena:

> Although localized in national—indeed, in subnational—settings, these processes are part of globalization in that they involve transboundary networks and entities connecting multiple local or "national" processes and actors, or the recurrence of particular issues or dynamics in a growing number of countries or localities. Among these entities and processes, I include, for instance, cross-border networks of activists engaged in specific localized struggles with an explicit or implicit global agenda, as is the case with many human rights and environmental organizations; particular aspects of the work of states—for example the implementation of certain monetary and fiscal policies in a growing number of countries, often with enormous pressure from the International Monetary Fund (IMF) and the United States, because those policies are critical to the constitution of global financial markets; and the fact that national courts are now using international instruments—whether human rights, international environmental standards, or WTO regulations—to address issues where before they would have used national instruments.[2]

This passage reflects Sassen's deliberate effort to build into her definition of globalization a transnationalist discourse.

But what we wish to emphasize here is a discourse employed by social movements that seek to challenge globalization "from below." It is important to recognize that not all who approach globalization from outside of political society do so with an aim to challenge or change the processes of globalization. Peter Evans distinguishes between two types of "globalization from below": (1) transnational networks, which seek to *adapt to* the power of global elites and (2) those that explicitly seek to *challenge* this power by "...pushing for different rules and by building different ideological understandings."[3]

The first type of globalization from below refers to cases like those of ordinary citizens from poor countries who build transnational communities that link them to wealthy countries where they build assets while remaining engaged in their communities of origin. As Evans points out, while such collective action reflects the adaptive ability of these people facing the challenges and opportunities of globalization, it does not challenge the dominant global rules or even the economic ideology invoked to legitimate them.[4]

The collective actions of those in the first category are extremely interesting. However, for the purposes of this chapter, we will be examining only the second type—the social movements that are what Evans calls "counter-hegemonic," that is to say, challenge neo-liberal globalization.[5] According to the transnationalist discourse, the question is not whether law, politics, and morality will shape our global economic future, but rather *whose* law, politics, and morality will shape it. All markets, including the global market that is currently under construction, depend upon rules and institutions to function. Who will shape their creation, and how will they be arranged? These are the critical questions, from a transnationalist perspective, that the neo-liberal globalization discourse does not address and, moreover, dangerously implies require no addressing.

The political opportunity to challenge neo-liberalism and influence the discursive constitution of globalization arises in contexts of political cultural struggle to influence which discourses do (and do not) become institutionalized through the politics of legislatures, the law enforcement of executive administrations, and the moral reasoning of judiciaries. To the extent that collective actors in civil society can continue to illuminate society's necessary role in regulating markets, they sustain the possibility of influencing the ideas around which we do organize such markets. As social theorist, and Brazil's Minister of Long-Term Planning, Roberto Unger argues:

> If we can change what free trade means and how it is organized, we can do the same more generally to globalization. And if we can have globalization on our terms, rather than on those of the supposedly irresistible forces that its contemporary form is claimed to represent, all bets are off: we are freer than we suppose to rethink and to reconstruct.[6]

Many social movements and networks of transnational activists are trying to influence the politics of globalization. However, it might be helpful to examine more closely one traditional social movement that has transformed into a transnational social movement, challenging not only the repressive policies of one state, but neo-liberal globalization as a whole. *Transnational social movements* are sustained contentious interactions with opponents by networks of actors that have common purposes linked across nation-state boundaries and that demonstrate a capacity to generate coordinated social mobilization in more than one country to publicly influence social change.[7] Examining the Free Burma movement as an example of a transnational social movement illuminates how the politics of influence might work in a globalizing world. It also highlights how social movement scholars will have to account for how globalization is changing social movements while at the same time some of those movements seek to change globalization.

The Free Burma Movement as Transnational Social Movement[8]

Throughout the fall of 2007, citizens around the world were horrified to learn that the military government of Myanmar (or, as referred to here, Burma)[9] was shooting and killing scores of innocent Buddhist monks as they peacefully marched in protest through the streets of Yangon and Mandalay. From August through October, the military junta arrested monks, students, and other citizens who marched with them to protest recent fuel price hikes and, more to the point, to call for democratic political change.

Such violent state repression on the part of Burma's military government was not new. This scene was similar to that of August 1988, when hundreds of thousands of citizens in statewide protest walked off their jobs and into the streets calling for an end to the ruling military's decades of economic mismanagement and for a democratic government. Then, too, the military government, which had first taken power by coup d'état in 1962, violently and indiscriminately repressed the public protest, killing over 3000 citizens.

Burma's pro-democracy movement emerged initially within a national scope of collective action. However, from 1990 to 1994, several factors altered the conditions challenging the pro-democracy movement, transforming it into a counterhegemonic transnational social movement. First, it was during this period that the pro-democracy movement's leaders came to realize that the Myanmar state was not its only obstacle to domestic political change. Transnational corporations and foreign investment in Burma buttressed the Myanmar state's power to repress the movement. Additionally, the Myanmar state refused to acknowledge the victory of Burma's powerful opposition party in the 1990 democratic elections.[10] Furthermore, the military adopted a new economic liberalization policy in an effort to draw badly needed foreign direct investment, just as the Cold War was ending and the neo-liberal discourse on globalization was increasing its hegemony. Transnational corporations (e.g., Total and Chevron) seeking to build a natural gas pipeline through Burma forged business partnerships with the military's state-owned oil and gas enterprise.

The pro-democracy movement began to organize transnational campaigns with other movements. *Transnational campaigns* are strategies or sets of tactics to publicly influence social change which are coordinated and shared by sets of actors linked across nation-state boundaries.[11] The actors participating in transnational campaigns do not necessarily construct a unitary transnational identity, but often deploy a transnationalist discourse. They also frequently link a variety of different social movements. For example, labor, environmental, human rights, and women's rights movements may band together temporarily to coordinate a single transnational campaign, only to later dissemble, scatter, and each reaggregate into separate transnational campaigns composed of new configurations of diverse social movements. These campaigns may be organized around either institutionalized or noninstitutionalized political tactics. The transnational campaigns organized by these Burmese pro-democracy activists, unlike the previous protests inside of Burma, were not centered directly on the Myanmar state. They instead targeted democratic states (such as the United States) and the transnational corporations chartered by those states that sought to profit from Burma's opening market.

In the process of organizing these campaigns, the pro-democracy movement developed into a transnational social movement. Important to the tranformation of the Free Burma movement was the development of alliances with other grass-roots movements and activists around the world. They waged the transnational campaigns (described in detail later) in alliance with local state and municipal governments in the United States and Australia, as well as nonstate actors, regional governing bodies like the European Union, nongovernmental organizations (NGOs) throughout East and Southeast Asia, international nongovernmental organizations (INGOs),[12] and voluntary associations on every continent and in over twenty-six countries. The movement also attracted preexisting transnational activists defending issues like human rights, women's rights, protection of the natural environment, labor rights, indigenous peoples' rights, and socially responsible corporate investment. They even created new *transnational advocacy networks*—configurations of nonstate actors, based usually on informal contacts, linked across nation-state boundaries, who share common values, discourses, and a dense exchange of information,[13] including one formed around the international "right to know" about the labor conditions and environmental impact of proposed development projects that are financed through transnational corporations in partnership with the state.

Significantly, the Free Burma movement began to develop a transnationalist discourse on corporate governance and globalization. This transnationalist discourse challenged several key neo-liberal assumptions that the Free Burma movement believed were propping up the repressive Myanmar government. First, the movement challenged the notion that market participants cannot or should not select their business partners on the basis of their moral positions. Then they challenged the idea that states are powerless to reign in transnational corporations. Finally, they challenged the claim that corporations are, unlike most governments, not required to respect universal human rights principles.

These transnational campaigns all took place in the United States. They were neither conceived nor launched simultaneously, and were not within the initial framework of an overarching, preconceived meta-discourse. These campaigns do, however, overlap in time, and each operates with an awareness of the others' strategies. Indeed, some of the actors participate significantly and simultaneously in more than one of these campaigns as they unfold over varying durations. Each campaign targets specific, neo-liberal discourses which various networks of actors (who eventually come to constitute a countermovement) invoke to promote continued investment and trade relations with Burma.

THE SELECTIVE PURCHASING LAW CAMPAIGN

The selective purchasing law campaign was initially successful at getting thirty municipal governments and the regional state of Massachusetts to legislate and enact "Free Burma" laws. This legislation restricted a government entity's own ability (including the ability of its agencies and authorities) to purchase goods or services from any individuals or corporations engaged in business with Burma. The strategy behind proposing selective purchasing laws was to use a government's purchasing power in a transnational marketplace where it procures contracts for goods and services to force not only domestic, but also foreign corporations to make a choice: either seek profitable contracts with the local or regional government that enacted the law *or* pursue contracts with the Myanmar state.

In practice, these selective purchasing laws were more effective at curbing business with the Myanmar state than were the economic sanctions policy discussed at the time but not implemented by many Western countries. The selective purchasing law campaign successfully persuaded all but one U.S.-based corporation and many foreign corporations as well to quit doing business with Burma. In doing so, it introduced a powerful challenge to neo-liberal discourse, which claims that the market should be amoral and that it should not matter with whom a company does business. The government entities that refused to do business not only with Burma, but also any companies that did business with Burma, were in effect saying that this was not true. They, as consumers, had an obligation to do business with companies that met their moral standards, those who did not do business with human rights violators.

The lone holdout was Unocal Oil Corporation. Unocal was the only remaining U.S.-chartered corporation still doing business in Burma. From the outset of the selective purchasing law campaign, it had been also the largest U.S.-based corporate investor in Burma.

THE CAMPAIGN TO DECHARTER UNOCAL CORPORATION

The next campaign targeted Unocal specifically, seeking to revoke its corporate charter on the basis of newly emerging evidence provided by NGOs that had documented Unocal's reliance on forced labor in constructing its natural gas pipeline through Burma.

The law in California emphasizes that corporations are legal entities that owe their existence to the regional state that created them. The law also specifies conditions under which corporations may be stripped of the charters that grant their right to exist. It provides a legal procedure allowing "the people of

California," acting through their attorney general, to initiate the charter revocation of any of its corporations that have violated existing law.

The campaign to revoke Unocal's corporate charter deployed a transnational strategy through which the Free Burma movement attempted to get the California State Attorney General to bring a lawsuit on behalf of the people of California that would decharter Unocal on the basis of "crimes against humanity," "environmental devastation," and other violations of international law that it has committed not only in California, but also in Burma and other foreign states.

The Free Burma movement's effort to petition the California sate attorneys general Lundgren and Lockyer, respectively, to bring a lawsuit against Unocal that would revoke its corporate charter had mixed results. Neither attorney general was persuaded to bring such a lawsuit against Unocal. But then again, this campaign's organizers never really expected that they would. The primary goal of this campaign strategy was to challenge the apologetic claim of California's regional state actors that they had no power to regulate the conduct—however morally questionable—of corporations choosing to do business with the Myanmar government in Burma. The problem, these politicians frequently suggested, is that the conduct of corporations in Burma falls within the administrative jurisdiction of the Myanmar government, and the Myanmar government has greeted these corporations and their conduct with open arms, despite their domestic citizenry's outcry to the international community for economic sanctions.

This campaign sought to educate the public about the legal power that regional states in the United States have to challenge the misconduct of the corporations that they charter, regardless of where in the world those corporations conduct their business. It sought to show that Unocal's violations of human rights in Burma could be stopped by California's legal administrators—if they had the political and moral will to do so—because the State of California had chartered Unocal and California's legal administrators have the legal grounds and power to revoke Unocal's charter. In doing so, the campaign employed a transnationalist discourse to suggest that, despite the protests of governments that they are powerless to rein in transnational corporations, local state and federal governments still held considerable power in the age of globalization. What the campaign pointed out was that states don't necessarily lack the power to act, but that they often lack the will.

THE ALIEN TORT CLAIMS CAMPAIGN

The final campaign focuses on the transnational legal space (a site for contesting the meaning of globalization) provided by the U.S. Alien Tort Claims Act (ATCA). The First Congress of the United States adopted this act in 1789, but it remained largely unused for the next two centuries. The statute asserts simply that "[t]he district courts shall have original jurisdiction of any civil action by an alien [non-U.S. citizen] for a tort [i.e., a harm or wrong] only, committed in violation of *the law of nations* or a treaty of the United States..." (28 U.S.C. §1350).[14] More recently, the statute has been invoked to hold states and their agents accountable for violations of international law committed *outside* the United States.

But in 1996, a dozen peasants from Burma filed a suit against Unocal Oil Corporation, alleging that it was complicit and even benefited from slave labor and other severe human rights abuses committed in Burma. In *Doe v. Unocal*, filed under the Alien Tort Claims Act, the movement actors (this time in the role of plaintiffs to the lawsuit and their supporters) deployed a transnational discourse to challenge the neo-liberal notion that corporations should be subject only to the laws of the country in which they were operating at that moment and that universal standards of morality or human rights did not apply to corporations.

The *Doe* plaintiffs asked that the court hold the corporation liable, even though the alleged acts occurred outside of the United States. What they were really asking was for the court to impose legal, ethical, and moral standards on a corporation and hold that those standards followed that corporation around the world, wherever it went. The peasants eventually settled with Unocal for a significant sum. It appeared that the corporation preferred to pay out a large sum of money rather than have the U.S. Supreme Court rule that corporations could be held liable for human rights abuses wherever they occurred.

What is significant about this case is that these transnational campaigns do not reflect a movement that has switched its focus to transnational corporations. Rather, they reflect the Free Burma movement activists' strategic choices to target the political, legal, and moral discourses that are embedded in, and that give meaning to, the rules and institutional arrangements that legitimate the transnational partnerships *between* these transnational corporations and the Myanmar state. These transnational partnerships are in many ways sustained by the states in which these transnational corporations are chartered, as these campaigns have demonstrated. In short, the targets of the movement have also become transnational.

As demonstrated in late 2007, local movement participation in Burma has not been completely deterritorialized. Citizens still living inside Burma continue to risk their lives to stage periodic symbolic protests in coordination with Free Burma movement actors outside the country. Even symbolic protest on behalf of democratic reform still represents a highly significant expression of commitment. This symbolic protest is not only expressive, it is strategic as well. Participants protest as a means of performing to an audience that has greatly expanded over the past two decades beyond the confines of Burma their solidarity with collective actors waging transnational campaigns for democratic change in Burma. They have also strategically coordinated the timing of their symbolic protest to show support for particular transnationalist discourses that the Free Burma movement operating outside of Burma periodically presents in the form of various nonviolent events to educate and remind the public of Burma's struggle for democracy.

Transnational social movements depend on both information exchange and coordinated tactics. But they also generate joint mobilization and, potentially, threaten to disrupt a social order. *Some* transnational social movements, like the Free Burma movement, have started to engage in a politics of influence that seeks to destabilize the complex cultural structures that are undergirding globalization. It is these movements that pose interesting questions regarding the future of social movements and the study of those movements.

New Directions for Social Movements and Research

The study of transnational social movements raises many new and difficult questions for political sociologists. Some promising avenues of future research include the impact that transnational corporations have on the political environment in which these movements operate, the effect that differently structured states (e.g., nation-states versus transnational governmental networks, or authoritarian versus democratic states) have on transnational social movements, and the differences between transnational social movements challenging globalization through nonviolent strategies versus transnational revolutionary movements that use terrorism to influence politics.

1. Where do transnational corporations fit into political sociology's effort to map transnational social movements and the influence that they wield on political society?

The transnational network of relations that the Myanmar state created with corporations not only profited those corporations which sought to take advantage of a labor force whose state offered it no legal protection, but also buttressed the power of the Myanmar state, facilitating its efforts to repress pro-democratic activism within Burma. But these same transnational business partnerships also created new opportunities for the movement.

First, it is because transnational corporations are embedded in the politics, law, and morality of the states that have created them, and not only of the states with which they develop trade and investment ties, that relations like those between the Myanmar state and Unocal have (unintentionally) provided their challengers with new opportunities.

Second, transnational corporations bring with them histories to the less socially protected states with which they seek new, more profitable partnerships. Unocal brought with it to Burma its history of interaction with Californians whose oceanic coasts it had polluted in an oil spill incident and for which it had failed to accept financial responsibility. Although most Californians could not locate Burma on a world map, and still fewer would recognize any reference to the Myanmar state, most of them know who Unocal is.

Transnational corporations not only span more than one nation-state, they link them. For their opponents in communities of one state, like Burma, they can provide an opportunity for mobilizing sympathetic opponents in communities of other states to which Unocal has links and a disreputable corporate identity.

In their path-breaking work on transnational advocacy networks, Keck and Sikkink tell us that when channels between the state and its domestic actors are blocked, a "boomerang pattern" of influence characteristic of transnational networks may occur: domestic NGOs bypass their state and directly search out international allies to try to bring pressure on their states from outside (Figure 11.1). This is most obviously the case in human rights campaigns.[15] Their model actually illustrates an additional step in this process whereby the domestic NGOs that have been blocked by their state activate the network *whose members pressure their own states* and (if relevant) a third-party organization, which in turn pressure the blocking, i.e., target, state.

This model focuses almost exclusively on interactions between states and civil society. They provide no conceptual space for examining interactions between markets and society. Corporations and market relations do not appear in Keck and Sikkink's conceptual model of how transnational social movements or transnational advocacy networks exert pressure for changing the human rights conditions that motivated their action. Yet, as we have seen in the case of the Free Burma movement, the trade relations between states and transnational corporations may constitute a very different kind of target and may require a different kind of pressure for affecting social change than that presumed by Keck and Sikkink's model.

Although Keck and Sikkink correctly emphasize the continuing significance of states, their reasons for doing so betrays, in light of the empirical evidence presented in this article, a questionable assumption regarding human rights practices and their implications for transnational movements. They claim that governments are the primary violators of rights.[16] Based upon this assumption, they build the conceptual logic of their boomerang pattern: "When a government violates or refuses to recognize rights, individuals and domestic groups often have no recourse within domestic political or judicial arenas. They may seek international connections finally to express their concerns and even to protect their lives."[17]

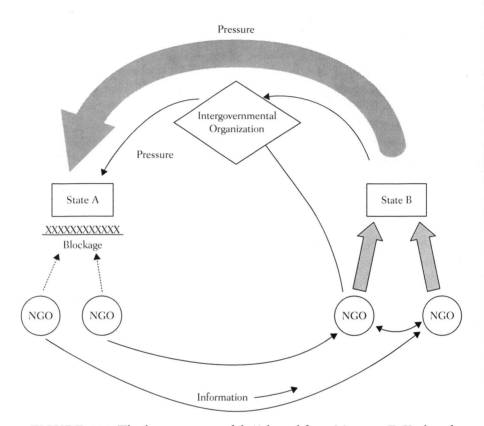

FIGURE 11.1 The boomerang model. (Adapted from Margaret E. Keck and Kathryn Sikkink, *Activists Beyond Borders: Advocacy Networks in International Politics* [Ithaca, NY: Cornell University Press, 1998], 13.)

One of the lessons that we should take from the transnational campaigns of the Free Burma movement is that transnational corporations, as much as governments, may be significant violators of human rights. In some cases, transnational corporations may even work together with states in violating them. Moreover, *Doe v. Unocal* and other cases filed against both corporate and state violators of human rights under the Alien Tort Claims Act reflect a transnational legal space where individuals and groups outside the United States may well find recourse within the judicial arenas of the U.S. Federal District Court. That is, the domestic state in which human rights victims hold their citizenship does not necessarily have a monopoly on their access to a judicial arena. Each of these points taken on its own may seem like trivial tinkering with Keck and Sikkink's model. Taken together, however, they begin to suggest an alternative pattern of transnational pressure that is distinctly different from the "international pressure" depicted in their model.

Keck and Sikkink's treatment of "international pressure" seems to suggest practices whereby foreign states are persuaded—via combinations of various types of politics (information, symbolic, leverage, and accountability)—to intervene in the affairs of the target state either directly or else through a mediating intergovernmental organization. However, the campaigns suggest a different pattern of pressure whereby foreign states intervene neither directly in the affairs of the target state nor through a mediating intergovernmental organization. The various types of politics identified by Keck and Sikkink are still important to this alternative pattern of pressure, but they are deployed within a transnational legal space over legislative, administrative, and judicial matters of U.S. law that mediate how global markets (in this case linking corporations chartered in the United States with the Myanmar government) become embedded in politics, law, and morality.

It is through these legislative, administrative, and judicial *dimensions* of state action, and at multiple spatial *levels* of state action (municipal, regional, and federal), that the United States exercises pressure—*transnational*, as opposed to international—on the transnational corporations that buttress the power of the Myanmar government. Keck and Sikkink focus on international pressure that states exert on other states (sometimes mediated through international nongovernmental organizations), but they provide no conceptual space for considering the transnational pressure that states exert on transnational corporations. Such pressure may well contribute to social change within the blocking state that has forged business relations with the targeted transnational corporations. Only with substantial conceptual stretching might one suggest that this pattern of pressure represents a state exerting pressure on another state.

2. Are states disappearing, weakening, or otherwise becoming obsolete as suggested by the neo-liberal globalization discourse? If so, what happens to movements that typically have the state as both their fulcrum and their target? Do they disappear too? Or do they appear in other forms, and, if so, how do social movement theorists describe and explain their activity? Both social movement activists and researchers will have to at least account for the claim, and deal with the way that states are transforming, even if they are not vanishing.

Typically the claim that states are weakening and soon to become obsolete is directed at states understood within a Weberian framework: a unitary actor (1) exercising monopoly over the legitimate use of violence in a given territory; (2) securing the territorial border and sovereignty; and (3) governing a particular population in a specific territory (see Chapter 3 for further discussion of these ideas).

Certainly there are many counterexamples to which we can point that question the utility and relevance of such a state. The United Nations peacekeeping missions, for example, organize volunteer forces from national militaries to impose order in states (without their consent) that are suffering internal conflict in the form of genocide or civil war.

Another example is the transnational human rights regime that investigates violations of human rights around the world and provides court venues for trying states, agents of states, and even citizens when states with jurisdiction to indict fail or refuse to do so. As Sarah Cleveland (2001) has cogently argued, this regime has been

> ...enunciated through a loose network of general treaties promulgated by the United Nations; rights-specific regimes which are promoted by intergovernmental entities and international organizations [e.g., the International Labor Organization]; regional regimes of conventions and oversight; and universal customary prohibitions that have evolved through treaties, the practices of states, and the efforts of nongovernmental and private actors.[18]

This human rights regime also consists of judges, tribunals, courts, covenants, truth commissions, activists, human rights organizations, witnesses, and testimonials. These institutions, organizations, and individuals act on a spatial scale that is different from that of nation-states. It does so in ways that challenge, if not trump, states' claims to sovereign control over their territory and citizens because its moral authority works through a transnational network of people, institutions, practices, rules, discourses, and norms that transcend the international system of nation-states.[19]

We can find more examples in the case of the "global war on terror." The U.S. policy of "preemptive warfare," which it has used to justify its attack and occupation of Iraq, obviously challenges the principles of national sovereignty, even though the United States claims that it did so to secure its own borders from terrorists who intended to harm the country with "weapons of mass destruction." At the same time today's transnational terrorist networks also challenge the notion that states are even capable of defending their own territory. And states' increasing reliance on corporate military firms to fight their enemies reflects a removal from the government of absolute control over the legitimate use of violence and the privatizing of it to the market.

All of these examples seem to support the claim that the Weberian monopoly of the state is breaking down.[20] However, we should not construe this to mean that states are disappearing or becoming irrelevant to the process of globalization. On the contrary, there is ample evidence to suggest that states are not only disaggregating but also reaggregating in the form of *transnational governmental networks*.

Today, not only corporations, but also pirates, money launderers, arms and drugs dealers, human and body parts smugglers all operate through transnational networks. So too do revolutionaries and reform-oriented protestors, using strat-egies ranging from terrorist tactics to legal campaigns. It should be no surprise, then, that governments are operating through transnational networks. As Anne-Marie Slaughter writes, "Networks of government officials—police investiga-tors, financial regulators, even judges and legislators—increasingly exchange information and coordinate activity to combat global crime and address com-mon problems on a global scale." [21]

These transnational governmental networks consist of more disaggregated state actors who still perform the basic functions of governments—legislative, judicial, and administrative—and interact with each other within their own nation-state, yet they also interact with their foreign and supranational counter-parts who relate through transnational regulatory, judicial, and legislative chan-nels. How are transnational social movements successfully inserting themselves and their discursive practices into these networks in the effort to transform the meaning and power of this kind of state action? What kind of social transforma-tion are they affecting?

Of course, it may be worth distinguishing transnational governmental net-works from *transnational networks of governance*. After all, it is not always just state actors who are transnationally organized to govern. Sometimes corpora-tions, nongovernmental organizations, and even activists are incorporated into these networks—often through a neo-liberal policy to privatize public services and "empower" (as well as coopt and make complicit) individuals and commu-nities to govern themselves.

3. Are the civil rights that social movement theory deems so vital to the emergence and power of social movements in danger as a result of a general weakening of states? Will social movements still be able to engage in a politics of influence? Is there a new terrain emerging, something akin to a global civil society, from which to target and influence these transnational governmen-tal networks and their private corporate partners? And if so, are transnational social movements more likely to be effective in influencing domestic policies in democracies than in authoritarian states because these regimes offer greater opportunities to organize?

Some political sociologists see transnational social movements emerging as a powerful new force in international politics and are transforming global norms and practices.[22] Others, as we have discussed, see transnational social movements as sources of challenge "from below" to globalization that target the authority and practices of states, transnational governmental networks, and international institutions and that play a role in shaping global governance. Some even claim to be mapping an emerging global civil society. While it is certainly too soon to say whether something like a coherent global civil society is forming that will be able to serve as an effective normative terrain from which to influence transnational politics, we can at least see that there are important transnational processes and mechanisms that are having a profound effect on local politics and that social movements are creating and effectively using to influence social, cultural, political, and economic change.

One of the lessons that we can take from the case of the Free Burma movement is how transnational discursive strategies can empower and increase the effectiveness of movements. Transnational discursive strategies help to erode powerful nationalist concepts and ideologies that too often prevent citizens living in separate nation-states from being able to understand, see, or even imagine how their action (or inaction) affects or is affected by that of citizens living in other nation-states. At the same time, transnational discursive strategies render visible connections between citizens that transcend nationalist boundaries of difference and thereby also reconfigure relations of community, class, race, ethnicity, and gender that the concept of nation mediates. This suggests new ways in which citizens might more powerfully coordinate their action across national boundaries and generate meaningful identities, solidarities, and representations of their interests that have not been already circumscribed and subjugated by oppressive states and market arrangements.

Furthermore, transnational discursive strategies produce alternative spatialities and temporalities that can empower movements. Transnational discursive strategies create a new space for socially constructing these alternative identities and representations and project a new space for collective action. This transnational space enables people to perceive political opportunities for challenging the repressive state and corporate power that exist outside of the cultural confines of nationalism and neo-liberal globalism. Transnational discursive strategies also create new temporalities—renarrating sequences of events and connecting the disparate histories of peoples whose experience and collective memory have been simultaneously, yet separately, interpreted through the cultural structures of competing nationalisms. By renarrating the sequential unfolding of events and, thus, the process of historical change, transnational discursive strategies also generate new understandings of what can be changed, by whom, and how.

Transnational movements that focus on influencing domestic policies in democracies are not necessarily less effective in enhancing representation of groups suffering under authoritarian rule. The case of the Free Burma movement illustrates how groups suffering under authoritarian rule may be repressed not only by the domestic policies of authoritarian states, but also by the domestic policies of democratic states that facilitate the undemocratic practices of the transnational corporations that they charter and which collaborate with authoritarian states in repressing for-profit groups that live there. We should recognize as well that these profits are often achieved through the lowering of costs of

production subsidized by democratic states that its tax-paying citizens economically underwrite, but do not necessarily morally support. When we pay closer
attention to these transnational connections between democratic and authoritarian states, their domestic policies, and their citizens, as well as the corporate
practices and partnerships that span the boundaries of democratic and authoritarian states, it blurs the binary conceptual distinction between them. This
provides the first step toward creating new possibilities for imagining effective
transnational legal action that investigates the hegemonic relations and discourses that sustain such a reified conceptual distinction between democratic
and authoritarian states.

4. Finally, we must not forget that some of today's transnational social
movements engage in a transnational politics of influence that are more revolutionary than reform oriented and that rely on violent tactics to achieve that
influence. For example, Jeff Goodwin makes a convincing case for framing al-
Qa'ida as a *transnational revolutionary movement*: "Al-Qa'ida not only has militants in more than one national society, which is by no means unusual among
revolutionary groups, but it also opposes and seeks to overthrow not just one, but
several political orders."[23] Al-Qa'ida, he explains, is a pan-Islamic revolutionary
project that perceives itself as the protectorate and leader of the transnational
Muslim community (*umma*) and perceives this multiethnic, transnational community as fragmented and oppressed by the violent practices of the "'apostate'
secular and 'hypocritical' pseudo-Islamic regimes, from Morocco to Minanao,
as well as by the 'Zionist entity' in Palestine."[24]

Yet, in contrast to the transnational social movements that we have emphasized in this chapter—those which seek to democratically reform the process of
globalization, and do so through nonviolent transnational strategies—al-Qa'ida's
transnational social movement employs violent transnational strategies for the
purpose of overthrowing several states within the Muslim world. Goodwin
defines *revolutionary terrorism* as the strategic use of violence and threats of
violence by a revolutionary movement [i.e., any organization or network and
its supporters which seeks to change the political and/or socioeconomic order
in more or less fundamental ways] against civilians or noncombatants, and
is usually intended to influence several audiences."[25] Al-Qa'ida believes that
propping up these repressive, un-Islamic regimes in the Muslim world is the
U.S. government (and other Western allies, especially the United Kingdom).
Al-Qa'ida's rationale is that if they are to successfully facilitate local struggles
against the "near enemy" in the Muslim world, then they must first force the
"far enemy" in the West to withdraw its troops.[26]

Al-Qa'ida's strategic choice of using terrorism indiscriminately against the
citizens of states that it is trying to influence, but not overthrow, reflects a novel
transnational strategy. If Goodwin's research on al'Qa'ida is correct, they view

the United States as a genuinely representative democracy in which ordinary citizens are therefore responsible for the violent actions of "their" government and indirectly for the repressive governments in Muslim governments that they support. Writes Goodwin:

> Al-Qa'ida views ordinary American citizens as complicitous civilians—morally culpable for the U.S.-sponsored 'massacres' of Muslims in a number of countries. [And believe that is therefore]...logical and indeed just for it to attack ordinary Americans in order to bring about change in 'their' government's policies.[27]

It is too soon to judge the extent to which this particular transnational social movement will succeed in achieving its goals.

Such examples, nevertheless, may point to the limits of emphasizing the democratizing influence of transnational social movements on civil society. Both of these movements seem to represent the kind of "globalization from below" that challenges counter-hegemonic globalization and antidemocratic regimes in the name of fighting marginalization. Yet, are there not significant differences in the substantive goals of the Free Burma movement and al-Qa'ida? The Free Burma movement seeks to democratize the values and norms and institutions embedded in its political culture. And although al-Qa'ida's movement seeks to resist the political and cultural imperialism of the United States and its allies and to overthrow the regimes of the Muslim world that it believes are repressing members of the *umma*, it is not clear whether the alternative political order it seeks to institutionalize or its strategy of using *indiscriminate* violence to influence civil societies that it sees as supporting its state oppressors is consistent with a democratizing agenda.

Still, it does seem that political sociology would benefit from exploring how transnational social movements and transnational governmental networks, too, choose among a variety of strategies and tactics available to them, including those of terrorism, to influence the politics of globalization.

NOTES

1. Michael Peter Smith, *Transnational Urbanism. Locating Globalization* (Oxford: Blackwell, 2001), 3.
2. Sakia Sassen, *A Sociology of Globalization* (New York: W. W. Norton, 2007), 6.
3. Peter Evans,. 2000. "Fighting Marginalization with Transnational Networks: Counter-Hegemonic Globalization." *Contemporary Sociology* 2000, 29: 1: 231.
4. Peter Evans, "Fighting Marginalization with Transnational Networks: Counter-Hegemonic Globalization," *Contemporary Sociology* 2000, 29(1), 230.
5. Peter Evans, "Fighting Marginalization with Transnational Networks: Counter-Hegemonic Globalization," *Contemporary Sociology* 2000, 29(1), 230.

6. Roberto Mangabeira Unger, *Free Trade Reimagined: The World Division of Labor and the Method of Economics* (Princeton, NJ: Princeton University Press, 2007), 2.

7. Sanjeev Khagram, Kathryn Sikkink, and James V. Riker, *Restructuring World Politics: Transnational Social Movements, Networks, and Norms* (Minneapolis: University of Minnesota Press, 2002), 8; and Sidney Tarrow, *Power in Movement: Social Movements, Collective Action, and Politics*, 2nd ed. (New York: Cambridge University Press, 1998), 184.

8. The following case study derives largely from my own research. See John Dale, "Transnational Conflict between Peasants and Corporations in Burma: Human Rights and Discursive Ambivalence under the U.S. Alien Tort Claims Act," in Mark Goodale and Sally Engle Merry, eds., *The Practice of Human Rights: Tracking Law between the Global and the Local* (Cambridge: Cambridge University Press, 2007), 285–319; and John Dale, *Transnational Legal Action: Global Business, Human Rights, and the Free Burma Movement* (Minneapolis, MN: University of Minnesota Press). (Forthcoming).

9. In the wake of international condemnation for its violent repression of the pro-democracy movement in 1988, the Myanmar military's ruling party, The State Law and Order Restoration Council (SLORC), initiated a series of measures intended to sublimate any collective memory of the illegitimate means by which it had secured its political domination over the state. One of the first measures that SLORC took was to rename the country that it ruled—from Burma to Myanmar. I will use "Myanmar" to refer to the post-1990 military government; yet, to resist playing too easily into the questionable intentions of this regime's project of collective forgetting, I retain the name "Burma" to refer to the country, and "Burmese" to refer to the state's citizens.

10. They had held these elections in the belief that they would win the vast majority of votes through intimidation, but they lost in a landslide victory to Aung San Suu Kyi's National League for Democracy party.

11. Sanjeev Khagram, Kathryn Sikkink, and James V. Riker, *Restructuring World Politics: Transnational Social Movements, Networks, and Norms* (Minneapolis: University of Minnesota Press, 2002), 7.

12. An INGO is a private, voluntary, nonprofit association whose chief aim is to influence publicly some form of social change. It has legal status and tends to be professionally staffed and more formally organized than a social movement. In general, this is true of all nongovernmental organizations, domestic as well as international. Indeed, both may have aims that are cross-national or international in scope. Yet, INGOs also have a decision-making structure with voting members from multiple countries. Examples include Oxfam International, Mercy Corps, World Vision International, and Save the Children Alliance. An INGO may be founded through private philanthropy, such as the Carnegie, Ford, MacArthur, or Gates Foundations, or as an adjunct to existing international organizations, such as the Catholic Church's INGO Catholic Relief Services.

13. *Transnational advocacy networks* are configurations of nonstate actors, based usually on informal contacts, linked across nation-state boundaries who share common

values, discourses, and a dense exchange of information. The exchange and use of information is the hallmark of the transnational advocacy network. See Margaret E. Keck and Kathryn Sikkink, *Activists Beyond Borders: Advocacy Networks in International Politics* (Ithaca, NY: Cornell University Press, 1998).

14. The "law of nations" is "the law of international relations, embracing not only nations but also...individuals (such as those who invoke their human rights or commit war crimes)" (*Black's Law Dictionary* 822, 7th ed., 1999). This is the same definition of the law of nations that the Ninth Circuit Court of Appeals used in *Doe v. Unocal*. According to the *Random House Compact Unabridged Dictionary, Special Second Edition*, the term "law of nations" first came into use some time between 1540 and 1550.

15. Margaret E. Keck and Kathryn Sikkink, *Activists Beyond Borders: Advocacy Networks in International Politics* (Ithaca, NY: Cornell University Press, 1998), 12.

16. Margaret E. Keck and Kathryn Sikkink, *Activists Beyond Borders: Advocacy Networks in International Politics* (Ithaca, NY: Cornell University Press, 1998), 12.

17. Margaret E.Keck and Kathryn Sikkink, *Activists Beyond Borders: Advocacy Networks in International Politics* (Ithaca, NY: Cornell University Press, 1998), 12.

18. Sarah H. Cleveland, "Norm Internalization and U.S. Economic Sanctions," *Yale Journal of International Law*, 2001, 26, 20.

19. Margaret E.Keck and Kathryn Sikkink, *Activists Beyond Borders: Advocacy Networks in International Politics* (Ithaca, NY: Cornell University Press, 1998); Aradhana Sharma and Akhil Gupta, *The Anthropology of the State: A Reader* (Malden, MA: Blackwell, 2006); and Saskia Sassen, *Losing Control? Sovereignty in an Age of Globalization. The Schoff Lectures* (New York: Columbia University Press, 1996).

20. P. W. Singer, *Corporate Warriors: The Rise of the Privatized Military Industry* (Ithaca, NY: Cornell University Press, 2003), 18.

21. Anne-Marie Slaughter, *A New World Order* (Princeton, NJ: Princeton University Press, 2004), 4.

22. Margaret E.Keck and Kathryn Sikkink, *Activists Beyond Borders: Advocacy Networks in International Politics* (Ithaca, NY: Cornell University Press, 1998); Sanjeev Khagram, Kathryn Sikkink, and James V. Riker, *Restructuring World Politics: Transnational Social Movements, Networks, and Norms* (Minneapolis: University of Minnesota Press, 2002).

23. Jeff Goodwin, "A Theory of Categorical Terrorism," *Social Forces*, 2006, 84(4), 2042.

24. Jeff Goodwin, "A Theory of Categorical Terrorism," *Social Forces*, 2006, 84(4), 2043.

25. Jeff Goodwin, "A Theory of Categorical Terrorism," *Social Forces*, 2006, 84(4), 2028.

26. Jeff Goodwin, "A Theory of Categorical Terrorism," *Social Forces*, 84(4), 2043.

27. Jeff Goodwin, "A Theory of Categorical Terrorism," *Social Forces*, 2006, 84(4), 2043.

Chapter 12

The Mass Media

In 1972, two young reporters for the *Washington Post*, Carl Bernstein and Bob Woodward, wrote a series of articles about a break-in at the offices of the National Democratic Committee in Washington, DC.[1] Their offices, located in the Watergate Hotel and apartment complex, had been entered by several men early on the morning of June 17. A security guard, Frank Mills, discovered the break-in when he was conducting a routine inspection of the building. At first it seemed to be a bungled burglary, but police soon uncovered evidence of an attempt by the men to bug the offices of members of the Democratic National Committee, including its chairman, Lawrence O'Brien. Shortly thereafter it was revealed that one of the men, James McCord, who had his own security firm, had actually been hired to be the security coordinator for the Committee to Reelect President Richard Nixon. All of this should have caused the public as well as the media some concern, yet most people and organizations paid no attention to it. The country was the middle of an election campaign and the War in Vietnam continued to occupy most people's attention. Bernstein and Woodward were alone among news reporters to track down and expand on the story. Aided by the support and enthusiasm of their editor, Ben Bradlee, the two journalists soon began to uncover more and more details about what seemed to be a darkly sinister plot.

The five men arrested for the break-in were eventually indicted by a grand jury and brought to trial. It turned out that several of them had various ties and connections to the Republican Party. As Bernstein and Woodward reported in a *Post* article on October 10, 1972, "FBI agents have established that the Watergate bugging incident stemmed from a massive campaign of political spying and sabotage conducted on behalf of President Nixon's re-election and directed by officials of the White House and the Committee for the Re-election of the President."[2] Such connections suggested something far more treacherous than a simple bungled effort to bug some offices. In fact, as the story unfolded it became clear that the robbery was carried out by people who had had a hand in other important political events and that their motives were very much wrapped up in political machinations. Bernstein and Woodward made even more important connections between the thieves and the act itself, suggesting that it likely was connected to the White House. The source of much of their information was someone they could only identify as "Deep Throat." Until 2005, when he was revealed to be W. Mark Felt, a former high official at the FBI, the identity of this person was the source of a great deal of speculation.

Bernstein and Woodward's revelations eventually prompted other news sources and agencies to unleash their own investigative reporters on the matter. The FBI and the Department of Justice had become involved almost immediately, providing much of the information on the background of the (burglars). Ultimately, congressional hearings were convened in 1973, involving both Senate and House Watergate committees. All the while the White House insisted that it had had no role in the matter whatsoever. Nixon appointed a special prosecutor, Archibald Cox, to the case, charging him to the get to the bottom of the matter. But Bernstein and Woodward, along with the broad forces of the government, persisted. Ties to the White House by the criminals meant something. But what exactly did they mean? Over the course of 1973 and then into the summer of 1974, the case for the White House began to unravel. Nixon eventually accepted the resignations of his top advisors, H. R. Haldeman and John Ehrlichman, and fired his chief counsel, John Dean.[3]

It was Dean, in fact, who became the key figure and informant in the congressional hearings, and who brought the president down. He claimed that the White House itself was somehow implicated in the robbery and that the president had been continuously involved in an effort to cover up the identities and motives behind the Watergate break-in. Unfortunately for Nixon, a former White House employee, Alexander Butterfield, revealed to authorities that Nixon had ordered the taping of all his conversations in the Oval Office beginning in 1971. Obviously, if the president were involved in a plot to cover up the forces behind the Watergate break-in, then evidence of his own misdeeds likely would be on those recordings. The Congress went ahead and subpoenaed the tapes. The President responded by declaring that he did not need to turn them over, citing executive privilege. On July 24, 1974, the Supreme Court, however, ruled against him.

All of us of course now know the outcome of those hearings. Nixon reluctantly agreed to release the transcripts of his tapes to Congress. They were not intact, however. There was an interval of about sixteen minutes missing from one of the tapes, and neither Nixon nor any of his associates, particularly his longtime secretary, Rosemary Woods, could account for what had happened to the sixteen minutes. But everyone had a pretty good idea. Nixon had tried to cover up the Watergate affair, and Republicans were deeply implicated in the effort to bug the Democratic National Committee. By August 1974, on the verge of being impeached, Richard Milhous Nixon became the first American president to resign his office.

Few moments in recent American history have been quite so riveting. And there are few such moments when journalists have been able to reveal so much about the inner workings of politics in America. Through their intrepid reporting, Woodward and Bernstein were able to bring to light the nefarious workings of the Republicans and the president. The episode made journalism, especially investigative journalism, seem very glamorous. Bernstein and Woodward became household names. It also gave journalists a sense of their own power and a pride in their profession. Politicians might do as they wish, but the press would always be there to report, check, and hold them accountable.

In this chapter we will consider how the press, and more broadly all the media, can serve to shape and to make the news and how, in the process, they act to form what we learn about the world of politics and the world, in general. Now, especially at the beginning of the twenty-first century, the media clearly are a powerful player in the workings of politics and the operation of basic social and political institutions. But how powerful are they? What do they shape? And is it possible that the Watergate affair was simply a one-time occurrence in the history of the press?

Highlights in the History of the Mass Media in America

American newspapers have been around for more than two hundred years.[4] It was in the nineteenth century, however, that they first became prominent. They came to be owned by men who were kingpins and powerhouses, and they were used not simply to tell the news but also to shape it to their interests of their owners. Newspapers became a way for getting inside the internal workings of politics and exposing the underbelly of American government.

Particular newsmen, such as Lincoln Steffens and Jacob Riis, grew famous for their special brand of uncovering the news, a style that was known as *muckraking* because it was intended to dig up the dirt about politics and politicians. Steffens was the most successful of these journalists, someone who had a nose for uncovering corruption and, more than that, spotlighting the men who used politics for their own gain. Riis was a somewhat different breed, but he turned his attention to stories about the way America's newcomers, immigrants, were adapting and how, in particular, they were barely surviving amidst the filth and poverty of the city. Newspapers, and journalists like Steffens and Riis provided a means not only for reporting about the world, but for protecting the public against the excesses engaged in by politicians.

Some kingpins in the newspaper business were enormously influential through their holdings and their control of the media. The most famous, perhaps, was William Randolph Hearst, who created a major empire of newspapers, among them, the *San Francisco Chronicle*. Hearst sought to use his newspapers to help portray his own views of the world and thereby to influence the course of history. He would become the prototype of many such figures, typically men who would use the newspaper to shape the news and voice their own views on matters. His fame was assured when he became the centerpiece in Orson Welles' famous movie, *Citizen Kane*. Other such persons who used the newspaper to their own advantages included Colonel Robert McCormick, owner of the *Chicago Tribune*. McCormick, a conservative Republican, was not shy about how he used his editorial pages, but he also used so-called news pages to express his own beliefs and thereby to influence over the way people thought.

One of the most famous illustrations of the McCormick bias came in the presidential election of 1948 that pitted the Republican Thomas E. Dewey against the Democratic incumbent president, Harry S. Truman. Truman, the underdog, had been running well behind Dewey until very late in the campaign. On the eve of the election, McCormick's *Chicago Tribune* printed a bold front-page headline saying that Dewey had won. In fact, Truman had come out the winner, and he is shown in a famous photograph holding up a copy of the *Tribune* with its Dewey headline.

The newspaper remained the chief source of news about the world well into the twentieth century. Yet once television came on the scene in the 1950s, it began to displace both the newspaper as well as the radio. Television, because of its visual images, proved to be a hot medium as compared to the cool medium of the printed page.[5] It provided an intimacy to the activities of its subjects, whether through news reporting or daytime soap operas, an intimacy that gave its messages a sense of authenticity the other media did not possess.

The power of television to shape politics was dramatically revealed during the presidential election of 1960. Several key figures, including Frank Stanton, the President of CBS News, decided it would be a good idea to have televised debates between the two leading candidates: Richard Nixon, the incumbent Republican vice president, and John F. Kennedy, the young Democratic congressman from Massachusetts. After much jockeying and negotiating, a series of four debates was arranged between the two men.

Unlike today, when debates are highly staged affairs, the first televised debates were rather awkward. Questions were posed to the two men by a single reporter. Each of the candidates addressed the television audience from behind a small podium. Since color television had not yet entered the American home in appreciable numbers, the telecast was in black and white. Prior to the first telecast, Richard Nixon had been in the hospital with a knee injury and had lost some twenty pounds. His clothing fit him loosely, and he refused to wear makeup. With his characteristic heavy beard, he appeared haggard, almost menacing. He rarely smiled and had a difficult time looking directly into the camera. By contrast, Kennedy, a far less accomplished politician, had just returned from a vacation. He looked tan and fit. At the same time he appeared far more comfortable in front of the camera. He came off as smooth and polished. Both men actually handled the questions well, and radio listeners thought Nixon to be the winner of the first debate. But television clearly gave the edge to Kennedy. In November, Kennedy narrowly defeated Nixon at the polls. Many observers looked back at the first debate, proclaiming not only that Kennedy had won the debate, but that television proved to have a compelling power unmatched by the print media and perhaps even unprecedented in American history.[6]

Today we are undergoing yet another dramatic shift in the nature and impact of the mass media around the world. More and more people have turned from the printed page and television to get their news from the Internet. This shift comes alongside a general shift of people away from the regular news sources of the past, such as television network news.

Consider some numbers from a recent survey by the Pew Research Center for the People & the Press.[7] The Pew Research Center conducts periodic sample surveys of the American public to find out how people use the media. Note in Table 12.1 the regular decline from 1993 to 2006 in the percentage of people who watch the nightly television network news. Note, too, the continuing decline in the percentage of people who read the newspaper—from 58 percent in 1993 to 40 percent in 2006. The only medium to have grown in popularity is that of online news: from only 2 percent in 1996, the percentage of those who get their news online has increased to 31 percent.

The Internet promises to introduce yet another revolution in the way that the mass media shape our sense of politics as well as in the way in which we get our news. As a recent report from the Columbia School of Journalism observes: "What is occurring, we have concluded, is not the end of journalism that some

TABLE 12.1. The Changing News Landscape

	Percent					
	1993	1996	2000	2002	2004	2006
Regularly watch:						
Local TV news	77	65	56	57	59	54
Cable TV news	—	—	—	33	38	34
Nightly network news	60	42	30	32	34	28
Network morning news	—	—	20	22	22	23
Listened/read yesterday:						
Radio	47[a]	44[a]	43	41	40	36
Newspaper	58[a]	50	47	41	42	40
Online news three or more days per week	—	2[b]	23	25	29	31

[a] From 1994.
[b] From 1995.
SOURCE: Pew Research Center for the People & the Press, "Online Papers Moderntly Boost Newspaper Readership" report from July 30, 2006.

have predicted. But we do see a seismic transformation in what and how people learn about the world around them.... Audiences are moving from old media such as television or newsprint to new media online."[8]

The Mass Media as a Vehicle of Corporate Capitalism

The empires of media moguls like William Randolph Hearst and Colonel Robert McCormick illustrated how men could become wealthy and influential using the media as the basis of their fortunes. Today it is no longer single individuals so much as it is large corporations that dominate the ownership of different forms of media. Major conglomerates such as Time Warner and Disney have emerged as leaders in the ownership of different forms and types of mass media. Many critics are concerned that the concentration of the media in just a few hands can seriously undermine the nature of American democratic institutions.[9]

Consider the major media giants of today and the variety of media forms that they control (Figure 12). Note that a vast array of media today, from print media to television to even the Internet, is controlled by a few dominant

NEWS CORPORATION

PRODUCTION
Twentieth Century
Fox Television
My Network TV
Fox Television Studios
Star Group Limited (STAR)
Fox Broadcasting Company
Fox Television
New York, WNYW, WWOR
Los Angeles, KTTV, KCOP
Chicago, WFLD, WPWR
Philadelphia, WTXF
Boston. WFXT
Plus 20 other stations

PROGRAMMING
Fox (77% of households reached)
Fox College Sports
Fox Reality
Fox Networks
Fox International Channels
Fox Sports Net
Fox Movie
Fox News Channel
Special Report With Brit Hume
Fox Report With Shepard Smith
On the Record With Greta Van Susteren
Fox News Sunday
Fox News Radio Network
The O'Reily Factor
Hannity & Colmes
National Geographic Channel [67%]
Fuel TC
Speed
Fox Sports International
Fox Sports World Middle East
Fox Pan American Sports [37.8%]
Fox Soccer

TELEVISION

FILM
Twentieth Century Fox
Twentieth Century Fox
Animation
Fox Searchlight Pictures
Fox 2000
Twentieth Century Fox Home
Entertainment
New Regency [20%]

BOOKS
HarperCollins Limited [UK]
HarperCollins Publishers [US]
Zondervan (evangelical
Christian imprint)
ReganBooks

INTERNET
Intermix
MyLeague.com
CasesLadder.com
FlowGo.com
Grab.com
MySpace
IGN.com
News.com.au
Foxnews.com
NYPost.com
MSN.FoxSports.com
WeeklyStandard.com
Scout.com
Broadsystem.com
NewsOptimus.co.uk
NewsOutdoor.com

NEWS CORPORATION
CEO: Rupert Murdoch
Number of Employees: 44,000

MISCELLANEOUS
Festival Mushroom Records
NDS ("open end-to-end
digital technology")
National Rugby League
Australia & New Zealand
[50%]

SATELLITE
SKY Italia
SKY News
FOXTEL [25%]
BSkyB [36.8%]
DirectTV Group [33.9%]
DirectTV Latin America
DirectTV US
Innova [30%]
SKYLatin America [49.7%]

PERIODICALS

MAGAZINES
News America
Marketing Group [US]
SmartSource
Weekly Standard [US]
News Magazines
[Australia]
INSIDEout
donna hay
Herald and Weekly Times
[Australia]
News Custom Publishing
Gemstar-TV Guide [41%]

NEWSPAPERS
(Publishes more
than 175 newspapers
worldwide)
New York Post [US]
News International [UK]
News of the world
The Sun
Sunday Times
The Times
TSL Education [UK]
Times Educational Supplement
Times Literary Supplement
Times Higher
Education Supplement
Nursery World
Daily Telegraph [Australia]
Sunday Tasmanian
Fiji Times
Papua New Guinea Post-Courier

FIGURE 12.

GENERAL ELECTRIC

MISCELLANEOUS
GE Commercial Finance
GE Insurance Solutions
Transportation Financial
  Services Group
GE Consumer Finance
GE Healthcare
GE Industrial
Plastics
Electrical Equipment
Silicones
Lightning
Household Appliances
Equipment Services
Securities Systems
GE Sensing
GE Infrastructure
Aircraft Engines
Aircraft Engines
  Maintenance
Commercial Aviation
  Financing
GE Energy
Energy Financial Services
Oil & Gas Turbomachinery
GE Water & Process
  Technologies
GE Transportation
Locomotives

FILM
Universal Pictures
Universal Studios
  Home Entertainment
Focus Features
Rogue Pictures

INTERNET
MSNBC.com
SciFi.com [80%]
msn.com
NBC.com
Telemundo.com

PARKS & RESORTS
Universal Parks and Resorts
Universal Studios
  Hollywood [40%]
Universal Studios Orlando [40%]
Universal Studios Japan [40%]

GENERAL ELECTRIC
CEO: Jeff Immelt
Number of Employees: 316,000

PERIODICALS

MAGAZINES
Sci Fi magazine [80%]

TELEVISION

PRODUCTION
NBC Universal
NBC Television
New York, WNBC
Los Angeles, KNBC
Chicago, WMAQ
San Jose/San Francisco, KNTV
Dallas/Fort Worth, KXAS
Plus 9 other stations
Telemundo
Los Angeles, KVEA/KWHY
New York, WNJU
Miami, WSCV
Chicago, WSNS
Dallas/Fort Worth, KXTX
NBC Universal Television
  Distribution
NBC Universal Television
  Studio
Law & Order franchise
Late Night With Conan O'Brien
The Tonight Show With Jay Leno

PROGRAMMING
NBC (99% of household
  reached)
NBC Network News
The Today Show
NBC Nightly News
  With Brian Williams
Dateline NBC
Meet the Press
Early Today
CNBC
Squawk Box
Mad money
Tim Russert
CNBC World
CNBC Arabia
CNBC-India TV-18
CNBC Asia [Part]
CNBC Europe [Part]
MSNBC [with Microsoft]
  (79% of households reached)
MSNBC Live
Hardball With Chris Matthews
Rita Cosby: Live and Direct
Scarborough Country
Sci Fi [Part]
Telemundo
Bravo
USA Network
Weather Plus
A&E [Part]
The History Channel [Part]
The Sundance Channel [Part]

FIGURE 12. *Continued*

DISNEY

RADIO
ABC Radio
  (73 stations)
ABC News Radio
ESPN Radio
Radio Disney

BOOKS
Hyperion [distribution
  by Time Warner]
Miramax
ESPN Books
ABC Daytime Press
Hyperion East
Hyperion Audiobooks
Disney Publishing
  Worldwide
Hyperion Books for
  Children
Disney Press
Disney Editions
Volo
Jump at the Sun
Disney Libri [Italy]
Disney Hachette JV [France]

PERIODICALS

MAGAZINES
FamilyFun
ESPN The Magazine
Disney Adventures
Buena Vista Magazines
Wondertime

INTERNET
Disney.com
ESPN.com
ABC.com
ABCNews.com
ABCSports.com
EXPN.com
ESPNdeportes.com
Soccernet
movies.com

MISCELLANEOUS
Disney Mobile
Mobile ESPN
Buena Vista Games
The Chronicles of Narnia
Chicken Little
Nightmare Before Christmas
Buena Vista Music Group
Walt Disney Records
Hollywood Records

FILM
Walt Disney Pictures
Touchstone Pictures
Hollywood Pictures
Miramax Films
Walt Disney Feature
  Animation
DisneyToon Studios
Buena Vista
  International
Buena Vista
  Theatrical Productions
Buena Vista
  Productions
Pixar

BOOKS
Hyperion [distribution
  by Time Warner]
Miramax
ESPN Books
ABC Daytime Press
Hyperion East
Hyperion Audiobooks
Disney Publishing Worldwide
Hyperion Books for Children
Disney Press
Disney Editions
Volo
Jump at the Sun
Disney Libri [Italy]
Disney Hachette JV [France]

PRODUCTION
ABC Television
New York, WABC
Los Angeles, KABC
Chicago, WLS
Philadelphia, WPVI
San Francisco, WKGO
Plus 5 other stations
Buena Vista Television
Touchstone Television
Walt Disney Television

TELEVISION

PARKS & RESORTS
Disneyland
Disneyland Resort
Disneyland California
  Adventure
Disneyland Paris [51%]
HongKong Disneyland [43%]
Euro Disney [40%]
Walt Disney World
Walt Disney World Resort
Magic Kingdom
EPCOT
Walt Disney Studio Park
Tokyo Disney
Tokyo Disney-Sea
Disney-MGM Studios
Disney's Animal Kingdom
Disney Crusine Line
Disney Vacation Club resorts
ESPN Zone restaurants

PROGRAMMING
ABC (97% of households reached)
ABC Entertainment
ABC Daytime
ABC Sports
ABC Kids
ABC News
Good Morning America
Nightline
World News Tonight
World News Now
20/20
Primetime
This Week With
  George Stephanopoulos
ESPN [80%]
ESPN Deportes
ESPN2
ESPN Classic
ESPNews
The Disney Channel
International Disney Channels
JETIX Europe [74.4%]
JETIX Latin America
A&E [37.5%]
E! Entertainment
  Networks [39.6%]
Style [39.6%]
Lifetime Television [50%]
The History Channel [37.5%]
The Biography Channel [37.5%]
History International [37.5%]
ABC Family
SoapNet
ToonDisney

DISNEY
CEO: Robert Iger
Number of Employees: 133,000

FIGURE 12. *Continued*

TIME WARNER
CEO: Richard D. Parsons
Number of Employees: 87,850

TIME WARNER

PERIODICALS

MAGAZINES
Time Inc. (publishes more than 145 magazines worldwide)
Time
People
Sports Illustrated
Fortune
Entertainment Weekly
InStyle
Essence Communications Partners
Essence
Synapse Group [92%]
IPC Media [UK]
Southern Progress Corporation
Southern Living
Sunset
Cooking Light
Health
Parenting Group
Parenting
Babytalk
E.C. Publications
MAD
DC Comics (publishes more than 50 comics worldwide)
Time4media (publishes 17 magazines worldwide)
Popular Science
Golf
Grupo Editorial Expansión (publishes more than 15 magazines in Mexico)

MISCELLANEOUS
Time Warner Telecom[44%]
Atlanta Braves

FILM

Warner Brothers Entertainment
Warner Brothers Pictures
Castle Rock
Warner Independent Pictures
Warner Home Video
New Line Cinema Corporation
New Line Cinema
Picturehouse Films

TELEVISION

INTERNET
AOL ["Strategic Alliance" with Google]
AOL High Speed
AIM
ICQ
Moviefone
MapQuest
AOL Call Alert
AOLbyphone
AOL Voicemail
AOL Europe
AOL Latin America (AOLA)
AOL Transit Data Network (ATDN)
CompuServe
Netscape
AOL Wireless
Advertising.com
CNN Interactive
CNN.com
allpolitics.com
NASCAR.com
PGA.com
CartoonNetwork.com
TheWB.com
DCComics.com
52theconomic.com
Time.com

PRODUCTION
Warner Brothers Television Production
Warner Bros. Animation
Warner Bros. Interactive Entertainment
Monolith Productions
Warner Bros. Consumer Products
Warner Bros. International Cinemas
Time Warner Cable
On Demand Services
Video on Demand
Digital Video Recorders
High Definition Television
High Speed Data Services
Digital Phone
Local News Channels

PROGRAMMING
Turner Broadcasting System
CNN (82% of households reached)
American Morning
CNN Live Today
Live From
The Situation Room
Lou Dobbs Tonight
Paula Zahn Now
Larry King Live
Anderson Cooper 360°
Turner Networks
TBS
TNT
Turner Classic Movies
Cartoon Network
Turner South
Boomerang
Home Box Office (HBO)
Cinemax
Court TV
WB
CW Network [50% with CBS]

FIGURE 12. *Continued*

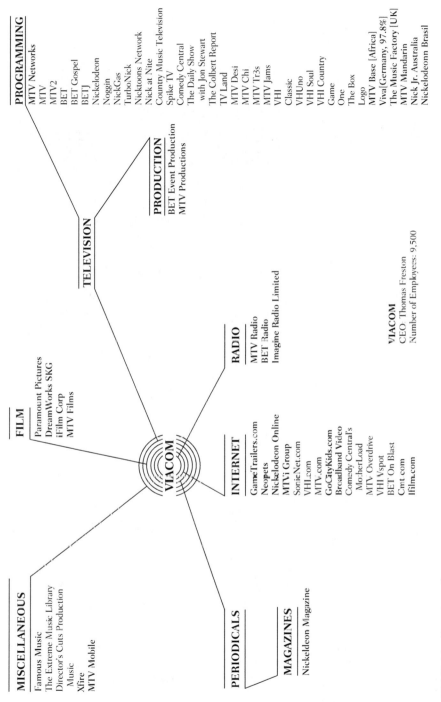

MISCELLANEOUS

Famous Music
The Extreme Music Library
Director's Cuts Production
    Music
Xfire
MTV Mobile

PERIODICALS

MAGAZINES

Nickeldeon Magazine

FILM

Paramount Pictures
DreamWorks SKG
iFilm Corp
MTV Films

INTERNET

GameTrailers.com
Neopets
Nickelodeon Online
MTVi Group
SonicNet.com
VH1.com
MTV.com
GoCityKids.com
Breadband Video
Comedy Central's
    MotherLoad
MTV Overdrive
VH1 Vspot
BET On Blast
Cmt com
Ifilm.com

RADIO

MTV Radio
BET Radio
Imagine Radio Limited

TELEVISION

PRODUCTION

BET Event Production
MTV Productions

PROGRAMMING

MTV Networks
MTV
MTV2
BET
BET Gospel
BET J
Nickelodeon
Noggin
NickGas
TurboNick
Nicktoons Network
Nick at Nite
Country Music Television
Spike TV
Comedy Central
The Daily Show
    with Jon Stewart
The Colbert Report
TV Land
MTV Desi
MTV Chi
MTV Tr3s
MTV Jams
VH1
Classic
VH1Uno
VH1 Soul
VH1 Country
Game
One
The Box
Logo
MTV Base [Africa]
Viva[Germany, 97.8%]
The Music Factory [UK]
MTV Mandarin
Nick Jr. Australia
Nickelodeonn Brasil

VIACOM
CEO: Thomas Freston
Number of Employees: 9,500

FIGURE 12. *Continued*

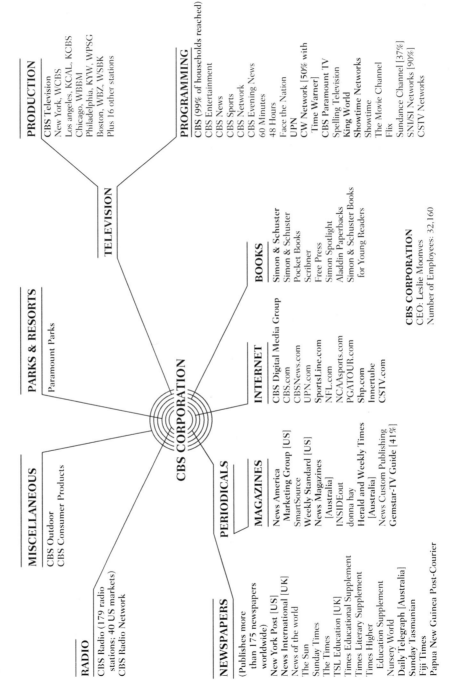

RADIO

CBS Radio (179 radio stations; 40 US markets)
CBS Radio Network

MISCELLANEOUS

CBS Outdoor
CBS Consumer Products

PRODUCTION

CBS Television
New York, WCBS
Los angeles, KCAL, KCBS
Chicago, WBBM
Philadelphia, KYW, WPSG
Boston, WBZ, WSBK
Plus 16 other stations

PROGRAMMING

CBS (99% of households reached)
CBS Entertainment
CBS News
CBS Sports
CBS Network
CBS Evening News
60 Minutes
48 Hours
Face the Nation
UPN
CW Network [50% with Time Warner]
CBS Paramount TV
Spelling Television
King World
Showtime Networks
Showtime
The Movie Channel
Flix
Sundance Channel [37%]
SNI/SI Networks [90%]
CSTV Networks

PARKS & RESORTS

Paramount Parks

TELEVISION

CBS CORPORATION

BOOKS

Simon & Schuster
Simon & Schuster Pocket Books
Scribner
Free Press
Simon Spotlight
Aladdin Paperbacks
Simon & Schuster Books for Young Readers

CBS CORPORATION
CEO: Leslie Moonves
Number of Employees: 32,160

INTERNET

CBS Digital Media Group
CBS.com
CBSNews.com
UPN.com
SportsLine.com
NFL.com
NCAAsports.com
PGATOUR.com
Shp.com
Innertube
CSTV.com

PERIODICALS

MAGAZINES

News America Marketing Group [US]
SmartSource
Weekly Standard [US]
News Magazines [Australia]
INSIDEout
donna hay
Herald and Weekly Times [Australia]
News Custom Publishing
Gemstar-TV Guide [41%]

NEWSPAPERS

(Publishes more than 175 newspapers worldwide)
New York Post [US]
News International [UK]
News of the world
The Sun
Sunday Times
The Times
TSL Education [UK]
Times Educational Supplement
Times Literary Supplement
Times Higher Education Supplement
Nursery World
Daily Telegraph [Australia]
Sunday Tasmanian
Fiji Times
Papua New Guinea Post-Courier

FIGURE 12. *Continued*

corporations. They are the News Corporation (owned by Rupert Murdoch), Disney, General Electric, Time Warner, Viacom, and the CBS Corporation. They control a wide range of outlets, from ABC, NBC, and CBS to Disney Productions and a host of others.

In the eyes of Marxists and other critics of modern capitalism, the ownership structure of the media illustrates two fundamental features of the nature of modern capitalism: one, the tendency for capital to become concentrated in fewer and fewer firms; and two, the effort by capitalists to use their resources in order to create a symbolic world, of ideology, that will support and buttress their economic ambitions. Insofar as our world is a symbolic one, fashioned by the news we read and the images we receive, this world is, in effect, created by a very small number of companies and individuals.

Indeed, ours is no longer a world like that first described by Alexis de Tocqueville, in which American democracy is to be found and reflected in the widespread availability of different and competing newspapers. Tocqueville argued emphatically that the cultural institutions of America promoted its democratic form of government, and perhaps no such institution was more significant than the newspaper. It was important, he argued, because it provided a vehicle for the public to express their views, but it was also important because, like much of the rest of America, its use and ownership was widespread. Today, however, it is clear that there are a few media giants who dominate what we get in the form of our news. But how much do they actually shape our views, and how does this take place?

The Mass Media and Their Influence in Society

In authoritarian governments, the nature of news and the media is carefully regulated by the government. In China today, for example, the government exercises considerable control over the content of the news, not only print and television news, but also increasingly the Internet. The government and its operatives can control who gets access to the Internet and the nature of the information that goes across it. The Chinese authorities, for example, periodically crack down on the local Internet cafes scattered across China, preventing people from using the local terminals. Moreover, the Chinese authorities also exercise great control over the content of the information that flows across the Internet. Recently, Google, the worldwide search engine giant, agreed to terms with the Chinese authorities that allowed the government to patrol and monitor the content of searches. Unlike in America, there are certain terms that cannot be used to generate information across the Internet in China.

In a society built upon democratic institutions, like that of the United States, the ability of the mass media, in theory, is far more circumscribed and limited.[10] The various media compete among themselves for the public's attention. And there are strategies, such as investigative reporting, that can be used to shed light on key political schemes. Moreover, federal agencies, such as the Federal Communications Commission, provide oversight over the activities by the various forms of media such as newspapers and television.

Despite all such ways of limiting and monitoring the power of the media, they continue to influence how and what we view.

AGENDA SETTING

One of the ways in which the media influence our view of the world is through a process known as *agenda setting*. This concept means what it says and derives from the workings of public meetings in which the officials in charge can set the agenda for what actually transpires during the meeting. Various critics of the workings of democracy charge that this process of agenda setting works across the wide range of governmental institutions and is the means whereby the government can limit the information and choices available to the public.[11]

In studies of the mass media, agenda setting has come to mean something similar. It refers to *the process whereby the media are able to shape the contents of what the public thinks about specific political figures and events as well as the importance they assign to specific types of policies and positions.* A great deal of the research done on agenda setting has been carried out by Maxwell McCombs and his associates.[12] McCombs, along with a colleague, Don Shaw, began simply studying the way that events and activities were reported by news media during a 1968 election and then doing a survey of how the public viewed such events, including the importance they assigned to them. Their basic hypothesis was, as they said, a strong one—that "the media agenda sets the public agenda."[13]

The study was conducted in Chapel Hill, North Carolina. The people they chose to interview were men and women who had not yet made up their minds about how to vote in the election. The researchers assumed that such citizens would be the most susceptible to the influence of the news media and their reports. The contents of several news sources, including both local and national newspapers as well as two television stations, were closely observed and recorded. The analysis of the data revealed a stunning fact. On the five issues that dominated both the media and the public's views during the campaign— foreign policy, law and order, economics, public welfare, and civil rights—both the media and the public assigned the same relative importance to all of the issues. In other words, the basic hypothesis was confirmed—the public's agenda was set by the media. The researchers also considered alternative explanations for the results, for example, that people only selectively read or listened to material that affirmed their opinions. But after careful examination of their data, it turned out that agenda setting provided the most powerful explanation for their findings.

Since this first rather primitive research, other research in different elections, on different issues, and in different places, including other countries, has basically confirmed the strong hypothesis proposed by McCombs and his colleagues. Moreover, the research has also provided nuances and embellished the basic notion behind agenda setting. For example, researchers have studied how the public views the attributes of specific candidates. It turns out that the way in which attributes, such as personal demeanor or specific views, are posed through the media is reflected in the way that the public tends to view a candidate. In addition, the research has moved beyond elections to consider broader arenas, such as debates about the importance of civil rights or crime. Again, the media portrayal tends to be reflected in the views of the public.

To round out and complete the portrait of the media as an agenda setter, McCombs and his colleagues also posed an even deeper question—who sets the media's agenda? They concluded that one of the key figures in setting the agenda for politics in America is the president. Their research showed, specifically, that the media agenda reflected that of the president. The presidency, in other words, can play a large role in determining what goes out across the media. This conclusion seems to match that of other work. Scholarship by historians finds that presidents such as Theodore Roosevelt, who started the notion of using the press as "bully pulpit," and, later, his cousin, Franklin Delano Roosevelt, who used the radio on Saturday mornings to read to his young listeners, were masters at shaping how the public thought of them and their policies.

We can even see these very influences in our own times and the work of more modern presidents. In recent years, the administration of George W. Bush has proven to be a master of using the media to shape the public's view of the world. Bush, for example, famously appeared in photographs and on television on board a naval ship to talk about how well the War in Iraq was going. He portrayed himself as the Commander in Chief, obviously something that resonates deeply in American political culture.

Yet, even the presidency has limits as to how it shapes the media's agenda. As the War in Iraq became more unpopular among Americans in 2005 and, especially, in 2006, President Bush proved far less able to command the details of the media agenda. One episode, in particular, illustrates this and, in so doing, reveals the decline of his presidency. This occurred in the fall of 2006, just after the decisive victories of Democrats in the November elections. There was widespread dissatisfaction with Bush and the way the War in Iraq was unfolding. Through their relentless and graphic images the television media made it clear, night after night, that there was widespread violence and countless deaths and killings in Iraq. Many, particularly those in the news media, had begun to label the War as a "civil war," a designation intended to portray just how deeply Iraq was divided. But Bush and his advisors would have none of it, and they continued to insist that it was not a civil war. Still, the portrait in the media of continued violence and massive resistance on the part of different parties to the American presence in Iraq seemed to say otherwise. And the media, plus the shift in public opinion, ultimately seemed to force the hand of the Bush administration in its conduct and pursuit of victory in Iraq. In the end it became clear that even the president can only have so much power in setting the media's and, in consequence, the public's agenda.

FRAMING

Another way in which the media can shape the public's view of the world is through the way they *frame* issues. Frames here are somewhat similar to the use of the notion of frames in the study of social movements: *they are schemes and templates for organizing experience according to certain rules and strategies.* When the notion of framing is used in terms of the mass media, it typically means the ways in which a specific story is told and organized: who are the protagonists; what is the logic, or argument, of the story; who did what to whom; and what were the substantive issues at stake. For instance, framing in the case of a story on crime could refer to the nature of the crime, who committed it, and why the crime took place.

Anyone who has read a newspaper, watched news on television, or read a story online is aware of the different types of stories and the way they are framed. Stories about crimes, for instance, talk about victims as well as perpetrators, and the characteristics of the criminals are often highlighted, along with their possible motives. The news media sometimes even reveal fundamental biases and prejudices in reporting crime stories. Likewise, stories about wars highlight the violence and the killings and, in the course of political debates about such wars, the way these stories are framed can deeply influence the thinking of the public. The ways in which the media portrayed the War in Vietnam, for example, have been said to have played a major role in the public's declining support for that war.

Frames then furnish ways for selectively highlighting and organizing the nature of a particular story about a particular event or series of events. They are not the truth, in some basic fundamental regard, but they are the way the truth and the story are organized. And in this sense, the story can potentially have a very powerful effect in communicating information to the public. Just as agenda setting has been the subject of careful empirical studies by social scientists, so, too, has framing. One of the most careful scholars on these matters is Shanto Iyengar, who has done a series of studies to understand the effects of framing on the public's view of events.[14]

Iyengar has done both experimental studies of the effects of framing on how people understand the news as well as surveys. One of the subjects he explored was how the attribution of responsibility for an event could affect how the public understood it. He suggested that if a story is organized in terms of being an episodic event, say a single crime perpetrated by a single criminal, then it led to one kind of understanding. But if the organization of the story tended to provide more thematic coverage, for example, it cast a person's poverty not as some single episode but rather as the result of some general social forces, then it led to another kind of understanding. And the difference proved fundamental to the way people think about the world. Iyengar examined and reexamined this argument in several ways, including exposing people to different portrayals of a televised program. His conclusions remained more or less intact: the way people attribute responsibility about things such as crime or poverty depends largely on the way the media construct and tell the story. The media, in other words, not only furnish images, but they provide a very powerful representation of the way we actually think about the world.

An Extended Illustration: The Media and SDS

It is clear from the evidence and studies cited here that the media can shape the way the public thinks about the world—the world of politics, but also the world of broad events. But can the media have a long and durable impact on shaping what transpires? There are a few extended case studies of these effects. One of the most interesting is a study by sociologist Todd Gitlin. Gitlin was curious about the way the media shape not only our understanding of the world but also whether they might influence the actual course of events. To test his ideas, he studied the way that the media, and, especially newspapers like *The New York Times*, reported on the efforts of the Students for a Democratic Society (SDS) during the 1960s.

SDS was one of the leading student organizations in the tumultuous sixties. Founded and organized by a group of young students, most of whom were from the University of Michigan, SDS helped to mobilize students and other young people to engage in various activities. Most of its work was devoted to promoting a view of "participatory democracy" in the United States; they believed that authentic democracy meant that people must be active in government in all respects, not simply in terms of voting during elections but also in terms of a wide range of possible political activities. SDS helped to encourage people to become active in the civil rights movement as well as to be active in local community organizations and events.

Gitlin traced the manner in which the *Times* treated and reported on SDS over the course of a few years. At the same time, he also traced the workings of the organization itself, how its fortunes rose and fell, and how it changed in terms of the interests and activities of its members. His research uncovered a number of interesting things. First, he discovered that in its early reports, beginning in 1965, the *Times* treated the organization rather well—as a group of young people pursuing high ideals. The first article, in 1965, by Fred Powledge, appeared prominently on the front page. The fortunes of the organization seemed to be enhanced by the reports in the paper as its membership grew and became a major part of the new politics of the time. But over a period of months and then years, the treatment by the *Times* began to change. Its reports about the organization grew increasingly critical and negative, although it was not at all evident that the organization itself had actually changed that much. The stories about SDS in the *Times* also moved from the front pages, where readers first turn to the news, to the inner pages of the paper. As this happened, the fortunes of the organization itself began to fade.

In the end, Gitlin concluded, the success and, eventually, the failure and decline of SDS depended not on the capacity and energies of its organizers and members alone, but as much, if not more, on the way that the media like the *Times* treated it. He argued that the media, in effect, provide "a spotlight" that shines brightly across the world of politics. And just as that spotlight can illuminate and enhance the outlines of this world, it can also "burn it to a crisp."[15]

Yet there was one part of the story that Gitlin failed to treat in depth but which is a reminder of the impact of SDS, regardless of the media's attention. Had it not been for this organization, and the many and various programs it pursued, our thinking about modern democracy would have remained embedded in the old institutional terms. SDS and its young adherents convinced many people that "participatory democracy" was an important ideal. Among those it convinced were such leading political theorists as Hannah Arendt and Benjamin Barber, both of whom incorporated such notions into their reworking of the ideas of democratic politics.[16]

The Media and the Business of Making the News

Although in theory the media are claimed to be organized with an eye to pursuing "the truth, and nothing but the truth," in fact, they are in just another kind of business. Because they must produce a product on a regular and timely basis, decisions about what is news and how to highlight it are often made on a last-minute basis rather than in terms of some kind of organized and strategic routine. Making the news is all about how news organizations go about their business and what they seek to cover.

The media tend to act as gatekeepers over what is seen to be the news in the world. They report on the material they believe to be the news, and thus we in the public come to believe the same thing. The media package the news, either on the front page of the daily paper, in the nightly news on the major channels, or in the continuing coverage that channels like CNN and Fox furnish during the day. And most journalists try to put together a good package.

In the process of putting out the news, moreover, certain figures exercise a great influence over the public and are seen by the public not simply as yet another staff writer or television personality, but as someone who can be trusted. This element of trust, it has been found, means a lot for the success of the medium of television. The great television journalist Walter Cronkite was said for years to be "the most trusted man in America," a compliment, but also a backhanded slap at the low regard for such political figures as President Richard Nixon. Today, on the national broadcast news, relatively young and new nightly broadcasts such as Brian Williams and Katie Couric seek to gain the same kind of influence as Cronkite once exercised.

Today research on news organizations also shows that, while they often work hard to produce the best and most objective news possible, they are very much constrained by economic forces. The mass media tend to keep their eye on the bottom line and thus to produce articles or shows that appeal to consumers. Bottom-line issues have led to various upheavals in recent years, particularly pressures on the print media. As *The New York Times* reported in the fall of 2006, "[t]he circulation of the nation's daily newspapers plunged during the latest reporting period . . . [continuing] the slide in a decades-long trend."[17] The decline was the steepest in fifteen years, they added. Television programs, moreover, are constantly monitored in terms of their audience reach by such organizations as ACNielsen. Demographics mean a lot, particularly to advertisers, and the media today are more concerned than ever about demographics. Is their audience young enough? Is it too heavily biased toward one gender rather than another?

The mass media now face forces that go well beyond the routines and schedules of their own work. More and more reporters, for example, are concerned that the news business is more about business than it is about news. A recent study by the Pew Research Center for the People & the Press found that an increasing number of journalists are worried that the quality and objectivity of their reports is suffering at the hands of the bottom line. The study, based on interviews with 547 journalists across America, found that 66 percent of national journalists, and 57 percent of local journalists, believed that economic pressures had begun to damage the quality of news reporting. These figures were up sharply from 1995, when 41 percent and 33per cent of national and local journalists, respectively, claimed that bottom-line pressures were taking their toll.[18]

The Public and Its View and Susceptibility to the Media

Although we have seen how the media work and the ways in which they shape our view of the world, how powerful are they, in fact, in exercising an influence over our basic political beliefs and views? Are they so powerful that they overwhelm other forces, such as our friends and family? This is an important matter, and it is one on which the evidence is mixed for now.

The early studies of elections and politics suggested that the media had only a minimal influence on the way people voted. Such classic studies as *Voting* and *The People's Choice*, studies of elections in the 1940s, found that it was people such as friends and family that were the more powerful influences in how people decided to vote.[19] Men and women tended to vote like the important figures in their lives—their wives or husbands, possibly their parents, or even their close friends. This initial evidence, in fact, helped to promote the notion that social ties and social networks represent the most prominent factors in the way people thought and acted about politics.

In addition, there is a good deal of research that shows that what we learn early about politics and the world tends to influence our basic views of politics.[20] The sociologist Karl Mannheim, for example, suggested that people grow up in cohorts, or what we now call generations (e.g., Generation X), and such generations can be influenced by defining events.[21] The War in Vietnam, for instance, was such a defining event for many people who came of age in the 1960s. So, too, was the civil rights movement for black Americans. People's basic orientations and attitudes can be indelibly shaped by such events. The events leave lasting marks on party choices as well as general attitudes about the political world as to whether people will tend to be either liberal or conservative.

Other research suggests a powerful influence of family backgrounds on how we think and picture the world. Children will often grow up to think like their parents because of direct learning and as a byproduct of social class.[22] Children from higher-income families have benefits, such as good schooling and other resources, that will tend to make them of the same political stripe as their parents. Family background, in other words, shapes our views of the world, not just the mass media, however powerful they seem to be.

This evidence notwithstanding, as we have seen in prior chapters of this book, there are fundamental changes now taking place in terms of political institutions that can leave us highly vulnerable to the effects of the mass media. Political parties are no longer as influential as they once were. Hence, more and more young people, like you, are growing up to see themselves as Independents. Research on agenda setting, in particular, has shown that people who are Independents, that is, have no fixed party affiliation, are also more likely to be influenced by the mass media and its choices.

The Future of the News and the News of the Future

We are living in revolutionary times, not only in terms of the reshaping of the global economy, but also in terms of the reshaping of the media. The print media is in decline. The sale and breakup of major newspaper organizations, such as that of the Knight Ridder newspaper chain in 2005, probably is a harbinger of major changes to come. Moreover, as we have shown above, more and more people, but especially younger generations, are turning to the Internet to get their news via various websites.

The next major changes are likely to come in the way that we in the public interact and use the Internet. During the presidential campaign of 2004, for example, websites like MoveOn.org exercised a major influence over the prospects of candidates. Howard Dean, a Democratic presidential candidates, raised a great deal of money over the Internet, virtually all of it from small donations— which, he claimed, gave his candidacy the stamp of popular approval. Other novelties, such as blogs, are also likely to produce dramatic shifts in the way we deal with the media, although the jury on blogs remains out at present.

Certainly one of the most vital questions here concerns the way in which the Internet can and will be used to promote democracy in democratic societies. The Internet allows for two-way conversations and more, such as the growth of specific online communities. Some political scientists have even suggested that it can provide a new and powerful way for people to vote in elections as well as to register their views on other political matters of interest to the government.[23] All of this opens up a myriad of possibilities for new forms of interaction and growth of new kinds of communities.[24] At the same time, however, it also opens the door to new ways for monitoring traffic on the Internet and who engages in specific practices. Indeed, one of the greatest struggles in democratic societies in coming years will most likely be between the forces for openness and those for governmental control in the use of the Internet.

NOTES

1. The chronology of the Watergate affair here comes from details provided by the *Washington Post* at its website, www.washingtonpost.com. It provides a general chronology as well as specific articles by Bernstein and Woodward, along with other reporters for the *Post*.
2. *Washington Post* website, October 10, 1972, A01.
3. *Washington Post* website, May 1, 1973, A01.
4. For an excellent set of essays on the history and form of the media, see Michael Schudson, *The Power of News, Part I, The News in Historical Perspective* (Cambridge, MA: Harvard University Press, 1995).
5. Marshall McLuhan, *The Medium Is the Message* (New York: Bantam Books, 1967).
6. Susan A. Hellweg, Michael Pfau, and Steven R. Brydon, *Televised Presidential Debates: Advocacy in Contemporary America* (New York: Praeger, 1992).
7. Pew Research Center for the People & the Press, "Online Papers Modestly Boost Newspaper Readership," July 30, 2006.
8. *The State of the News Media: An Annual Report on American Journalism*, "An Overview," at www.stateof thenewsmedia.org/2006.
9. See, for example, the excellent set of essays in *The Nation*, "The 10th Anniversary National Entertainment State," 2006, 283(1).
10. But see the writings of Noam Chomsky, for example, which take a more cynical view of the ways in which corporate media can influence our views.
11. See, for example, Arthur Vidich and Joseph Bensman, *Small Town in Mass Society* (Princeton, NJ: Princeton University Press, 1968); and Matthew Crenson, *The Unpolitics of Air Pollution* (Baltimore, MD: Johns Hopkins University Press, 1971).
12. Maxwell McCombs, *Setting the Agenda: The Mass Media and Public Opinion* (Cambridge, UK: Polity Press, 2006).
13. Ibid., 5.
14. Shanto Iyengar, *Is Anyone Responsible? How Television Frames Political Issues* (Chicago: The University of Chicago Press, 1994).
15. This image of Gitlin's research comes from Doris Graber, *Mass Media & American Politics*, 6th ed. (Washington, DC: CQ Press, 2002), 182.
16. See, for example, John McGowan, *Hannah Arendt: An Introduction* (Minneapolis, MN: University of Minnesota Press, 1997); and Benjamin Barber, *Strong Democracy* (Berkeley, CA: University of California Press, 2001).
17. *The New York Times*, October 31, 2006, C1.
18. The Pew Research Center for the People & the Press, "Bottom-Line Pressures Now Hurting Coverage, Say Journalists," May 23, 2004.
19. Paul Lazarsfeld, Bernard Berelson, and Hazel Gaudet, *The People's Choice* (New York: Columbia University Press, 1944).
20. See, for example, Robert D. Hess and Judith Torney-Purta, *The Development of Political Attitudes in Children* (Garden City, NY: Doubleday, 1968); M. Kent

Jennings and Richard G. Niemi, *Generations and Politics: A Panel Study of Young Adults and Their Parents* (Princeton, NJ: Princeton University Press, 1981); and also Anthony M. Orum, ed., *The Seeds of Politics: Youth and Politics in America* (Englewood Cliffs, NJ: Prentice-Hall, 1972).

21. Karl Mannheim, "The Problem of Generations," in Karl Mannheim, *Essays in the Sociology of Knowledge* (London: Routledge & Kegan Paul, 1952).

22. See, for example, M. Kent Jennings and Richard Niemi, op. cit.

23. See, for example, Caroline J. Tolbert and Ramona S. McNeal, "Unraveling the Effects of the Internet on Political Participation," *Political Research Quarterly*, 2003, 56(2), 175–85.

24. See, for example, Barry Wellman and Caroline Haythornwaite, *The Internet in Everyday Life* (Oxford: Blackwell Publishers, 2002).

Chapter 13

Political Participation
and the Pursuit of Democracy

Introduction

It is difficult to tie together the threads of a long and complex textbook such as this one. Indeed, many textbooks forgo that process altogether because it represents such a challenge. But the field of political sociology is not only, or even merely, the study of abstract theory and how it applies to the world. It is also a discipline that was created by men and women who, in their effort to understand the world, also hoped to change it. Karl Marx, the most activist of our theorists, was the most explicit about this in his short and famous thesis on the work of Ludwig Feuerbach: "The philosophers have only interpreted the world, in various ways; the point, however, is to change it." [1]

All sociologists possess the same passion and aim for the same goal as Marx. How can political sociology help us to achieve that end? We can do so, we believe, by focusing our attention on two elements of the modern world: participation and democracy. Both elements, we believe, underlie any effort to shape or reshape the world in which we live. Indeed, both are inextricably tied to one another: most, though not all, theories of democracy make it clear that such a system requires the widespread and active participation by people in the making of their own social and political worlds. We would go so far as to claim that such participation is absolutely essential to the workings of democracy itself.

284

Here we shall focus our attention on these two central points to how we might have an impact on the world. We shall consider at length the nature and importance of participation by people in politics. We shall consider participation first in the context of theories of democracy. Here we shall expand on some ideas and notions we first introduced in Chapter 7. Then we shall consider some of the critical intellectual challenges to democracy and participation, in particular the very profound challenge presented by theories of rational choice and action. These theories, as the recent *Handbook of Political Sociology* makes clear, now provide a substantial challenge to the panoply of ideas and assumptions that underlie the writings and thinking of many political sociologists.[2] Only by engaging these ideas, and examining their consequences, can the field of political sociology find firm ground for its own particular claims and stance on the world.

Next we shall turn to the empirical examinations of political participation to show in some detail what we know about the facts of such participation. Of special interest will be the ways in which social cleavages make themselves evident in differences in rates and types of participation. Thus we shall show how participation varies by gender, by race and ethnicity, and by social class. We shall consider here not merely the numbers and ways in which participation varies between people, but also some of the competing explanations for why it varies.

Finally, we shall consider the forces and factors that might, on the one hand, promote greater participation by the public and, on the other hand, limit such participation. Of particular interest here is the argument that, in contrast to much of the thinking in political sociology, participation should be seen not simply as a voluntary activity, prompted by the desires and aims of people, but also as an activity that is channeled and directed by, for lack of a better phrase, specific agents of mobilization. In the past sociologists have written about participation as though people merely chose on the basis of their own inclinations to participate. But political scientists have known for a long while that people do not simply decide to act: they often must be mobilized by outside forces to act. In effect, then, we want to theoretically bridge the orientation of sociology, with its emphasis on voluntary action, to the orientation of political science, with its emphasis on mobilization.[3]

In this chapter, then, we shall consider the avenues through which people in their everyday lives might engage in their own self-governance and in the workings of their own lives. Although we all do so, as members of families, of course, even as friends, certain theories of democracy make it imperative that we also participate in politics as members of a larger public, as engaged citizens. It is in these public roles, as writers like Robert Putnam point out, that we must engage in debate and exchange with one another. For that is what democracy is really all about: the everyday give and take of ideas, and exchange with one another, about the things we believe to be meaningful—not simply to ourselves, alone, but to our children and to all future generations.

Democratic Theory and Participation

Democratic theory is all about how governments should operate in order to advance and to implement the desires and goals of their citizens. As compared to nondemocratic forms—in particular, authoritarian and totalitarian regimes—democracies are built on institutions that seek to implement the wishes of the public. Such institutions include elements like congresses or parliaments in which representatives, elected by the public, engage in debate and make policies on behalf of the public.

Now there are all sorts of variations on these themes and the elements that theorists of different persuasions seek to emphasize. Some theorists stress the importance of free elections in which the public can participate with impunity and choose specific figures to present their interests. Other theorists, such as John Stuart Mill, recognizing the difficulty of direct participation of all the people in a large society, highlight the importance of representation and how representatives can work to implement the will of the public in a fair and just manner.[4]

Yet there are some elements of democratic theory that are not open to question. The most significant of these is participation by people in their own governance. No one ever put it more plainly or more clearly than Abraham Lincoln: a government for the people by the people and of the people. Democracy, in other words, such as that of the United States is, at root, an institution that seeks to represent the people as well as to advance their collective interest.

A CLASSIC VIEW OF DEMOCRACY AND ITS CRITICS

What is regarded in many quarters as the seminal statement of modern democracy, the writings of Jean Jacques Rousseau, makes clear that a true democracy is one in which the will of the people is represented in the workings of government—and that no government can be called a democracy if such public involvement is absent. The will of the people means the collective judgment of the public taken in an open and visible manner. Only if people are permitted to exercise their own individual wills, and those actions then are aggregated and recorded, can one actually call a government democratic. Anything short of such a free, open, and visible (or public) activity is not, at least in the eyes of Rousseau, worthy of being called a democratic government.[5]

How, then, can such an expression of the will of the people be achieved? Some theorists of democracy argue that such a radical public demonstration of the will of the people is not only impossible, as Mill would insist, but, ironically, that it is also quite dangerous. The notion here is that if people are actually permitted to freely exercise their own individual judgments and everyone proceeds to do so, the result could be chaotic. Modern critics of the ideas of figures like Rousseau actually claim that the mass participation of people in political projects can lead to dangerous consequences (see Chapter 6). Indeed, such critics seem to believe that participation by the public in their own governance is fine just as long as it is limited.

But why would such participation be so detrimental? One may understand Mill's reservations about direct democracy, given the scope of modern societies, but what can possibly go wrong if all people are permitted some choice in their own lives and their own governance? The flaw in the reasoning of the critics of full democracy lies, we think, in the imagery they associated with the participation of the public. The critics of participation, such as Bernard Berelson, had in their own lifetimes witnessed the evils and terror associated with the rise of Fascist regimes in Europe—in particular, the Nazi regime in Germany. They seemed to believe that all widespread participation by the public would become something that resembled the massive parades and marches orchestrated by the Nazis during the infamous Nuremberg rallies. But political participation, particularly in regimes that contain democratic institutions, such as a parliament, but more importantly free and open elections, need not turn into rallies led by demagogues. Indeed, it is an entirely specious argument put forward by such critics, the effect of which is to support their own beliefs that democracies are fine as long as the people participate in only a minimal fashion.

We do not agree with such critics as Berelson or others. We believe, along with Rousseau, that the central element of a democracy today—the defining element of democracy, in fact—is that people are free to participate in the actions that govern and direct their own lives and fates. Such participation is essential to sustaining democratic governments and institutions. If people refuse, decline, or are unable to participate, it simply permits public officials to take actions that advance their own interests and goals. Participation by the public provides, in other words, a check and a constraint on the actions of public officials. But more than that, participation provides the means whereby the interests of the public can be articulated and represented to the officials of government.

WHY PUBLIC PARTICIPATION IS ESSENTIAL TO THE WORKINGS OF DEMOCRACY

Participation by people in the workings of their own public lives is, as writers like Carole Pateman and Benjamin Barber argue, a good thing not only for the workings of democratic institutions but also for citizens themselves.[6] In effect, participation creates citizens out of otherwise passive subjects. Participation in public life provides an important way for people to develop and to articulate their own visions of what the nature of government should be about. It also provides a chance for people to develop skills and a sense of effectiveness about their own abilities, as much research on political behavior shows. Participation, as Barber points out, can also be transformative: it takes the potential abilities of people and transforms those abilities into action, into activities that help to advance their own goals. Participation is also, by its very nature, a public and visible event: it is something that people do in common, and, therefore, it is the one opportunity that they have to act together, in concert. It furnishes people with an opportunity to share and to test out their ideas with others; to get feedback, including criticism; to reformulate and to reframe what they think. Participation, in brief, is an activity taken by individuals but done so in conjunction with one another, and thus a public activity that, as Rousseau put it, furnishes a sense of the common will of the people.

Still, it would be a mistake to romanticize participation entirely. Participation can be abused by public officials if the central institutions of democratic government are not firmly in place. There must be, among other things, representative institutions through which the will of the people operates. There also must be legal institutions, built on constitutional foundations, so that there are certain procedures and guidelines that can be followed in carrying out the public will. Such institutional foundations are critical to the workings of democracy. But they are nothing, of course, if there is no opportunity available to, or taken by, the public at large to voice and to act upon their beliefs, interests, and ideals.

In short, the *sine qua non* of democratic government is free and equal participation by the people in the public sphere of their own lives. Anything less than that cannot be judged to be democracy. It is because of this central imperative to the workings of modern democracy that observers, like Robert Putnam but also many others, are so concerned today about the workings of governments like that of the United States. If, as it appears, relatively few people take an active interest in the workings of government and public institutions, and if relatively small numbers turn out to vote in national elections, can we actually call this a democratic system of government?

A Challenge to Democratic Theory: Rational Choice

Theories of democracy, such as those of Rousseau and, later, Barber and Pateman, are based on the premise that the participation of the public is essential both for the operation of democratic governments and for the lives of their citizens. For the governments, the full and active participation by people means that the leaders of the government—the political officials—can learn of the various needs and desires of their citizens. For the citizens, such actual participation can be, as Barber suggests, transformative: it takes their ideas and wishes and, through the magic of actual participation, transforms them into activities done in common and with real consequences for the workings of the polity. Now, what if participation was neither transformative for the lives of people nor productive? What then?

Those questions arise because of serious intellectual challenges posed to political sociology and to the sociologically informed brand of democratic theory, in particular. In the 1960s, a new brand of theory began to take root among political scientists; since then, it has spread like wildfire, challenging many of the assumptions and the basic foundations of political theory itself. Along the way it has also challenged the very grounds and foundations of many sociological theories.

Rational Choice and Collective Action

One of the seminal writings on rational choice, or public choice, theory is that of the political scientist Mancur Olson.[7] Olson provided a theory for explaining the nature of collective action in the pursuit of "public goods." Such goods include things such as public parks, new sports arenas, improved public highway systems, and other such items that are shared, and indivisible, among the public. Olson insisted that individuals likely will participate in collective action designed to achieve such goods to the extent that they believe their actions will advance the acquisition of public goods.

Thus, he claimed, people are apt to participate in groups that are fairly small because in such groups they will recognize that their action can be decisive to the outcome of the decision. If people desire a public park, and that action can only happen if they take an active role in its acquisition—by vote or even by contributing materially to its purchase—then any individual, or small group of individuals, will be motivated to join and to participate actively in that effort.

But most such collective action intended to acquire public goods never involves a small number of participants. Public goods are precisely that: goods that are indivisible and are to be shared among the members of the public. And the public often, if not always, involves a wide variety of people who will benefit from the decision. So Olson reasons further that collective action intended to achieve public goods generally will involve large numbers of people. And, as it does so, any single individual will come to recognize that, no matter how much that individual participates either by way of real activity, time, or even material contribution, to the campaign, as the numbers expand the payoff will diminish. If everyone benefits from the development, let us say of a new public park, then any single individual is likely to refrain from actual participation because he will benefit regardless of his effort in the campaign for the park.

THE PROBLEM OF THE FREE RIDER

Olson's argument rests on a particular way of thinking about the individual and his choice to act. It assumes that every individual will calculate the costs and benefits of his actions. If the benefits of collective action remain the same, as they will with any public good, then the costs to the individual become the operative force. In large-scale collective actions, the individual will reason, according to Olson, that he can enjoy the public goods regardless of his own action because, as in the case of a new park, they are available to all by being public. Thus, it makes little sense for him to participate in the action; moreover, because so many people are actually involved in the pursuit, one person's action will add little of consequence to the overall effect of the collective action. In other words, that person's participation is unlikely to affect the outcome.

The upshot is, then, that in large-scale collective actions there is little incentive for any single person to participate. The individual will still benefit from a positive outcome. Olson called this the problem of the *free rider*. Members of the public, in other words, can still enjoy the benefits of a new public good, whether a park or stadium, without putting forth any costs, of time or money, on their own. They become, in effect, free riders on the outcome. The question then arises—and this is the profound issue raised by Olson: Why should any single individual participate in any collective action designed to obtain a specific good? If the individual reasons, as Olson suggests he does, then why should anyone participate in any large-scale collective action in pursuit of public goods?

Until Olson's work and that of other rational choice theorists, sociologists had taken the position that individuals will voluntarily, or freely, choose to act in ways that will promote their own interests. Further, sociologists tended to think of such interests in terms of certain basic values, or ends, that people wish to pursue in the course of the workings of society. They rarely, if ever, invoked a model of human reasoning that would apply to all such actions like the one assumed by Olson. But Olson clearly shows that, if we think in terms of costs and benefits, individuals will find no rational grounds to pursue any collective action on behalf of public goods. The theoretical burden then shifts from explaining the grounds for individual action, on the basis of free choice, to explaining how organizations, governments, social movements, and other groups get people to act on behalf of broad public projects.

SELECTIVE INCENTIVES

Olson proposes that organizations must provide an array of *selective incentives* that will encourage people to participate in actions of specific interest to the organization, whether local government or local neighborhood group. Such incentives might include such actual material benefits as money, or simply symbolic benefits, such as the sheer fun and joy of participating with people in an act that is seen to be important and vital to the organization. Other rational choice theorists take up a similar line of reasoning, arguing, for example, that it is the duty, or a similar kind of imperative, that will motivate people to participate in collective actions above and beyond issues of the relative costs and benefits of such action.[8]

The theoretical challenge posed by Olson and other rational choice theorists to the free and open workings of democracy is immense.[9] Essentially they claim that even if people are free to participate in a collective action, as they are in a society with democratic institutions, such as free and open elections, they are not entirely free: their thinking, and action, are still bound to an assessment of the costs and benefits to be obtained from their action. And such thinking can seem to be entirely rational insofar as people in everyday life make similar kinds of calculations about the purchase of goods or even about leisure activities with members of their family.

Public Participation in Everyday Social Life

The theoretical challenge then to theories that insist on the underlying importance of participation both to the livelihood of the individual and democratic institutions is to furnish a persuasive argument that counters the claims and logic of theories of rational choice. We must be able, as political sociologists, to justify the importance of participation in such a way that we move the concept outside the realm simply of the costs and benefits assigned to it by individual actors. Indeed, we must view it, as the rational choice theorists do, as something that appears as natural and transparent to individuals as the other things they pursue in their everyday lives. The argument must be a realistic one by invoking features of daily social life people find around them, much as rational choice theorists invoke features of economic life.

The main solution, as we see it, is that participation must feel so natural to the lives of people, so much a part of their everyday circumstances, that it feels both important and necessary to the workings of their lives. People must think that participation and involvement in public issues and in the public arena—the physical and institutional space they share with others—is not simply something imposed upon them. It must seem as comfortable as getting up on a sunny morning, or as driving the car to work, or as as taking the dog for a walk. Public participation must be a taken-for-granted part of people's lives; yet, at the same time, it must be something that is felt as imperative and essential to the way their lives work.

Another way of saying the same thing is to say that public participation must arise out of the everyday social and cultural circumstances of the lives of people. In classic democratic theory, as invoked by, among others, Hannah Arendt, citizens became involved in public affairs because the public arena was a natural part of their lives.[10] Granted, as in the case of the Greeks, citizenship only covered a small proportion of the population, nevertheless, citizenship was not simply imposed on people as a means of satisfying certain constitutional obligations; it was, as it were, a skin in which they felt entirely comfortable. So, too, participation in public projects must feel the same way today to citizens of a democracy. It must feel both so comfortable and yet so important that people are willing to do it in a way as to move it beyond questions of costs and benefits: it becomes, in other words, a responsibility but not one that feels as though it were a burden.

How, then, can this sense emerge? We believe that it must emerge naturally from the workings of society and the elements of culture of a particular society. In his great analysis of democracy in America, Alexis de Tocqueville pointed to those various features of America that promoted the formation of democratic society. As we noted earlier, such features included an active involvement of people in associations and the public life. This broad sector is what is often known as *civil society*, the underlying social basis of the world (see Chapter 5). But de Tocqueville put it even more powerfully: the elements of America that helped to create it as a working and effective democracy were the *customs* of Americans—the manners and, as we would say today, the nature of American culture. It is the working elements of such a culture that people take for granted in the operations of their world.

Why people then choose to participate in public issues is because such participation feels perfectly natural to their way of doing things, so natural that not to do it would be disruptive of their own lives and of the order they see in their lives. It is of course a stretch to see participation in this light. Indeed, many observers note that the workings of our world, in a country like the United States, is moving in the very opposite direction—away from a sense of a shared public arena and public concerns to an ever-greater sense of individualism and private self-absorption.[11]

Yet although the world may be moving in a different direction, one in which the economy, with its emphasis on private property and private calculation, continues to invade our lives, the promise and hope of democracy is that participation can become part and parcel of everyday life. Benjamin Barber was willing to advance his theory by invoking various kinds of institutional agents that, in some ways, seem to have been so ideal as to be entirely impractical. But rather than simply looking for practical circumstances, we should look for those real working circumstances where participation, by the nature of life, occurs and is valued. And some societies do this much better than others.

For democracy to work and to succeed, participation by the public is vital. It is so vital as to remove it from a simple cost-and-benefit set of calculations. We now want to turn to empirical examinations of actual political participation and to discover the social circumstances and conditions that help to promote participation among people. They should give us much better insight into precisely the kinds of conditions that not only promote participation but that, if one wishes to reshape the world, must be put into place to make participation possible for the widest variety of citizens.

Political Participation and Social Cleavages

Democratic theory urges the importance of participation so that nations can work like democracies. Rational choice theories suggest, however, that there are real limits to the conditions under which people will participate in public projects. But what does the empirical world, of people and participation, reveal to us about the actual conditions for participation: Who actually participates and why? We turn now to consider an array of empirical studies and findings about the levels of political participation by people. Most of these results come from studies of American politics, but a few are based upon studies of other countries as well. These results will help provide a realistic appreciation of the hope and possibilities for participation by the public and the successful pursuit of democracy.

RATES AND TYPES OF POLITICAL PARTICIPATION

People participate in different ways and to different degrees in the public activities of democratic nations. Some people participate a great deal: they may run for political office or they may actively engage in political campaigns, contributing money and/or time to getting others elected to political office. There have been a number of studies over the years that get into the details of such participation, and they consistently reveal certain results.

The most common activity of people is that of voting in elections, in particular, presidential elections. Something on the order of about one of every two registered voters actually votes in elections; more people tend to vote in presidential contests than in local ones. Ordinarily only about 30–40 percent of registered voters actually vote in local governmental elections.

Both turnout and voting registration differ among voters from different countries. Turnout has been consistently higher in European countries, in part because people are automatically registered to vote in Europe and the government renews those registrations regularly.[12] Moreover, in the United States, the rates of registration to vote vary among different groups. People who are wealthier or better educated tend to register in higher numbers than those who are poorer or less well educated. These differences in the rates of registration are so striking and so consistent that recent laws have been enacted that now make it easier for all people to register to vote.[13]

While voting is the most common form of political participation, it also has declined among citizens over the past few decades. As recently as the 1960s, there was a fairly substantial rate of voting: about six of every ten registered voters turned out to vote in presidential elections. But over time there has been a gradual but relentless decline in voting turnout in the United States as well as in European nations.[14] This decline has been seen repeatedly in any number of studies, and it has been the source of a great deal of discussion and concern among various students of democracy.[15] We shall return to it later for more in-depth discussion.

There are other ways in which people can and have participated in politics. In their pioneering research on these matters, the political scientists Sidney Verba and Norman Nie classified people in terms of the types of participation in which they engaged.[16] They found that people, for example, sometimes participated in local community affairs and avoided participation in other kinds of political activities. Other people tended to participate in political campaigns and were especially involved in electoral activities beyond voting. Of the public in general, they identified several specific patterns in the participation of people: *inactive, or those who are not at all active in politics* (22 percent); *voting specialists, or those who only vote* (21 percent); *parochial participants, or those who only make specialized political contacts* (4 percent); *communalists, or those who are active in community affairs but low in campaign activities* (20 percent); *campaigners, or those who are active in campaigns but low in community affairs* (15 percent); and *complete activists* (11 percent). Other important studies tend to confirm these same patterns.[17]

SOCIAL CLASS AND PARTICIPATION

Participation in politics does not occur evenly among the members of all groups and strata. In fact, there are certain specific social differences that appear time and again in empirical studies of participation, and one of the most central of these concerns social class and rates of participation.

The work of Sidney Verba and Norman Nie was the first to actually propose a basic model of participation whose foundations lay in class differences. The model clearly and emphatically shows that rates of political participation are far higher for the members of higher social classes than they are for members of lower ones: or, to put it another way, there is a positive correlation between the likelihood of participation and an individual's social class ranking.[18] Verba and Nie showed that the model helped to explain differences in the rates of overall participation, where participation is based upon a set of discrete activities such as involvement in campaigns as well as in local affairs. But it also holds for each specific type of participation as well. Thus, for example, the higher the social class background of a person, the more likely he will vote in presidential elections.

We also know that social class is composed of different elements. In particular, research on social class generally creates measures which combine the ranking of people on such items as their level of education, type of occupation, and annual family income. These measures actually referred to as measures of a person's socioeconomic status. All of these measures, when considered separately, reveal once again the same basic pattern of results: the higher the annual income of a person, for example, the more likely he will participate in politics.

Yet of the three elements, it is a person's level of education that turns out to be the most important.[19] ducation, in other words, makes a much bigger difference in the likelihood of participation—especially voting—than either family income or occupation.

Table 13.1 reveals this pattern for voting turnout in the 1996 presidential election, for example; other research comes up with much the same kind of pattern.[20] Note that the rate of voting turnout increases generally as the education of respondents increases. As people acquire more education, in other words, they vote in much higher numbers. The difference shows up most clearly in this table between people who have not completed high school and those who have

TABLE 13.1. Education by Vote in 1996 Presidential Election

EDUCATION	DID NOT VOTE	VOTED	NUMBER OF CASES
Grade school or less	46%	54%	411
Some high school	53%	47%	776
High school graduate	34%	66%	2,228
Some college	29%	71%	2,103
College graduate or more	14%	86%	896
Number of cases	2,095	4,319	6,414

SOURCE: American National Election Studies University of Michigan, Ann Arbor.

at least a college education. Political scientists Raymond Wolfinger and Steven Rosenstone conclude that education has a number of important consequences for people: it enhances their cognitive abilities, thus their capacity to understand politics; it improves their sense of citizen duty and responsibility; and it helps them to overcome the specific procedural matters involved both in voting registration and in voting itself.

One of the best studies ever of political participation was done by Sidney Verba, Kay Lehman Schlozman, and Henry Brady.[21] It goes even more deeply into these issues. Verba and his colleagues develop a special and compact theory of political participation, the "civic voluntarism model." They argue that people are able to participate in politics based upon three central factors: *resources*, such as time available to them; *engagement*, such as their psychological interest in politics; and *recruitment*, or contact by political parties and other organizations. Each of these components acts separately to promote the likelihood of participation, but resources may be, in their view, the most important. And it is not only resources of time that matter, but also those of energy and, of course, money as well.

The theory is a comprehensive one and furnishes a full and satisfying way to explain differences in the interest and capacity of people to participate in politics. It is particularly useful for capturing the differences in social class. People of higher social classes clearly have a number of advantages that other people do not have: they have more time; they have more money; and they also have more education. And once again, it is the educational component that makes the biggest difference of all because

> circumstances of initial privilege have consequences for educational attainment which, in turn, has consequences for the acquisition of nearly every other participatory factor: income earned on the job; skills acquired at work, in organizations, and, to a lesser extent, in church; psychological engagement with politics; exposure to requests for activity.[22]

We shall revisit this particular finding later when we consider ways in which the opportunities for people to participate in politics might be enhanced.

GENDER AND PARTICIPATION

Men and women have tended to differ consistently in their rates of participation in politics in countries like the United States. In part, these are simply matters of historical fact and political realities, as we noted in Chapter 7. Women did not possess the right to vote in the United States until 1920 and the passage of the Nineteenth Amendment to the American Constitution. Yet even after its passage, women have tended to participate in smaller numbers than men in politics.

Sidney Verba and Norman Nie, for instance, found that women generally had lower rates of participation than men.[23] In their subsequent study, Verba and his colleagues found that there were gender differences, but they were not nearly as pronounced as shown in previous studies.[24] Coupled with other evidence, in fact, there seems to have been a decline in recent decades in the gender gap between men and women in their overall rates of participation in politics.[25]

Beyond the simple indices of participation, women in recent years have become more and more involved in running and winning political office. Although women remain a minority today in the U.S. Congress, the gap with men is narrowing. As of late 2006, before the mid-term elections, 13 women (10 Democrats and 3 Republicans) served in the U.S. Senate, while 61 women (43 Democrats and 18 Republicans) held seats in the House of Representatives. Four of the Senators and seven Representatives were serving their first terms in Congress.

While the social class differences in participation can be explained by the different resources and energies available to people, explaining gender differences proves to be a much more complicated matter. It does not come down simply to a matter of resources.[26] As we noted, part of the difference can be explained by laws that have prevented women from participating in politics as fully as men. But there are other ways to explain these differences, especially those that continued after the franchise became available to women.

Some theorists suggest that there are structural circumstances that continue to make it more difficult for women to participate. In part, it may be, as some feminists suggest, that there remains an old boy network that can limit the entry of women to various forms of political engagement. In part, too, it may be that as more and more women have entered the labor force as part of two-income families, the responsibilities of women, both for raising children and for supporting the household, have simply doubled and become more difficult.[27]

A more likely line of analysis lies in seeking an explanation for the gender differences in the upbringing and socialization of men and women. A number of early studies done in the 1960s found that boys and girls tend to be socialized in ways that lead to later differences in their interests and engagement in politics. Boys, for example, tend to be far more interested in news and matters of war than girls, interests that converge with a general interest in politics.[28] More recent research suggests that such childhood and early adulthood experiences may hold the key to explaining gender differences. Nancy Burns and her colleagues, at the conclusion of their impressive study into the source of gender differences in politics, observe that "[w]e saw that women are less likely than men to be psychologically engaged with politics: less likely to be politically interested, informed, or efficacious. This attitudinal deficit contributes substantially to the gender gap in activity."[29]

RACE, ETHNICITY, AND PARTICIPATION

Race and ethnicity are as powerful as class and gender in affecting the likelihood that people will participate in politics. In the United States, in particular, there have been a number of studies of the rates and differences in participation among African Americans, Latinos, and whites. Most of the work has been devoted to uncovering the nature of differences between blacks and whites.[30]

Typically it has been found that blacks participate in politics at lower rates than whites. Table 13.2 shows data from the study by Verba, Schlozman, and Brady. Note, for example, that African Americans tend to vote less than whites, but that Latinos are the least politically active of the three groups. The lower rate of political activity among Latinos is generally consistent with the findings from a great deal of other research.[31]

One of the early discoveries about the differences in participation between blacks and whites revealed that, with social class controlled, blacks actually participated somewhat more heavily in politics than whites. That is, as compared to whites of comparable social class, blacks tended to be more active in politics. There were various explanations designed to account for this difference. The most popular explanation was that the strength of their ethnic community helped to propel blacks and to enhance the rate of their participation in politics.[32] Some recent research, however, casts some doubt on this particular explanation.[33]

TABLE 13.2. Political Activities by Race (percent active)

ACTIVITY	ANGLO WHITES	AFRICAN AMERICANS	LATINOS	LATINO CITIZENS
Vote	73	65	41	52
Campaign work	8	12	7	8
Campaign contributions	25	22	11	12
Contact	37	24	14	17
Protest	5	9	4	4
Informal community activity	17	19	12	14
Board membership	4	2	4	5
Affiliated with a political organization	52	38	24	27

SOURCE: Sidney Verba, Kay Lehman Schlozman and Henry E. Brady, Voice and Equality, Harvard University Press, 1995.

One of the more important findings in recent years comes from the research of Lawrence Bobo and Franklin Gilliam, Jr.[34] They argue that the local context of participation deeply influences the rate and involvement of African Americans in politics. In fact, they found that in cities where blacks hold positions of power, they are more active and participate at higher rates than whites of comparable socioeconomic status. In other words, they argue, blacks in such cases have moved beyond mere political activity to expanding and building upon their political resources.[35] Other research also highlights the important role that context and organizations, especially religious ones, can have on the political participation of African Americans.[36]

As for the case of Latinos, most research has shown that Latinos, especially Mexican immigrants, the largest of the Latino groups in the Untied States, tend to participate at much lower rates than both blacks and whites. Some of this difference in the rate of activity of Latinos can be attributed to differences in the resources available to them, as compared to blacks and whites. That is, since many Latinos are found in lower social classes and lack the money and time as resources for activity, they will participate less than whites. But there are other factors that can offset those differences in resources. In particular, the involvement of blacks and Latinos in churches seems to provide an important incentive for higher levels of interest and activity. Moreover, other elements, such as language, that can promote a greater sense of group identity, and thus interest in group activities, can also work in the same way to enhance and to benefit the rates of participation by Latinos.[37]

SUMMARY

We have seen that there are important differences in the ways and rates at which people participate in politics. The pursuit of democracy may require that everyone have the chance to be active in politics, but unless the obstacles to the participation of some groups are overcome, the differences by class, gender and ethnicity, and race are likely to remain. How might the playing field of politics be leveled? What can be done? We turn now to consider some of the strategies that could, and that actually have been, deployed.

Promoting Political Participation in the Pursuit of Democracy

The American government, led by President George W. Bush, embarked on the War in Iraq in the effort to bring democracy to that region of the world. Although the government toppled the regime of Saddam Hussein, the effort to establish democracy has been far more difficult. Many observers had thought it would be. Democracy is not simply a matter of creating a (puppet) government, consisting of elected officials and the apparatus of democracy, such as a parliament, but it is foremost a government that works only if it is built upon solid social and cultural foundations. Most of all, it must permit and encourage the widespread participation of the public in its workings and deliberations.

We have seen that there are obstacles to such participation even in Western nations where there are institutions that support and encourage participation. As the rational choice theorists warn us, people will not participate in efforts to secure major public projects, whatever they might be, on their own. Most people will simply conclude that their efforts are too costly in terms of the time and money required or simply that they have better things to do with their time. Further, as we have seen, the facts suggest beyond the criticism of the rational choice theorists that some groups of people simply lack the resources and/or the opportunities to participate.

In light of these problems, then, there are several strategies that could be pursued. As the noted political scientists Frances Fox Piven and Richard Cloward claim, the major obstacle to the participation of many people to be overcome is a simple one: many people have neither the time nor the opportunity to register to vote, hence, they don't.[38] As a result, Piven and Cloward helped promote an effort that resulted in the passage of a major American law, the National Voter Registration Act of 1993, that provides people with easier access to register to vote. The results have been encouraging. Yet, as Piven and Cloward point out, the new law has not captured all, or even many, of the people who fail to participate. And even with the increase in voter registration, voter turnout has continued to decline.

Another answer is a structural one that lies at the foundations of the social order. A key structural difference between those who participate and those who do not lies in the extent of their educational training, their schooling. People with more education tend to have more opportunities to develop the skills that will facilitate their participation. Some of these skills are simple ones, such as knowing the procedural mechanics of registration. But others are deeper ones, such as having the ability to communicate with large numbers of people and, for those who are willing, to master and digest important facts about politics and the public arena.

The problem with seeking to remedy the educational deficit, as with any major structural obstacle, is that deficits are the result of a series of cumulative advantages and disadvantages. Well educated citizens typically come from homes of well-educated parents.

Such homes have many privileges and resources unavailable to the families of people who are less well educated. Income, while not as important to turnout and participation, in general, as education, could help reduce the difference. But efforts to narrow the economic gap between the rich and the poor in countries like the United States face major obstacles themselves. Indeed, in the past ten to fifteen years, the income inequalities between the richest and poorest segments of America have become more marked than in the past.

Perhaps one of the most important and accessible strategies to employ to open the political arena to the participation of more and more people lies in concerted efforts to mobilize people who typically do not participate in elections or other forms of politics. A major work by Steven Rosenstone and Mark Hansen argues that the usual way of understanding the roots and causes of political participation is only half-right.[39] They insist, as do Mancur Olson and other rational choice theorists, that participation is not simply the result of the free and open choice of people. In fact, they show, the rate of political participation actually increases when organizations use direct and concerted means to draw out voters or to engage in other types of political campaigns. Mobilization, in other words, is as central to the process of participation—hence, to the broader effort to achieve democracy—as reliance on the voluntary choices of individuals. In fact, it is more significant because it can help to offset such things as the educational deficits that some people face or the deficits in resources that poorer groups confront.[40]

Finally, we would argue here, once again, that in order for participation to take root among people, it must feel like a natural and important extension of their real lives. People will only participate in politics if they believe it to be an integral element of their everyday social life. Though it may be hard to achieve, there must be something like a cultural imperative to participate, one that flows out of the everyday circumstances in the routines of people's lives. We believe that to be essentially the most important and profound lesson that political sociology can teach us about the pursuit of democracy in the modern world.

NOTES

1. Karl Marx, "Theses on Feuerbach," in Robert C. Tucker, editor, *The Marx-Engels Reader*, 2nd ed, (New York: W.W. Norton & Company, Inc., 1978), 145.
2. Thomas Janoski, Robert R. Alford, Alexander M. Hicks, and Mildred A. Schwartz, eds., *The Handbook of Political Sociology: States, Civil Societies, and Globalization* (New York: Cambridge University Press, 2005), Introduction.
3. This is a lesson that has been made abundantly clear in the literature on social movements; indeed, this literature was probably the first to give a decisive role to agents of mobilization in sociological studies of politics.
4. John Stuart Mill, *Utilitarianism, Liberty and Representative Government*, Introduction by A. D. Lindsay (New York: E.P. Dutton & Company, Inc., 1951).

5. *The Essential Rousseau*, translated by Lowell Bair (New York: New American Library, 1974).

6. Benjamin R. Barber, *Strong Democracy: Participatory Politics for A New Age*, 20th Anniversary Edition with a New Preface (Berkeley, CA: University of California Press, 2003); and Carole Pateman, *Participation and Democratic Theory* (Cambridge, UK: Cambridge University Press, 1970).

7. Mancur Olson, *The Logic of Collective Action: Public Goods and the Theory of Groups* (Cambridge, MA: Harvard University Press, 1971).

8. John H. Aldrich, "Rational Choice and Turnout," *American Journal of Political Science*, 1993, 37(1), 246–78. This is an excellent article on the application of rational choice models to voter turnout, providing a clear explication of the nature of rational choice models and also at the same time whether, and how, they might apply to collective actions, like voting, which involves both low costs and low benefits to the individual.

9. On this matter also see Kay Lehman Schlozman, Sidney Verba, and Henry E. Brady, "Participation's Not a Paradox: The View from American Activists," *British Journal of Political Science*, 1995, 25(1), 1–36.

10. Hannah Arendt, "On Public Happiness," in *The Frontiers of Democratic Theory* ed. Henry Kariel (New York: Random House, Inc., 1970), especially p. 5.

11. See, for example, Richard Sennett, *The Fall of Public Man* (New York: W.W. Norton & Co., 1992), plus many others.

12. Russell J. Dalton, *Citizen Politics: Public Opinion and Political Parties in Advanced Industrial Democracies*, 3rd ed. (New York: Seven Bridges Press, 2002), 36–38; also Ruy A. Teixeira, *The Disappearing American Voter* (Washington, DC: Brookings Institution, 1992), 13–18.

13. For the political history of these efforts, see Frances Fox Piven and Richard A. Cloward, *Why Americans Still Don't Vote* (Boston: Beacon Press, 2000), especially Chapter 11.

14. Dalton, op. cit., Chapter 3.

15. See, for example, Teixeira, *The Disappearing American Voter*, as well as the discussion and many fine analyses cited in Aldrich, "Rational Choice and Turnout."

16. Sidney Verba and Norman H. Nie, *Participation in America: Political Democracy and Social Equality* (New York: Harper & Row Publishers, 1972).

17. Lester W. Milbrath and M. L. Goel, *Political Participation: How and Why Do People Get Involved in Politics?* (Chicago: Rand McNally, 1977); and Sidney Verba, Norman H. Nie, and Jae-On Kim, *Participation and Political Equality: A Seven-Nation Comparison* (Chicago: University of Chicago Press, 1978).

18. Verba and Nie, op cit.

19. See, for example, Dalton, Chapter 3.

20. Raymond E. Wolfinger and Steven J. Rosenstone, *Who Votes?* (New Haven, CT: Yale University Press, 1980).

21. Sidney Verba, Kay Lehman Schlozman, and Henry E. Brady, *Voice and Equality: Civic Voluntarism in American Politics* (Cambridge, MA: Harvard University Press, 1995).

22. Verba, Schlozman, and Brady, p. 514.
23. Verba and Nie, op cit.
24. Verba, Scholzman, and Brady, op cit.
25. M. Margaret Conway, Gertrude A. Steuernagel, and David W. Ahern, *Women and Political Participation: Cultural Change in the Political Arena*, Third Edition (Washington, DC: CQ Press, 2005).
26. Nancy Burns, Kay Lehman Schlozman, and Sidney Verba, *The Private Roots of Public Action: Gender, Equality, and Political Participation* (Cambridge, MA: Harvard University Press, 2001).
27. But the research of Burns, Schlozman, and Verba found very little evidence for this kind of structural explanation.
28. Fred I. Greenstein, *Children and Politics* (New Haven, CT: Yale University Press, 1969); Robert D. Hess and Judith V. Torney, *Development of Political Attitudes in Children* (Garden City, NY: Doubleday Anchor, 1968).
29. Burns, Scholzman, and Verba, op cit., p. 360.
30. An extensive list of such studies can be found in Jan E. Leighley and Arnold Vedlitz, "Race, Ethnicity, and Political Participation: Competing Models and Contrasting Explanations," *The Journal of Politics*, 1999, 61(4), 1092–114.
31. See, for example, M. Margaret Conway, *Political Participation in the United States* (Washington, DC: CQ Press, 2000), 31. Also see Rodolfo O. de la Garza et al., *Latino Voices: Mexican, Puerto Rican and Cuban Perspectives on American Politics* (Boulder, CO: Westview Press, 1992).
32. Marvin E. Olsen, "Social and Political Participation of Blacks," *American Sociological Review*, 1970, 35(4): 682–97.
33. Leighley and Vedlitz, op cit.
34. Lawrence Bobo and Franklin Gilliam, Jr., "Race, Sociopolitical Participation, and Black Empowerment," *American Political Science Review*, 1990, 84(2), 377–93.
35. Ibid., p. 387.
36. See, for example, Frederick C. Harris, "Something Within: Religion as a Mobilizer of African-American Political Activism," *The Journal of Politics*, 1994, 56(1), 42–68; Doug McAdam, *Political Process and the Development of Black Insurgency: 1930–1970* (Chicago: University of Chicago Press, 1982; 1999); and Aldon D. Morris, *The Origins of the Civil Rights Movement: Black Communities Organizing for Change* (New York: Free Press, 1984).
37. Verba, Schlozman, and Brady, op cit., 492–95.
38. Frances Fox Piven and Richard A. Cloward, *Why Americans Still Don't Vote* (Boston: Beacon, 2000).
39. Steven J. Rosenstone and John Mark Hansen, *Mobilization, Participation and Democracy in America* (New York: Macmillan, 1993).
40. Piven and Cloward, ibid., Chapter 12.

Index

Note: Page numbers in *italics* denote figures and tables.

of state, 16–17, 28, 41, 138–139
  in the U.S., 125–127, 143–145
  in war-making state, 127–128
Powledge, Fred, 278
Precinct captains, 188
Preemptive warfare, U.S. policy of, 254
Presidential democracy, 108, 118n.20
Press, 74. *See also* Mass media
Primogeniture, 72
Private realm, 112
Pro-democracy movement, Burma, 245–246
Production
  Marxian view, 13, 14, 15
  Poulantzas view, 31
Professionalism, 40, 45
Progressive movement, 209
Proletariat. *See also* Workers
  Marxian view, 13–14, 35n.9
  politicization, 21
  relative misery, 19
Proletarization, 19
Propaganda, 189, 196
Property
  ownership, 13
  valuation, 171
Proportional representation, 76, 191, 192–193
Prosperity, 139, 172
Protest movement, 52, 53. *See also*
  Opposition
Protestant Ethic, 37, 43
Protestantism, 37, 40, 43, 209
Prussia, 56
Pudong, 179
Punishments, 44, 67
Putnam, Robert, 64, 82–83, 84, 172, 211,
  285, 288

Quadagno, Jill, 138

Race. *See also* Ethnic groups
  and equality, 148
  Tocqueville view, 74
Racism, 79, 175
Rank and file, 191, 196, 197–198, 199
Ratcliff, Richard, 141
Rational actors, 224
Rational choice, 288–291
  and collective action, 289–291
    free rider problem, 290–291
    selective incentives, 291
Rationality
  Marcuse view, 29–30
  and voting, 210, 211

Weber view, 29, 40, 42
Reagan, Ronald, 129, 130, 131, 203
Real estate, 167, 168, 170–171, 172, 176
Real estate developers, 167–168, 170–171
Realignment theory, 203–204
Rebellions. *See* Revolution
Regional governments, 82–83
Regionalism, 166
Regions, geographical, 52
Religions
  Bellah view, 78–79
  civic, 78–79
  Durkheim view, 67
  Marxian view, 14
  in totalitarian regime, 113
  in the U.S., 78–79
  Weberian view, 40
Repertoire, of collective action, 53, 227, 229
Representation, proportional, 76, 191, 192–193
Representative government, 105
Repression, 29, 53, 115, 224, 230, 245, 259n.9
Republican Party, 166, 183, 188, 262
Resource mobilization, 222–226
  vs. collective behavior, 223
  criticisms on, 225–226
  and NGOs, 225
  and rational actors, 224
Resources
  and authority, 131
  and politics, 39
  and U.S. corporations, 130–131
Revolution. *See also* Coup d'état
  Lenin view, 23–24
  Marxian view, 11–12, 18–22, 20
  Skocpol view, 55–57
  Tillyian view, 54
Revolutionary movements, 217
Revolutionary terrorism, 257
Rights, 147–152. *See also* Civil rights; Human
  rights
Riis, Jacob, 264
Rituals
  Bellah view, 79
  Durkheim view, 67–68
Roosevelt, Franklin, Delano, 55, 94, 123, 127,
  128, 203, 275
Roosevelt, Theodore, 192, 275
Rosenstone, Steven, 296, 301
Ross, Thomas, 133
Rotating credit association, 81
Rousseau, Jean Jacques, 286
  on democracy, 99
  general will, 64, 66